You Are Here

*Readings on Higher Education
for College Writers*

Russel K. Durst

University of Cincinnati

Prentice
Hall

Upper Saddle River, New Jersey 07458

Library of Congress Cataloging-in-Publication Data

DURST, RUSSEL K., (date)
  You are here : readings on higher education for college writers / Russel K. Durst.

    p. cm.
  Includes bibliographical references.
  ISBN 0–13–027761–4 (alk. paper)
    1. Education, Higher.   2. English language—Rhetoric.   I. Title: Readings on higher
  education for college writers.   II. Title.
  LA174.D87 2003
  378—dc21   2002022479

Editor-in-Chief: *Leah Jewell*
Sr. Acquisition Editor: *Corey Good*
Editorial Assistant: *John Ragozzine*
Executive Managing Editor: *Ann Marie McCarthy*
Production Liaison: *Fran Russello*
Editorial/Production Supervision: *Kim Gueterman*
Prepress and Manufacturing Buyer: *Mary Ann Gloriande*
Cover Director: *Jayne Conte*
Cover Designer: *Bruce Kenselaar*
Permissions Specialist: *Jill Dougan*
Copyeditor: *Donna Mulder*
Marketing Manager: *Brandy Dawson*

This book was set in 10/12 Palatino by DM Cradle Associates.
and was printed and bound by R.R. Donnelley & Sons Company.
The cover was printed by Phoenix Color Corp.

For permission to use copyrighted material grateful acknowledgment is made to the
copyright holders starting on page xv, which is hereby part of the copyright page.

© 2003 by Pearson Education, Inc.
Upper Saddle River, New Jersey 07458

Printed in the United States of America
10   9   8   7   6   5   4   3   2

ISBN   0-13-027761-4

Pearson Education LTD., *London*
Pearson Education Australia Pty, Limited, *Sydney*
Pearson Education Singapore, PTE. Ltd.
Pearson Education North Asia Ltd., *Hong Kong*
Pearson Education Canada, Ltd., *Toronto*
Pearson Educación de Mexico, S.A. de C.V.
Pearson Education—Japan, *Tokyo*
Pearson Education Malaysia, Pte. Ltd.
Pearson Education, *Upper Saddle River, New Jersey*

Contents

Contents

Dear Student

As a college composition teacher and administrator for two decades, I have found it especially difficult—but also especially rewarding—to teach the critical reading and writing course. This course imparts literacy and intellectual skills so crucial to a college education and to life after college. Topics I have covered include popular culture, the environment, the influence of advertising and other media on consumer attitudes, American values, and many more. Unfortunately, students often say they find the readings irrelevant and boring. I generally respond by pointing out ways in which I believe the course material really does connect with students' lives. However, I've long wanted a book for the critical reading and writing class whose relevance to students would be more immediately evident. Despite years of searching, I couldn't find such a book, so with the help of a number of excellent teachers at the University of Cincinnati, I created one. The topic is college itself, the opportunities, challenges, and complexities it offers and how to make the most of them. What topic could be more relevant to students just starting out on their journey through the often-mysterious world of higher education?

Throughout the United States, more than 1 million students are currently enrolled in first-year college composition. As one of those students, perhaps planning to major in business, biology, education, architecture, engineering, music, pharmacy, or some other preprofessional subject, you may well be wondering why you need to take this composition class in the first place. After all, haven't you already taken 12 years of English? What exactly is the point of yet another? One answer is that the class in which this book is being used focuses on key literacy skills that need to be developed at a higher level than was necessary for high school. Mastering these skills will help you considerably in your work as a college student, in your public role as an educated citizen, and in your career (or careers, since most people do not stay in the same field for their entire working lives).

The Book's Purposes

The goals of this course concern critical thinking, communication, and research skills, tools that are crucial no matter what field you may find yourself in.

- The reading and writing assignments included in this anthology will improve your ability to analyze, synthesize, and evaluate arguments, something you will doubtless be called on to do frequently in the years to come.
- The materials in this book will help you construct your own written arguments and interpretations, a process that also involves taking into consideration the views of others.
- In addition, the book will improve your ability to do research, using not only library and online sources but also field research techniques such as interview and field observation.
- Just as importantly, this book will also help you make the most of your college education by examining the following question from a variety of perspectives: What does it mean for me to be a college student? You will have the opportunity to read, write, think, and talk about this question and to do a research project investigating your intended major.
- Taken seriously, this book will help you gain a richer, clearer, and more complex sense of your own goals for being in college, and this improved understanding will help you in your subsequent coursework and beyond.

You are no doubt hoping to be successful in your college studies. However, as a close examination of the readings in this book will reveal, success is not simply about achieving high grades and attaining a high-paying job, important though these considerations may be. Success is also about finding satisfaction and fulfillment, about figuring out what you most want to do in life, about growing intellectually, and about making a difference in the lives of others. If this book is successful, it will help you gain a greater understanding of the many forms of success and of your own potential to achieve each.

The Book's Subject Matter

You Are Here: Readings on Higher Education for College Writers consists of some of the best writing that has been done on this important topic. The book makes you a part of key conversations about schooling that have been taking place throughout our society. The readings examine questions that you may have been asking yourself about your expectations and experiences in college. The essays also introduce you to ideas and issues—ways of thinking about higher education—that will be new to you and that will help you make sense of the variety of purposes underlying postsecondary education in the United States.

- Unit One examines the relationship between education and the surrounding cultures, considering ways in which male and female students' school experiences may differ and investigating the perceptions of students from a variety of backgrounds, perhaps including your own. It also looks at the nature and role of education in American society.

- Unit Two moves to an analysis of college life as experienced by students and teachers alike, illuminating some of the differences in perspective between these two groups.
- Unit Three offers a variety of possible answers to the question, "Why go to college in the first place?"
- Unit Four looks at a range of issues regarding testing and assessment, from an examination of the prominent role standardized tests play in education to a consideration of classroom testing, grading, and assessing for learning disabilities.

Critical Reading, Writing, and Thinking

The pieces in this book concern issues directly relevant to you as a college student and very significant for our society as a whole. Thus, the essays are meant to be read rigorously and thought about in depth. That's what this course is all about. Readings are not simply to be skimmed over, restated, and slotted mechanically into an essay with a thesis statement and three supporting points. You will need to work on these readings actively, taking the authors' ideas seriously enough to understand them but also to question and critique them. You will need to use what you already know and think about a subject to help you understand what the writer is saying.

In a particular reading, for example, you may find points with which you agree as well as others with which you disagree. You may question specific evidence and/or arguments a writer provides in support of his or her views. You may dislike an author's conclusions but find his or her argument and support compelling nonetheless, or you may like the author's conclusions but find the argument lacking in some way. These readings and the issues they discuss are complicated, and your responses to them should be complicated as well. Accordingly, you will need to have a strong sense of what the author is arguing, how he or she constructs and supports that argument, and how it relates to other pieces you have read, as well as to your own past experiences and observations. You will also need to develop your own interpretations of the readings. These interpretations should be thought through and carefully supported, not simply based on your immediate and unreflective response. If you don't already have an opinion on a particular issue, you might think of the assignment as an opportunity to develop your own view.

Your teacher will expect you to read and write about each assigned essay carefully. Toward that end, an apparatus has been provided to support you in your work. Before each reading, you will find, first of all, a short summary of the essay along with some background information about the author and the text. Reading this introductory material is essential. It's not an optional extra to be skipped in order to save yourself a little time, but rather an important first step to help you make sense of a complex piece of writing.

Following this opening information will be a short paragraph entitled "To Consider." Here you will find questions and issues that place the reading in an intellectual context and that direct you toward its primary themes. Most likely, you have had some experience in the past with prewriting as preparation for English class essays. You might think of the "To Consider" section as prereading intended to prepare you for the essay that awaits. Carrying out this preparatory work prior to reading the essay itself will aid your understanding and put you in a stronger position for the reading and writing activities that follow.

After you complete the "To Consider" section, it is time to read the essay itself. The readings in this book are designed to make you think, to help you learn, and to give you something to write about. Don't short circuit the thinking, learning, and writing process by reading quickly and superficially in your haste to complete the assignment. A shallow reading will almost certainly lead to shallow writing, in particular because writing assignments will require you to examine carefully and discuss extensively the ideas elaborated in the readings. When reading an essay, keep in mind the preparatory questions you have been asked to consider. Reading is a very active process. When we read, we are not passively receiving the material but are actively constructing meaning. We construct meaning by using what we already know—about the subject at hand, about our own beliefs and prior experiences, about reading, about the culture in which we live, and, if the text under scrutiny is from a different time or place, the culture in which the work was produced. We apply these different types of knowledge to the text at hand to figure out what the author is saying and what we think about it.

As you read, annotate the text to help you make sense of it:

- Underline or highlight what seem to you to be key points and comment on their significance in the margins.
- Point out places where you agree or disagree with what the author is saying, or where you don't understand.
- Circle words that you might need to look up in the dictionary, although you might want to see first if you can figure the word out from its context.
- Use the margins as a place to ask questions, make connections, express opinions, outline the main ideas of the text, and reflect on the meaning and implications of what you are reading.

Annotating a text is an important part of understanding it and often leads to better understanding and, therefore, better performance on essays. Included next is a short sample essay published in 1975 by Russell Baker, longtime columnist for *The New York Times*, entitled "School vs. Education," along with my own annotations.

School vs. Education

Russell Baker

That's odd. I thought education began at 6, not ended.

By the age of six the average child will have completed the basic American education and be ready to enter school. If the child has been attentive in these preschool years, he or she will already have mastered many skills.

From television, the child will have learned how to pick a lock, commit a fairly elaborate bank holdup, prevent wetness all day long, get the laundry twice as white, and kill people with a variety of sophisticated armaments.

Oh, I see

From watching his parents, the child, in many cases, will already know how to smoke, how much soda to mix with whiskey, what kind of language to use when angry, and how to violate the speed laws without being caught.

Stage 2

At this point, the child is ready for the second stage of education, which occurs in school. There, a variety of lessons may be learned in the very first days.

The implicit lessons of school

The teacher may illustrate the economic importance of belonging to a strong union by closing down the school before the child arrives. Fathers and mothers may demonstrate to the child the social cohesion that can be built on shared hatred by demonstrating their dislike for children whose pigmentation displeases them. In the latter event, the child may receive visual instruction in techniques of stoning buses, cracking skulls with a nightstick, and subduing mobs with tear gas. Formal education has begun.

Sad but largely true.

During formal education, the child learns that life is for testing. This stage lasts twelve years, a period during which the child learns that success comes from telling testers what they want to hear.

Expectations are key

Early in this stage, the child learns that he is either dumb or smart. If the teacher puts intelligent demands upon the child, the child learns he is smart. If the teacher expects little of the child, the child learns he is dumb and soon quits bothering to tell the testers what they want to hear.

Everyone passes anyway, so why try?

At this point, education becomes more subtle. The child taught by school that he is dumb observes that neither he, she, nor any of the many children who are even dumber, ever fails to be promoted to the next grade. From this, the child learns that while everybody talks a lot about the virtue of being smart, there is very little incentive to stop being dumb.

What is the point of school, besides attendance? the child wonders. As the end of the first formal stage of education approaches, school answers this question. <u>The point is to equip the child to enter college.</u>

Why shouldn't the system favor the smart?

Children who have been taught they are smart have no difficulty. They have been happily telling testers what they want to hear for twelve years. Being artists at telling testers what they want to hear, they are admitted to college joyously, where they promptly learn that they are the hope of America.

remedial ed.

Children whose education has been limited to adjusting themselves to their school's low estimates of them are admitted to less joyous colleges which, in some cases, may teach them to read.

At this stage of education, a fresh quotation arises for everyone. If the point of lower education was to get into college, what is the point of college? The answer is soon learned. <u>The point of college is to prepare the student</u>—no longer a child now—<u>to get into graduate school.</u> In college the student learns that it is no longer enough simply to tell the testers what they want to hear. Many are tested for graduate school; few are admitted.

Not the work world?

Tough world out there

Those excluded may be denied valuable certificates to prosper in medicine, at the bar, in the corporate boardroom. <u>The student learns that the race is to the cunning and often, alas, to the unprincipled.</u>

Thus, *the student learns the importance of destroying competitors* and emerges richly prepared to play his role in the great simmering melodrama of American life.

Afterward, the former student's destiny fulfilled, his life rich with Oriental carpets, rare porcelain, and full bank accounts, he may one day find himself with the leisure and the inclination to open a book with a curious mind, and start to become educated.

He's saying that education and school have very little to do with one another. To a point, he may be right. But I think education, real learning, is at least possible in school, though one may have to work against the grain to achieve it.

Marking a text in this way can be an enormous help when it comes time to write an essay in which you discuss the text, because the annotations help you work through the author's argument and develop your own responses to it.

Following each reading is an informal writing activity entitled "Reflective Writing." These entries should be a page or two in length and should be completed after carrying out the assigned reading. The reflective writing prompt provides an opportunity for you not only to summarize but also to interpret and mull over the arguments discussed in the reading. In many cases, you will be asked to relate an author's points to your own experience and understanding. However, the views you put forward should not involve unsupported personal opinion or emotional response alone; you must ground your discussion in the specifics of the text you are writing about. This sort of writing is informal in the sense that the quality and complexity of your ideas are more important than the correctness of your grammar, punctuation, and spelling. You should use these assignments as a chance to reflect, or think on paper, about what an author is trying to say and how it relates to what others, including you, have said and thought. Reflection involves consideration not only of other people's ideas but of your own views as well. You will need to consider the rationale or justification for your own developing opinions about the issues discussed in the readings. Taking the reflective writing seriously will help you do your best work on the formal essay assignments of the course.

In addition to the informal reflective writing activities concerning the individual readings, for each unit there is a formal, extended essay assignment drawing in detail on several of the readings in the unit. Several possible essay topics appear at the end of each unit.

An important point is that although personal experience and opinions are crucial considerations in writing critical essays, these assignments are *not* meant to produce personal essays in which you focus exclusively on your own ideas and experiences. Rather, you should aim to develop a well-elaborated discussion of an important issue, using your own background knowledge but drawing on, and examining in depth, specific points from the assigned readings in order to put forward your own informed perspective on the issue in question.

For these essay assignments, your teacher will expect you to engage seriously with the readings. You should use material from the readings in a variety of ways, the most common of which is to support your own views. But many students think that points from the readings should only be used for support. I strongly encourage you to branch out into other uses of text. Of course, where appropriate, you should include the words and ideas and evidence of others to back up your own views. However, and this is where students often have trouble, you should also bring in the readings for other purposes. For example, you may bring in points from a reading:

- to argue or disagree with the authors
- to look for connections or points of contrast among ideas
- to speculate about
- to explore an idea in detail and from different perspectives
- to examine the relations between the texts and your own goals, insights, and experiences.

The most important and challenging intellectual work of the course will center around your engagement with the readings as you construct your own interpretations and arguments about education.

An Invitation

This course will be intellectually challenging, but I hope it will also be interesting and useful in your own development as a college student. As you use this book in your class or after you finish working with it, I invite you to drop me a note with a question, comment, or criticism. I do so because this book, like your own approach to college studies, is in a continual process of development. Good luck in your coursework, and happy reading and writing.

ACKNOWLEDGEMENTS

I would like to thank the following people for their help in putting together an earlier draft of this collection. Sherry Cook Stanforth, Christina Court, Matt DeWald, Megan Fitzpatrick-Jones, Kelly Fuller, Michele Griegel, Vive Griffith, Alli Hammond, Rob Hartzell, Brent Heckerman, Ron Hundemer, Kurt Jaenicke, Francis Janosco, Peter LePage, Ann McClellan, Shirley McKee, Rebecca Meacham, Sandi Nieman, Julie Perry, Jay Peterson, Anna Priebe, Carol Rainey, Nan Reitz, Cynthia Ris, Wendy Rountree, Lynn Shaffer, Adam Sol, Sheila Townsend, and Brad Vice. Diana Becket gave many valuable suggestions for the reflective reading and writing prompts. Maggy Lindgren and Lucy Schultz offered excellent critical feedback on all aspects of the book. Corey Good, my Prentice-Hall editor, kept the publication process moving smoothly and efficiently. Kim Gueterman helped me turn my unpublished manuscript into a finished book.

Professor Russel Durst
Cincinnati, OH
e-mail: russel.durst@uc.edu

Credits

UNIT ONE

Education and Culture

Schools function not only as isolated entities but also as part of the larger society, an important part, to be sure. Accordingly, and in important ways, schools both influence and are influenced by that larger society. The goals of schooling, the ways our educational institutions are structured and funded, the entrance and graduation requirements, how students and teachers are expected to behave, and the kinds of educational aspirations people allow themselves are all aspects of American education and reflect the cultural context in which schooling exists in the United States.

A country's educational system reflects the particular society in which the system is embedded. For example, choice and flexibility are extremely important values in U.S. culture, and we are affluent enough as a society to offer what might seem to citizens of many other countries to be a vast array of alternatives. So, at many points in the American educational system, students may choose particular courses to take from a range of options—what some critics have called the "shopping mall" curriculum: home economics, shop, music or art, and mini-courses in literature, creative writing, journalism, and speech. Students generally also have a choice of which school to attend, and where college is concerned, they potentially have enormous choice with literally thousands of institutions of higher learning in the United States. In other countries that emphasize the importance of tradition and that legislate a national curriculum, students may have almost no choice in determining what to study or where to attend school. Choice in itself is not necessarily altogether a good thing or a bad thing—one can have too many choices, or resources can be spread too thin in an effort to offer desired alternatives. But the point is that the importance of choice is ingrained in us as consumers and as Americans. And this notion, like other cultural phenomena characteristic of this country—such as an emphasis on competitive team sports and the idea that just about everyone should have the opportunity for postsecondary schooling—is built into our educational system.

Besides influencing how schools are structured, there is another very important way in which culture influences how students experience education. The culture from which a student comes can have a significant effect on the student's perception of and performance in school. Of course, there are many factors influencing school success, including individual ability, interest, and motivation, as well as family background and expectations. But at the same time, the culture a student grows up in—including such features as neighborhood, community, ethnicity, religion, and social class—can have a profound and lasting impact on a student's schooling. There is a very strong correlation among social class, college attended, and career chosen. The higher a student's social class, for example, as determined by such factors as parents' income, level of education, occupation, and neighborhood, the more likely that student is to be well prepared for school, to attend a prestigious college, to be academically successful, and to go on to a lucrative career. Conversely, the lower a student's social class, in terms of these same measures, the more likely that student will attend weaker schools, drop out, not go on to college, and end up in a low-paying job. Surely there are students from privileged backgrounds who fail in school, and there is a long tradition in this country of students from poor families who distinguish themselves in school and go on to fine careers. Indeed, one purpose of public education in this country is to provide a means by which the less privileged can compete with more advantaged members of our society. But in a general sense, and for most people, cultural variables such as social class correlate strongly with academic achievement and career options.

The readings in this unit examine some of the many ways in which education and cultural difference can intersect. To make sense of the essays, you will need to do more than memorize their main points. To read and write about them in the critical, reflective way that is expected in college, you will need to understand the readings thoroughly. You will also need to consider the points they raise in light of your own experience as a student in elementary and high school as well as your current status as a college student. You will need to consider what you have observed or heard from others, books and articles you have read, and movies and television shows you have seen. All of these sources contribute in different ways to your understanding. If you read the unit's essays closely and consider all of these other sources carefully, you should begin to construct your own complex view of the relationship between culture and education.

Readings focus on different aspects of the larger culture as it impinges on students' education. The first reading deals with the intersection of education and socioeconomic class. In the essay, former U.S. Secretary of Labor Robert Reich argues that university admissions policies favor the most privileged and increase already sizeable inequities. The next three readings examine issues of gender and education. In recent decades, women have made great strides in American education, as in other areas of society. Yet some observers argue that inequities remain. The essay by researcher Peggy Orenstein examines students at what the author suggests is a fairly typical middle school. Based on extensive observation and interviews, she argues that the school's curriculum and teaching approaches tend to favor male students at the expense of females and states that single-sex schools may be a better alternative for many female students. The next essay, by writer and cultural critic Wendy Kaminer, finds fault with some of Orenstein's conclusions and argues instead that coeducational schools offer substantial benefits to females. Educational critic Christina Hoff Sommers's essay argues that boys are not being well served in schools; she suggests that educators are ignoring boys' problems in the mistaken belief that schools discriminate against female students.

The following essays investigate ways in which ethnicity, social class, and sexual orientation can help to shape students' school experiences. Benjamin P. Bowser and Herbert Perkins chronicle the effective strategies and positive learning environments of successful African-American male high school students. Journalist Ron Suskind contributes an essay from his Pulitzer prize–winning study of an African-American young man who struggles against great odds to go from a low-achieving, inner-city high school to one of the nation's most prestigious universities. The authors of these pieces also consider ways in which the populations they are writing about can be better served by the schools and take greater advantage of available educational opportunities. The next essay, by educational researcher Andi O'Conor, explores the situation of gay and lesbian high school students, who often face hostility from their peers, indifference from their teachers, and rejection from their own families.

The final reading of the unit shifts gears, looking at the effects of American culture in a larger sense—in particular the practical, hands-on spirit that characterizes us as a nation—on our educational system. This reading is an excerpt from Alexis de Toqueville's nineteenth-century classic *Democracy in America*. Taken together, these readings provide a wealth of ideas and issues for your consideration. Before you read, think about your own assumptions regarding education and cultural differences, and then consider how your views relate to those presented by the authors.

How Selective Colleges Heighten Inequality

Robert B. Reich

In many ways, college is the great equalizer, the institution that helps make it possible for hardworking students from disadvantaged backgrounds to be successful. Or at least that's how we like to think about college. But is this view correct? In this essay from the Chronicle of Higher Education, *Robert B. Reich argues that admissions and recruitment policies at colleges and universities today may actually be decreasing opportunities for less privileged students, while increasing opportunities for wealthier students who already have plenty of options. Reich is a former U.S. Secretary of Labor and is currently a professor of economic and social policy at Brandeis University.*

To Consider: *Outline the arguments that Reich makes in this essay. What support does he provide? What assumptions does he make regarding what is best for individual students and for the country as a whole? How might your own situation as a college student relate to the author's argument?*

Not long ago, the president of a prestigious university (not the one in which I now teach) was explaining his strategy to me. "We're very selective, but we need to become even more selective," he said. "Our SATs are rising, but not as fast as I'd like. We should be on par with . . . ," and he named several institutions even more selective than the one he led. "We're going to market ourselves more intensively to high-school stars," he told me.

I asked him about his new capital campaign, and how much of the money raised would go to awarding scholarships to needy students or expanding the size of the entering class. Apparently, none. "We're going to build a new student center, upgrade the dorms, and use the rest to attract some faculty and student stars," he answered. "That's what our competitors are doing. We can't afford not to."

I nodded sympathetically. Still, it struck me that, if most college presidents were thinking the same way, the competition for the best and brightest (measured in conventional ways) was going to become more heated than it already is, and a lot of children from lower-income families weren't going to stand a chance.

Meanwhile, children from middle-income families continue to apply to four-year colleges in ever greater numbers, and competition for admission to the most selective and prestigious institutions is rising steeply. Acceptance rates at the most selective institutions are dropping, even though high-school guidance counselors have been trying to make students more realistic about their chances. For example, according to data published in a popular guide to colleges, in 1980 Harvard accepted 16 percent of its applicants; the most recent data, from 1998, show Harvard accepting 12 percent. Parents and students are similarly finding out that Stanford accepts only 13 percent of its applicants these days; 20 years ago, it accepted 19 percent. The pattern has been much the same at prestigious state universities like the University of Michigan at Ann Arbor, where the rate of acceptance dropped from 72 percent to 59 percent over the same interval, or at the University of California at Berkeley, where acceptances plummeted from 70 to 28 percent.

With colleges seeking to be more selective, and more students seeking admission to the most selective, it's no surprise that the pressure on students and their families is rising. Even sixth graders are feeling it, according to a front-page story in *The New York Times* this summer. The father of one 11-year-old introduced the boy to a university admissions officer, who advised him to take Spanish rather than Latin and to sign up for calculus as soon as possible. Other sixth graders are surfing college home pages on the Web, eyeing future majors and financial-aid opportunities.

That such competitive pressures are building, among both colleges and their prospective students, seems an accepted aspect of contemporary American life. Yet, in my view, inadequate attention is being paid to the larger social consequences of the trend—especially to how higher-education resources are being allocated in this era of widening inequality.

Two broad forces are behind the headlong rush toward greater selectivity. The most basic is that the economic stakes of getting a degree from a reputable four-year college or university have become much higher, as disparities in income and wealth have widened nationwide. By the end of the 1990s, according to data contained in the Census Bureau's annual Current Population Survey, the income gap between the top and bottom 10 percent of earners was wider than at any time since the 1920s. During the prosperous '90s, the incomes of people at or near the top grew twice as fast as those in the middle, while the wealthiest 10 percent of families got about 85 percent of the value of all the gains in the booming stock market, and the wealthiest 1 percent got over 40 percent of the gains. Such changes have large consequences: At the end of the 20th century, the richest 1 percent of American families, comprising 2.7 million people, had just about as many dollars to spend, after they had paid all taxes, as the bottom 100 million. And they owned most of America's marketable assets. That represents the largest concentration of both income and wealth in more than a century.

The purpose of college shouldn't be solely about earning a good income after graduation, of course, but the growing correlation between the amount of education and the level of earnings is striking. In 1998, according to the Census Bureau, the average income of families headed by someone with no more than a high-school diploma was $48,434, which was 8 percent higher than it had been in 1990 (adjusted for inflation). But family income was $63,524 when the household head had a two-year-college degree, 10 percent higher than in 1990. A B.A. lifted family income to $85,423, marking a 13 percent increase; an M.A. raised earnings to $101,670, a 17 percent jump. With a professional degree, family income was $147,170, a whopping 24 percent increase from 1990.

It should not be surprising, then, that more high-school seniors are seeking to attend college—and more are graduating. But that's not all: Parents and their offspring also assume that future earnings will be higher with a degree from a more selective institution. They figure that future employers will use institutional selectivity as a proxy for the quality of a prospective employee, and that prestigious institutions will offer an abundance of valuable connections to the job market. While the assumption of a direct correlation between selectivity and future earnings is not borne out by research, the tenacity with which it's held says much about how parents view the opportunities and risks faced by young people today. Middle-class and upper-middle-class boomers are determined to do whatever is necessary to increase the chances that their youngsters will do well in the new economy.

The second reason for the lurch toward selectivity has to do with technologies that are knitting together the nation—and the globe. More students than ever are competing nationally (and some internationally) for admission to the same limited set of colleges and universities. Two decades ago, bright high-school seniors with good records typically aimed for the best university in their state or region. But rapidly improving technologies of information, transportation, and communication are on their way to creating a single national, and eventually global, market for higher education.

Today, high-school students and their parents have an abundance of comparative data about colleges—including standardized ratings such as the annual listings compiled by *U.S. News & World Report*—as well as a flood of information available on the Internet. As a result, bright high-school seniors with good grades and test scores are more likely to apply to the big national brands, competing for admission with other students from around the country. Even the sixth graders in the *Times*'s sample worried about attending a local or regional university. One child intoned, "C is community college, B is state college, A is Ivy League school."

At the same time, and for much the same reason, every major college and university want a reputation for being among the places that attract the nation's best and brightest. And colleges and universities have access to much more information than they used to about who and where those students are, and they are able to communicate with prospects with ever greater ease.

What does all this mean for us as a society? The danger is that the increasing competition—to be selected and to be selective—will exacerbate the widening inequalities that are raising the stakes in the first place.

There is no single, simple cause of the growing inequality in the United States, but a large part of it relates to supply and demand. In the old economy that dominated the 20th century, profits and productivity gains depended on making more and more of the same thing. Large numbers of production workers were needed to undertake relatively routine tasks. Those workers did not, in general, require much education. In the new economy of the 21st century, by contrast, businesses depend largely on innovation. To stay competitive, they have to generate products and services that are better or cheaper than those of their rivals, and they must innovate faster than their rivals. Thus, demand is growing for people who can spur innovation by identifying and solving new problems or figuring out what clients and customers might need or want.

Even though more young people than ever are attending postsecondary institutions, the demand for workers with the education and skills needed to innovate is rising faster than the supply. By contrast, demand for people with relatively few skills and little education is static or shrinking. And such people are in abundant supply; in fact, many of them can be readily replaced with overseas labor or smart machines. Those trends help explain why the incomes of people with more education have been increasing faster than the incomes of people with less education. As long as the economy remains reasonably healthy, less-educated people will continue to have jobs—but their jobs will pay comparatively little.

A society concerned about widening inequality—and its corrosive effects on democracy, social solidarity, and the moral authority of a nation—would logically turn its attention to increasing the supply of people capable of doing the work that the new economy rewards. It would, in particular, do so by broadening access to postsecondary education for children from lower-income families.

Yet almost all the increase in the proportion of 18- to 24-year-olds in postsecondary institutions in recent years is attributable to children from middle- and upper-income families. As the economist Thomas Kane has noted, from 1977 to 1993, about 70 percent of 18- and 19-year-olds from families with incomes in the top quarter attended postsecondary institutions, and that percentage has been rising since then. Slightly more than 50 percent of children from families in the second-highest quartile attended, and 50 percent of children from families in the quartile below that did so. But less than 30 percent of children from families in the bottom quarter enrolled in postsecondary education—a percentage that has been dropping since 1993, even as college enrollments among more affluent students have been rising.

There is a danger that the current competitive rush toward selectivity will make it even less likely that lower-income children will gain access to higher education. That's because college and university administrators have incentives to spend more resources to attract those whom they consider the best students, rather than accommodating more lower-income students whose credentials and test scores do not add to an institution's luster.

Too many colleges and universities are using scarce scholarship resources to lure student stars, who often come from advantaged families and good secondary schools—and who already have every chance of succeeding in life. In fact, an increasing number of institutions are engaging in quiet bidding wars for such students. *The New York Times* reported last year that Pittsburgh's Carnegie Mellon University, for example, explicitly reassures star applicants that it will match or surpass any offers they receive from other colleges. "We believe competition among schools is healthy," Carnegie Mellon's admissions director was quoted as saying. "We are trying to encourage dialogue, and we have set aside enough dough to do it." Harvard's admissions materials hint at a similar policy: "We expect that some of our students will have particularly attractive offers from the institutions with new aid programs," it writes to newly admitted students, "and those students should not assume that we will not respond."

Harvard's almost-bottomless endowment allows it to match any bid without skimping on aid to needier students, but that's not the case for most colleges. What's doled out to the stars is almost certainly given at the expense of some needier students who qualify academically, but cannot afford the costs. Across the country, "need-blind" admissions policies are vanishing. "It used to be, providing aid was a charitable operation," Michael S. McPherson, the president of Macalester College, told the *Times*. "Now, it's an investment, like brand management."

A second way that colleges and universities have been pumping up the applicant pool of good students, ratcheting up average SAT scores, and enhancing selectivity is through direct marketing to high schools and families in the middle-class and upper-middle-class communities where high achievers can easily be found. An increasing slice of university budgets is now dedicated to mailings, brochures, visits by recruiters to suburban high schools, telephoners, elaborately staged visiting days on campuses, Web pages, and videos. Similarly, money for recruiting minority candidates is often aimed at middle-class African-American and Asian-American families already intent on sending their children to college. Such marketing invites similar responses from competing institutions, in what has become an escalating round of promotion.

Here, too, the result is often less money to finance the much harder job of recruiting high-school students from outside the mainstream—diamonds in the rough who could benefit enormously from college but who don't know it because they and their families are too poor, or their high-school teachers and administrators too overwhelmed, to become aware of the possibility; or because their performance on standardized tests may not reveal their real promise.

The same competition for the best students is driving many colleges and universities to expand and upgrade student centers, improve campus landscaping, make current dormitories more comfortable, and add other amenities. Administrators argue that they must do so in order to keep up with other colleges in attracting star students and improving institutional rankings. But when such expenditures are passed on to students in the form of higher costs, the consequence is reduced accessibility for needy students who cannot afford the tab.

Alternatively, those expenditures are financed from the proceeds of capital campaigns, which might otherwise be used to expand enrollments and provide more scholarship assistance to the needy. One administrator (again, I should note, not at the institution in which I now teach) explained the logic to me in commendably candid terms: "Our goal is to add more students but to reject more students. If anything, we want a smaller entering class. That way, we look more selective."

Public resources are not being allocated to counter such trends. From 1988 to 1998, according to the *Digest of Education Statistics*, the average price of attending a public college or university rose 22 percent, after adjusting for inflation (it rose 28 percent at private colleges and universities).

The new fashion among states to provide merit awards to high-school students who score well on standardized examinations is not helping, because children from lower-income families are less likely to succeed on such tests than are students from higher-income families. Last spring, for example, 63 percent of white high-school students who took the Michigan Educational Assessment Program test qualified for a $2,500 Michigan merit scholarship, while only 2.2 percent of African-American students who took the test qualified. Most of the white students were from families with higher incomes than the families of the African-American students.

If we are serious about reversing the larger trend toward widening inequality of income and wealth in the United States—or, at the very least, about slowing it—we need to make it easier, not harder, for children from relatively poor families to gain access to postsecondary education. As institutions of higher education, as well as state legislatures, debate issues like how to allocate student aid, recruit students, prioritize capital construction, and even create a presence on the Internet, they need to keep in mind the importance of making higher education available across the economic spectrum.

In light of the nation's widening inequalities of income and wealth, it seems to me that scarce scholarship resources should be reserved for students who need them, rather than for student stars who do not.

Colleges should refrain from informally bidding against one another for stars, and from spending significant resources marketing themselves to middle-class families who already are being marketed to death. Resources should be used, instead, to recruit potential students from lower-income families, for whom a college education would be beneficial, but who do not show that by conventional measures. And rather than spending funds on amenities that make campuses more attractive to middle-class children whose families can bear the added costs, colleges should keep a lid on tuition, room, and board so that more lower-income kids could afford to attend. Colleges and universities might also consider how to efficiently expand their enrollments to provide better access to more students at lower cost. That could include using the Internet to extend the reach of instructional programs to people who now have little or no access to higher education.

Some people will say that the competitive pressures forcing colleges and universities toward more selectivity cannot be reversed. I accept that some institutional competition is inevitable, even desirable. But I see no inherent reason why the terms of competition must converge on standardized test scores, numerical rankings in such publications as *U.S. News & World Report,* or any such uniform calculus. Institutional success could as well be measured in ways that better respond to the nation's problem of widening inequality—for example, by reference to the proportion of promising new admits from lower-income families.

If the challenge is framed more broadly—as how to help more young people from lower-income families gain the skills they need to succeed in the new economy—other directions may suggest themselves. For example, colleges and universities might offer associate degrees in various technical fields; or they might "adopt" high schools in some of the poorer communities in their regions. They could encourage undergraduates to tutor students in those communities and professors to give refresher courses to the high-school faculties, and they could aim scholarships and admissions slots at promising students from those schools.

By the same token, state legislatures could expand resources and provide more scholarships for students at community colleges and technical institutes that offer skills that are in demand. More states could also adopt variations of plans, already in effect in some areas, to grant automatic admission to the top public universities to all state students graduating at the tops of their high-school classes. Because lower-income students increasingly tend to be concentrated in lower-income communities, such policies would enhance the access of those students to college.

The rush toward selectivity and exclusivity in higher education is exactly the wrong direction to take for a society that is already becoming less equal, and in which higher education is the fault line separating winners from losers. We should—and can—reverse course.

Reflective Writing: *Former Secretary of Labor Reich believes that colleges today should provide more opportunities for poorer students to attend college and that colleges spend too much time competing for a core group of high-ability, privileged students. Looking carefully over his argument, consider how you, as a college student with a certain academic and economic background, fit into Reich's picture. What, in your view, would be the advantages and disadvantages of colleges adopting the policies he suggests?*

Learning Silence:
Scenes from the Class Struggle

Peggy Orenstein

Are boys and girls treated differently in school? Do girls get the short end of the stick? In the following excerpt from her book Schoolgirls: Young Women, Self-Esteem, *and the* Confidence Gap *(1994), journalist Peggy Orenstein answers yes to these questions. Drawing upon a yearlong, nationwide study commissioned by the American Association of University Women, the author describes classroom scenes at a California middle school (one of several schools that she studied) and lets teachers and female students speak for themselves about ways in which gender seems to influence learning. The author, formerly managing editor of* Mother Jones *magazine, has published in* The New York Times Magazine, Esquire, Vogue, The New Yorker, *and other magazines.*

To Consider: *As you read this piece, think carefully about the nature of Orenstein's argument as well as the evidence that she uses to support it. You may also want to consider your own experiences as a student, ways in which they did or did not conform to the patterns Orenstein describes, and possible alternative explanations for the behaviors depicted.*

Weston, California, sits at the far reaches of the San Francisco Bay Area. The drive from the city takes one through a series of bedroom communities, carefully planned idylls in which, as the miles roll by, the tax brackets leap upward, the politics swing right, and the people fade to white. But Weston is different: once an oddly matched blend of country folk and chemical plant workers, this is an old town, the kind of place where people still gather curbside under the bunting-swathed lampposts of Maple Street to watch the Fourth of July parade. Many of the businesses in Weston's center—doughnut shops, ladies' clothing stores, a few hard drinkers' bars, and picked-over antiquaries—haven't changed hands in over thirty years. There are a few fern bars and one café serving espresso here, but if people want high tone, they go to the city.

Not that Weston has remained suspended in time. The ramshackle houses downtown may still be populated by the families of mechanics, plant

12

workers, and, in shoddy apartment complexes, a small community of working poor, but the hills that ring the town's edge have been gobbled up by tract homes where young professionals have hunkered down—a safe distance from urban ills—to raise their children. There's even a clean, modern supermarket by the freeway, built expressly for the new suburbanites, with a multiplex cinema across the street for their occasional evenings out.

The only place where Weston's two populations converge regularly is at Weston Middle School, a crumbling Spanish-style edifice just up the street from the post office, city hall, and, more important to the student body, a McDonald's. This is the town's sole middle school, and as such, it serves nearly nine hundred students a year from this disparate population. The bumper stickers on the cars dropping off the children reflect the mix: Toyota vans advertising the local National Public Radio affiliate pull up behind rusty pickups that proclaim: "My wife said if I buy another gun she'll divorce me; God, I'll miss her!" There is also a staunch Christian population here—Mormons, Seventh-Day Adventists, and other, less austere sects whose cars remind other residents that "Jesus Loves You!"

In recent years, Weston Middle School has fulfilled its mandate well: the school entrance is draped with a "California Distinguished School" banner, earned last year by the students' estimable standardized test scores as well as the staff's exemplary performance. The teachers are an impressive, enthusiastic group who routinely seek methods of instruction that will inspire a little more engagement, a little more effort on the part of their pupils: an eighth-grade history teacher uses a karaoke microphone to juice up his lessons; an English teacher videotapes students performing original poems to bring literature to life; a science teacher offers extra credit to students who join him in cleaning up the banks of a local river. There is also some concern about gender issues in education: Weston's history teachers have embraced the new, more inclusive textbooks adopted by the state of California; in English, students write essays on their views about abortion and read, among other books, *Streams to the River, River to the Sea*, a historical novel which recasts Sacagawea as an intrepid female hero.

Yet the overt curriculum, as fine as it may be, is never the only force operating in a classroom. There is something else as well. The "hidden curriculum" comprises the unstated lessons that students learn in school: it is the running subtext through which teachers communicate behavioral norms and individual status in the school culture, the process of socialization that cues children into their place in the hierarchy of larger society. Once used to describe the ways in which the education system works to reproduce class systems in our culture, the "hidden curriculum" has recently been applied to the ways in which schools help reinforce gender roles, whether they intend to or not.

The Daily Grind: Lessons in the Hidden Curriculum

Amy Wilkinson has looked forward to being an eighth grader forever—at least for the last two years, which, when you're thirteen, seems like the same thing. By the second week of September she's settled comfortably into her role as one of the school's reigning elite. Each morning before class, she lounges with a group of about twenty other eighth-grade girls and boys in the most visible spot on campus: at the base of the schoolyard, between one of the portable classrooms that was constructed in the late 1970s and the old oak tree in the overflow parking lot. The group trades gossip, flirts, or simply stands around, basking in its own importance and killing time before the morning bell.

At 8:15 on Tuesday the crowd has already convened, and Amy is standing among a knot of girls, laughing. She is fuller-figured than she'd like to be, wide-hipped and heavy-limbed with curly, blond hair, cornflower-blue eyes, and a sharply upturned nose. With the help of her mother, who is a drama coach, she has become the school's star actress: last year she played Eliza in Weston's production of *My Fair Lady.* Although she earns solid grades in all of her subjects—she'll make the honor roll this fall—drama is her passion, she says, because "I love entertaining people, and I love putting on characters."

Also, no doubt, because she loves the spotlight: this morning, when she mentions a boy I haven't met, Amy turns, puts her hands on her hips, anchors her feet shoulder width apart, and bellows across the schoolyard, "Greg! Get over here! You have to meet Peggy."

She smiles wryly as Greg, looking startled, begins to make his way across the schoolyard for an introduction. "I'm not exactly shy," she says, her hands still on her hips. "I'm *bold.*"

Amy is bold. And brassy, and strong-willed. Like any teenager, she tries on and discards different selves as if they were so many pairs of Girbaud jeans, searching ruthlessly for a perfect fit. During a morning chat just before the school year began, she told me that her parents tried to coach her on how to respond to my questions. "They told me to tell you that they want me to be my own person," she complained. "My mother *told* me to tell you that. I do want to be my own person, but it's like, you're interviewing me about who I am and she's telling me what to say—that's not my own person, is it?"

When the morning bell rings, Amy and her friends cut off their conversations, scoop up their books, and jostle toward the school's entrance. Inside, Weston's hallways smell chalky, papery, and a little sweaty from gym class. The wood-railed staircases at either end of the two-story main building are worn thin in the middle from the scuffle of hundreds of pairs of sneakers pounding them at forty-eight-minute intervals for nearly seventy-five years. Amy's mother, Sharon, and her grandmother both attended this school. So will her two younger sisters. Her father, a mechanic who works on big rigs, is a more recent Weston recruit: he grew up in Georgia and came here after he and Sharon were married.

Amy grabs my hand, pulling me along like a small child or a slightly addled new student: within three minutes we have threaded our way through the dull-yellow hallways to her locker and then upstairs to room 238, Mrs. Richter's math class.

The twenty-two students that stream through the door with us run the gamut of physical maturity. Some of the boys are as small and compact as fourth graders, their legs sticking out of their shorts like pipe cleaners. A few are trapped in the agony of a growth spurt, and still others cultivate downy beards. The girls' physiques are less extreme: most are nearly their full height, and all but a few have already weathered the brunt of puberty. They wear topknots or ponytails, and their shirts are tucked neatly into their jeans.

Mrs. Richter, a ruddy, athletic woman with a powerful voice, has arranged the chairs in a three-sided square, two rows deep. Amy walks to the far side of the room and, as she takes her seat, falls into a typically feminine pose: she crosses her legs, folds her arms across her chest, and hunches forward toward her desk, seeming to shrink into herself. The sauciness of the playground disappears, and, in fact, she says hardly a word during class. Meanwhile, the boys, especially those who are more physically mature, sprawl in their chairs, stretching their legs long, expanding into the available space.

Nate, a gawky, sanguine boy who has shaved his head except for a small thatch that's hidden under an Oakland A's cap, leans his chair back on two legs and, although the bell has already rung, begins a noisy conversation with his friend Kyle.

Mrs. Richter turns to him, "What's all the discussion about, Nate?" she asks.

"*He's* talking to *me*," Nate answers, pointing to Kyle. Mrs. Richter writes Nate's name on the chalkboard as a warning toward detention and he yells out in protest. They begin to quibble over the justice of her decision, their first—but certainly not their last—power struggle of the day. As they argue, Allison, a tall, angular girl who once told me, "My goal is to be the best wife and mother I can be," raises her hand to ask a question. Mrs. Richter, finishing up with Nate, doesn't notice.

"Get your homework out, everyone!" the teacher booms, and walks among the students, checking to make sure no one has shirked on her or his assignment. Allison, who sits in the front row nearest both the blackboard and the teacher, waits patiently for another moment, then, realizing she's not getting results, puts her hand down. When Mrs. Richter walks toward her, Allison tries another tack, calling out her question. Still, she gets no response, so she gives up.

As a homework assignment, the students have divided their papers into one hundred squares, color-coding each square prime or composite—

prime being those numbers which are divisible only by one and themselves, and composite being everything else. Mrs. Richter asks them to call out the prime numbers they've found, starting with the tens.

Nate is the first to shout, "Eleven!" The rest of the class chimes in a second later. As they move through the twenties and thirties, Nate, Kyle, and Kevin, who sit near one another at the back of the class, call out louder and louder, casually competing for both quickest response and the highest decibel level. Mrs. Richter lets the boys' behavior slide, although they are intimidating other students.

"Okay," Mrs. Richter says when they've reached one hundred. "Now, what do you think of one hundred and three? Prime or composite?"

Kyle, who is skinny and a little pop-eyed, yells out, "Prime!" but Mrs. Richter turns away from him to give someone else a turn. Unlike Allison, who gave up when she was ignored, Kyle isn't willing to cede his teacher's attention. He begins to bounce in his chair and chant, "*Prime! Prime! Prime!*" Then, when he turns out to be right, he rebukes the teacher, saying, "*See,* I told you."

When the girls in Mrs. Richter's class do speak, they follow the rules. When Allison has another question, she raises her hand again and waits her turn; this time, the teacher responds. When Amy volunteers her sole answer of the period, she raises her hand, too. She gives the wrong answer to an easy multiplication problem, turns crimson, and flips her head forward so her hair falls over her face.

Occasionally, the girls shout out answers, but generally they are to the easiest, lowest-risk questions, such as the factors of four or six. And their stabs at public recognition depend on the boys' largesse: when the girls venture responses to more complex questions the boys quickly become territorial, shouting them down with their own answers. Nate and Kyle are particularly adept at overpowering Renee, who, I've been told by the teacher, is the brightest girl in the class. (On a subsequent visit, I will see her lay her head on her desk when Nate overwhelms her and mutter, "I hate this class.")

Mrs. Richter doesn't say anything to condone the boys' aggressiveness, but she doesn't have to: they insist on—and receive—her attention even when she consciously tries to shift it elsewhere in order to make the class more equitable.

After the previous day's homework is corrected, Mrs. Richter begins a new lesson, on the use of exponents.

"What does three to the third power mean?" she asks the class.

"*I know!*" shouts Kyle.

Instead of calling on Kyle, who has already answered more than his share of questions, the teacher turns to Dawn, a somewhat more voluble girl who has plucked her eyebrows down to a few hairs.

"Do you know, Dawn?"

Dawn hesitates, and begins "Well, you count the number of threes and . . ."

"But I know!" interrupts Kyle. *"I know!"*

Mrs. Richter deliberately ignores him, but Dawn is rattled: she never finishes her sentence, she just stops.

"I know! ME!" Kyle shouts again, and then before Dawn recovers herself he blurts, *"It's three times three times three!"*

At this point, Mrs. Richter gives in. She turns away from Dawn, who is staring blankly, and nods at Kyle. "Yes," she says. "Three times three times three. Does everyone get it?"

"YES!" shouts Kyle; Dawn says nothing.

Mrs. Richter picks up the chalk. "Let's do some others," she says.

"Let me!" says Kyle.

"I'll pick on whoever raises their hand," she tells him.

Nate, Kyle, and two other boys immediately shoot up their hands, fingers squeezed tight and straight in what looks like a salute.

"Don't you want to wait and hear the problem first?" she asks, laughing.

They drop their hands briefly. She writes 8^4 on the board. "Okay, what would that look like written out?"

Although a third of the class raises their hands to answer—including a number of students who haven't yet said a word—she calls on Kyle anyway.

"Eight times eight times eight times eight," he says triumphantly, as the other students drop their hands.

When the bell rings, I ask Amy about the mistake she made in class and the embarrassment it caused her. She blushes again.

"Oh yeah," she says. "That's about the only time I ever talked in there. I'll never do that again."

Voice and Silence

I had chosen Amy, along with two of her friends, Evie DiLeo and Becca Holbrook, as three of the subjects for this book partly because, within minutes of our first meeting—and months before I ever saw them in a classroom—they announced to me that they were not like other girls at Weston: they were, they proudly announced, feminists. Amy explained that to them "feminism" meant that as adults they plan to be economically independent of men. Until that time, though, it means "knowing that boys aren't all they're cracked up to be."

I had hoped that these girls, with their bold credo, would defy the statistics in the AAUW survey *Shortchanging Girls, Shortchanging America*. Yet although they spoke of themselves in terms of grit and independence, those qualities were rarely on display in the classroom. Whereas their male classmates yelled out or snapped the fingers of their raised hands when they wanted to speak, these girls seemed, for the most part, to recede from class proceedings, a charge they didn't deny.

"I don't raise my hand in my classes because I'm afraid I have the wrong answer and I'll be embarrassed," Becca, who is gangly and soft-spoken, explains one day during lunch. "My self-confidence will be taken away, so I don't want to raise my hand even if I really do know."

"I hate when teachers correct you," says Evie, who, dark-haired and serious, is enrolled in Weston's gifted students' program. "And it's worse when they say it's okay to do things wrong in that voice like 'It's okay, honey.' I can't handle it. I get really red and I start crying and I feel stupid."

"I think," Amy says slowly, "I think girls just worry about what people will say more than boys do, so they don't want to talk so much."

I mention to Amy that the boys freely volunteer in the math and science classes I've observed, even though their answers are often wrong. They seem to think it's okay to say "I think," to be unsure of a response.

Amy nods in agreement. "Boys never care if they're wrong. They can say totally off-the-wall things, things that have nothing to do with class sometimes. They're not afraid to get in trouble or anything. I'm not shy. But it's like, when I get into class, I just . . . " She shrugs her shoulders helplessly. "I just can't talk. I don't know why."

Girls' hesitance to speak out relative to boys is not mere stylistic difference; speaking out in class—and being acknowledged for it—is a constant reinforcement of a student's right to be heard, to take academic risks. Students who talk in class have more opportunity to enhance self-esteem through exposure to praise; they have the luxury of learning from mistakes and they develop the perspective to see failure as an educational tool. Boys such as Kyle and Nate feel internal permission to speak out whether they are bright or not, whether they are right or wrong, whether their comments are insightful, corrosive, combative, or utterly ridiculous. The important thing is to be recognized, to assert the "I am."

"I think my opinions are important, so I yell them out," Nate tells me one day after Mrs. Richter's math class. "The teacher'll tell you not to do it, but they answer your question before the people who raise their hands. Girls will sit there until the bell rings with their hands up and never get their question answered." He waves his hand in the air as if brushing the girls aside and says contemptuously, "Forget that."

According to gender equity specialists Myra and David Sadker, students who participate in class hold more positive attitudes toward school, and those attitudes enhance learning. Yet they also found that, in the typical classroom, boys overwhelmingly dominate the proceedings: they consistently command more of the teacher's time and energy than girls, receiving more positive reinforcement, more remediation, and more criticism. Nor is the difference just one of quantity: in the Sadkers' observations of one hundred classrooms in four states, they found that the boys were routinely asked more complex questions than girls, and were commended for their academic acumen, while girls were commended for social skills and docility.

In every class I visit at Weston there is at least one boy like Nate or Kyle, a boy who demands constant and inappropriate attention and to whom the teacher succumbs: if she doesn't, after all, she won't get much done during that period. In a straight count of who talks in Weston class-rooms—who yells out answers, who is called on by the teacher, who com-mands the most interaction—the ratio hovers roughly around five boys to one girl. Compared to other schools, however, this constitutes progress: the Sadkers placed the rate at eight to one. Even in English class, traditionally girls' turf, Weston boys received roughly three times the recognition of their female classmates.

The argument can be made that boys as well as girls suffer from the hidden curriculum. Boys such as Nate may be learning an unfortunate self-centeredness along with a lack of respect for their female classmates. Yet they still profit from the attention they receive. Ignored by their teachers and belittled by their male peers, girls lose heart: they may become reluctant to participate at all in class, unable to withstand the small failures necessary for long-term academic success. Even girls such as Amy, Evie, and Becca, who frequently proclaim that "guys are so obnoxious," have absorbed the hidden lessons of deference to them in the classroom, and, along with it, a powerful lesson in self-abnegation.

Several days after joining Amy in her math class, I visit Ms. Kelly's English class. Ms. Kelly is a second-year teacher: freckle-faced and snub-nosed, dressed in a T-shirt and khaki skirt, she barely looks older than her students. The class has been studying Greek mythology; today Ms. Kelly, who has placed the desks in clusters of six, instructs the students to write out the discussion they imagine took place between Zeus and Hera when she discovered he had fathered an illegitimate child.

"Any questions?" she asks, after explaining the assignment.

Two girls, Kathy and Amanda, raise their hands and she calls on Amanda. Amanda glances at Kathy, who sits in the group of desks next to hers. "Well, can you help me when you've answered her question?" she says politely. The teacher tends to Kathy, and then to a boy in another group who is misbehaving; she never returns to Amanda, who becomes frustrated.

"What are we supposed to do?" she mutters. "I don't get it." She puts her pencil down and looks over the shoulder of the girl sitting next to her. After a few minutes, she sighs wearily and begins to write.

I walk around the room, asking the students if I can read their works-in-progress. Amanda, who will eventually get an A on her paper, covers hers when I ask to see it.

"Oh," she says, "mine's so stupid you wouldn't want to read it."

Kathy reluctantly hands me her work. As I skim through it, one of the boys shoves his paper at me.

"'Don't you want to read mine?" he asks.

I smile politely, as unwilling as the teachers to chastise him for interrupting, and take his paper. The dialogue he's written is almost incoherent and laced with misuses of the archaic forms of "you," as in "Hera, I'll whip thou butt for that."

He smirks as I read.

"Good, huh?" he says, then takes the paper back to read to his seatmates.

During an earlier lesson, the students have composed their own original myths, and have voted on the one they think is the best in the class. At the end of today's period, Ms. Kelly reads the winner, written by a wiry, sharp-featured Latina girl named Amber. The tale is surprisingly artful, the story of a young boy's search for the answers to questions that his father says are unsolvable. His quest takes him through enchanted woods, where he encounters talking animals who help him unlock the secret of a magic waterfall. He attains wisdom through risk and adventure, and, in the end, brings insight as well as treasure home to lay before his father.

After class I ask Amber why she chose to make a boy, not a girl, the central character in her story. She shrugs. "I used a boy because little girls don't go into creepy places and explore things," she says. "And it was an adventure; it wouldn't be right if you used a girl."

I ask Ms. Kelly to lend me the students' stories from all of her class periods and flip through the stack. Although many girls chose men and boys as the embodiments of bravery, strength, and wisdom, it did not surprise me to find that not a single boy had imagined a female hero.

Certainly some girls at Weston act out, demand attention, clown in class, but when they try those tactics, using disruption as a tool to gain individual attention and instruction, they are not met with the same reward as boys.

In mid-November, Mrs. Richter is giving out grades to Amy's class. The teacher sits at her desk in the back corner of the room, and the students come up one by one, in reverse alphabetical order; their faces are tense on the way up, then pleased or disappointed on the way back.

When Dawn's turn comes, Mrs. Richter speaks sharply to her.

"You're getting a B," the teacher says, "but for citizenship, you're getting 'disruptive.' You've been talking a lot and there have been some outbursts."

Dawn scrunches her mouth over to one side of her face, lowers her eyes, and returns to her seat.

"Disruptive?" yells Nate from across the room where the teacher's voice has carried. "*She's* not disruptive, *I'm* disruptive."

Mrs. Richter laughs. "You've got that right," she says.

When his turn comes, Nate gets a B plus. "It would've been an A minus if you turned in your last homework assignment," Mrs. Richter says. As predicted, his citizenship comment is also 'disruptive,' but the bad news isn't delivered with the same sting as it was to Dawn—it's conferred with an indulgent smile. There is a tacit acceptance of a disruptive boy, because boys *are* disruptive. Girls are too, sometimes, as Dawn illustrates, but with different consequences.

So along with fractions and exponents, Dawn has learned that she has to tamp down assertive behavior, that she has to diminish herself both to please the teacher and to appease the boys, with whom she cannot compete. Meanwhile, Nate has learned that monopolizing the class period and defying the teacher gets him in trouble, but he also garners individual attention, praise, and answers to his questions.

Over the course of the semester, Dawn slowly stops disrupting; she stops participating too. At the semester break, when I check with Mrs. Richter on the classes' progress, she tells me, "Dawn hardly talks at all now because she's overpowered by the boys. She can't get the attention in class, so she's calmed down."

Nate, however, hasn't changed a bit, but whereas Dawn's behavior is viewed as containable, the teacher sees Nate's as inevitable. "I'll go through two weeks of torture before I'll give him detention," Mrs. Richter says. "But you have to tolerate that behavior to a certain extent or he won't want to be there at all, he'll get himself kicked out.

"I know his behavior works for him, though," she continues. "He talks more, he gets more answers out there, and he does well because of it. I try to tell him that we need to let others talk so they can understand too. But when I do, I begin and end with positive things about his behavior and sandwich the bad stuff in the middle. I'm never sure which part he really hears."

Unbalanced Equations: Girls, Math, and the Confidence Gap

Although the skewed equations of voice and silence are not the exclusive province of math or science, they are arguably the most damaging in those classes, where the tradition of male dominance is most entrenched. *Shortchanging Girls, Shortchanging America* showed that girls and boys who like math and science have higher levels of self-esteem than other children (and, for that matter, that children with high self-esteem tend to like math and science). For girls in particular, those subjects are also tied to ambition: girls who like math and science—who are, perhaps, more resistant to traditional gender roles—are more likely to aspire to careers as professionals. As adults, women who have taken more than two math courses in college are the only ones who subsequently achieve pay equity and even earn more than their male counterparts.

Unfortunately, girls are far less likely than boys to retain their affection for math and science. As they move through school, their confidence in their mathematical abilities falters and their competence soon follows suit. It's important to note that the confidence drop often *precedes* the competence drop: even in early adolescence, girls who perform as well as boys often evaluate their skills as lesser. By their senior year, convinced of their ineptitude, they become less persistent in solving problems than their male peers and less likely than boys with poorer grades in the same class to believe they can pursue a math-related career.

Amy is one of those girls who has little faith in her math skills, although her performance is well above average. "School is important to me," she says during lunch one day, when I catch her struggling with a homework assignment. "I want to do good in school and be proud of myself. I don't want to be a lazy bum. And I'll need math when I'm older. There's math in everything, no matter what, so it's important to learn. So I know I should have a better attitude, but I just want to give up. It's not that I don't try, it's just that I don't believe in myself and I don't get it. I'm just so *slow*." She glares down at her paper.

Amy goes on to say that a person has to be smarter to do well at math than at English. She also believes that girls—herself included—have a natural bent toward English and boys toward math, which, by her logic, would make girls less intelligent than boys. When I point this out, she begins to backtrack, but then stops, leans forward, and drops her voice, continuing in a solemn, confidential tone. "Boys do better in math, believe me, they do. Girls, we have other things on our minds, I guess."

Yet in spite of this purported genetic disadvantage, during the same class in which Dawn receives her disappointing citizenship mark, Amy receives an A in math, which clinches her spot on the school honor roll. The news doesn't change her assumptions one whit.

"It's not hard to get an A in here," she says. "Basically you just have to show up. And I still think I've done it wrong every day. I'll probably be in, like, special ed. math next year."

From her vantage point in the front of the class, Mrs. Richter says she can see the girls' waning interest in her subject, and it frustrates her. She is especially disturbed by a trend she's recently noticed: the boys in her class tend to improve over the course of the school year—some even jump from D's to B's or A's—while girls stay exactly where they were in September: the good students remain good students, the poor students remain poor. She worries that, for the girls, the holding pattern is simply temporary. Next year, perhaps the year after, even the good students may begin to slide; they simply don't trust their ability.

"The boys see math as something that shows they're brainy and they like being able to show off that way," Mrs. Richter explains. "And they're more risk-taking than the girls, so they'll do better on tests every time, even if the girls turn in all their work and the boys don't. It's like the girls set themselves up to fail. They do the work. I see them practice one kind of problem over and over because I've told them it'll be on a test. But then the test comes and they miss it anyway. I've heard them say, 'Oh no, I got that kind of problem wrong last time.' So even though they practiced it, they go and get it wrong again. Amy does that. She'll look at a problem and say, 'There's no way I can do this,' and give up, even though I know she has the skills. But the boys are different: they can get all the homework wrong, but they don't care as long as they tried. And then they figure out *why* it's wrong instead of being embarrassed about it. That makes them more confident."

Mrs. Richter considers parents, more than teachers, to be responsible for girls' confidence gap. Every year, she says, her female students tell her, "My mother said she couldn't do math either," as if math skills are genetic, which, the teacher hastens to add, they are not. Still, she admits, the classroom culture can further undercut the girls. "I try to teach them the same; I try to call on them the same. But I know I don't always hold them accountable the same way. I let the girls off the hook because they get so embarrassed when they're wrong. And the boys want control of the class, so sometimes they get it . . . " She trails off, shaking her head. "I don't know," she says. "We try, but somehow we're still not getting to the girls, and we're going to lose them."

Bad Chemistry: "Guys Like It When You Act All Helpless"

It is another late-fall morning under the oak tree at Weston. Amy, Becca, and Evie huddle together slightly apart from the other students, the intimate turn to their shoulders making it clear that they're exchanging the juiciest gossip. A squadron of seventh-grade boys on bicycles zips by and the girls look up, annoyed, sidling to the left to avoid being hit.

A few seconds later, Becca, usually the most reserved of her friends, shrieks.

"Get that away from me!"

The bikers are forgotten as the girls scatter, screaming, their faces flushed, revealing Carl Ross, a boy from Evie's math class, whose feet are firmly planted where the girls once stood. An uncapped jar labeled "Felicia" dangles from his left hand. Until a minute ago, it held a large spider he'd captured for extra credit in science class. Felicia is currently hanging from a dead pine needle in his other hand, her legs tucked in and body contracted in fear.

Becca runs about ten feet and turns around. When she smiles, she reveals a mouth full of braces. "I'm *deathly* afraid of spiders," she says, her eyes shining as she looks back at her tormentor.

The other two girls run up to her. "God, me too!" Amy says breathlessly, clutching her friend's arms. "When I saw *Arachnophobia* my dad had to go check my room for me. He had to look under the bed!"

Evie's cheeks are pink and her dark hair is falling from its bun. She tucks the wayward wisps back in place as a second boy lets the bug drop from his finger by a lengthening strand of web. "Yuck, how disgusting," she says, widening her eyes. "I hope he doesn't come near me with that."

As a woman standing among these girls, I wasn't sure how to react. I desperately wanted them to stand up to the boys who increasingly joined in the game. I wanted them to be brave, to marvel at the spider's jewel-green body, to ask for a turn at holding it and watching it try to spin its escape. But I felt the pressure too: a real girl, a girl who wants a boy to like her, runs screaming from spiders. The more she likes a boy, the more she allows him to terrorize her, and the more helpless she pretends to be. Showing any real interest in spiders would've been imprudent for the girls, a denial of their newly important femininity. During my year at Weston, I saw girls run from spiders innumerable times; with each flight toward traditional femininity, I thought about who has permission, who has the right in our culture, to explore the natural world, to get dirty and muddy, to think spiders and worms and frogs are neat, to bring them in for extra credit in science. In fact, to be engaged in science at all.

"I'm not *really* afraid of that stuff, except snakes and blood," Amy admits later, after the hoopla. "But guys like it if you act all helpless and girly, so you do."

As with math, there is a circular relationship among girls' affection for science, their self-esteem, and their career plans. But unlike in math, the achievement gap between girls and boys in science is actually widening: the National Assessment of Educational Progress found that, for thirteen-year-olds, gender differences in all areas of science performance except biology actually increased during the 1980s, with boys' skills improving and girls' slipping during that time. This is particularly disturbing when one considers that today's young people are growing up in an era of rapid technological change; without a solid grounding in science, girls will not only be unable to participate in shaping that change, they will be helpless in the face of it.

Certainly, the culture outside the classroom discourages scientific competence in girls. Boys still have more casual exposure to science—whether it's light meters, chemistry sets, or, like Carl and his friends, spiders—and they're more likely to have computers at home. Science toys are still marketed almost exclusively toward boys, with boys featured on packages (or, worse still, girls *watching* boys) and the world of video games seems constructed with an entirely male audience in mind.

In school, girls opt out—or are pushed out—of science at every stage of advancement. In high school, boys and girls take introductory biology and chemistry in similar numbers, but far more boys go on to physics or advanced chemistry, while girls, if they take science at all, continue with biology. And although the numbers of women who pursue the sciences have skyrocketed, there were formerly so few that even huge jumps yield small results: for instance, the number of female engineers grew 131 percent during the 1980s, but women still make up only 8 percent of that field. In fact, a scant 16 percent of currently employed scientists are female, and that figure may well have peaked: by the late 1980s, the numbers of women pursuing degrees in science and engineering (excluding the social sciences) had leveled off and were dropping, especially in advanced physics and computer science.

Nonetheless, in spite of the achievement gap, today's girls believe that they can excel in science; the trouble is, boys (perhaps prejudiced by the overreaction to spiders and snakes) do not share that belief about their female classmates. Because of that disparity, science laboratory groups—in which boys grab equipment from girls, perform experiments for them, and ridicule girls' contributions—can become less an opportunity for partnership than a microcosm of unintended lessons about gender.

Amy's science class is taught by Mr. Sinclair, a mustachioed fellow with a receding hairline, who chose teaching as a profession during what he describes as his idealistic youth in the late 1960s. He periodically considers changing careers, mostly for financial reasons, but he enjoys his work too much to quit. Instead, he stays sharp by attending conferences on science instruction, subscribing to newsletters, seeking out new ways to teach. He tries hard to be creative because, he says, the kids tend not to like physical science very much. But judging from what happens in his classroom, it's really the girls who don't like it.

Like Mrs. Richter, Mr. Sinclair never intentionally discriminates against the girls in his class; both he and the other eighth-grade science teacher at Weston—who is also male—are quick to point out the few girls who do participate (although in further conversation I found that many of those girls felt neither affection nor affinity for the subject). What I saw instead, even more than in the math classes I observed, was a kind of passive resistance to participation by the girls that went unquestioned by the teacher. Call it gender bias by omission. When, week after week, boys raised their hands to ask or answer questions in far greater numbers than girls, when only boys shouted out responses, when boys enthusiastically offered up extra-credit demonstrations, the teacher simply didn't notice.

The very morning that Amy flees shrieking from Felicia the spider, Mr. Sinclair invites me to observe as her section of his physical science class performs an easy, fun experiment called "The Cartesian Diver." Each group of three students is given an empty dishwashing liquid bottle, an eyedropper, and a beaker of water. The idea is to fill the bottle with water, drop in the dropper, and, through some magical process that the students must determine (which turns out to be placing a little water in the dropper in advance, then squeezing the bottle to cause mass displacement), make the dropper sink and float at will.

In Amy's lab group there is another girl, Donna, and a boy, Liam, who sits between them. Liam performs the experiment as the two girls watch, occasionally offering encouragement, but no criticism. When he is successful, Amy squeals and pats him on the arm. Eventually Liam lets Donna and Amy each try the diver exactly once; then he recovers it and continues to play.

In another group of two girls and one boy directly behind Amy, Roger stands behind the girls, supervising . . . sort of.

"You're doing it wrong, ha-ha," he taunts in a singsong voice. Roger has a long rattail and a pierced ear; he wears an oversized tie-dyed T-shirt. The girls, who have styled their long blond hair identically, huddle together, trying to ignore him, and continue to attempt the experiment. Roger watches them a moment longer, then grabs the bottle from them, pours the water into the beaker, and walks away with the dropper. The girls do not protest. When he comes back a few minutes later, the girls have refilled the bottle, but, still uncertain about how to proceed, have decided to empty it again and start over.

"Oh, smart," Roger says sarcastically. "*Real* smart." He grabs the bottle again. "*I'll* do it." He refills the bottle, puts the dropper in, and completes the experiment while the girls watch in silence.

I wander to the far corner of the room, where Allison, from Amy's math class, and Karla, a round-faced Latina girl with deep dimples and black hair pulled into a topknot, are having trouble with their diver. There are several girls sitting around them, yet they have asked a boy for help.

"I told him he could do it for us because he has man's hands," Karla, who once told me she wants to be an astronaut, tells me, smiling.

A second boy is watching the scene. When his friend completes the experiment, he pumps his fist in the air. "Yes!" he says. "A *man* had to do it!"

"But *how* did you do it?" Allison asks.

"I have magic hands," the first boy answers. "*Man* hands," and he laughs.

The girls laugh too—acting appropriately "helpless and girly"—but they never learn how to do the experiment. Instead, like the girls in the other groups, they have become outsiders in the learning process, passive observers rather than competent participants. In truth, "man hands" do complete most of the experiments in the room.

Later, Mr. Sinclair tells me that his classroom is free of gender bias. "I try to emphasize the subject for both," he tells me. "I never tell girls they can't do something." But there was much that he didn't see. When I ask whether he's noticed that boys speak out more—sometimes exclusively—in his class, and are more eager to perform extra-credit demonstrations, he looks up at the ceiling and squints thoughtfully. "Yeah," he says, "that's true. I'm guessing they're more mechanical, doing stuff with machines outside of school. Boys probably do have that, and it's probably true that gives them an advantage I hadn't thought of."

We discuss the marketing of science toys and again he slowly nods his head. "I didn't think about that either," he says. "Yeah, that's probably true, the toys are geared toward boys; that would give them an advantage too."

Finally I tell him what I've seen in lab groups.

"Man hands," he says, looking bemused. "Really? Well, hopefully they picked up that it's the level of water and not gender that does it."

You Can Say "I Think" in There

Teachers at Weston varied tremendously in their reactions to boys' dominance in their classroom. Some, like Mr. Sinclair, simply didn't see it. Others fought the boys for control: one eighth-grade history teacher—who proudly told me that his wife had founded the local NOW chapter—would break into class discussions to say, "We haven't heard from any of the girls in the room. What do *you* think?" The girls seemed to be uncomfortable with such attention at first, but, as the year progressed, they became increasingly vocal. During a lesson on England's debtor's prisons one girl even yelled out, "What about the women? What happened to them?"

Another teacher, Liz Muney, who runs the district's gifted program and teaches sixth grade at Weston, told me that when *Shortchanging Girls, Shortchanging America* was first released, she discussed its findings with her class. She explained that, from now on, she was going to call equally on girls and boys, and, just to make sure that she did, she held her attendance roster during class.

"After two days the boys blew up," she told me one afternoon during a break between classes. "They started complaining and saying that I was calling on the girls more than them. I showed them it wasn't true and they had to back down. I kept on doing it, but for the boys, equality was hard to get used to; they perceived it as a big loss."

Like the teachers, the girls I interviewed were not always aware that they were being ignored in class (in some classes, such as math, they even preferred it), but their favorite teachers just happened to be the ones who actively wrestled with the hidden curriculum. For Amy, Evie, and Becca that teacher is Ms. Nellas, with whom they study American history.

"She teaches good," Becca assures me one day during lunch.

"Yeah," Evie says. "She makes you want to strive to be better. She'll do 'the power clap' and say how good you're doing . . . "

"Even if your work sucks," interrupts Amy, whose work rarely "sucks." "So you try really hard. And you can say what you want in there and no one ever says you're wrong; it's like, you're not afraid to say 'I think.'"

Becca returns to her original assessment: "She teaches good," she says, nodding her head.

Amy's demeanor in Ms. Nellas's class is utterly different than it is in math, science, or even English: she uncrosses her legs and plants both feet on the floor. She sits up straight, leans forward, and thrusts her hand in the air. Once, she even gives an impatient (and uncharacteristic) little wave for attention.

This is election year, and when I first visit Ms. Nellas's class in late October, she is discussing the electoral college. She stands at the front of the room, a craggy-faced woman with an easy smile, and offers a blunt explanation of that esoteric organization: "The reason there's an electoral college is that people who wrote the Constitution—who were all men—*didn't* really want everyone to participate in electing officials," she says. "They only trusted people like themselves, so they said, 'We don't want the common people to vote. They can't read or write and we can't trust them to elect leaders.' And they certainly didn't trust *women*, so they weren't about to let *them* vote."

During the lesson, boys raise their hands roughly twice as often as girls, but Ms. Nellas has a trick for making sure that girls who do volunteer are recognized: after she asks a question she looks around the room to see whose hands are up, then says, "Okay, first Randy, then Jeffrey, then Amy." If she inadvertently continues without exhausting the list, the slighted students are quick to protest. She also promotes a more tolerant culture through her classroom decor: among the encouraging messages she has posted on the classroom walls are "You Have a *Duty to Assist* Anyone Who Asks for Help" and the somewhat convoluted "Everybody Is Good at *Some* of the Abilities." Under the clock, in the most strategic spot in the room, there is a yellowed poster depicting a teacher in Renaissance garb saying to his student, "Columbus, will yer [sic] sit down and stop asking all those dumb questions?" Beneath it a caption reads: "'Dumb' questions lead to learning. Don't be afraid to ask."

Amy's class meets just before Ms. Nellas's free period, so, one afternoon after the bell rings, I linger behind to chat. Ms. Nellas invites me to sit at one of the students' recently vacated desks and settles in opposite me. As a veteran teacher—she's been in the profession for over twenty years—Ms. Nellas is comfortable discussing both her strengths and weaknesses. She looks pleased when I tell her that girls seem to feel the most comfortable in her class, but adamantly denies that she's solved the gender dilemma.

"I definitely play to the boys," she says, shaking her head. "I know I do. The squeaky wheel gets the grease and they're louder."

She mentions Andrew, a curly-haired, slightly pudgy boy in Amy's class who shoots his hand up—sometimes snapping his fingers for attention—whenever she asks a question. When called on, he tends not only to answer but to offer up an additional mini lecture of his own.

"Andrew's into history," Ms. Nellas says. "He knows a lot and teaches the class things with what he has to say, so he's a good resource and I like that. But on the other hand, he's loud, and, like a lot of boys he pulls my attention. I know that means they walk out of here with greater self-esteem, they feel more valued. For the girls it seems more important that they feel a personal bond, that makes them feel valued. I have that with Amy, Evie, and Becca, but I don't have that with all of them. I try to make it up some by encouraging the girls to talk, by stressing that a question is a question and every question is worthwhile"—Ms. Nellas gestures to her Columbus poster—"but I know some girls end up feeling bad, they feel reduced by the experience of my class."

Like many teachers at Weston, Ms. Nellas is an advocate of cooperative learning: students collaborating on projects in groups, each with an assigned role. Cooperative learning—in which success is not contingent on quick response time or a loud voice—is said to be especially beneficial for girls and has become somewhat voguish in progressive schools. But, as with lab groups, the interactions, if not effectively monitored, can merely reinforce the students' stereotypes. "I've noticed that when they do group work, the boys want to be the leader," Ms. Nellas says, "and the girls always take the recorder role and that's a problem. I suppose I let it happen, too, but I don't want to assign them the roles in groups because I'm afraid of my own prejudices. I think I'd pick the quick students to lead the group, and so I might end up with the boys too, although I think I'd pick more girls than they do.

"The dynamics are already in place when they get here," she continues, "and they don't improve as they get older: when I teach high school, boys put their arm around me, pat my head like I'm a pet or something because I'm a woman. It can be funny, but it's still a power play. It's all about control, about who's in charge. When they really act out, though, I'll just stop the class and wait, even if it takes thirty seconds and it's driving me crazy. That sounds like a long time, but it's less of a waste, in the end, than sending them to the principal or yelling at the student. That way, they don't get the power, they don't get the attention, and they don't get the control. And *maybe* you can make it a little more equal."

Reflective Writing: *Author Peggy Orenstein mostly tells the story of what she observed in a California middle school, but her story is also an argument about the problems female students often have in classroom situations. Try to piece together that argument. Specifically, why is it, according to Orenstein, that so many girls learn to be silent? In what ways does she observe boys as favored in certain classes? How does what she is saying relate to your own experiences and observations in school? If she is correct in asserting that female students are often not well served by schools, what would be the implications of that situation for society as a whole? What further research needs to be done examining how male and female students are treated in our schools?*

The Trouble with Single-Sex Schools

Wendy Kaminer

A number of educators have responded to perceived gender inequities in the schools by advocating single-sex education, particularly for female students. In this 1998 essay from the Atlantic Monthly *magazine, author Wendy Kaminer, herself a graduate of a leading women's university, critically examines the evidence and arguments for the greater effectiveness of single-sex schools for females; she finds little support for this position. The author also presents some arguments in favor of coeducational learning. Kaminer, a lawyer and social critic, is a Public Policy Fellow at Radcliffe College, contributing editor at the* Atlantic Monthly, *and the author of five books and numerous articles on social and cultural issues.*

To Consider: *What specific problems does the author have with the arguments in favor of single-sex education? In considering Kaminer's critique of this position, try to imagine what features of coeducational schooling she finds most valuable, for both female and male students.*

American women won the opportunity to be educated nearly a hundred years before they won the right to vote, not coincidentally. In the beginning women were educated for the sake of family and society: the new republic needed educated mothers to produce reasonable, responsible male citizens. But although the first all-female academies, founded in the early 1800s, reflected a commitment to traditional gender roles, which reserved the public sphere for men, they reinforced a nascent view of women as potentially reasonable human beings—endowed with the attributes of citizenship.

Education also contributed to women's restlessness and impatience with domesticity. It may or may not have produced better mothers, but it did seem to produce fewer mothers. Young female secondary-school graduates of the mid-1800s tended to marry later than their uneducated peers or not at all. "Our failures only marry," the president of Bryn Mawr, M. Carey Thomas, famously remarked in the early 1900s.

The first generations of educated women were products of single-sex secondary and undergraduate schools, with few exceptions (Oberlin became the country's first coed college, in 1837). The Seven Sisters opened their doors in the last decades of the nineteenth century and evolved into a female Ivy League, educating the daughters of elites and providing social and professional mobility to some members of the middle class. Such schools were essential to the nineteenth-century women's movement. They not only inspired activism in women and prepared them to work outside the home but also created wage-earning work, as schoolteaching became one of few respectable professional options for unmarried females.

Still, single-sex education was not exactly a choice; it was a cultural mandate at a time when sexual segregation was considered only natural. Early feminists hoped eventually to integrate men's schools as well as voting booths, and equal educational opportunities proved much easier to obtain than equal electoral rights. By the turn of the century more girls than boys were graduating from high school and coeducation was becoming the norm. In 1910, out of the nation's 1,083 colleges 27 percent were exclusively for men, 15 percent exclusively for women, and the remaining 58 percent coed.

Today females outnumber males among college graduates, and a mere 1.3 percent of all women awarded B.A. degrees graduate from single-sex colleges. Now that the Ivy League is coed, academically elite women's colleges—Smith, Wellesley, Mount Holyoke—are apt to lose the best-credentialed students to schools like Harvard, Brown, and Yale. In the 1970s, after men's colleges and universities began accepting women, the SAT scores of Smith College applicants declined; they stabilized and rose slightly during the 1980s.

The image of women's colleges has improved in the past five years, thanks partly to Hillary Rodham Clinton, Wellesley class of 1969. Applications to women's schools have steadily increased—but so has the number of college applicants overall. It's highly unlikely that with competition from the Ivy League and in the aftermath of the Sexual Revolution, women's colleges will ever recover the popularity and prestige they once enjoyed. Only about 3 percent of female high school seniors even consider attending any of the nation's eighty-two women's colleges. But if single-sex college education seems to generate relatively low demand among young women, support for it is on the increase among their elders.

Having gained entry to virtually all the nation's public and private universities (and military academies), many women are questioning the benefits of coeducation at every level, but especially in secondary schools. According to popular feminist wisdom, coed schools are detrimental to the self-esteem of girls; they discourage rather than inspire girls' achievement, particularly in math and science. Many parents of girls seem to share these beliefs—or they want their daughters protected from the attentions and temptations of boys. (For gay and bisexual girls, however, single-sex schools can be fraught with sexual tension.) All-girls elementary and secondary schools are in the midst of a "renaissance," according to Whitney Ransome, the director of the National Coalition of Girls' Schools. Since the early 1990s applications have increased by 21 percent and four new all-girls secondary schools have been established.

Pursuant to federal law, single-sex education is primarily a private prerogative; public schools are generally barred from discriminating on the basis of sex or race. But separatism has been enjoying a resurgence among some feminists and advocates of racial justice, who are challenging restrictions on segregated public classrooms. The belief that segregation necessarily sends a message of inferiority, which underlays the Supreme Court's 1954 decision in *Brown v. Board of Education,* has been upended. Now segregated schools are heralded for raising self-esteem in disadvantaged groups.

Of course, integrationists still have the law on their side. In 1991 three public schools proposed for African-American males in Detroit were quickly and successfully challenged in a federal district court by the parents of girls in the city's public schools, along with a coalition of feminist and civil-rights groups. In that suit, *Garrett v. Board of Education,* the court held that the all-boys schools violated the Fourteenth Amendment and federal equal-education laws. Supporters of these schools characterized them as a response to a crisis facing young African-American males, who as a group suffered inordinately high dropout, unemployment, and homicide rates. But, as the court observed, there was no evidence that the presence of girls in class increased the risks faced by boys or interfered with efforts to help them: "Although co-educational programs have failed, there is no showing that it is the co-educational factor that results in failure." Besides, girls were in crisis as well. Sex was "inappropriately" invoked as a "proxy for 'at risk' students."

Undeterred by this decision, advocates for single-sex education recently established a public all-girls school in New York City. Named The Young Women's Leadership School, and known informally as the East Harlem Girls' School, it opened in September of 1996 with one seventh-grade class of fifty girls, and was immediately challenged by the New York Civil Liberties Union, the New York City chapter of the National Organization for Women, and the New York Civil Rights Coalition.

Last September the U.S. Department of Education's Office of Civil Rights issued an informal preliminary finding that the school appeared to violate federal law. Two remedies were suggested: sexually integrate the school or establish a separate but equal school for boys. (The state of California has recently initiated a pilot program encouraging the establishment of single-sex academies for middle and high school students.) But New York City's school chancellor, Rudy Crew, has said that he will neither admit boys to the East Harlem Girls' School nor establish a brother school, and civil-rights activists would fight attempts to establish a separate but equal boys' academy anyway. Compromise appears unlikely. The battle rages between those who pursue equality through integration and those who pursue it through separate institutions for the presumptively disadvantaged.

Supporters of the East Harlem school have cast the debate as a class struggle. The school serves Latinas from lower-income families, and Latina activists have denounced its opponents, NOW in particular, as upper-middle-class meddlers out of touch with the needs of less affluent minorities. The image of NOW as a group of elite feminists does not reflect reality (Anne Conners, the former president of the New York chapter, observed that the average income of members was $20,000), but wealth is relative. As outsiders to the East Harlem community, NOW activists may be "meddling"— but so were northerners who fought for an end to Jim Crow laws in the South. A commitment to civil rights assumes a responsibility to meddle.

Of course, whether the establishment of public all-girls schools retards or advances civil rights and social equality is a central question in this case. Supporters of The Young Women's Leadership School assert that it provides low-income families with the option of single-sex education that has always existed for the upper classes. Rich parents send their daughters to all-female schools; why shouldn't the daughters of the poor enjoy similar advantages?

That's an appeal bound to elicit sympathy, especially from guilty liberals, but it begs the question of whether the daughters of the rich benefit from single-sex education. Perhaps they benefit merely from being rich and attending elite private schools with favorable student-teacher ratios and superior facilities and curricula. Perhaps many would fare better at elite coed schools. In any case, the tendency of some affluent parents to choose single-sex schools is not evidence that single-sex education provides advantages for girls. The traditions of the rich, such as coming-out parties, are not necessarily progressive.

In fact, challengers of the East Harlem school charge that its establishment is part of a campaign by conservative elites to dismantle the public school system through privatization. The school was conceived and partly funded by Ann Rubenstein Tisch and her husband, Andrew Tisch, the chairman of the Loews Corporation management committee. It represents the initiative and ideals of upper-class meddlers, whose motives the middle-class meddlers suspect.

Does The Young Women's Leadership School represent a small step toward the goal of equality or a step away from it? The more that girls' schools are celebrated for nurturing achievement and self-esteem, the more futile efforts to improve public coeducation may seem. And feminist supporters of girls' schools are often opposed to boys' schools, so the prospect of success presents them with a quandary: which girls will be sacrificed to coed schools in the hope of socializing the boys?

The debate over single-sex education is complicated, and replete with the usual ironies: The Young Women's Leadership School can count among its defenders feminists who opposed single-sex admissions policies at the state-run Virginia Military Institute and anti-feminists who supported the exclusion of women from VMI and the Citadel. Feminist supporters of the East Harlem school distinguish its establishment as affirmative action, intended to remedy the discrimination that girls are said to encounter in coed classrooms—and in having been excluded from schools like VMI. Thus, conservative advocates of the East Harlem school, who generally oppose affirmative action, find themselves defending one putative form of it. Conservatives who are generally unsympathetic to arguments about self-esteem, dismissing them as an expression of liberal "victimism," find themselves extolling the virtues of a nurturing, supportive environment that builds girls' confidence and capacity to lead. In their defense of girls' schools, however, they rely primarily on a traditional belief that maintaining separate schools for males and females is only natural, considering presumed differences in their developmental needs and learning styles.

It is the belief in cognitive and characterological sex-based differences that unites conservative and liberal advocates of single-sex education—at least when the exclusion of males is at issue. Feminism is inconsistent on the subject of sex-based differences. Some of the same women who praise The Young Women's Leadership School for attending to the special needs of girls lambasted VMI for arguing that the special needs and sensibilities of young women made them unlikely to succeed in the harsh, highly competitive environment of a military academy. Feminists who complain about the male ethic that pervades law-school classrooms and male learning styles that are inimical to women suddenly, when the integration of VMI was at issue, started talking about the capacity of women to compete with men as equals in presumptively masculine environments.

In defense of male exclusivity, witnesses for VMI spouted popular feminist truths: women are less aggressive and more emotional, more cooperative and less competitive, than men. To substantiate these assertions and justify separation of the sexes, the state relied on Carol Gilligan's work on female moral development, which, of course, is regularly cited by feminists to support the exclusion of males from institutions like The Young Women's Leadership School.

In addition to assumptions about female learning and relational styles, proponents of all-girls schools rely on social science to support the claim that segregation by sex fosters achievement in girls. "Studies show . . ." is the usual lead-in to any defense of single-sex education. In fact studies do not show that girls fare better in single-sex schools. "There does not seem to be research support for this perspective," the sociologist Cynthia Epstein politely observes. Epstein, the author of *Deceptive Distinctions: Sex, Gender, and the Social Order* (1988), adds that there is no consensus among psychologists as to the existence of psychological or cognitive differences between the sexes, and that the evidence for the need for single-sex education and the justice of single-sex schools are highly equivocal.

Many social science studies [of sex-based differences] do not support the idea that deep-rooted male and female natures require separate education, or that segregated education can provide members of each sex with the same opportunities and development of skills.

What, then, is the basis for the claim that "studies show" the advantages of all-female schools? Perhaps the most frequently cited studies were conducted by M. Elizabeth Tidball, who reviewed the educational backgrounds of female achievers. In her first, widely cited study, published in 1973, Tidball examined a random sample of women included in *Who's Who* and found that disproportionate numbers were graduates of women's colleges. In subsequent studies Tidball found that women's colleges produced more than their share of graduates who went on to medical school or received life sciences.

What do these studies tell us about the relationship between single-sex education and achievement? Virtually nothing. Tidball made the common mistake of confusing correlation with causation. As Faye Crosby, a professor of psychology at Smith College, and other critics have observed, Tidball did not control for characteristics of women's colleges, apart from sexual homogeneity, that might well account for the success of their graduates. She did not allow for the socio-economic privileges shared by many graduates of elite women's colleges or for the selectivity of the schools.

Tidball's 1973 study focuses on women who graduated from women's colleges in the years before elite men's colleges were integrated; until the mid-1970s ambitious, high-achieving females gravitated to Seven Sister schools because they were among the most selective and prestigious institutions open to women. Students at these schools were self-selected for success, like their male counterparts in the Ivy League. They also tended to be well connected; many may have owed their success to the males present in their families more than to the absence of males from their classes.

Tidball's subsequent finding, that single-sex schools produce more female achievers in the sciences and medicine, also collapses under scrutiny. Faye Crosby and her Smith colleagues found in a comparison of similarly selective single-sex and coeducational schools that "women's colleges are not more productive." There are no definitive comparative data on the benefits of single-sex colleges for women. "Data are slim," Crosby writes, "but they indicate that coeducational schools are as likely to produce women scientists as are women's colleges."

Crosby's assertion challenges conventional wisdom about the risks of coeducation, which is becoming increasingly fashionable in secondary schools. A recent, widely cited study commissioned by the American Association of University Women (prepared by the Wellesley College Center for Research on Women) decries the current system. Titled "How Schools Shortchange Girls," the AAUW report declares that "the educational system is not meeting girls' needs." The executive summary cites "gender bias as a major problem at all levels of schooling," asserting that girls are plagued by sexual harassment, even at the grade school level, and neglected by sexist teachers, who pay more attention to boys. As a consequence, it seems, girls fall behind their male classmates: "Girls and boys enter school roughly equal in measured ability. Twelve years later, girls have fallen behind their male classmates in key areas such as higher-level mathematics and measures of self-esteem."

These remarks might awaken the anxieties of many parents with daughters in coed schools. But the dire tone of the summary is belied by the underlying findings of the AAUW study. Reviewed in its entirety, it presents a more complex, nuanced view of the female educational experience, which varies with race and class. In fact, "socioeconomic status," not sex, is said to be "the best predictor of both grades and test scores."

Are schools "shortchanging girls"? Reading the entire AAUW report, it's hard to say. "There is considerable evidence that girls earn higher grades than boys throughout their school careers," the report acknowledges. And the sexes seem to be approaching parity in skills. Recent research indicates that "sex differences in verbal abilities have decreased markedly . . . [and] differences in mathematics achievement are small and declining." Findings regarding achievement in science, however, are discouraging: girls are not catching up to boys and may even be falling further behind. Both sexes tend to lose interest in math and science as they proceed through school, but the loss is more pronounced for girls. Girls also exhibit less confidence in their mathematical abilities than boys, although it's worth remembering that girls are generally socialized to be relatively self-effacing; boys are expected to brag.

These differences in social conditioning complicate the task of measuring girls' relative self-esteem. The AAUW study suggests that high school girls have less self-esteem than boys and that the self-esteem of girls declines dramatically after puberty. How did researchers measure self-esteem? They counted the number of elementary school and high school students who reported being "happy the way I am." Sixty-nine percent of elementary school boys and 60 percent of elementary school girls declared that they were indeed happy with themselves. But among high school students 46 percent of boys were "happy the way I am," and a mere 29 percent of girls.

It's impossible to know what this survey means. Maybe it is evidence that girls have low self-esteem, as the AAUW report suggests. Or maybe it demonstrates that girls are less complacent and more ambitious than boys, and more likely to hold themselves to high standards of performance. Maybe boys are in a rut. Maybe not. By itself, Are you happy with yourself? is a useless survey question, because interpretations of the answer are hopelessly subjective.

What additional evidence is there to support the common assumption that girls are more likely to suffer a drop in self-esteem as they enter their teens? The AAUW report cites recent work, by Carol Gilligan, Lyn Mikel Brown, and Annie Rogers, documenting "the silencing of girls" in junior high and high school. But even if their findings on a loss of confidence in girls are accurate, these tell us very little about sexism or sex difference, because they offer no comparable study of boys. Maybe a loss of self-esteem is a function of adolescence, not of sex. Maybe boys are silenced too, metaphorically if not in fact. Maybe they make noise to drown out their fears. Maybe not.

A review of the usual studies of female development and education is most likely to result in uncertainty. The overall effects of coeducation are open to question, but evidence that single-sex secondary schools are especially beneficial for girls is scarce. One of the leading researchers in this area, Valerie Lee, a professor of education at the University of Michigan, found that students in Catholic girls' schools enjoyed advantages over female students in Catholic coeducational schools. Her subsequent study of independent schools, however, "produced equivocal results." She found "no consistent pattern of results favoring either single sex or coeducational schools, either for girls or boys."

Lee's work also challenged the assumption that girls' schools are considerably less sexist than coed schools. Her findings suggest that they may simply exhibit different styles of sexism. Comparing a sample of coeducational, all-boys, and all-girls independent schools, Lee found that "the frequency of [sexist] incidents was similar in the three types of schools, [but] the forms of sexism were different." Sexism was most severe in boys' schools; in coed schools it was most blatant and frequent in chemistry classes; girls' schools did pay the most attention to equality between the sexes, but, they also "perpetuated a pernicious form of sexism: academic dependence and nonrigorous instruction." In all-girls chemistry classes, for example, "undue attention was paid to neatness and cleanliness as well as to drawing parallels between domesticity and chemistry activities." It's not surprising to learn, after reviewing this study, that at The Young Women's Leadership School many walls are painted pink.

The sexism in girls' and women's schools is insidious. Whether manifested in feminine decor or in an approach to teaching that assumes a female penchant for cooperative, or "connected," learning, stereotypical notions of femininity often infect institutions for women and girls. Many of them encourage female academic achievement, but they discourage academic competition with males. They encourage heterosexual women and girls to separate their social and intellectual lives, reinforcing the dissonance bred into many achievement-oriented females.

That, at least, is what I learned about single-sex education as a student at Smith College, where I realized that the restraints of femininity are often self-imposed. In 1971, during my senior year, the college conducted a survey on coeducation, which a majority of students opposed. Many reported that they preferred not competing with men intellectually. As conversations made clear, they were concerned not about discrimination but about appearing unfeminine. Many students stressed that they liked being at a women's school because they didn't have to worry about their appearance in class.

Social convention can be blamed for their inclination to dress and act differently around men, I suppose. But adhering to convention is as much a choice as is challenging it. Single-sex education allowed female students to exercise the choice of being smart on weekdays and pretty on weekends. The prospect of being intellectually assertive and sexually appealing simultaneously, every day of the week, was barely considered or, perhaps, even desired.

To me, student opposition to coeducation at Smith underscored the need for it. The survey of student attitudes crystallized the danger that a single-sex school would pander to women's fears of masculinizing themselves. It was at least arguable that women's colleges were accepting the limits of femininity rather than challenging them.

Social mores on campus reflected this embrace of traditional gender roles, since males and females existed for each other as dates, objects of desire, not classmates. In protecting young women from the attractions and distractions of men, single-sex schools can unwittingly contribute to their sexual objectification. There interactions between the sexes are primarily romantic, not collegial—and collegiality is crucial to social equality. Laws against sexual harassment may not be nearly as effective in preventing it as the daily experiences of men working with competent, intelligent female colleagues.

This is not to suggest that many women don't benefit from attending single-sex schools; other graduates of women's colleges will offer testimony very different from my own. But it is important to acknowledge what sexual separatism can cost.

Since their inception in the nineteenth century, all-girls schools have fostered femininity along with feminism. They are models of equivocation, reinforcing regressive notions of sex difference at the same time that they educate women and help to facilitate their entry into the professions. In the beginning these contradictions were unavoidable: coeducation was not an option, and female chauvinism was essential to building the women's movement. Today the case for single-sex education is much less clear. The Young Women's Leadership School is intended to prepare girls for college and careers, and is apt to succeed, given that it is a new, well-equipped, well-funded school that currently serves about 150 students; it is also a school with something to prove. But there is little if any evidence that a small coed school of equal quality would not succeed as well.

It's tempting to conclude with a recognition that some students prosper in single-sex schools and some benefit more from coeducation. Why not allow for the establishment of sexually segregated public schools in order to provide educational choice? That's a little like asking why the Supreme Court denied people the choice of racially segregated schools, which many parents and students preferred. The Constitution and various civil-rights statutes prohibit the state from choosing to discriminate on the basis of race or sex. (In some cases the law prohibits acts of private discrimination as well.) Federal law does provide narrow exceptions for the maintenance of historically female and black colleges and single-sex secondary schools. But as the federal district court in *Garrett v. Board of Education* pointed out, "No case has ever upheld the existence of a sex-segregated public school that has the effect of favoring one sex over another."

Why should boys in East Harlem be deprived of the opportunity to enroll in what *The New York Times* described as a "haven" from "bad schools, tough streets, and bleak prospects"? It's hard to make a case for the establishment of The Young Women's Leadership School as a form of affirmative action when poor girls from minority communities are no more at risk than poor boys. It was equally hard for the Board of Education in Detroit to justify establishing schools for African-American boys when girls were at risk too. Affirmative action is supposed to compensate members of historically disadvantaged groups for the unfair advantages enjoyed by others. The version of affirmative action offered by supporters of The Young Women's Leadership School promises to pit one disadvantaged group against another.

Should we resolve the competition by establishing a comparable public school for boys in East Harlem? Only if we're willing to abandon efforts to ensure that coed schools are free of gender bias. And only if there is compelling evidence that girls and boys are most likely to prosper in segregated schools. So far, proponents of single-sex education have primarily relied on conventional assumptions about male and female skills, learning styles, and sensibilities (which dominated the defense in the VMI case)—along with unsubstantiated assertions about the evils of sexual integration. That is not enough to justify the revision of civil-rights laws against sex discrimination.

Forty years ago the Supreme Court struck down racial segregation, relying in part on empirical evidence that racially separate schools were inherently unequal. We ought not to embrace a standard of separate but equal schools for males and females without equivalent empirical evidence that they are needed and likely to make progress toward equality. A hundred and fifty years ago the drive to establish separate but equal schools for men and women was necessitated by the separation of the sexes in social and political life. A hundred and fifty years ago, when women were excluded from men's academies, women's academies did indeed represent affirmative action. Today a return to separate single-sex schools may hasten the revival of separate gender roles. Only as the sexes have become less separate have women become more free.

Reflective Writing: *Wendy Kaminer is herself a successful graduate of Smith, a distinguished women's college. Yet she appears to oppose single-sex education for women. List the reasons for her opposition and write your own response to her views. In responding, be sure to consider the specific points Orenstein makes in the previous essay.*

The War Against Boys

Christina Hoff Sommers

The notion that female students are discriminated against in education, advanced by Peggy Orenstein and others, generated a great deal of discussion on the part of educators and policy makers. Not everyone has agreed with that assessment. Christina Hoff Sommers, a philosopher and author of Who Stole Feminism? How Women Have Betrayed Women, *published in 1999, takes an opposing view. She draws on existing studies to argue that male students, rather than females, are being poorly served by the nation's educational institutions. The author is currently a W.H. Brady Fellow at the American Enterprise Institute.*

To Consider: *What research does the author draw on to advance her argument? What strategies does she employ to critique authors whose views differ from her own?*

It's a bad time to be a boy in America. The triumphant victory of the U.S. women's soccer team at the World Cup last summer has come to symbolize the spirit of American girls. The shooting at Columbine High last spring might be said to symbolize the spirit of American boys.

That boys are in disrepute is not accidental. For many years women's groups have complained that boys benefit from a school system that favors them and is biased against girls. "Schools shortchange girls," declares the American Association of University Women. Girls are "undergoing a kind of psychological foot-binding," two prominent educational psychologists say. A stream of books and pamphlets cite research showing not only that boys are classroom favorites but also that they are given to schoolyard violence and sexual harassment.

In the view that has prevailed in American education over the past decade, boys are resented, both as the unfairly privileged sex and as obstacles on the path to gender justice for girls. This perspective is promoted in schools of education, and many a teacher now feels that girls need and deserve special indemnifying consideration. "It is really clear that boys are Number One in this society and in most of the world," says Patricia O'Reilly, a professor of education and the director of the Gender Equity Center, at the University of Cincinnati.

The idea that schools and society grind girls down has given rise to an array of laws and policies intended to curtail the advantage boys have and to redress the harm done to girls. That girls are treated as the second sex in school and consequently suffer, that boys are accorded privileges and consequently benefit—these are things everyone is presumed to know. But they are not true.

The research commonly cited to support claims of male privilege and male sinfulness is riddled with errors. Almost none of it has been published in peer-reviewed professional journals. Some of the data turn out to be mysteriously missing. A review of the facts shows boys, not girls, on the weak side of an education gender gap. The typical boy is a year and a half behind the typical girl in reading and writing; he is less committed to school and less likely to go to college. In 1997 college full-time enrollments were 45 percent male and 55 percent female. The Department of Education predicts that the proportion of boys in college classes will continue to shrink.

Data from the U.S. Department of Education and from several recent university studies show that far from being shy and demoralized, today's girls outshine boys. They get better grades. They have higher educational aspirations. They follow more-rigorous academic programs and participate in advanced-placement classes at higher rates. According to the National Center for Education Statistics, slightly more girls than boys enroll in high-level math and science courses. Girls, allegedly timorous and lacking in confidence, now outnumber boys in student government, in honor societies, on school newspapers, and in debating clubs. Only in sports are boys ahead, and women's groups are targeting the sports gap with a vengeance. Girls read more books. They outperform boys on tests for artistic and musical ability. More girls than boys study abroad. More join the Peace Corps. At the same time, more boys than girls are suspended from school. More are held back and more drop out. Boys are three times as likely to receive a diagnosis of attention-deficit hyperactivity disorder. More boys than girls are involved in crime, alcohol, and drugs. Girls attempt suicide more often than boys, but it is boys who more often succeed. In 1997, a typical year, 4,483 young people aged five to twenty-four committed suicide: 701 females and 3,782 males.

In the technical language of education experts, girls are academically more "engaged." Last year an article in *The CQ Researcher* about male and female academic achievement described a common parental observation: "Daughters want to please their teachers by spending extra time on projects, doing extra credit, making homework as neat as possible. Sons rush through homework assignments and run outside to play, unconcerned about how the teacher will regard the sloppy work."

School engagement is a critical measure of student success. The U.S. Department of Education gauges student commitment by the following criteria: "How much time do students devote to homework each night?" and "Do students come to class prepared and ready to learn? (Do they bring books and pencils? Have they completed their homework?)" According to surveys of fourth, eighth, and twelfth graders, girls consistently do more homework than boys. By the twelfth grade boys are four times as likely as girls not to do homework. Similarly, more boys than girls report that they "usually" or "often" come to school without supplies or without having done their homework.

The performance gap between boys and girls in high school leads directly to the growing gap between male and female admissions to college. The Department of Education reports that in 1996 there were 8.4 million women but only 6.7 million men enrolled in college. It predicts that women will hold on to and increase their lead well into the next decade, and that by 2007 the numbers will be 9.2 million women and 6.9 million men.

Deconstructing the Test-Score Gap

Feminists cannot deny that girls get better grades, are more engaged academically, and are now the majority sex in higher education. They argue, however, that these advantages are hardly decisive. Boys, they point out, get higher scores than girls on almost every significant standardized test—especially the Scholastic Assessment Test and law school, medical school, and graduate school admissions tests.

In 1996 I wrote an article for *Education Week* about the many ways in which girl students were moving ahead of boys. Seizing on the test-score data that suggest boys are doing better than girls, David Sadker, a professor of education at American University and a co-author with his wife, Myra, of *Failing at Fairness: How America's Schools Cheat Girls* (1994), wrote, "If females are soaring in school, as Christina Hoff Sommers writes, then these tests are blind to their flight." On the 1998 SAT boys were thirty-five points (out of 800) ahead of girls in math and seven points ahead in English. These results seem to run counter to all other measurements of achievement in school. In almost all other areas boys lag behind girls. Why do they test better? Is Sadker right in suggesting that this is a manifestation of boys' privileged status?

The answer is no. A careful look at the pool of students who take the SAT and similar tests shows that the girls' lower scores have little or nothing to do with bias or unfairness. Indeed, the scores do not even signify lower achievement by girls. First of all, according to *College Bound Seniors*, an annual report on standardized-test takers published by the College Board, many more "at risk" girls than "at risk" boys take the SAT—girls from lower-income homes or with parents who never graduated from high school or never attended college. "These characteristics," the report says, "are associated with lower than average SAT scores." Instead of wrongly using SAT scores as evidence of bias against girls, scholars should be concerned about the boys who never show up for the tests they need if they are to move on to higher education.

Another factor skews test results so that they appear to favor boys. Nancy Cole, the president of the Educational Testing Service, calls it the "spread" phenomenon. Scores on almost any intelligence or achievement test are more spread out for boys than for girls—boys include more prodigies and more students of marginal ability. Or, as the political scientist James Q. Wilson once put it, "There are more male geniuses and more male idiots."

Boys also dominate dropout lists, failure lists, and learning-disability lists. Students in these groups rarely take college-admissions tests. On the other hand, the exceptional boys who take school seriously show up in disproportionately high numbers for standardized tests. Gender-equity activists like Sadker ought to apply their logic consistently: if the shortage of girls at the high end of the ability distribution is evidence of unfairness to girls, then the excess of boys at the low end should be deemed evidence of unfairness to boys.

Suppose we were to turn our attention away from the highly motivated, self-selected two fifths of high school students who take the SAT and consider instead a truly representative sample of American schoolchildren. How would girls and boys then compare? Well, we have the answer. The National Assessment of Educational Progress, started in 1969 and mandated by Congress, offers the best and most comprehensive measure of achievement among students at all levels of ability. Under the NAEP program 70,000 to 100,000 students, drawn from forty-four states, are tested in reading, writing, math, and science at ages nine, thirteen, and seventeen. In 1996, seventeen-year-old boys outperformed seventeen-year-old girls by five points in math and eight points in science, whereas the girls outperformed the boys by fourteen points in reading and seventeen points in writing. In the past few years girls have been catching up in math and science while boys have continued to lag far behind in reading and writing.

In the July 1995 issue of *Science*, Larry V. Hedges and Amy Nowell, researchers at the University of Chicago, observed that girls' deficits in math were small but not insignificant. These deficits, they noted, could adversely affect the number of women who "excel in scientific and technical occupations." Of the deficits in boys' writing skills they wrote, "The large sex differences in writing . . . are alarming. . . . The data imply that males are, on average, at a rather profound disadvantage in the performance of this basic skill." They went on to warn,

> The generally larger numbers of males who perform near the bottom of the distribution in reading comprehension and writing also have policy implications. It seems likely that individuals with such poor literacy skills will have difficulty finding employment in an increasingly information-driven economy. Thus, some intervention may be required to enable them to participate constructively.

Hedges and Nowell were describing a serious problem of national scope, but because the focus elsewhere has been on girls' deficits, few Americans know much about the problem or even suspect that it exists.

Indeed, so accepted has the myth of girls in crisis become that even teachers who work daily with male and female students tend to reflexively dismiss any challenge to the myth, or any evidence pointing to the very real crisis among boys. Three years ago Scarsdale High School, in New York, held a gender-equity workshop for faculty members. It was the standard girls-are-being-shortchanged fare, with one notable difference. A male student gave a presentation in which he pointed to evidence suggesting that girls at Scarsdale High were well ahead of boys. David Greene, a social-studies teacher, thought the student must be mistaken, but when he and some colleagues analyzed department grading patterns, they discovered that the student was right. They found little or no difference in the grades of boys and girls in advanced-placement social-studies classes. But in standard classes the girls were doing a lot better.

And Greene discovered one other thing: few wanted to hear about his startling findings. Like schools everywhere, Scarsdale High has been strongly influenced by the belief that girls are systematically deprived. That belief prevails among the school's gender-equity committee and has led the school to offer a special senior elective on gender equity. Greene has tried to broach the subject of male underperformance with his colleagues. Many of them concede that in the classes they teach, the girls seem to be doing better than the boys, but they do not see this as part of a larger pattern. After so many years of hearing about silenced, diminished girls, teachers do not take seriously the suggestion that boys are not doing as well as girls even if they see it with their own eyes in their own classrooms.

The Incredible Shrinking Girl

How did we get to this odd place? How did we come to believe in a picture of American boys and girls that is the opposite of the truth? And why has that belief persisted, enshrined in law, encoded in governmental and school policies, despite overwhelming evidence against it? The answer has much to do with one of the American academy's most celebrated women—Carol Gilligan, Harvard University's first professor of gender studies.

Gilligan first came to widespread attention in 1982, with the publication of *In a Different Voice*, which this article will discuss shortly. In 1990 Gilligan announced that America's adolescent girls were in crisis. In her words, "As the river of a girl's life flows into the sea of Western culture, she is in danger of drowning or disappearing." Gilligan offered little in the way of conventional evidence to support this alarming finding. Indeed, it is hard to imagine what sort of empirical research could establish such a large claim. But she quickly attracted powerful allies. Within a very short time the allegedly vulnerable and demoralized state of adolescent girls achieved the status of a national emergency.

Popular writers, electrified by Gilligan's discovery, began to see evidence of the crisis everywhere. Anna Quindlen, who was then a *New York Times* columnist, recounted in a 1990 column how Gilligan's research had cast an ominous shadow on the celebration of her daughter's second birthday: "My daughter is ready to leap into the world, as though life were chicken soup and she a delighted noodle. The work of Professor Carol Gilligan of Harvard suggests that some time after the age of 11 this will change, that even this lively little girl will pull back [and] shrink."

A number of popular books soon materialized, including Myra and David Sadker's *Failing at Fairness* and Peggy Orenstein's *Schoolgirls: Young Women, Self-Esteem, and the Confidence Gap* (1994). Elizabeth Gleick wrote in *Time* in 1996 on a new trend in literary victimology: "Dozens of troubled teenage girls troop across [the] pages: composite sketches of Charlottes, Whitneys and Danielles who were raped, who have bulimia, who have pierced bodies or shaved heads, who are coping with strict religious families or are felled by their parents' bitter divorce."

The country's adolescent girls were both pitied and exalted. The novelist Carolyn See wrote in *The Washington Post* in 1994, "The most heroic, fearless, graceful, tortured human beings in this land must be girls from the ages of 12 to 15." In the same vein, the Sadkers, in *Failing at Fairness*, predicted the fate of a lively six-year-old on top of a playground slide: "There she stood on her sturdy legs, with her head thrown back and her arms flung wide. As ruler of the playground, she was at the very zenith of her world." But all would soon change: "If the camera had photographed the girl . . . at twelve instead of six . . . she would have been looking at the ground instead of the sky; her sense of self-worth would have been an accelerating downward spiral."

A picture of confused and forlorn girls struggling to survive would be drawn again and again, with added details and increasing urgency. Mary Pipher, a clinical psychologist, wrote in *Reviving Ophelia* (1994), by far the most successful of the girls-in-crisis books, "Something dramatic happens to girls in early adolescence. Just as planes and ships disappear mysteriously into the Bermuda Triangle, so do the selves of girls go down in droves. They crash and burn."

The description of America's teenage girls as silenced, tortured, and otherwise personally diminished was (and is) indeed dismaying. But no real evidence has ever been offered to support it. Certainly neither Gilligan nor the popular writers who followed her lead produced anything like solid empirical evidence, gathered according to the conventional protocols of social-science research.

Scholars who do abide by those protocols describe adolescent girls in far more optimistic terms. Anne Petersen, a former professor of adolescent development and pediatrics at the University of Minnesota and now a senior vice-president of the W. K. Kellogg Foundation, reports the consensus of researchers working in adolescent psychology: "It is now known that the majority of adolescents of both genders successfully negotiate this developmental period without any major psychological or emotional disorder, develop a positive sense of personal identity, and manage to forge adaptive peer relationships with their families." Daniel Offer, a professor of psychiatry at Northwestern, concurs. He refers to a "new generation of studies" that find 80 percent of adolescents to be normal and well adjusted.

At the time that Gilligan was declaring her crisis, a study conducted by the University of Michigan asked a scientifically selected sample of 3,000 high school seniors, "Taking all things together, how would you say things are these days—would you say you're very happy, pretty happy, or not too happy these days?" Nearly 86 percent of the girls and 88 percent of the boys responded that they were "pretty happy" or "very happy." If the girls polled were caught in "an accelerating downward spiral," they were unaware of it.

Contrary to the story told by Gilligan and her followers, American girls were flourishing in unprecedented ways by the early 1990s. To be sure, some—including many who found themselves in the offices of clinical psychologists—felt they were crashing and drowning in the sea of Western culture. But the vast majority were occupied in more-constructive ways, moving ahead of boys in the primary and secondary grades, applying to college in record numbers, filling challenging academic classes, joining sports teams, and generally enjoying more freedom and opportunities than any other young women in history.

The great discrepancy between what Gilligan says she discovered about adolescent girls and what numerous other scientists say they have learned raises obvious questions about the quality of Gilligan's research. And these questions loom larger the more one examines Gilligan's methods. Carol Gilligan is a much-celebrated figure. Journalists routinely cite her research on the distinctive moral psychology of women. She was *Ms.* magazine's Woman of the Year in 1984, and *Time* put her on its short list of most-influential Americans in 1996. In 1997 she received the $250,000 Heinz Award for "transform[ing] the paradigm for what it means to be human." Such a transformation would certainly be a feat. At the very least, it would require a great deal of empirical supporting evidence. Most of Gilligan's published research, however, consists of anecdotes based on a small number of interviews. Her data are otherwise unavailable for review, giving rise to some reasonable doubts about their merits and persuasiveness.

In a Different Voice offered the provocative thesis that men and women have distinctly different ways of dealing with moral quandaries. Relying on data from three studies she had conducted, Gilligan found that women tend to be more caring, less competitive, and less abstract than men; they speak "in a different voice." Women approach moral questions by applying an "ethic of care." In contrast, men approach moral issues by applying rules and abstract principles; theirs is an "ethic of justice." Gilligan argued further that women's moral style had been insufficiently studied by professional psychologists. She complained that the entire fields of psychology and moral philosophy had been built on studies that excluded women.

In a Different Voice was an instant success. It sold more than 600,000 copies and was translated into nine languages. A reviewer at *Vogue* explained its appeal: "[Gilligan] flips old prejudices against women on their ears. She reframes qualities regarded as women's weaknesses and shows them to be human strengths. It is impossible to consider [her] ideas without having your estimation of women rise."

The book received a mixed reaction from feminists. Some—such as the philosophers Virginia Held and Sara Ruddick, and those in various fields who would come to be known as "difference feminists"—were tantalized by the idea that women were different from, and quite probably better than, men. But other academic feminists attacked Gilligan for reinforcing stereotypes about women as nurturers and caretakers.

Many academic psychologists, feminist and nonfeminist alike, found Gilligan's specific claims about distinct male and female moral orientations unpersuasive and ungrounded in empirical data. Lawrence Walker, of the University of British Columbia, has reviewed 108 studies of sex differences in solving moral problems. He concluded in a 1984 review article in *Child Development* that "sex differences in moral reasoning in late adolescence and youth are rare." In 1987 three psychologists at Oberlin College attempted to test Gilligan's hypothesis: they administered a moral-reasoning test to 101 male and female students and concluded, "There were no reliable sex differences . . . in the directions predicted by Gilligan." Concurring with Walker, the Oberlin researchers pointed out that "Gilligan failed to provide acceptable empirical support for her model."

The thesis of *In a Different Voice* is based on three studies Gilligan conducted: the "college student study," the "abortion decision study," and the "rights and responsibilities study." Here is how Gilligan described the last.

> This study involved a sample of males and females matched for age, intelligence, education, occupation, and social class at nine points across the life cycle: ages 6–9, 11, 15, 19, 22, 25–27, 35, 45, and 60. From a total sample of 144 (8 males and 8 females at each age), including a more intensively interviewed subsample of 36 (2 males and 2 females at each age), data were collected on conceptions of self and morality, experiences of moral conflicts and choice, and judgments of hypothetical moral dilemmas.

This description is all we ever learn about the mechanics of the study, which seems to have no proper name; it was never published, never peer-reviewed. It was, in any case, very small in scope and in number of subjects. And the data are tantalizingly inaccessible. In September of 1998 my research assistant, Elizabeth Bowen, called Gilligan's office and asked where she could find copies of the three studies that were the basis for *In a Different Voice*. Gilligan's assistant, Tatiana Bertsch, told her that they were unavailable, and not in the public domain; because of the sensitivity of the data (especially the abortion study), the information had been kept confidential. Asked where the studies were now kept, Bertsch explained that the original data were being prepared to be placed in a Harvard library: "They are physically in the office. We are in the process of sending them to the archives at the Murray Center."

In October of 1998 Hugh Liebert, a sophomore at Harvard who had been my research assistant the previous summer, spoke to Bertsch. She told him that the data would not be available until the end of the academic year, adding, "They have been kept secret because the issues [raised in the study] are so sensitive." She suggested that he check back occasionally. He tried again in March. This time she informed him, "They will not be available anytime soon."

Last September, Liebert tried one more time. He sent an e-mail message directly to Gilligan, but Bertsch replied,

> None of the *In a Different Voice* studies have been published. We are in the process of donating the college student study to the Murray Research Center at Radcliffe, but that will not be completed for another year, probably. At this point Professor Gilligan has no immediate plans of donating the abortion or the rights and responsibilities studies. Sorry that none of what you are interested in is available.

Brendan Maher is a professor emeritus at Harvard University and a former chairman of the psychology department. I told him about the inaccessibility of Gilligan's data and the explanation that their sensitive nature precluded public dissemination. He laughed and said, "It would be extraordinary to say [that one's data] are too sensitive for others to see." He pointed out that there are standard methods for handling confidential materials in research. Names are left out but raw scores are reported, "so others can see if they can replicate your study." A researcher must also disclose how subjects were chosen, how interviews were recorded, and the method by which meaning was derived from the data.

"Politics Dressed Up as Science"

Gilligan's ideas about demoralized teenage girls had a special resonance with women's groups that were already committed to the proposition that our society is unsympathetic to women. The interest of the venerable and politically influential American Association of University Women, in particular, was piqued. Its officers were reported to be "intrigued and alarmed" by Gilligan's research. They wanted to know more.

In 1990 *The New York Times Sunday Magazine* published an admiring profile of Gilligan that heralded the discovery of a hidden crisis among the nation's girls. Soon after, the AAUW commissioned a study from the polling firm Greenberg-Lake. The pollsters asked 3,000 children (2,400 girls and 600 boys in grades four through ten) about their self-perceptions. In 1991 the association announced the disturbing results, in a report titled *Shortchanging Girls, Shortchanging America:* "Girls aged eight and nine are confident, assertive, and feel authoritative about themselves. Yet most emerge from adolescence with a poor self-image, constrained views of their future and their place in society, and much less confidence about themselves and their abilities." Anne Bryant, the executive director of the AAUW and an expert in public relations, organized a media campaign to spread the word that "an unacknowledged American tragedy" had been uncovered. Newspapers and magazines around the country carried reports that girls were being adversely affected by gender bias that eroded their self-esteem. Sharon Schuster, at the time the president of the AAUW, candidly explained to *The New York Times* why the association had undertaken the research in the first place: "We wanted to put some factual data behind our belief that girls are getting shortchanged in the classroom."

As the AAUW's self-esteem study was making headlines, a little-known magazine called *Science News,* which has been supplying information on scientific and technical developments to interested newspapers since 1922, reported the skeptical reaction of leading specialists on adolescent development. The late Roberta Simmons, a professor of sociology at the University of Pittsburgh (described by *Science News* as "director of the most ambitious longitudinal study of adolescent self-esteem to date"), said that her research showed nothing like the substantial gender gap described by the AAUW. According to Simmons, "Most kids come through the years from 10 to 20 without major problems and with an increasing sense of self-esteem." But the doubts of Simmons and several other prominent experts were not reported in the hundreds of news stories that the Greenberg-Lake study generated.

The AAUW quickly commissioned a second study, *How Schools Shortchange Girls.* This one, conducted by the Wellesley College Center for Research on Women and released in 1992, focused on the alleged effects of sexism on girls' school performance. It asserted that schools deflate girls' self-esteem by "systematically cheating girls of classroom attention." Such bias leads to lower aspirations and impaired academic achievement. Carol Gilligan's crisis was being transformed into a civil-rights issue: girls were the victims of widespread sex discrimination. "The implications are clear," the AAUW said. "The system must change."

With great fanfare *How Schools Shortchange Girls* was released to the remarkably uncritical media. A 1992 article for *The New York Times* by Susan Chira was typical of coverage throughout the country. The headline read

"BIAS AGAINST GIRLS IS FOUND RIFE IN SCHOOLS, WITH LASTING DAMAGE." The piece was later reproduced by the AAUW and sent out as part of a fundraising package. Chira had not interviewed a single critic of the study.

In March of last year I called Chira and asked about the way she had handled the AAUW study. I asked if she would write her article the same way today. No, she said, pointing out that we have since learned much more about boys' problems in school. Why had she not canvassed dissenting opinions? She explained that she had been traveling when the AAUW study came out, and was on a short deadline. Yes, perhaps she had relied too much on the AAUW's report. She had tried to reach Diane Ravitch, who had then been the former U.S. assistant secretary of education and was a known critic of women's-advocacy findings, but without success.

Six years after the release of *How Schools Shortchange Girls, The New York Times* ran a story that raised questions about its validity. This time the reporter, Tamar Lewin, did reach Diane Ravitch, who told her, "That [1992] AAUW report was just completely wrong. What was so bizarre is that it came out right at the time that girls had just overtaken boys in almost every area. It might have been the right story twenty years earlier, but coming out when it did, it was like calling a wedding a funeral. . . . There were all these special programs put in place for girls, and no one paid any attention to boys."

One of the many things about which the report was wrong was the famous "call-out" gap. According to the AAUW, "In a study conducted by the Sadkers, boys in elementary and middle school called out answers eight times more often than girls. When boys called out, teachers listened. But when girls called out, they were told 'raise your hand if you want to speak.'"

But the Sadker study turns out to be missing—and meaningless, to boot. In 1994 Amy Saltzman, of *U.S. News & World Report*, asked David Sadker for a copy of the research backing up the eight-to-one call-out claim. Sadker said that he had presented the findings in an unpublished paper at a symposium sponsored by the American Educational Research Association; neither he nor the AERA had a copy. Sadker conceded to Saltzman that the ratio may have been inaccurate. Indeed, Saltzman cited an independent study by Gail Jones, an associate professor of education at the University of North Carolina at Chapel Hill, which found that boys called out only twice as often as girls. Whatever the accurate number is, no one has shown that permitting a student to call out answers in the classroom confers any kind of academic advantage. What does confer advantage is a student's attentiveness. Boys are less attentive—which could explain why some teachers might call on them more or be more tolerant of call-outs.

Despite the errors, the campaign to persuade the public that girls were being diminished personally and academically was a spectacular success. The Sadkers described an exultant Anne Bryant, of the AAUW, telling her friends, "I remember going to bed the night our report was issued, totally exhilarated. When I woke up the next morning, the first thought in my mind was, 'Oh, my God, what do we do next?'" Political action came next, and here, too, girls' advocates were successful.

Categorizing girls as an "under-served population" on a par with other discriminated-against minorities, Congress passed the Gender Equity in Education Act in 1994. Millions of dollars in grants were awarded to study the plight of girls and to learn how to counter bias against them. At the United Nations Fourth World Conference on Women, in Beijing in 1995, U.S. delegates presented the educational and psychological deficits of American girls as a human-rights issue.

The Myth Unraveling

By the late 1990s the myth of the downtrodden girl was showing some signs of unraveling, and concern over boys was growing. In 1997 the Public Education Network (PEN) announced at its annual conference the results of a new teacher-student survey titled *The American Teacher 1997: Examining Gender Issues in Public Schools*. The survey was funded by the Metropolitan Life Insurance Company and conducted by Louis Harris and Associates.

During a three-month period in 1997 various questions about gender equity were asked of 1,306 students and 1,035 teachers in grades seven through twelve. The MetLife study had no doctrinal ax to grind. What it found contradicted most of the findings of the AAUW, the Sadkers, and the Wellesley College Center for Research on Women: "Contrary to the commonly held view that boys are at an advantage over girls in school, girls appear to have an advantage over boys in terms of their future plans, teachers' expectations, everyday experiences at school and interactions in the classroom."

Some other conclusions from the MetLife study: Girls are more likely than boys to see themselves as college-bound and more likely to want a good education. Furthermore, more boys (31 percent) than girls (19 percent) feel that teachers do not listen to what they have to say.

At the PEN conference, Nancy Leffert, a child psychologist then at the Search Institute, in Minneapolis, reported the results of a survey that she and colleagues had recently completed of more than 99,000 children in grades six through twelve. The children were asked about what the researchers call "developmental assets." The Search Institute has identified forty critical assets—"building blocks for healthy development." Half of these are external, such as a supportive family and adult role models, and half are internal, such as motivation to achieve, a sense of purpose in life, and interpersonal confidence. Leffert explained, somewhat apologetically, that girls were ahead of boys with respect to thirty-seven out of forty assets. By almost every significant measure of well-being girls had the better of boys: they felt closer to their families; they had higher aspirations, stronger connections to school, and even superior assertiveness skills. Leffert concluded her talk by saying that in the past she had referred to girls as fragile or vulnerable, but that the survey "tells me that girls have very powerful assets."

The Horatio Alger Association, a fifty-year-old organization devoted to promoting and affirming individual initiative and "the American dream," releases annual back-to-school surveys. Its survey for 1998 contrasted two groups of students: the "highly successful" (approximately 18 percent of American students) and the "disillusioned" (approximately 15 percent). The successful students work hard, choose challenging classes, make schoolwork a top priority, get good grades, participate in extracurricular activities, and feel that teachers and administrators care about them and listen to them. According to the association, the successful group in the 1998 survey is 63 percent female and 37 percent male. The disillusioned students are pessimistic about their future, get low grades, and have little contact with teachers. The disillusioned group could accurately be characterized as demoralized. According to the Alger Association, "Nearly seven out of ten are male."

In the spring of 1998 Judith Kleinfeld, a psychologist at the University of Alaska, published a thorough critique of the research on schoolgirls titled "The Myth That Schools Shortchange Girls: Social Science in the Service of Deception." Kleinfeld exposed a number of errors in the AAUW/Wellesley Center study, concluding that it was "politics dressed up as science." Kleinfeld's report prompted several publications, including *The New York Times* and *Education Week*, to take a second look at claims that girls were in a tragic state.

The AAUW did not adequately respond to any of Kleinfeld's substantive objections; instead its current president, Maggie Ford, complained in *The New York Times* letters column that Kleinfeld was "reducing the problems of our children to this petty 'who is worse off, boys or girls?' [which] gets us nowhere." From the leader of an organization that spent nearly a decade ceaselessly promoting the proposition that American girls are being "shortchanged," this comment is rather remarkable.

Boys and Their Mothers

Growing evidence that the scales are tipped not against girls but against boys is beginning to inspire a quiet revisionism. Some educators will admit that boys are on the wrong side of the gender gap. In 1998 I met the president of the Board of Education of Atlanta. Who is faring better in Atlanta's schools, boys or girls? I asked. "Girls," he replied, without hesitation. In what areas? I asked. "Just about any area you mention." A high school principal from Pennsylvania says of his school, "Students who dominate the dropout list, the suspension list, the failure list, and other negative indices of nonachievement in school are males by a wide margin."

Carol Gilligan, too, has begun to give boys some attention. In 1995 she and her colleagues at the Harvard University School of Education inaugurated "The Harvard Project on Women's Psychology, Boys' Development and the Culture of Manhood." Within a year Gilligan was announcing the existence of a crisis among boys that was as bad as or worse than the one afflicting girls. "Girls' psychological development in patriarchy involves a process of eclipse that is even more total for boys," she wrote in a 1996 article titled "The Centrality of Relationship in Human Development."

Gilligan claimed to have discovered "a startling pattern of developmental asymmetry": girls undergo trauma as they enter adolescence, whereas for boys the period of crisis is early childhood. Boys aged three to seven are pressured to "take into themselves the structure or moral order of a patriarchal civilization: to internalize a patriarchal voice."

This masculinizing process is traumatic and damaging. "At this age," Gilligan told *The Boston Globe* in 1996, "boys show a high incidence of depression, out-of-control behavior, learning disorders, even allergies and stuttering."

One can welcome Gilligan's acceptance of the fact that boys, too, have problems while remaining deeply skeptical of her ideas about their source. Gilligan's theory about boys' development includes three hypothetical claims: 1) Boys are being deformed and made sick by a traumatic, forced separation from their mothers. 2) Seemingly healthy boys are cut off from their own feelings and damaged in their capacity to develop healthy relationships. 3) The well-being of society may depend on freeing boys from "cultures that value or valorize heroism, honor, war, and competition—the culture of warriors, the economy of capitalism." Let us consider each proposition in turn.

According to Gilligan, boys are at special risk in early childhood; they suffer "more stuttering, more bedwetting, more learning problems . . . when cultural norms pressure them to separate from their mothers." (Sometimes she adds allergies, attention-deficit disorder, and attempted suicide to the list.) She does not cite any pediatric research to support her theory about the origins of these various early-childhood disorders. Does a study exist, for example, showing that boys who remain intimately bonded with their mothers are less likely to develop allergies or wet their beds?

Gilligan's assertion that the "pressure of cultural norms" causes boys to separate from their mothers and thus generates a host of early disorders has not been tested empirically. Nor does Gilligan offer any indication of how it *could* be tested. She does not seem to feel that her assertions need empirical confirmation. She is confident that boys need to be protected from the culture—a culture in which manhood valorizes war and the economy of capitalism, a culture that desensitizes boys and, by submerging their humanity, is the root cause of "out-of-control and out-of-touch behavior" and is the ultimate source of war and other violence committed by men.

But are boys aggressive and violent because they are psychically separated from their mothers? Thirty years of research suggests that the absence of the male parent is more likely to be the problem. The boys who are most at risk for juvenile delinquency and violence are boys who are *physically* separated from their fathers. The U.S. Bureau of the Census reports that in 1960 children living with their mother but not their father numbered 5.1 million; by 1996 the number was more than 16 million. As the phenomenon of fatherlessness has increased, so has violence. As far back as 1965 Senator Daniel Patrick Moynihan called attention to the social dangers of raising boys without benefit of a paternal presence. He wrote in a 1965 study for the Labor Department, "A community that allows a large number of young men to grow up in broken families, dominated by women, never acquiring any stable relationship to male authority, never acquiring any rational expectations about the future—that community asks for and gets chaos."

The sociologist David Blankenhorn, in *Fatherless America* (1995), wrote, "Despite the difficulty of proving causation in the social sciences, the weight of evidence increasingly supports the conclusion that fatherlessness is a primary generator of violence among young men." William Galston, a former domestic-policy adviser in the Clinton Administration who is now at the University of Maryland, and his colleague Elaine Kamarck, now at Harvard, concur. Commenting on the relationship between crime and one-parent families, they wrote in a 1990 institute report, "The relationship is so strong that controlling for family configuration erases the relationship between race and crime and between low income and crime. This conclusion shows up time and again in the literature."

Oblivious of all the factual evidence that paternal separation causes aberrant behavior in boys, Carol Gilligan calls for a fundamental change in child rearing that would keep boys in a more sensitive relationship with their feminine side. We need to free young men from a destructive culture of manhood that "impedes their capacity to feel their own and other people's hurt, to know their own and other's sadness," she writes. Since the pathology, as she has diagnosed it, is presumably universal, the cure must be radical. We must change the very nature of childhood: we must find ways to keep boys bonded to their mothers. We must undercut the system of socialization that is so "essential to the perpetuation of patriarchal societies."

Gilligan's views are attractive to many of those who believe that boys could profit by being more sensitive and empathetic. But anyone thinking to enlist in Gilligan's project of getting boys in touch with their inner nurturer would do well to note that her central thesis—that boys are being imprisoned by conventional ideas of masculinity—is not a scientific hypothesis. Nor, it seems, does Gilligan regard it in this light, for she presents no data to support it. It is, in fact, an extravagant piece of speculation of the kind that would not be taken seriously in most professional departments of psychology.

On a less academic plane Gilligan's proposed reformation seems to challenge common sense. It is obvious that a boy wants a father to help him become a young man, and belonging to the culture of manhood is important to almost every boy. To impugn his desire to become "one of the boys" is to deny that a boy's biology determines much of what he prefers and is attracted to. Unfortunately, by denying the nature of boys, education theorists can cause them much misery.

Gilligan talks of radically reforming "the fundamental structure of authority" by making changes that will free boys from the stereotypes that bind them. But in what sense are American boys unfree? Was the young Mark Twain or the young Teddy Roosevelt enslaved by conventional modes of boyhood? Is the average Little Leaguer or Cub Scout defective in the ways Gilligan suggests? In practice, getting boys to be more like girls means getting them to stop segregating themselves into all-male groups. That's the darker, coercive side of the project to "free" boys from their masculine straitjackets.

It is certainly true that a small subset of male children are, as Gilligan argues, desensitized and cut off from feelings of tenderness and care. But these boys are not representative of their sex. Gilligan speaks of boys in general as "hiding their humanity," showing a capacity to "hurt without feeling hurt." This, she maintains, is a more or less universal condition that exists because the vast majority of boys are forced into separation from their nurturers. But the idea that boys are abnormally insensitive flies in the face of everyday experience. Boys are competitive and often aggressive, yes; but anyone in close contact with them—parents, grandparents, teachers, coaches, friends—gets daily proof of their humanity, loyalty, and compassion.

Gilligan appears to be making the same mistake with boys that she made with girls—she observes a few children and interprets their problems as indicative of a deep and general malaise caused by the way our society imposes gender stereotypes. The pressure to conform to these stereotypes, she believes, has impaired, distressed, and deformed the members of both sexes by the time they are adolescents. In fact—with the important exception of boys whose fathers are absent and who get their concept of maleness from peer groups—most boys are not violent. Most are not unfeeling or antisocial. They are just boys—and being a boy is not in itself a failing.

Does Gilligan actually understand boys? Does she empathize with them? Is she free of the misandry that infects so many gender theorists who never stop blaming the "male culture" for all social and psychological ills? Nothing we have seen or heard offers the slightest reassurance that Gilligan and her followers are wise enough or objective enough to be trusted with devising new ways of socializing boys.

Every society confronts the problem of civilizing its young males. The traditional approach is through character education: Develop the young man's sense of honor. Help him become a considerate, conscientious human being. Turn him into a gentleman. This approach respects boys' masculine nature; it is time-tested, and it works. Even today, despite several decades of moral confusion, most young men understand the term "gentleman" and approve of the ideals it connotes.

What Gilligan and her followers are proposing is quite different: civilize boys by diminishing their masculinity. "Raise boys like we raise girls" is Gloria Steinem's advice. This approach is deeply disrespectful of boys. It is meddlesome, abusive, and quite beyond what educators in a free society are mandated to do.

Did anything of value come out of the manufactured crisis of diminished girls? Yes, a bit. Parents, teachers, and administrators now pay more attention to girls' deficits in math and science, and they offer more support for girls' participation in sports. But do these benefits outweigh the disservice done by promulgating the myth of the victimized girl or by presenting boys as the unfairly favored sex?

A boy today, through no fault of his own, finds himself implicated in the social crime of shortchanging girls. Yet the allegedly silenced and neglected girl sitting next to him is likely to be the superior student. She is probably more articulate, more mature, more engaged, and more well-balanced. The boy may be aware that she is more likely to go on to college. He may believe that teachers prefer to be around girls and pay more attention to them. At the same time, he is uncomfortably aware that he is considered to be a member of the favored and dominant gender.

The widening gender gap in academic achievement is real. It threatens the future of millions of American boys. Boys do not need to be rescued from their masculinity. But they are not getting the help they need. In the climate of disapproval in which boys now exist, programs designed to aid them have a very low priority. This must change. We should repudiate the partisanship that currently clouds the issues surrounding sex differences in the schools. We should call for balance, objective information, fair treatment, and a concerted national effort to get boys back on track. That means we can no longer allow the partisans of girls to shape the discussion and to write the rules.

Reflective Writing: *What specific evidence and arguments does Christina Hoff Sommers provide to support her view that it is boys, not girls, who are disadvantaged by school? How do her arguments correspond to your own experiences and observations?*

Success Against the Odds:
Young Black Men Tell What It Takes

Benjamin P. Bowser and Herbert Perkins

We hear a lot in the media about African-American students, especially young males, who are not doing well in school. But what about the increasing numbers of African-American students who are successful in school? This article, by sociology professor Benjamin Bowser of California State University, Hayward, and anthropology professor Herbert Perkins of Lawrence University in Wisconsin, examines the factors that account for academic success in African-American male students. The article, based on interviews with successful students, originally appeared in Bowser's 1991 book, Black Male Adolescents: Parenting and Education in Community Context.

To Consider: _Bowser and Perkins asked students what they did to perform well in school; who in their family, school, community, and peer groups played important roles; what were the barriers; was race a factor; and how would they account for peers' lack of success? As you read through this article, highlight areas that provide answers to these questions. What factors seem most important to you and why?_

The relatively poor academic performance of many ethnic minorities has been documented in a number of studies, some of which are cited by Allan Ornstein and Daniel Levine in "Social Class, Race, and School Achievement." Although many scholars and journalists have attempted to account for this phenomenon, the authors of the following article have taken a more direct approach, interviewing Hispanic and African-American students who succeed academically.

While there are many aspects of a young person's life which can be judged as a success or failure, their educational achievement is decisive. Success in school is a prerequisite for maximizing life chances and for taking advantage of new opportunities. Ironically, the single most difficult piece of information to find is what goes on in the lives of academically successful Black and Hispanic adolescents. How do they beat the odds? The importance of this information is obvious. If we can find out what successful Black and Hispanic students do and have in common, then we have some idea of what can be done to intervene into the circumstances of the majority who are not succeeding.

The Interviews

There is research under way that looks directly at the lives of successful Black students. The primary focus is on the role that parents play in their academic success. At different times since 1960 the schools, community, peers and parents have been identified as primary factors in academic success and failure. Researchers have more often found the family to be the most important factor. Because of this history, the authors developed a series of questions to be used by focus group leaders to probe student relations with parents, relatives, teachers, peers, other people and organizations within their community.

The students who participated in our focus groups consisted of forty Black and Hispanic high school sophomores through seniors. Roughly half of the students were males and most of the males were Black. The students were evenly divided across the three academic years. They had 3.0 plus grade point averages in college preparatory tracks and were the top minority academic achievers in three integrated suburban high schools in California. What made this group of students interesting to us is that it cut across virtually all categories. Most had attended segregated junior high schools. They were doing well in integrated suburban high schools where the academic programs were very competitive and demanding. Virtually all of these students came from working-class households and half had single parents. Their parents worked, for example, as nurses, bus drivers, mechanics, stock clerks, physical education instructors, part-time ministers and hospital attendants. Only three students had parents who were professionals—a lawyer, teacher and engineer. Also their community reflected what will be the more common circumstance for Blacks and Hispanics in the next century. They are mostly from working-class households living in suburban racial ghettos.

Several years ago, their high school district realized that they had very few academically successful minority students. The district principals decided that the first step was to identify the few who were doing well and encourage their efforts. They developed a district program where any minority student in their schools who achieved a 3.0 plus grade point average (GPA) was to be rewarded and encouraged with field trips, recognition and opportunities to meet, interact and encourage one another. These students represented a unique opportunity to derive insight on what makes for academic success for working-class minority students in suburban integrated schools. These students were brought to the California State University at Hayward campus and spent an afternoon divided into six focus groups, led by student service staff and faculty. We asked the students to tell us in taped discussions: What did they do to perform well in school; who in their family, school, community and peer groups played important roles; what were the barriers; was race a factor; and how would they account for their peers' lack of success?

The students were assured that their individual identities would be kept confidential. With the formalities over, they lit up and had a lot to say. No one had asked them these questions before, so they were eager to respond. In no session did the focus group leader dominate the discussion. The students responded to the questions with amazing candor and detail. While we had a special interest in what the young Black men had to say, it was very clear right from the beginning of the sessions that the students' experiences and insights cut across gender and ethnicity. The following is what they told us, based on a review of the tape recordings of each session.

Students' Reflections on Academic Success

Relations with Family

Past and current research suggests that there is a very close relation between student academic success and parents. Early in each focus group a number of students said that their parents were important as sources of encouragement. These students reported that their parents always had time for them, would help them with their homework, clearly rewarded success, punished failure and were generally "on their case." One student had a mother who corrected her papers and a father who tutored her in mathematics. But when we probed this response and got all of the students in the discussion, a far more complex picture of relations with parents emerged. Most of the students had a different situation. After the groups became more comfortable, several "acknowledgers" as well as most who had remained quiet said that their immediate parents were really not their main source of support. The key persons, who they named as their main sources of family support for high academic achievement, consisted of grandparents or, more often, older brothers or sisters. While parents may or may not have been "on their case" and were pleased that the student was doing well, it was actually some other member of the family who helped the student to define his long-term career goals and who turned him on to high academic achievement.

> My older sister really got me going. She is in the Navy, is doing well and has told me many times what I need to do to be successful. I have admired her and have always listened to her.

Ironically, most of the people who were reported as the main source of family motivation were not successful in school. Many of our high achievers as elementary and junior high school students had watched their parents struggle with older siblings. These older brothers and sisters had made all sorts of mistakes, primary of which was failure in school. The outcomes in troubled lives, purposelessness, underemployment and unemployment are now very apparent within each family. It turns out that the experiences of these older brothers and sisters serve as a powerful source of motivation to take some other route. The students said repeatedly that they would do anything not to end up like their older siblings who were models of the consequences of underachievement. In many cases, these older siblings became directly involved in making certain that their younger brother or sister did not end up as they did. One student who was the sixth and youngest boy in his family reported:

> All five of my older brothers did not do well in school and have been in some form of trouble at one time or another. One day they got together and sat me down in the middle of them and told me that they wanted me to do better and that I had to get A's and B's in school. No matter what they're doing, they all check my report card. If it's good, they really make me feel great. If it's bad, they'll kick my ass.

Another student said, "All I have to do is look at how my parents ended up unhappy and fighting all the time and I know I have to do well in school—I work harder and harder." Other students reported that what got them achieving was an older sister's struggle to graduate from high school as a single parent, defiance aided by an older brother against parents who don't believe "I can do it," and a brother's trouble in college because he was not well prepared. What all of these high achieving students had in common is that there was somebody outside of school in their immediate or extended family who was "on their case" and who more often served as a direct example of what happens to those who do not achieve.

Relations with School

It is overly simplistic to assume that home motivation, regardless of its source, translates directly into high academic achievement. Work which focuses exclusively on family and academic achievement makes such an assumption by default. In reality, schools can either take advantage of or frustrate home-based motivation to achieve. It is also necessary to look at the related influence of schools on individual academic achievement. Otherwise, schools appear to be culturally neutral and totally objective entities—an impossibility. Our high achievers come to school with very strong motivation from home to do well. But it is also clear from the focus group that family motivation is not all that it takes to maintain a 3.0 plus grade point average in college preparatory courses.

What was said in all of the focus groups was that someone at school took a personal interest in each student's work. There was at least one teacher who held each student in high regard and who told them repeatedly that they could do well. The students reported that these "mentor" teachers then worked with them.

The "mentor" teachers were important to the initial translation of personal and home derived motivation into actual high grades. Several students reported having a series of supportive teachers who showed them that they could do good work—repeatedly. Others had only one teacher now and then who took a special interest in them. In addition to a "mentor" teacher all of the high achievers had counselors. The fewer supportive teachers they had, the more important were these counselors. Even with a series of supportive teachers, caring counselors were essential to monitoring, encouraging and getting students into good classroom experiences.

Active counselors were also reported to be essential in their role as in-school advocates and for coaching students through classes with unsupportive teachers who could have easily broken their motivation and early successes.

Several focus group leaders explored with their students the nature of the relation the students reported having with "mentor" teachers and counselors. Amazingly the responses were consistent across each of the focus groups. The students reported that the people in school who were supportive treated them more like friends or close relatives than like students. It was very important that the formal student-teacher and student-counselor relation be reduced to a more personal one-on-one relation.

> Mrs. X treats us like her son. She is excited about me, shares with me her feelings, makes me feel special and a part of her life. I even have her home telephone number.

The students reported that it was easier and even fun to study with a teacher who really cared and "did not talk down to you." Teachers who would stop them in the hall while they were with other students and ask how they were and how were things going were well regarded. One student said that he really did not believe that he could do superior work until he realized that two of his teachers were willing to stay after school to work with him on science and math problems. But besides being personal and supportive, these significant school persons held high expectations and did not hesitate to monitor each student's progress, in which case, the students' relations with their "mentor" teachers and counselors became additional motivation to do well. Poor grades and lack of effort would have violated these positive personal relations and would have hurt and disappointed their mentors.

In contrast, teachers who insisted on being impersonal, who showed no signs of caring and had no time or interest in the student, drew angry, hurt comments. "Mr. Y would see me on the street and wouldn't even say 'hello' and, if you ask him a question in class, he would tell you 'go look it up—I already talked about that in class.'" Especially hurtful were teachers who were clearly very positive toward their White students, but were very impersonal with minority students in the same class.

One of the more fascinating elements in the students' discussion about school was when they began to realize that they really could be high achievers. The first time they attained their 3.0 plus in high school was not the point at which they realized that their achievement was special. The seniors had had at least two years of high grades and had no doubts about accepting and identifying with their achievement. The seniors told us that their earlier confidence was closer to what the sophomores reported. The less experienced achievers said that, while they knew that they were doing well, they still did not think that what they had done was exceptional or important—even after making the dean's list several times and being part of a program for high achieving minority students! One student had a 3.9 GPA at the end of his freshman year and seriously considered dropping out for a temporary labor job. He knew that a 3.9 was a high average, but he had no sense of its meaning in his own life or what he could attain by maintaining that average. Another student had so thoroughly identified with the stereotype that minority students do poorly in school that she assumed that her 3.6 was simply not good enough.

High initial attainment in itself was not sufficient to be a source of motivation for continued effort nor did it mark special status. One of the Black males with high grades was also a top athlete. Like the others, he did not think of his academic achievements as important. At first, his only concern about his grades was that they be high enough for him to continue playing ball. The turning point for him and the others came with some public declaration that their academic achievement was "special." The athlete did not fully realize that he was also an exceptional student until the city newspaper sent a reporter and photographer to his home. They took pictures and did a story with a focus on him as an athlete who was also a top student. Another student was called to the principal's office. He thought that he was in some sort of trouble. Instead, the principal gave him an award for his academic achievement.

The other students indicated that the minority scholars' annual awards and recognition banquet was the turning point for them. At this banquet each student received an academic award with their peers and parents present. A number of students had part-time jobs after school—they were assisted in placement by their school counselors. People on their jobs were aware of their academic achievements and also encouraged them. The students were asked by the people they worked with if they ever considered going to particular colleges and universities. The students had always assumed that these schools were beyond their means and abilities. They were asked if they knew about various fields of study in college. Again they either had no knowledge or simply never associated themselves with the fields. On some of these jobs there were college students who offered to help them with their homework and told them to consider going to their university—they could get in. These events impressed on them that what they were doing was important and was not to be taken for granted. But it was equally important that the point be made to their parents, friends and peers. After public acknowledgment, each student had a new identity to live up to and a sense that the opportunities before them were real.

Finally, if you ever thought that high academic performance was largely due to proper study skills, what these young people reported was shocking. They violated every rule for efficient and effective study. They studied with their radios on. They studied lying down. They studied in between classes and on the run. They studied when they were tired. They studied for examinations the night before or just an hour before. Occasionally, they did not study at all! Only a couple of students reported studying consistently several hours per night. Out of the entire group only two students studied together and at the library. Ironically, they all knew how they were supposed to study, but the proper way was simply not how they did it. With regard to study habits, they seemed to have only two points in common: They all did some sort of studying and they were all diligent about completing homework assignments on time. But they may have had an additional and very subtle point in common. Several students mentioned that they paid very close attention to what went on in each class and practiced recalling what they learned right after classes. I suspect that there is a close relation between their relations with teachers and how well they retained information. Being personally close to teachers makes recall easier, while the formal social distance common to the teacher-student relation makes retention and recall more difficult.

Relations with Community

Virtually all of these high achievers lived in low income, working-class suburban communities which are segregated by race and by economic class. The students were asked if there were other nonfamily members in their community who contributed to their academic achievement. The most common response was emphatically "none." In exploring their community experiences we found a rough and tragic terrain. The students saw academic achievement as a way out of depressed and dangerous environments. One student said, "You do whatever you can to get out of X."

Others commented that their community was varied by income and people and was not all negative. Everyone's concern was that others, especially their White peers at school, held consistently negative stereotypes about their communities and all of the people who lived there. People who lived in X community were considered to be "stupid, lazy and criminal." This stereotype was a formidable barrier to how others treated the students. Only one student said that his community motivated him. He wanted to get an education so that he could return to help turn it around. Another student realized that education was the only way out after having worked during a summer on a survey project. The households he interviewed that had the least education were the poorest and the most troubled.

Virtually all of these high achievers conveyed a sense of walking a fine line in their community lives. The subject that got them all especially animated was drug trafficking in their communities. This was the most threatening aspect of their community life. They could live with poverty and the stereotyping, but drug trafficking was another matter. They had family members involved as sellers and users. Neighbors and friends also used and sold "crack." This is what the "crowd" did and there was considerable peer pressure on them to also get involved. One student said "you can't act like they [drug sellers and users] don't exist. They are family, neighbors and friends. You got to live with them." But the fine line is that "you have to not be a part of them while they are all around you." Another student said, "I stay by myself away from the crowd and spend as much time as possible outside of the community." The consensus was that you either do well in school or you do drugs. There was literally no other option. Focusing on school was banking on the future because in the present those who sold drugs clearly had the money, cars, clothes and high regard of the "crowd."

We asked about church and other institutions in their community. Were community institutions viewed as supportive of their high achievement? The responses were mostly negative. One church was mentioned where the pastor acknowledged student academic achievement in the congregation. He always asked, "How are you doing in school?" and never forgot to tell them "to keep up the good work." But most of the other churches the students attended only gave lip service to the need for students to do well in school. Individual student achievements were not recognized or acknowledged. There is no place in the format or tradition of the Catholic masses for this sort of acknowledgment. And as one student put it, his church was so down on young people that they wouldn't know how to recognize him even if they knew of his work. Two female students, whose families were Pentecostal and Jehovah's Witnesses respectively, told stories of how their churches actually opposed their focus on school. The time they spend at school would be better spent at church and it was not good to become too much a part of "the world." Only three students talked of being a part of youth groups in their communities. A number of organizations for young people existed some years ago, but not anymore—there is no money for them and people are now scared of the dope.

Relations with Peers

"It helps to have someone to talk to and work with." But more typically these students did not have peers whom they were really close to. They had many acquaintances but few close friends. Even participation in the three schools' minority scholars program did not change their relative isolation. There were enough differences among these students that they rarely got together outside of program activities. They were also spread across three high schools and several communities. The lack of close friends highlighted the need for open and warm friendships with teachers and counselors. The students gave a variety of explanations for their situation. One of the Black males said "When the kids I used to hang with found out that I was doing well [in school], they didn't want to hang with me no more." Most of the students reported that very few of the young people they spent their time with were doing well in school. When the achievers were together with their friends, they simply did not talk about school. In some cases, friends who were doing poorly were pleased to have a partner who was "smart" and encouraged their achieving friend to continue doing well.

Friends were mostly of the same sex and race. But occasionally support and motivation came from unanticipated places. Several female students spoke of their boyfriends as being very supportive of their achievement—especially friends in colleges who were a year or two older. One male student said, "I wanted to be friends with a girl who was a good student. But she don't want to be bothered with me when my grades were bad. When your grades are good, you can go out with a lot more girls." Most White students expected the minority students to do poorly and were often openly hostile to those who managed to be exceptions. Several of our achievers had experiences similar to a student who said, "When the White students in my classes found out that I was getting As, they stopped talking to me. At first they thought I was there for their entertainment—to talk about sports. Several said to me that Blacks aren't supposed to get As—especially those from my community." Another student said, "When I answer questions correctly in class, the White students turn and look at me in amazement."

Not all of the White students constantly mirrored prejudice. One student told of an incident in one of his classes when an examination was being returned. A White student asked, what grade did he get? Before he could answer another White student said laughingly, "He probably got a D." The comment hurt and the Black student resented it, but he and the White student who made the comment are now good friends. Another student told the group that, if it had not been for a White friend from junior high school, he would not have enrolled in college preparatory courses.

His White friend kept after him to get into the right classes—he had no idea that a decision in the eighth grade would make a difference.

As part of the focus group questions, each facilitator asked the students to tell us why they felt other "bright" Blacks and Hispanics did poorly in school. The achievers began discussing other students who were smart and did better work than they did in junior high school. Their explanations ranged across school, peers, family and community. They pointed out that if there was no one in the family who actively cared, the young person was finished. A student not on the college track by the ninth grade was also finished—"Nobody is going to go back to take the right courses." They called for more guidance counselors and wondered why, the very year their district high schools were integrated, the guidance departments were cut out. They also pointed out that the low achievers were unwilling to give up their friends for school. Other comments were that their peers did not believe in themselves—just as our scholars had not. The low achievers thought that they could not do any better because deep down they really believed that Blacks and Hispanics are dumb—precisely what many White teachers and students believe. So there was no point in committing themselves to studies. The worst part of what they reported was that alienation from school fed directly into alienation in the community. There were no opportunities for a young person to simply make mistakes, sort out their lives and mature. The drug scene was there waiting with open arms.

The Significance of Race

We asked the students, had they experienced racism and, if so, did it have any effect on their academic performance? Most replied that they had no direct experience with racism. What they meant was that they had not experienced blatant and obvious discrimination like that which existed in the South during Jim Crow segregation. Instead, what they experienced were actions directed at them personally that kept them guessing whether it was or was not racist. Not really knowing was worse than the acts. There were key teachers in the college preparatory track who seemed friendly toward their White students, but were cold and matter-of-fact with Black and Hispanic students. One student with a B average in the class got a D as a final grade. The teacher said it was because he did poorly on the final examination. When the student's counselor and father demanded to see the examination, the teacher claimed that it was lost. The grade was changed. Another "unfriendly" teacher wanted to give the student a failing grade for one unexcused absence. The student knew of White students in his class with unexcused absences who were not failed. It turned out that the teacher could not fail this minority student after all, because he had really not been absent. Another student remarked, "It seems like they [unsupportive teachers] are just laying for you and looking for an excuse to mark you down. It is hard to go all semester and make no mistakes."

In listening to the focus group tapes it was interesting to note that only males reported that teachers were "laying for them." The female students also experienced covert mistreatment, but there appeared to be greater tolerance among unsupportive teachers for Black and Hispanic females being exceptional students. White students exhibited covert racism by assuming that all Black and Hispanic students were dumb and by wanting to maintain this belief even when they encountered exceptions. Sometimes underlying racial hostility would be manifested in actions. Students reported occasionally opening their lockers and finding notes stuffed in through the air holes. The contents of these anonymous notes were personally insulting, racist and derogatory. These covert acts of racism took a much greater toll in anger and personal hurt than the overt acts. "It is hard to get your mind off of it [an anonymous act of racism] and study, especially when it came from a teacher." In addition, those who held jobs pointed out that they saw racist behavior on the job. It was usually directed at Blacks and Hispanics, in lower-level roles. In these cases, racism was an incentive to study in order to be better employed.

Conclusion

What we have uncovered from these interviews are insights from the lives of a group of Black and Hispanic students as to why they are successful in school. They have also given us a glimpse of the price they are paying for choosing to focus on school.

What these students provided in one intense afternoon is by no means the whole story. Black and Hispanic students from other social class and community circumstances could undoubtedly give us additional insight on what it takes to be academically successful. This small group of students went quickly beyond the demographic and statistical picture of success and got into the factors and processes that account for their achievement. Others may wish to use this information to design surveys to see just how representative the experiences are of the students who participated in our focus groups. If we learned anything from these group discussions, it was the value of involving teens in an inquiry about their lives and experiences.

There are a number of specific points which the students raised that are well worth testing and considering:

1. Both family and school involvement and encouragement are essential to student motivation to succeed. Also both sources of motivation have to be complementary.
2. A student's family should be defined more broadly so that it includes extended relations. We should note that there is a bias toward crediting parent(s) with influence even when the primary motivation comes from some other, non-parent family member.

3. Students can be motivated to succeed by family and friends who are not themselves "successful" role models.

4. An effective and motivating relation between students and their teachers and counselors begins when teachers and counselors take a personal interest in the students and work with them. Willingness to drop the formal teacher-student or counselor-student role is important.

5. Public acknowledgment and identification of an achieving student are essential to those students' realization that they are indeed doing exceptional work and can qualify for opportunities in the larger society outside of their community. Acknowledgment is also very important for encouraging continued support from a high achiever's peers and family.

6. The specific study strategies that lead to high academic achievement are primarily to study consistently, to pay close attention in class and to be diligent in turning in assignments. Specific study techniques or number of hours per day of study are of secondary importance.

The Black and Hispanic students we interviewed are paying a very high price in being shunned and isolated from their peers and community. They have to literally disassociate themselves from their communities and normal friendships in order to maintain their motivation to academically succeed. Also they cannot afford to make mistakes in walking the fine lines in their communities, between drug trafficking and resentment over their choice or at school between racist teachers "laying for them" and White students who do not accept their competitiveness. The personal price these students are paying for their academic achievement is remarkable and ironic. It is remarkable because they have to pay such a price at all. It is ironic because all well-meaning individuals and institutions in American life profess to support and would applaud their achievement. Yet they are isolated, shunned and could not achieve without a system of special support. The problem is that for these students professions willing to have them as important players in the larger society are too far away from their day-to-day reality.

The Community Factor

The students we interviewed are doing well academically because of extraordinary efforts from their schools which have made it possible for individual teachers and counselors to take interest in each student and to work with them. Their achievement also required someone at home to convince each student to forgo the immediate world around them and to count on school and the future for a better life—another extraordinary effort. Why are these extraordinary efforts necessary in order to produce high achievers? It is very clear that if motivators at home or at school had not taken special interest and given attention to these students, we would not have had any Black and Hispanic high achievers to interview. These young people would be indistinguishable from their peers—many of whom are just as talented.

The answer can be found by looking at the factor the students found least supportive and hoped to escape from: the community.

Researchers may be able to conceptually separate families from communities and then research the relation between families and academic achievement as if the community were not a factor. But the family lives of the young people we interviewed would suggest that to separate family from community is to ignore very important factors in student motivation. The community more than any other factor is a reflection of the morale, expectations and life conditions of its residents. It is also the community that serves as the immediate environment for family life. If we focus on what the students told us about their parents and older brothers and sisters, we get a glimpse of a real struggle. That struggle is not simply between family members; it is about the family living in its environment. It was through the community that older brothers and sisters got into their troubles. It was peers in the community that parents competed against in shaping their children's lives and in controlling them amidst fast money and other potentially destructive distractions.

Current research suggests that Black student academic achievement is largely due to family influences, in which case declining achievement is due to declining family support. What researchers might be really looking at is declining community morale and declining social resources mediated through the family. By overlooking community influence, one can focus on the extraordinary uphill struggles of those few families who do produce a high achiever and overcome their communities. But this is to ignore the obvious. The obvious is that if the majority are failing because of community influences, the majority can also succeed if community becomes positive and supportive. Our students' older brothers and sisters and friends are a testimony to this fact. The interviewers asked each group of students to name the one thing which could be done to produce more academically successful students like themselves. We fully expected them to focus on improvements within their schools such as expanding special programs. To our surprise the most common answer had to do with community improvement—get rid of drugs and get more jobs.

Reflective Writing: *Based on this reading, can you construct a portrait of a successful student and that student's home and school environment? How is your own student profile similar to and/or different from this portrait? What might families, schools, and communities do to help more students fit this positive profile?*

Something to Push Against

Ron Suskind

In this 1998 book, A Hope in the Unseen, *the author tells the story of Cedric Jennings, a young man of great academic promise and determination attending a tough inner-city high school from which few students go on to succeed in higher education. This chapter from the book describes Cedric's efforts to distinguish himself, with the help of teachers and administrators, while many of his peers are far less supportive and even hostile. Ron Suskind is a reporter for* The Wall Street Journal. *He spent four years researching the book and observing Cedric in his day-to-day life. He won a Pulitzer prize for this work.*

To Consider: *What factors do you think account for Cedric's fierce desire to succeed against the odds? Why do many other students appear to take such a negative view of his efforts?*

A hip-hop tune bursts forth from the six-foot-high amplifiers, prompting the shoulder-snug slopes of black teenagers to sway and pivot in their bleacher seats. It takes only a second or two for some eight hundred students to lock onto the backbeat, and the gymnasium starts to thump with a jaunty enthusiasm.

Principal Richard Washington, an aggressive little gamecock of a man, struts across the free throw line to a stand-up microphone at the top of the key as the tune (just a check for the speaker system) cuts off. He dramatically clears his throat and sweeps his gaze across the students who happen to be present today—a chilly February morning in 1994—at Frank W. Ballou Senior High, the most troubled and violent school in the blighted southeast corner of Washington, D.C. Usually, he uses assemblies as a forum to admonish students for their stupidity or disrespect. Today, though, he smiles brightly.

"Ballou students," he says after a moment, "let's give a warm welcome to Mayor Marion Barry."

The mayor steps forward from a too-small cafeteria chair in his dark suit, an intricately embroidered kufi covering his bald spot. He grabs the throat of the mike stand. "Yes," he says, his voice full of pride, "I like what I see," a comment that draws a roar of appreciation. The mayor's criminal past—his much publicized conviction for cocaine possession and subsequent time served—binds him to this audience, where almost everyone can claim a friend, relative, or parent who is currently in "the system."

The mayor delivers his standard speech about self-esteem, about "being all you believe you can be" and "please, everyone, stay in school." As he speaks, Barry surveys an all-black world: a fully formed, parallel universe to white America. Providing today's music are disc jockeys from WPGC, a hip-hop station from just across the D.C. line in Maryland's black suburbs. A nationally famous black rhythm and blues singer—Tevin Campbell—up next, stands under a glass basketball backboard. Watercolors of George Washington Carver and Frederick Douglass glare from display cases. All the administrators are black, as are the ten members of the muscular security force and the two full-time, uniformed cops, one of whom momentarily leaves his hallway beat to duck in and hear the mayor.

Along the top rows of both sets of bleachers, leaning against the white-painted cinder blocks, are male "crews" from nearby housing projects and neighborhoods in expensive Fila or Hilfiger or Nautica garments and $100-plus shoes, mostly Nikes. Down a few rows from the crews on both sides of the gym is a ridge of wanna-bes, both boys and girls, who feel a rush of excitement sitting so close to their grander neighbors. All during the assembly, they crane their necks to glimpse the crews, to gauge proximity. Next in the hierarchy are the athletes. Local heroes at most high schools but paler characters at Ballou, they are clustered here and there, often identifiable by extreme height or girth. They are relatively few in number, since the school district's mandatory 2.0 grade point average for athletic participation is too high a bar for many kids here to cross.

The silent majority at Ballou—spreading along the middle and lower seats of the bleachers—are duck-and-run adolescents: baggy-panted boys and delicately coifed girls in the best outfits they can manage on a shoestring budget. They mug and smile shyly, play cards in class, tend to avoid eye contact, and whisper gossip about all the most interesting stuff going on at school. Hot topics of late include a boy shot recently during lunch period, another hacked with an ax, the girl gang member wounded in a knife fight with a female rival, the weekly fires set in lockers and bathrooms, and that unidentified body dumped a few weeks ago behind the parking lot. Their daily lesson: distinctiveness can be dangerous, so it's best to develop an aptitude for not being noticed. This, more than any other, is the catechism taught at Ballou and countless other high schools like it across the country.

As with any dogma, however, there are bound to be heretics. At Ballou, their names are found on a bulletin board outside the principal's office. The list is pinned up like the manifest from a plane crash, the names of survivors. It's the honor roll, a mere 79 students—67 girls, 12 boys—out of 1,389 enrolled here who have managed a B average or better.

With the school's dropout/transfer rate at nearly 50 percent, it's understandable that kids at Ballou act as though they're just passing through. Academics are a low priority, so few stop to read the names of the honor students as they jostle by the bulletin board. Such inattentiveness drives frustrated teachers to keep making the board's heading bolder and more commanding. Giant, blocky blue letters now shout "WALL OF HONOR."

The wall is a paltry play by administrators to boost the top students' self-esteem—a tired mantra here and at urban schools everywhere. The more practical effect is that the kids listed here become possible targets of violence, which is why some students slated for the Wall of Honor speed off to the principal's office to plead that their names not be listed, that they not be singled out. To replace their fear with pride, Principal Washington has settled on a new tactic: bribery. Give straight-A students cash and maybe they'll get respect, too. Any student with perfect grades in any of the year's four marking periods receives a $100 check. For a year-long straight-A performance, that's $400. Real money. The catch? Winners have to personally receive their checks at awards assemblies.

At the start, the assemblies were a success. The gymnasium was full, and honor students seemed happy to attend, flushed out by the cash. But after a few such gatherings, the jeering started. It was thunderous. "Nerd!" "Geek!" "Egghead!" And the harshest, "Whitey!" Crew members, sensing a hearts-and-minds struggle, stomped on the bleachers and howled. No longer simply names on the Wall of Honor, the "whiteys" now had faces. The honor students were hazed for months afterward. With each assembly, fewer show up.

Today's gathering of the mayor, the singer, and the guest DJs carries an added twist: surprise. There was no mention of academic awards, just news about the mayor's visit, the music, and the general topic of "Stay in School."

As the R&B singer takes his bows, Washington steps forward, his trap in place. "I'll be reading names of students who got straight A's in the second marking period. I'd like each one to come forward to collect his $100 prize and a special shirt from WPGC. We're all," he pauses, glaring across the crowd, "very, *very* proud of them." A murmur rumbles through the bleachers.

Washington takes a list from his breast pocket and begins reading names. He calls four sophomore girls who quietly slip, one by one, onto the gym floor. Then he calls a sophomore boy. Trying his best to vanish, the boy sits stone still in the bleachers, until a teacher spots him, yells, "You can't hide from me!" and drags him front and center. A chorus of "NEEERD!" rains down from every corner of the room.

Time for the juniors. Washington looks at his list, knowing this next name will bring an eruption. "Okay then," he says, mustering his composure. "The next award winner is . . . Cedric Jennings."

Snickers race through the crowd like an electrical current. Necks are craning, everyone trying to get the first glimpse.

"Oh Cedric? Heeere Cedric," a crew member calls out from the top row as his buddies dissolve in hysterics.

Washington starts to sweat. The strategy is backfiring. He scans the crowd. No sign. There's no way the boy could have known about the surprise awards; most teachers didn't even know. And Jennings, of all people. Jennings is the only male honor student who bears the cross with pride, the one who stands up to the blows. The only goddamn one left!

The principal clutches the mike stand, veins bulging from a too-tight collar, and gives it all he's got, "Cedric Jenningsssss. . ."

Across a labyrinth of empty corridors, an angular, almond-eyed boy is holed up in a deserted chemistry classroom. Cedric Jennings often retreats here. It's his private sanctuary, the one place at Ballou where he feels completely safe, where he can get some peace.

He looks out the window at a gentle hill of overgrown grass, now patched with snow, and lets his mind wander down two floors and due south to the gymnasium, where he imagines his name being called. Not attending was a calculated bet. He'd heard rumors of possible academic awards. Catcalls from the assemblies of last spring and fall still burn in his memory.

Off in the distance are skeletons of trees and, behind them, a low-slung, low-rent apartment complex. His eyes glaze as he takes in the lifeless scene, clenching his jaw—a little habit that seems to center him—before turning back to the computer screen.

"Scholastic Aptitude Practice Test, English, Part III" floats at eye level, atop a long column of words—"cacophony," "metaphor," "alliteration"—and choices of definitions.

He presses through the list—words from another country, words for which you'd get punched if you used them here—and wonders, scrolling with the cursor, if these are words that white people in the suburbs use. A few screens down, a familiar-sounding noun appears: "epistle." Sort of like "apostle," he figures, passing by choice "A) a letter" and clicking his mouse on "B) a person sent on a mission."

He looks quizzically at his selection. Probably wrong, but he likes the sound of that phrase—"a person sent on a mission." Sort of like me, he thinks, on a mission to get out of here, to be the one who makes it.

Cedric Jennings is not, by nature, a loner, but he finds himself ever more isolated, walking a gauntlet through the halls, sitting unaccompanied in class, and spending hours in this room. He is comforted by its orderliness, by the beach-blanket-sized periodic table above his head against the back wall and the gentle glow of the bluish screen.

He scrolls back to the top of the vocabulary list and reaches for a dictionary on the computer table. The classroom's occupant, chemistry teacher Clarence Taylor, wanders into the room and registers surprise. "Didn't go down there, today, huh?" asks Taylor, a bearlike man in his mid-thirties, short but wide all over. "I'm disappointed in you."

Cedric doesn't look up. "They give out the awards?" he asks nonchalantly.

"Yep," says Mr. Taylor.

"Glad I didn't go, then. I just couldn't take that abuse again," he says evenly, this time glancing over at the teacher. "I'll just pick up the check later. They have to give it to me, you know?"

Mr. Taylor offers a mock frown, now standing over the boy, eyes wide, brows arched. "That's not much of an attitude."

Cedric flips off the power switch with a long, dexterous finger. "I know," he murmurs. "I worked hard. Why should I be ashamed? Ashamed to claim credit for something I earned? I hate myself for not going."

He sits and stares at the darkened screen. He can hear Mr. Taylor ease away behind him and unload an armful of books on the slate-topped lab table near the blackboard. He knows the teacher is just fussing, walking through a few meaningless maneuvers while he tries to conjure a worthwhile response to what Cedric just said.

Mr. Taylor's moves are familiar by now. The teacher has personally invested in Cedric's future since the student appeared in his tenth grade chemistry class—back then, Cedric was a sullen ninth grader who had just been thrown out of biology for talking back to the teacher and needed somewhere to go. Taylor let him sit in, gave him a few assignments that the older kids were doing, and was soon marveling at flawless A papers. Taylor took Cedric for an after-school dinner at Western Sizzlin', and they were suddenly a team.

In the last two years, Taylor has offered his charge a steady stream of extra-credit projects and trips, like a visit last month with scientists at the National Aeronautics and Space Administration. He challenges Cedric with elaborate intellectual riddles, withholding praise and daring the pupil to vanquish his theatrical doubting with a real display of intellectual muscle. It's call and response, combative but productive. Mr. Taylor even sets up competitions among the top students, like a recent after-school contest to see who could most swiftly write every element in the periodic table from memory. As usual, Cedric rose to crush the competition, reeling off all 109 elements in three minutes, thirty-nine seconds.

Cedric is still staring at the dead screen when he finally hears Mr. Taylor's squeaky wing tips coming back around the lab table.

"You see, Cedric, you're in a race, a long race," the teacher says as Cedric swivels toward him, his arms crossed. "You can't worry about what people say from the sidelines. They're already out of it. You, however, are still on the track. You have to just keep on running so . . ."

"All right, I know," says Cedric, smirking impatiently. With Mr. Taylor, it's either a marathon metaphor or a citation from Scripture, and Cedric has heard the race routine many times before. "I'm doing my best, Mr. Taylor. I do more than ten people sometimes."

Mr. Taylor clams up. So much for *that* race *metaphor*, Cedric thinks to himself, delighted to employ an SAT word. He jumps up from the chair and paces around the classroom, picking up things and putting them down, looking caged.

"So, did you mail the application yet?" Taylor asks, trying to keep the conversation alive.

"Yeeeess, I maaaiiiled it," Cedric says, rolling his eyes.

This is not just any application. It's a bid for acceptance into a special summer program for top minority high school students at the Massachusetts Institute of Technology. It's highly competitive, drawing from a nationwide pool and taking kids for an intensive six-week program between their junior and senior years. It offers academic enrichment but also sizes up whether the students could cut it at MIT. About 60 percent are eventually offered a blessed spot in the university's freshman class for the following year.

Cedric does not dare speak about it to anyone except Mr. Taylor, who helped him with the application. He feels too vulnerable. His yearning is white hot. It's his first real competition against invisible opponents—minority kids from far better schools—in what Cedric rightly knows is a dry run for the college applications that must be mailed in the coming school year. It could even mean a slot, eventually, at MIT.

It will be nearly two months before he hears whether he's accepted, but the program is quickly consuming Cedric's thoughts. His notebooks in math, physics, and English have MIT doodles—the three magic letters Gothic here, three-dimensional there, then crossing over one page and written fifty times on the next. Being accepted there would be the reward for years of sacrifice.

"You think I'll get in?" he asks, awkward and momentarily exposed, but catches himself. "I mean, you know, whaaaatever. What does it matter?"

"Will you get in?" begins Mr. Taylor, launching another discursive riff. "Well, let me note . . ." The class bell rings, interrupting him, and Cedric prepares to go, having lost his taste for an answer.

The hallways fill as a wave of students from the gymnasium washes through the school. Leaving the chemistry classroom, Cedric keeps his eyes fixed forward on a shifting spot of linoleum about a yard ahead of his front foot. He hears someone from behind, a boy's voice, yell, "Where was you Cedric—hiding in the bathroom?" followed by a burst of nearby giggles, but he won't look up. *Just don't get into it,* he says over and over in his head, trying to drown out the noise.

Today, though, it's no use. He wheels around to see a contingent behind him, two hard-looking boys he barely knows and an accompaniment of girls.

"Why don't you just shut up," he barks, facing them while back-pedaling. "Just leave me alone." Fortunately, his math class is the next doorway and he slips into the almost empty classroom, relieved to have avoided an altercation.

"Ready for the test today, Cedric?" asks Joanne Nelson from her desk across the room. She's a round, soft-spoken, dark-skinned black woman who also had Cedric in tenth grade.

"Uh-huh," he nods, regaining some composure. "Yeah, I mean, I think I'm in real good shape."

The test is in Unified Math, his favorite subject. Each day, Cedric looks forward to this class, composed of eighteen kids from Ballou's special math and science program.

With the program, Ballou is attempting a sort of academic triage that is in vogue at tough urban schools across the country. The idea: save as many kids as you can by separating out top students early and putting the lion's share of resources into boosting as many of them as possible to college. Forget about the rest. The few kids who can manage to learn, to the right; the overwhelming majority who are going nowhere, flow left.

Cedric, like some other math/science students, applied to the program and arrived a year early to Ballou, which allows a handful of ninth graders to arrive with the eight-hundred-student tenth grade class. While at Ballou, the math/science students mix with the general student body for subjects like English and history but stay separated for math and science classes, which are called "advanced" but are more at a middle level of classes taught at most of the area's suburban high schools.

Slipping into a favorite desk, Cedric watches as the rest of the class arrives, mostly girls, many of them part of a tiny middle-class enclave from nearby Bolling Air Force base. He is friendly with a few of the girls, but today the room is tense and hushed, so he just nods a quick hello or two. Soon, everyone is lost in the sheaves of test papers.

It takes only a few moments for a calm to come over him. Knowing the material cold is Cedric's best antidote to the uncertainty that sometimes wells up inside him, the doubts about whether any amount of work will be enough to propel him to a new life. He takes out his ruler and confidently draws two vertical lines, noting points for asymptotes, limits, and intercepts. He moves easily through the algebraic functions on the next few questions, hunched close to his paper, writing quickly and neatly, the pencil's eraser end wiggling near his ear. For half an hour, he is steady and deliberate, like someone savoring a fine meal.

When he arrives at the last question—which asks students to write about the topic they have found most interesting thus far in the semester—he starts tapping his pencil on the desk. So much to choose from.

Finally, he begins to write: "The part that most interested me was finding the identity of the trigonometric functions. I had a little bit of trouble with them at first, but they became easy!" He reels off ten lines of tangent, sine, and cosine functions, an intricate equation springing effortlessly from his memory, and arrives at a proof. Cedric sits back to admire his work. It's so neat and final, so orderly. So much confusion, all around, such a long way to travel to get out of this hole, but here, at least, he can arrive at modest answers—small steps—that give him the sensation of motion.

He's done and puts down his pencil. Still ten minutes to the period bell. Then, suddenly, he smiles for the first time in days and again grabs the dull No. 2. Across the bottom, he scribbles "I LOVE THIS STUFF!"

Each afternoon, there is a choice of bus stops. The stop right in front of the school is usually quiet and empty late in the afternoon, while another one, a few hundred yards away on bustling Martin Luther King Avenue, is always hopping.

At 5:02 P.M. on this day, a week after the awards assembly, Cedric Jennings emerges from Ballou's side entrance, having already finished his homework and another SAT practice test in Clarence Taylor's room. He slings his bookbag over his shoulder, freeing his hands to pull closed his three-year-old black parka with the broken zipper. Day by day, he's hearing fewer barbs in the hallways about the awards assembly, and his spirits lift a bit as he sees a fading late afternoon sun shining across the teachers' parking lot. He pauses to look at it a moment—there hasn't been much sun lately—and decides today to opt for Martin Luther King.

In a moment, he's strolling on the boulevard—Southeast's main street of commerce, legal and otherwise—and taking in the sights. There's a furious bustle at this time of day. Darkness, after all, comes earlier here than in those parts of Washington where the streetlights work, where national chains have stores with big neon marquees, and where everything stays open late. In those places, the churn of commerce isn't halted, as it is here, by a thoroughly rational fear that seems to freeze the streets at nightfall.

Cedric huddles against the cloudy plastic window of the bus stop hut and watches the drug dealers near the intersection at 8th Street. He wonders what draws him out to the avenue bus stop, where—God knows—he could get killed. People do, all the time; he muses today, as he often does when he stands at this stop, about whether coming out here means he's going a little crazy.

Two crack dealers are chatting about twenty feet away. Both guys are in their early twenties, with hair mottled from being outside all day—one in a fine-looking long-sleeve Redskins football jersey and the other in a soft leather jacket. Cedric cranes his head around the hut's aluminum edge to pick up the conversation. He's sure they're armed, and he spots telltale bulges on each with his trained eye.

"So, you see, this bitch, she sucked my dick just to get her a little rock," says the Redskins jersey.

"Hey, next time you send her to me," says the soft leather, throwing his head back in a toothless laugh. "I'll give her what she needs real bad."

Cedric listens, not breathing, and then pulls back behind the plastic wall just as the one in leather turns toward him.

Hidden behind the bus shelter, he replays the dialogue in his head, where he will continue to chew on it for days afterward. He smells the rich greasy aroma of Popeye's Fried Chicken wafting from across the street, hears a saxophonist just up the boulevard, playing for quarters. A few guys he recognizes from Ballou, including some crew members, wander into view and he watches them flirt—or "kick some game"—with some cute girls who are rolling their eyes but definitely not walking away.

Spending so much time alone, he finds it hard to resist observing the fiery action all around. No diving in, not for him, not ever, but what's the harm in watching a little, picking up bits of this or that? He spots the bus a few blocks down. Clenching his molars to flex muscle at the bend of his still smooth, boyish jaw, he steps out into the wind.

Apartment 307 on the third floor of the blond brick High View apartments at 1635 V Street, Southeast, is empty, dark, and warm at 6:04 P.M., when Cedric unlocks the door. There hasn't always been heat, with overdue bills and whatnot, and he always appreciates the warmth, especially after the long walk from the Anacostia bus and subway station in the icy dusk wind.

He slips out of his coat and backpack and goes from room to room turning on lights, something he's done since he was a small kid, coming home alone to apartments and tiptoeing, with a lump in his throat, to check if intruders were lurking inside closets and under beds.

It's not a very big place—two bedrooms, a small bathroom, a kitchenette, and an attached living and dining room—but it's one of the better apartments that he and his mother, Barbara, have lived in. He's even got his own bedroom in the far back corner.

He flips on the switch. It's like a bear's winter cave of strewn matter—a thick padding of clothes, magazines, rubber-soled shoes, books, loose papers, and more clothes.

Cedric turns on his beloved Sharp Trinitron, a 19-inch color TV that his mother rented for him in ninth grade from a nearby Rent-a-Center (just paid off a month ago at an astonishing total price of nearly $1,500) and flops onto the bed. Like his proclivity for spying on street hustlers, the TV is a vital element of Cedric's secondhand life. He loves the tube, especially the racy, exhibitionist afternoon talk shows, which he watches for a few minutes tonight before turning to the local news—the lead story about a shooting not far from here—and then flipping to *The Flintstones,* a favorite.

He hears the thump of a door slamming.

"Lavar, you home?" comes the voice—calling him, as his mother always has, by his middle name—but he doesn't get up, figuring she'll wander back. In a moment, Barbara Jennings, hands on hips, is standing in the doorway.

In the sixteen and a half years since Cedric's birth, Barbara Jennings has been on a path of sacrifice and piety that has taken her far from the lighthearted haughtiness of her earlier self—the woman with a blonde wig, leather miniskirt, white knee-high boots, and a taste for malt liquor. Cedric has seen pictures of that skinny young thing, a striking girl with a quick smile who, as he has discerned from his mother's infrequent recollections, searched for love and found mostly trouble.

She stopped searching long ago. Barbara is a churchwoman now. On weekdays she works in a data input job at the Department of Agriculture, where she has been for almost eleven years, and splits the rest of her time between a church in a rough section of Washington north of the Capitol dome and this small, messy apartment.

Cedric looks her up and down and smiles thinly. Today, like most days, she has opted for a black dress and sensible shoes, an outfit most appropriate to her general mood, needs, and heavier frame. But her features—her smallish nose and pretty, wide-set eyes—have held up well, even at forty-seven and without makeup.

"I thought you would have made dinner by now," she says, slipping a thin chain with her dangling Department of Agriculture photo ID from around her neck. "How long you been home?"

"Only a couple of minutes," Cedric says, turning back to the tube. "What we got to eat?"

"I don't know, whatever's in there," she says curtly before disappearing into her room to change out of her work clothes. Taking his cue, Cedric moves into the kitchen and begins breaking up ground beef into a frying pan. He pours in a can of navy beans, some oil, chopped onions, some pepper, salt, a little paprika, and other condiments. He does this without complaint or enthusiasm—it's what he does most nights—and soon there are two heaping plates of steaming hash.

"Hey, it's ready and all," he calls around a short breakwall behind the stove to Barbara, who's sitting in a bathrobe on the white living room couch watching TV.

Usually, he takes his plate to his room and she eats on the low, wide living room coffee table—each sitting in front of their own TV. Tonight, though, she clears away newspapers and unopened bills from the dining room table.

"I haven't talked to you in ages, it seems," she says softly as they sit down to eat.

"I've been around," he says, grateful for her attentions. "Just been a lot going on—at school and whatever."

So it ends up being a night that they talk. It happens every couple of weeks. It's not needed more than that, Cedric figures. He knows that his mom wants to give him his space, now that he's sixteen and, by his reckoning, almost grown up, so she doesn't bother him in his room, where he spends most of his time. Maybe too much time, she tells him sometimes, but it's the only place he feels he has any privacy. After all, it's not as if he goes out late on weekend nights with friends, like most kids at school. Inside his room is the only place he can really relax.

He describes last week's assembly, about his not going, and she shakes her head dismissively. "What did I tell you? Before you know it, you'll be leaving them all behind. Just pay them no mind."

"Okay, okay," he says, "but what if I get rejected by MIT? That'd kill me." Barbara heeds this more carefully. It was she, after all, who found a description of the program in a scholarship book that someone gave to her at the office.

"You can't be worrying about MIT, Lavar. Just pray about it. If God has meant it to happen, it will." She looks up between bites and sees he's not convinced. "Look, your grades are perfect, your recommendations are good. What can they not like?"

"Yeah, I guess," he concedes.

"What's the point of getting down on yourself?" she says. "People will see that you're special."

He nods, letting her words sink in, and they eat for a while in silence—just the two of them, the way it has been for years. Barbara's two older girls, Cedric's half-sisters, are twenty-six and thirty-one and long gone, leaving mother and son to rely on each other in more ways than they can count.

Through years of ups and downs—times when he was certain that he was unworthy of success or love or any reasonable hope of getting something better—her faith in him has been his savior. It always amazes him. Having finished dinner quickly, he watches her clean her plate contentedly, and he shakes his head. She's just rock solid certain that he's going to MIT. Who knows, he wonders as he busses their plates and begins washing the dishes. Maybe she's right.

Both return to their customary evening routines—Barbara back to the couch and her sitcoms while Cedric dries and puts away the dishes and silverware. Quieter now, with the sink water not running, he hears what sound like pops from outside, almost certainly gunshots. He looks over at his mother sitting by the window but she doesn't react, so he begins wiping down the kitchen counters.

Gunshots are part of the background score here. Listen on most nights and a few pops are audible. The corner nearest the house—16th and V—is among the worst half-dozen or so spots in the city for crack cocaine dealing. The corner a block north—16th and U—is, of late, the very worst. There has been lots of shooting on both corners recently, but still they're open all night, and the traffic of buyers on 16th remains strong and steady in all weather.

Cedric knows that the surrounding mayhem is not something he and his mother need to talk much about. Still, it's always there, ionizing the air in the apartment, lending it some extra gravity, which, Cedric told his mother a couple of weeks ago, gives him "a little something to push against."

Cedric hangs up the wet dish towel on a drawer handle and strides toward the short hallway leading to his room. He glances quickly at Barbara as he passes and realizes that the TV is on but she's no longer watching it. Her eyes are on him.

He stops. "What you looking at?"

She pauses as though she's trying to remember something. "What did I once tell you?" she asks finally, in a tentative voice.

"Ma, what are you talking about, talking crazy?"

"What did I once tell you, Lavar?"

"I don't know. You tell me lots of things."

She stands, tying her robe closed, and slowly points a finger at him, buying an extra moment to get the words from Scripture just so: "The race," she says with a satisfied smile, "goes not to the swift nor the strong, but he who endureth until the end."

Oh yes, that's a good one, Cedric agrees, and nods. Hasn't heard that one in a while. "Thank you, Jesus," he says to her with a wry smile as he makes his way toward the back bedroom. Stopping at the threshold, he turns and calls back: "But it wouldn't be so terrible to be all swift and strong—just once in a while—and let some other people do all the enduring."

Barbara, sunk back into the couch, can't help but laugh.

ATTENTION, STUDENTS. WE ARE IN CODE BLUE."

Cedric Jennings gazes at the silvery mesh intercom speaker above the blackboard in Advanced Physics. Images of tumult form in his head.

"REPEAT. IT'S A CODE BLUE!" barks the scratchy voice of the assistant principal, Reggie Ballard. "EVERYONE SHOULD BE WHERE THEY'RE SUPPOSED TO BE . . . OR ELSE."

Through the open door to the physics classroom, the sounds of frenzy become audible for Cedric and fifteen other math/science students. The rules of this game are simple: anyone in the halls during a "code blue"— called from time to time when students are supposed to be settled into class after a period change—is hauled to the cafeteria and cataloged for after-school detention. With the warning duly issued, ten security guards with walkie-talkies—large black men in plain clothes—fan out through the halls, grabbing students by the collars and sleeves.

Everyone in physics sits still, ears perked up, as light footsteps tap down the hallway of the school's science wing, followed by heavy slaps on linoleum and then a shout from the nearby stairwell: "DAMN YOU, LET GO OF MY CLOTHES!"

It's an unseasonably warm day in early March, a day to make one think that spring is already here. It's also one of those bad days at Ballou, when anarchy is loosed and it suddenly becomes clear to kids, teachers, and administrators—all at once—that no one is even remotely in charge. Some random event tends to trigger it. Early this morning, for instance, a teacher got punched by a student and bled. The news traveled, and other kids, looking for any excuse to blow, were emboldened.

At a few minutes after 10 A.M., there was a fire in the downstairs bathroom, forcing everyone out into the parking lot as four fire trucks arrived to drench a flaming bathroom trash can. Afterward, kids milled about the halls, and two separate scuffles ignited on different corners of the first floor. Security crews moved to one but neglected the other, and a social studies teacher—a large, heavily built man—jumped in to break it up. He avoided injury, other than getting his glasses knocked across the hall.

Like other students, Cedric kept himself apprised of the morning's commotion, but he had other business to occupy him. Before physics—as Ballard was consulting with Washington about preparations for calling the code blue— Cedric sauntered into the administration office and leaned against the chest-high Formica counter. He spotted the assistant principal and started right in. "Hey, Mr. Ballard. Look, Mr. Dorosti gave me a B+ on the midterm in computer science and I deserved an A, and I've got all my weekly quizzes to back it up," Cedric said, trying to give a little bass to his voice. "He can't mark something I did as correct on a quiz and then mark the same thing wrong on a test—right?"

"I guess not," Ballard replied. "Bring me what you've got and I'll take it under advisement."

"You better, and Mr. Dorosti better, 'cause I'm fighting this one."

As Cedric turned to stalk out, Ballard whispered to Washington, "That Cedric . . . nothing but trouble. Quick tongue and too proud."

Pride. Cedric's 4.02 grade point average virtually ties him for first in the junior class with a quiet, studious girl named LaCountiss Spinner. Pride in such accomplishment is acceptable behavior for sterling students at high schools across the land, but at Ballou and other urban schools like it, something else is at work. Educators have even coined a phrase for it. They call it the crab/bucket syndrome: when one crab tries to climb from the bucket, the others pull it back down. The forces dragging students toward failure— especially those who have crawled farthest up the side—flow through every corner of the school. Inside the bucket, there is little chance of escape.

The code blue excitement subsides, and Mr. Momen, an Iranian immigrant with a thick accent, closes the classroom door. "All right, every one of you, listen," he says. "We have today, for you, some exercises that have to be done by the end of class. No exceptions." He passes out the core teaching tool at Ballou: the worksheet. Attendance is too irregular and books too scarce, even in the advanced sections, to actually teach many lessons during class. Often, worksheets are just the previous day's homework, and Cedric can finish them quickly.

Today, though, he runs into trouble. A few minutes in, he looks up and realizes that a girl in the next row is copying his work.

"Hey, what're you doing?" he snaps. She begins to giggle and then parlays his attention into a sexual jibe.

"Listen, Cedric, if you looking for something hot and wet, I'll give it to you."

Guffaws all around.

"Yeah, and I'll give you something hard and dry right back," he counters as the class erupts in catcalls. Cedric is removed from the room. "I put in a lot of hours, a lot of time, to get everything just right," he says to Mr. Momen from a forest of beakers and microscopes in the adjoining lab area. "I shouldn't just give answers away."

"Cedric," Mr. Momen says as he turns back to the others, "you have to figure out a way to get along better with people. Other students try hard, too. They're not all trying to get you."

Cedric sits for a moment, alone again, and quietly pushes through the worksheet, calculating, at the very least, what's being asked of him in physics. He leads the class—including his rival, LaCountiss—in grade points for the semester.

After class, he makes his way across the width of the building toward the cafeteria, thinking about what Mr. Momen said and what it's supposed to mean. How can he possibly get along with kids who hate him, he asks himself as he walks, lifting his gaze from the floor and searching the faces of kids flowing in the opposite direction in the hallway. Hate? Well, maybe not hate exactly, he decides. It's more that they hate what he represents, or something.

As he watches them pass, Cedric struggles with something that he would rather not know and that he manages, day in and day out, to keep safely submerged: that these kids are not all that different from him, that what mostly differentiates him are transferable qualities like will and faith. Just like him, they are almost all low-income black kids from a shadowy corner of America. His exile is, in large measure, self-induced and enforced. If he changed, soon enough he'd be accepted.

He knows all this but pushes the thoughts out of his head. Reaching out to any fellow ghetto kids is an act he puts in the same category as doing drugs: the initial rush of warmth and euphoria puts you on a path to ruin. His face, uncharacteristically open and searching a moment ago, slips into its customary pursed-lipped armor. Don't give up, don't give in. Other kids, passing him in the hall, pick it up. No one's a fool here. They recognize Cedric's face—pinched, dismissive, looking right past them. They've seen this look before, on the faces of white people, and they respond accordingly.

"Can you believe that sorry ass Cedric," whispers a pudgy boy, leaning against a locker as Cedric passes.

A boy on his left—a tall drink of water in a Nike shirt—nods. "Right, just look at him, would you? Kind of pants are those?"

"He needs a good beating," murmurs a third, just loud enough for Cedric to hear.

Cedric cuts forward like a torpedo. Around the next bend comes Phillip Atkins, a tough, popular fellow junior sporting a C– average who is, lately, in Cedric's face.

"Oh, look, it's the amazing nerdboy," Phillip chides as he approaches. Cedric tries to slip by, but there's a crowd up ahead watching a craps game in the hall, causing a backup. There's nowhere to go.

"Come on nerdboy, you and me, let's do it, right now," says Phillip, feigning a punch as a girl holds him back and two boys, standing nearby, giggle. Phillip is known for his sense of humor.

"Why don't you leave me be, Phillip?" says Cedric after a moment. "What'd I ever do to you?"

Phillip, satisfied at getting a rise, just smiles. The two stand for a minute, eye to eye: Cedric in a white shirt, khakis, and black felt shoes, math book in one hand, the other hand clenched in a fist, shaking nervously; Phillip, a bit shorter and wiry, dressed in a brown T-shirt with jeans pulled low. The latter offers a menacing deadeye stare, copied immaculately from the gang leaders he admires, and Cedric breaks it off, looking away, flustered.

The craps game is over, and his exit has cleared. Throwing a side-long scowl at Phillip, Cedric slips forward through the dispersing mob, in the midst of which Delante Coleman collects his dice and rises from a crouch. Delante, known to all as "Head" because he helps run one of the school's largest gangs, the Trenton Park Crew, is short and stocky, with caramel-light skin, hazel eyes, and the temerity of a killer. He helps manage a significant drug dealing and protection ring, directs a dozen or so underlings, drives a Lexus, and, in his way, is every bit as driven as Cedric. It's what each does with his fury and talents that separates these two into a sort of urban black yin and yang.

Cedric passes tight against the lockers, and Head, flirting with some girls, doesn't see him—which is just as well. Head and some of his crew enjoy toying with honor students, or "goodies," as he calls them, messing with their hair, taking their books (if they're foolish enough to carry any), scuffing them up a bit.

By now, Cedric has cut hard to the left into a different hallway, one that leads toward the cafeteria, which is a few feet ahead. He often tries to eat in empty classrooms—the cafeteria being the type of free-fire zone that some-one of his lowly social status is wise to avoid—but today a friend of his, a girl, convinced him to meet her at the cafeteria. Just inside the side entrance, she is waiting for him.

" 'Bout time you got here, Cedric. I'm starving," says LaTisha Williams, arms folded but smiling radiantly. "It's wrong to keep your boo waiting."

Cedric says nothing, just smirks at her and rolls his eyes. LaTisha is not his "boo," slang for girl- or boyfriend. She's bubbly and has a pretty face, but she's huge—five-foot-two and maybe 250 pounds. She's an outcast, just like he is. But, he concedes, handing her a pinkish tray, she usually manages to cheer him up.

Mostly, she talks and he laughs, offering modest rejoinders, and now off she goes again. Today she's doing a riff—mostly for the benefit of another girl with them in line—about Cedric's long-ago flirtation with Connie Mitchell, a gorgeous, light-skinned ingénue from the Bolling Air Force base area, who arrived here midway through tenth grade.

"You see, Cedric goes up to her and says, 'Hi. Hi, you new here? Can I do anything for you. Can I, can I?'" says LaTisha. "He was on her like a dog, sniffing her up and down." Cedric chuckles at this, appreciating any story showing that, sexually speaking, his clock ticks in the traditional fashion. He's made passes at other girls, though it never amounts to much, and he's begun to see himself through other people's eyes, wondering if he's just not manly enough to have any success with women. Though his voice has yet to change, he has no feminine affectations. He's pleasant looking and tallish, his dress unflamboyant but neat and usually color coordinated. He suspects that it is this terrain that's atypical and upside down—but he's not sure. All he knows is that, here, no one wants to be with an honor student—a pariah—except maybe LaTisha, who has few alternatives. Cedric Jennings simply has no social currency at Ballou.

"Cedric, you just ain't a woman's man," LaTisha says a few minutes later, once they're seated, certain she'll get a rise out of him. But Cedric, increasingly glum about the subject and anxious to leave the cafeteria, bears down on his grilled cheese and doesn't get into it. LaTisha quietly eats her undressed salad and leaves to get a second one.

Looking across the raucous cafeteria crowd, Cedric is reminded of the assembly—probably most of these kids were there—and what he said that day to Mr. Taylor, about how not going made him feel ashamed.

Ashamed. The word has been smoldering inside him for weeks. What he said, it didn't track somehow. Was he ashamed of getting all A's? No, he was proud of that. So why wouldn't he show his face? Is it maybe that he's ashamed of being alone all the time, of being so lame? No girlfriend. No close guy friends. He tears at an empty carton of milk with his long, agile fingers. No, that doesn't seem right either. That's all part of his solitary mission to get out of here and off to a famous college.

LaTisha comes back. "You okay, Cedric? You look kind of bad."

"Yeah," he says. "I'm all right. Just been thinking about why I feel the way I do."

With the afternoon temperature reaching seventy, students start slipping out early from one of Ballou's ten exits. Cedric sits through his afternoon classes and finds himself absently watching the clock. After the dismissal bell, he runs into LaTisha in the hallway and tells her he's not going to stay his usual two hours or so after school. He thinks he'll just "go home, watch TV, and crash."

She says she's going home, too, and they walk outside to the bus stop just in front of the school. In the very late afternoons, when Cedric often leaves the building, this stop is empty. At 3:30, though, it's jammed and rowdy with kids who've been cooped up for the winter in nearby public housing projects, small apartments, or modest homes, all now feeling the free sunshine on their faces.

He and LaTisha take different buses home, so she's talking fast to fill the few moments they'll have before parting. He's nodding and half listening. Then something happens.

A boy a few feet away from them grabs another boy around the neck, pulls out a pistol, and holds it to the other kid's head. People are screaming and trying to get away, bumping into each other, not sure which direction to run. Cedric, backing onto the grass, turns to see the gun again and feels himself flinching. He sees that LaTisha has fallen down, her great girth slumped onto the concrete.

And then it's over. The kid with the gun runs across the street and disappears. No shots were fired, and some kids murmur about whether the gun, which was an odd greenish color, was real.

Cedric's bus comes and, after helping LaTisha up, he gets on, shaken, and finds a seat. He pushes himself tight into the seat's corner, leaning his shoulder against the bumpy tin siding as the bus rolls up to the avenue stop. The dealers are out in force today, and, looking at them, he realizes that he's been fooling himself, that there is no safe distance, no safe place to go, not in school, not on the street, not anywhere.

His breath feels short. He closes his eyes, presses his fingers against them, and feels that his hands are trembling. In the dark field behind his closed lids, he sees clearly the gun, the terrified face of the kid with the barrel pressed against his temple, and LaTisha falling. He jerks his eyes open, tries to push the images away, and finds himself recalling something that happened in school a year ago. It was just a day or two after last spring's awards ceremony. A kid came up to him in the hall, a smallish kid in a green army jacket. The kid said something about not liking Cedric's face and how he saw him get his $100 award check and it made him sick—and there was a bulge in the army jacket's pocket. The heavy green fabric was tented into a triangle pointing out from the kid's hip. Cedric looked down and could see the back of a rat-gray steel handle.

Cedric can't remember much else—just that he couldn't speak, that he ran through a cluster of kids into the bathroom, terrified, and decided not to tell Mr. Washington or anyone about it, afraid that there'd be retaliation if he squealed. He never saw the kid again.

He hasn't thought about any of that for almost a year. He just pushed it out of his mind. But now, as the bus rumbles through the gritty circus on Martin Luther King Avenue, it suddenly dawns on him. Maybe that's why he didn't go to the awards assembly. It wasn't that he was ashamed of his achievements or too weak to face the razzing. He was scared. Maybe that kid's still out there. That's why he hid. He's scared right now. Nothing wrong with that.

He lets out a little high-pitched laugh, drawing an anxious stare from an old woman sitting next to him. He smiles at her and she looks away. Yes sir, he muses, feeling a weight lift. His absence didn't mean they'd won and he'd lost. He was simply scared to death. That's something he can live with.

Reflective Writing: *This chapter describes a high-achieving, academically engaged young man trying hard to succeed in a school where most students seem to place little value on academic success, and some even scorn it. How might you compare Cedric's situation at Ballou High School to the situation of a successful student at the high school you graduated from? What factors made possible Cedric's success? What barriers did he have to overcome?*

Who Gets Called Queer in School?

Lesbian, Gay, and Bisexual Teenagers, Homophobia, and High School

Andi O'Conor

Drawing on interviews with students and on an extensive research literature, this essay explores the problems associated with being a gay student in high school. The essay, from the book The Gay Teen: Educational Practice and Theory for Lesbian, Gay, and Bisexual Adolescents, *focuses on problems of acceptance, rejection, alienation, and threats of violence but also looks at innovative programs designed to help gay and lesbian students. When she wrote this article in 1995, Andi O'Conor was a doctoral student at the University of Colorado conducting research on attitudes toward homosexual students in secondary schools.*

To Consider: *Gay student Tommy states: "Our parents hate us, our teachers hate us, straight kids hate us, adults hate us." Author O'Conor gives statistics and anecdotal information suggesting that Tommy speaks for many young people in his situation. O'Conor goes on to comment, "As a result, gay and lesbian teenagers often feel they have no place to go, that there is no room in the world for them to exist." While you read this article and afterwards, consider your own reactions to the account of the experiences of homosexual teenagers in school, and ponder the question of why such treatment exists.*

Discussions of heterosexism, homophobia, and the lives of lesbian, gay, and bisexual youth have been noticeably absent in the educational literature. As Reed (1993) states: "Not only does the group remain invisible, the existence of and problems associated with gay youth are largely denied by public school educators, particularly school administrators."

In 1992, I spent several months observing and interviewing a group of gay, lesbian and bisexual teenagers in a support group setting. The group met at the local gay and lesbian community center, and about twenty to forty teenagers attended each week. Attendance fluctuated a great deal, and while I got to know the core group of youths fairly well, I actually observed over a hundred different teens. Many sought me out to tell their stories; many told their stories to the entire group. Part of my goal in conducting this research project was to give voice to these teenagers. However, having your story printed and published can be very risky for gay teens, many of whom had not disclosed their sexual identity to their parents, friends, or peers.

In order to give voice to these teenagers and protect their identities, I constructed a composite narrative. In the narrative, only two voices are portrayed—one male, one female, named fictitiously "Christi" and "Tommy." Though their names are fictitious, their experiences are not. Each word they utter in the narrative is taken verbatim from my notes or from interviews. Christi and Tommy represent a wide range of teenagers—black, white, Asian, Latino/a, working and middle class. Their conversation reflects some of the most common and important experiences of these teenagers—isolation, alienation, rejection by gay adults, hostility by parents, and problems with homophobia in and out of school. It also portrays some of their humor and heart, their courage and compassion for each other.

A Conversation with Christi and Tommy

We sit having coffee at a downtown coffee shop, a fast-food place on the main drag in the city. It is filled with businesspeople, street people, waitresses in tired brown uniforms.

Tommy takes a drag of his cigarette; "I don't know which was worse," he says, "home or school." He fingers the ragged scars at his wrists. "My mom, has, um . . . a drinking problem. After I came out to her, she got drunk and told me I was a faggot and she didn't want no queer in her house. My brother, he called me a sick fag. So I figured it was either stay and take their shit or leave. So here I am." He stops talking and looks out the window again.

"School was a definite hellhole," says Christi. "H-E-L-L hole. No lie. Like, you sit in class, right, and all these girls are talking about which boys they like and all that crap. And you make stuff up, like 'oh, yeah, *he's* really cute.' You don't know how many times I wanted to lean over and say, 'Hey, what about Julia Roberts? Some fox, huh . . .' And class was such a joke. Teachers were such a joke. This one English teacher, all these girls have such a big crush on him. I *know* this guy is gay, he has to be. And he avoids me like the plague for two years. Like he KNOWS I KNOW and I'm going to turn him in or something. Fucking chicken. He could have helped me. He could have talked to me. But nooo . . ."

Tommy: "When I was about, I don't know, fifteen I guess, people at school decided I was gay. I didn't even know what they were talking about at first. They just started calling me 'faggot' this and 'fag' that, and all of a sudden I didn't have any friends anymore. So when people started calling me faggot and queer and stuff, and I thought, Yeah, I'm gay. That's what I am. I saw what happened to other kids who got called queer at school. I dropped out. I got a job. My mom thought that was cool. I didn't tell her until later, and that's when things got sort of bad."

Christi turns to me. "I used to call guys faggots in school. We thought it was real funny. 'You fag, you faggot.' We used to call guys gay, if they were skinny or nerdy. 'You sissy, you queer.' We'd hit them, punch them in the halls and stuff. I'd get in trouble and they'd call my mom. Poor Mom. She was so clueless. She'd sit me down and say, 'We are ladies, you and I.' I'd say yeah, yeah. And I'd try to be more ladylike. I mean, I wear makeup and stuff. When I came out to my mom she said, 'But you're so pretty!' Like I had to be ugly to be a lesbian!

"Mom and Dad are pretty cool. I mean, they haven't kicked me out or sent me to a shrink or anything. My mom's even gone to P-FLAG [Parents and Friends of Lesbians and Gays] a couple of times. She goes and cries with other parents. My dad just went, 'uh, huh.' He's clueless. He just, like, reads the newspaper and doesn't say anything. Who knows if they talk about it. I think Mom is really bummed because she, like, wanted me to be a Chanel runway model or something."

Tommy gives a sarcastic sigh. "I always wanted to be a Chanel runway model myself." We laugh.

We order more coffee and watch people walk by on the street. A man and a woman walk by, holding hands. "See that?" Christi says. "No way could I do that with my girlfriend on this street. I'd get killed. No lie. It pisses me off, kind of. That Jo and I can't walk down the street like that. Just like everyone else. I mean, people throw stuff at you . . . really. It's not that they just yell stuff, but they really get mean."

"Yeah," Tommy sighs. "I don't have a boyfriend right now, but everywhere I go I think: Am I safe here? Is someone waiting to get me? So many people get bashed. I mean, we can't even go to bars unless we sneak in, so there's no gay places to even hang out, but I'm still afraid. I mean, I don't even look gay. I go to the park and I hang out with my friends, and we have to plan an escape route before we even sit down. It's such a drag. Last summer we were in the park and this car full of guys drove through screaming 'FUCKING FAGGOTS' and threw bottles from the car. They drove on the lawn, trying to run guys over and stuff. The cops got there later, way later, and looked at us like we were dirt. 'So no one got hurt,' they said. Yeah, right. No one got hurt."

"It's so sad," Christi says. "But I think things are better. I mean, better for us than for people our parents' age. You know, we have this group, we have P-FLAG, we have the center. And there are groups in schools now, in high schools and stuff. We don't have any bars, and that's a drag. And the adult gay community thinks we're babies." "Or jail bait," Tommy adds. She laughs. "Yeah, or like we don't really know we're gay because we're too young. Like they were never young. Like *they* never went to high school. But really, it's better. Since AIDS, people know that we exist, at least."

Tommy lights another cigarette. "But they still hate us," he says. "Our parents hate us, our teachers hate us, straight kids hate us, adults hate us . . .'"

His voice falters a little. Christi leans over the table and takes his hand. "But WE don't hate us, dummy. *We* don't hate us."

Christi and Tommy's conversation brings to light many of the problems experienced by gay, lesbian, and bisexual teenagers in high schools today. Tommy speaks of his problems at home, dealing with the hostility of his mother and brother. His brother calls him a "sick fag"; his mother calls him a "queer" and "faggot." Unlike teenagers from other oppressed minority groups, gay teenagers find little or no support or understanding at home for their societal difference. Most often, family members are the most difficult people to reveal sexual orientation to, and are often the last to know. Considering the consequences, this is often a wise choice. Many teenagers who reveal their sexual orientation (or "come out") to their parents face extreme hostility, violence, or sudden homelessness. As one gay youth stated, "growing up gay in my family is like being Jewish in a Nazi home" (Friend, 1993).

In contrast, Christi states that her parents are "clueless" even though they know she's a lesbian. Though they haven't kicked her out of the house, they don't discuss her lesbianism. Many parents of gay teenagers refuse to acknowledge their son's or daughter's sexual orientation, and even formerly close relationships can be torn apart.

School is also a hostile and dangerous environment for most gay and lesbian teenagers. As Christi says, "a definite hellhole." A recent U.S. Department of Justice report states that gays and lesbians are the most frequent victims of hate crimes, and school is the primary setting for this type of violence (Herek, 1989). Comstock (1991) writes, "Lesbian and gay crime victims report greater frequency of incidents in school settings than do victims of crime in general (25 percent lesbian/gay, 9 percent general)." People of color and men experience greater incidence of violence in schools than do whites and women.

Silence on the part of teachers and administrators also makes schools unsafe places for gay and lesbian teens. While teachers often punish students who make racist remarks, homophobic comments are typically unchallenged, and sometimes even perpetrated by teachers themselves (Friend, 1993). As Tommy says, "I saw what happened to other kids who got called queer at school."

Often in order to survive in school, many gay and lesbian teens have to construct a false, heterosexual self. As Christi says above, "You make stuff up, like, 'Oh yeah, *he's* really cute.'" Some teenagers have sex with members of the opposite sex to prove they are straight, and to avoid being called "queer" or "dyke." Lesbian and gay youth may also engage in antigay violence in an attempt to hide their homosexuality. Christi describes beating up boys who were feminine or different. Others participate in name-calling, or join in the laughter at "fag" or "dyke" jokes.

Gay and lesbian teens are also often isolated from gay, lesbian, and bisexual adults. Because of societal misconceptions about gay people as "recruiters" of youth, gay, lesbian, and bisexual adults (particularly teachers) often avoid interacting with gay and lesbian teenagers. Christi describes the situation well when she talks about her English teacher. "I *know* this guy is gay . . . and he avoids me like the plague for two years. Like he KNOWS I KNOW and I'm going to turn him in or something." Unlike other minority teachers, who can serve as role models to minority youth, gay and lesbian teachers nearly always hide their sexual identity and distance themselves from gay and lesbian youth.

Many youths face exclusion from the adult gay and lesbian community. As Christi and Tommy state, "The adult gay community thinks we're babies . . . like we don't really know we're gay because we're too young." Gay and lesbian youth are excluded from many community activities as well, since they often lack transportation and are too young for gay bars and social events.

Thus, gay, lesbian, and bisexual youth often go through the difficult period of adolescence ostracized and isolated from family members, teachers, peer groups, and the adult gay and lesbian community. As Tommy says, "Our parents hate us, our teachers hate us, straight kids hate us, adults hate us." As a result, gay and lesbian teenagers often feel they have no place to go, that there is no room in the world for them to exist. As Tommy says, "Everywhere I go I think, 'Am I safe here? Is someone waiting to get me?'"

Fortunately, as Christi says, "things are better." With the advent of groups like Parents and Friends of Lesbians and Gays (P-FLAG), parents can learn more about their gay, lesbian, and bisexual children, and can understand their unique difficulties. Support programs such as Project 10 in Los Angeles and the Harvey Milk School in New York offer safe environments for gay and lesbian youth. In-school support groups are being started in high schools throughout the country, and many gay and lesbian community centers offer support groups specifically for teenagers. These programs offer a critical bridge between gay and lesbian teenagers, their parents, friends, and the adult gay and lesbian community. They provide buffer zones where teenagers can learn who they are in a positive environment, away from the dangers of home and school. Support groups and programs both in and out of school provide these teenagers with a critical sense of community and self-esteem. They provide an alternative to alienation and suicide, a place to learn, as Christi says, that "*We* don't hate us."

I'd like to close with a quote by Aaron Fricke. As a teenager, Fricke sued his high school and won the right to take a male date to his senior prom. As a result, he became nationally known and soon after wrote a book called *Reflections of a Rock Lobster, A Story About Growing Up Gay* (1981). This book is an invaluable source of information for teachers, students, parents, and educational researchers interested in the lives of gay and lesbian youth. In this passage, Fricke reflects on what turned out to be a tense but uneventful senior prom:

I thought of all the people who would have enjoyed going to their proms with the date of their choice but were denied that right; of all the people in the past who wanted to live respectably with the person they loved but could not; of all the men and women who had been hurt or killed because they were gay; of the rich history of lesbians and homosexual men that had so long been ignored. Gradually we were triumphing over ignorance. One day we would be free.

That freedom, I hope, can be won by speaking out, and by sharing the stories of gay, lesbian, and bisexual youth. By refusing to tolerate name-calling, gay-bashing, and other forms of homophobia, and by recognizing gay, lesbian, and bisexual teenagers as a high school population at risk, teachers, students, parents, and administrators can help break the silence and truly "triumph over ignorance." We can help end homophobia and antigay violence, and work toward a day when no one gets called "queer" in school.

Many thanks to Matthew Goldwasser, Pat McQuillan, Margaret Eisenhart, and Cheryl Schwartz for their valuable input and ongoing support of my work. Special thanks to S.C.

References

Comstock, G.D. (1991). *Violence Against Lesbians and Gay Men.* New York: Columbia University Press.

Fricke, A. (1981). *Reflections of a Rock Lobster: A Story About Growing Up Gay.* Boston: Alyson Publications.

Friend, R. (1993). "Choices, Not Closets: Heterosexism and Homophobia in Schools." In *Beyond Silenced Voices.* Lois Weis and Michelle Fine, eds. Albany, NY: SUNY Press.

Herek, G.M. (1989). "Hate Crimes Against Lesbians and Gay Men: Issues for Research and Policy." *American Psychologist* 44, pp. 948–955.

Reed, D. (1993). "High School Gay Youth: Invisible Diversity." Paper presented at the Annual Meeting of the American Educational Research Association, April, Atlanta, GA.

Reflective Writing: *What are the specific instances of discrimination faced by the homosexual students discussed in the essay? Have you ever observed or experienced such treatment, and how would you explain it? How does discrimination in a school setting differ from what one might find in the home or with peers? What are your own views about the author's assertion that gay and lesbian students are treated unfairly in schools?*

Why the Americans Are More Addicted to Practical Than to Theoretical Science

Alexis de Toqueville

The other readings in this unit all look at subgroups within American society. This excerpt, from the classic 1835 book Democracy in America, *attempts to generalize about U.S. society as a whole. In 1831, a 26-year-old French aristocrat named Alexis de Toqueville was sent by his government to study the American penal system. Instead, he wrote a sweeping book about the people making up the world's youngest and most important democracy. Still considered to be one of the most distinguished—and most accurate—studies of the American character ever written, de Toqueville's book depicts Americans as a "hands-on," "can-do" people, far less interested in theoretical abstraction than in practical application and with a particular interest in business, industry, and commerce.*

To Consider: *De Toqueville tries to explain the reasons for Americans' practical orientation and lack of interest in high theory by pointing to this country's traditions of democracy and equality of opportunity. As you read, highlight the reasons he suggests for his opinion. In what ways do you agree with him? What alternatives can you think of to this practical focus? Can you think of examples from your own experience to illustrate and/or counter the argument he is making?*

If a democratic state of society and democratic institutions do not retard the onward course of the human mind, they incontestably guide it in one direction in preference to another. Their efforts, thus circumscribed, are still exceedingly great; and I may be pardoned if I pause for a moment to contemplate them.

We had occasion, in speaking of philosophical method of the American people, to make several remarks, which must here be turned to account.

Equality begets in man the desire of judging of everything for himself: it gives him, in all things, a taste for the tangible and the real, a contempt for tradition and for forms. These general tendencies are principally discernible in the peculiar subject of this chapter.

Those who cultivate the sciences amongst a democratic people are always afraid of losing their way in visionary speculation. They mistrust system; they adhere closely to facts, and study facts with their own senses.

As they do not easily defer to the mere name of any fellow-man, they are never inclined to rest upon any man's authority; but, on the contrary, they are unremitting in their efforts to find out the weaker points of their neighbors' doctrine. Scientific precedents have little weight with them; they are never long detained by the subtlty of the schools, nor ready to accept big words for sterling coin; they penetrate, as far as they can, into the principal parts of the subject which occupies them, and they like to expound them in the vulgar tongue. Scientific pursuits then follow a freer and safer course, but a less lofty one.

The mind may, as it appears to me, divide science into three parts.

The first comprises the most theoretical principles, and those more abstract notions, whose application is either unknown or very remote.

The second is composed of those general truths which still belong to pure theory, but lead nevertheless by a straight and short road to practical results.

Methods of application and means of execution make up the third.

Each of these different portions of science may be separately cultivated, although reason and experience prove that neither of them can prosper long, if it be absolutely cut off from the two others.

In America, the purely practical part of science is admirably understood, and careful attention is paid to the theoretical portion, which is immediately requisite to application. On this head, the Americans always display a clear, free, original, and inventive power of mind. But hardly any one in the United States devotes himself to the essentially theoretical and abstract portion of human knowledge. In this respect, the Americans carry to excess a tendency which is, I think, discernible, though in a less degree, amongst all democratic nations.

The greater part of the men who constitute these nations are extremely eager in the pursuit of actual and physical gratification. As they are always dissatisfied with the position which they occupy, and are always free to leave it, they think of nothing but the means of changing their fortune, or increasing it. To minds thus predisposed, every new method which leads by a shorter road to wealth, every machine which spares labor, every instrument which diminishes the cost of production, every discovery which facilitates pleasures or augments them, seems to be the grandest effort of the human intellect. It is chiefly from these motives that a democratic people addicts itself to scientific pursuits,—that it understands and respects them. In aristocratic ages, science is more particularly called upon to furnish gratification to the mind; in democracies, to the body.

You may be sure that the more a nation is democratic, enlightened, and free, the greater will be the number of these interested promoters of scientific genius, and the more will discoveries immediately applicable to productive industry confer gain, fame, and even power, on their authors. For in democracies, the working class take a part in public affairs; and public honors, as well as pecuniary remuneration, may be awarded to those who deserve them.

In a community thus organized, it may easily be conceived that the human mind may be led insensibly to the neglect of theory; and that it is urged, on the contrary, with unparalleled energy, to the applications of science, or at least to that portion of theoretical science which is necessary to those who make such applications. In vain will some instinctive inclination raise the mind towards the loftier spheres of the intellect; interest draws it down to the middle zone. There it may develop all its energy and restless activity, and bring forth wonders. These very Americans, who have not discovered one of the general laws of mechanics, have introduced into navigation an engine which changes the aspect of the world.

Assuredly I do not contend that the democratic nations of our time are destined to witness the extinction of the great luminaries of man's intelligence, or even that they will never bring new lights into existence. At the age at which the world has now arrived, and amongst so many cultivated nations perpetually excited by the fever of productive industry, the bonds which connect the different parts of science cannot fail to strike the observer; and the taste for practical science itself, if it be enlightened, ought to lead men not to neglect theory. In the midst of so many attempted applications of so many experiments, repeated every day, it is almost impossible that general laws should not frequently be brought to light; so that great discoveries would be frequent, though great inventors may be few.

I believe, moreover, in high scientific vocations. If the democratic principle does not, on the one hand, induce men to cultivate science for its own sake, on the other, it enormously increases the number of those who do cultivate it. Nor is it credible that, amid so great a multitude, a speculative genius should not from time to time arise inflamed by the love of truth alone. Such a one, we may be sure, would dive into the deepest mysteries of nature, whatever be the spirit of his country and his age. He requires no assistance in his course,—it is enough that he is not checked in it. All that I mean to say is this: permanent inequality of conditions leads men to confine themselves to the arrogant and sterile research of abstract truths, whilst the social condition and the institutions of democracy prepare them to seek the immediate and useful practical results of the sciences. This tendency is natural and inevitable: it is curious to be acquainted with it, and it may be necessary to point it out.

If those who are called upon to guide the nations of our time clearly discerned from afar off these new tendencies, which will soon be irresistible, they would understand that, possessing education and freedom, men living in democratic ages cannot fail to improve the industrial part of science; and that henceforward all the efforts of the constituted authorities ought to be directed to support the highest branches of learning, and to foster the nobler passion for science itself. In the present age, the human mind must be coerced into theoretical studies; it runs of its own accord to practical applications; and, instead of perpetually referring it to the minute examination of secondary effects, it is well to divert it from them sometimes, in order to raise it up to the contemplation of primary causes.

Reflective Writing: *According to de Toqueville, what attitudes and expectations characterized Americans in the early nineteenth century? Think about your own aspirations and interests, and those of the people you know. How well does the author's analysis of national characteristics from almost 170 years ago seem to fit our nation today? Also, what sort of educational emphasis does he recommend, and what do you think about his recommendation? To what extent would you say that his suggestions have been followed in setting up our higher education system?*

Possible Essay Topics

For this assignment, choose one of the following topics and write a three- to four-page essay. In your essay, be sure to draw significantly on readings from this unit of the anthology. But rather than merely summarizing or restating ideas from the essays, you will also want to add your own discussion and analysis of the readings and how they relate to your own ideas and experiences. Make sure your points are well developed and your prose carefully edited and proofread.

1. Orenstein in "Learning Silence," Kaminer in "The Trouble with Single-Sex Schools," and Sommers in "The War Against Boys" all argue that gender can play a key role in schooling. However, they come down on very different sides in discussions about differential treatment of male and female students and about the appropriateness and effectiveness of single-sex schools. Drawing on the readings from this unit, as well as your own observations and experiences, and being as specific as you can, develop your own argument about the possible roles of gender in education and the desirability of single-sex institutions.

2. The essays we're reading in this unit mainly discuss how such factors as gender, race, socioeconomic class, and ethnicity affect students in the early years of schooling. Now that you find yourself in college, you are probably in a more diverse environment in all kinds of ways than you were previously.

   For this writing assignment, think about your own experiences since beginning college, as well as your past experiences in elementary and high school. Pick one or two of the cultural factors discussed earlier (e.g., gender, race, class, ethnicity) and consider what role it or they might have had (and may continue to have) in shaping your own experiences and perceptions as a student. Draw significantly on at least two of the readings from this unit in writing your essay.

3. Drawing on de Toqueville's analysis, consider the ways in which schooling in this country (as reflected in your own experiences and in what you have observed around you) has been influenced by the pragmatic, "hands-on" emphasis discussed in the reading. Examine and critique some of the effects of

this emphasis. In your view, how is this pragmatism related to our democratic traditions?

4. The pieces by Reich, Bowser and Perkins, and Suskind deal in different ways with issues of social class and privilege and their role in education. Consider in some detail what these authors are saying, and then use your own experiences, observations, and ideas to respond to the authors. Your essay should include a summary and analysis of the essays to which you choose to respond, as well as your own interpretations of the relationship between social class and education, which you should relate to the interpretations put forward in the readings.

5. The essays by Bowser and Perkins and Suskind examine issues facing African-American students. Think carefully about the authors' arguments in these essays. Relate them to one another, considering similarities and differences. Then discuss your own life history—and the development of your own ways of looking at the world—in light of the readings. Think of specific ways in which your background and ideas conform to or depart from the patterns discussed in the readings.

UNIT TWO

Being in College

The first colleges in the United States—Harvard in Massachusetts and William and Mary in Virginia—were established more than 300 years ago. Although originally all-male schools that primarily prepared students from wealthy families for the ministry and that required the study of ancient Greek, Latin, and Hebrew, many aspects of college life from these earlier times would be familiar today. Although academic standards were generally high, students' interests frequently gravitated toward socializing, many prided themselves on cheating and on doing as little schoolwork as possible, and rowdy, even violent behavior was far more common than students today might think.

In Helen Horowitz's 1987 book, *Campus Life*, in a chapter entitled "College Men: The War Between Students and Faculty," the author describes the often unsuccessful attempts of college authorities "to control the unruly bands of young men who gathered for instruction" (23). She provides examples of problematic student behavior, ranging from youthful hijinks to truly destructive acts of violence, taking place at a number of schools including the most prestigious institutions.

> Records of youthful hedonism and collegiate customs in North America go back to Harvard's beginnings. Its poverty, simplicity, piety, and small scale may have initially inhibited adolescent enthusiasm, but Harvard in the heart of Puritan New England caught its students playing cards, drinking, and stealing the turkeys of their Cambridge neighbors. As early as 1667, the Overseers complained that upperclassmen were sending freshmen out on private errands. . . . High spirits continued to plague college authorities. By the eighteenth century the faculty recorded a new kind of misdemeanor: students put live snakes in their tutor's room and drank his wine (23–24).

At similarly distinguished Princeton University in 1800, after three students were expelled for disrupting chapel service, violent rebellion ensued. As Horowitz tells the story, "When their fellow students learned of this harsh penalty, they set off a riot. They shot pistols, crashed brickbats against walls and doors, and rolled barrels filled with stones along the hallways of Nassau Hall, the principal college building" (24). The campus eventually calmed down, but several weeks later, one of the originally expelled students returned to campus and assaulted the tutor he believed had turned him in for misbehavior. This incident led to another riot, which ended only when the president of Princeton threatened to close the college. Similar instances took place at numerous other institutions, including the University of North Carolina, where "students horsewhipped the college president, stoned two professors, and threatened the other members of the faculty with personal injury" (25). The student demonstrations of the 1960s and the more recent drunken rowdiness on college campuses pale in comparison to these earlier incidents.

In previous periods, many students could afford to take a casual attitude toward their schooling because very few students were able to attend college in the first place and because their family position assured them a comfortable living after college. Today students still find ways to relax and have fun, and campus protests still take place, but in general students have a more business-like approach to their studies and a more subdued approach to campus life.

As a relatively new college student, you are probably still in the process of figuring out how best to spend your time. Coursework; participation in organizations such as a fraternity, sorority, or campus club; interaction with friends; a job; sports: All or most of these activities may be competing for your time in a hectic schedule. This dizzying array of activities can make it difficult even to consider the fundamental question: What does being in college mean? Consideration of this question can help you decide how best to spend your own time throughout the coming years.

The readings in this unit examine from different perspectives this complex issue of competing demands on students' time and attention in college. In the first essay, philosopher Jack Meiland looks at the differing intellectual demands of high school and college courses, making explicit a distinction that is rarely spelled out. He argues that college demands a more critical, questioning approach than does high school. The next pieces, by English professor Mark Edmundson and writer Earl Shorris, respectively, originally published together in *Harper's Magazine*, offer a contrast between bored, affluent students in humanities classes at an expensive, elite university and deeply engaged, disadvantaged students learning philosophy and literature in an antipoverty program. The following piece, by classical Greek philosopher Plato, extends the discussion of thinking and learning by distinguishing between the world of the senses and the world of knowledge.

Next, from the perspective of the sciences, Duke professor Stuart Rojstaczer examines the intellectual demands of college science courses, questioning the rigor and faculty expectations of these courses. The following essay, by national education policy analyst Jacqueline King, examines the statistics on college student involvement in outside employment and argues that too many students are spending too much time working, sometimes even when they don't really need the money, and to the detriment of their education. Murray Sperber, English professor at Indiana University and critic of big-time college sports, contributes an essay placing college students into four categories based on their approaches to college academic and social life. Former university president Thomas Ehrlich discusses the recent trend creating opportunities for students to carry out—and learn from—community service projects. Finally, French professor Michael Randall defends traditional teaching methods of lecture, discussion, and the slow but steady consideration of complicated ideas, in light of the increasing emphasis on speed, efficiency, and technology in teaching today.

The Difference Between High School and College

Jack Meiland

This essay comes from the author's 1981 book, College Thinking: How to Get the Best out of College. *In the essay, Meiland, a philosophy professor at the University of Michigan who died in 1997 after a distinguished career, discusses the kinds of thinking students are asked to do in college. He contrasts these with the kinds of thinking students may have engaged in during high school. In particular, he argues, college requires students to treat subject matter not as unchanging fact but as beliefs or conclusions that have been reached through investigations. This orientation, he argues, demands an entirely different intellectual approach to the material than was needed in high school, and Meiland lays out suggestions for what that approach should entail.*

To Consider: *Examine the examples of higher-order thinking that the author provides. What skills and strategies might you need to work on in order to carry out this kind of academic work? In what ways have your previous schooling and experiences prepared you for such work?*

Since you know what high school work is like, we can approach the nature of college work by comparing college with high school. College freshmen believe that there must be a difference between high school and college, but their ideas about what the difference is are often radically mistaken. Students often see the function of high school as the teaching of facts and basic skills. They see high school as a continuation of elementary and junior high school in this respect. In senior high school, one learns physics and chemistry, trigonometry, American and world history—all subjects in which the "facts" to be learned are harder, but in which the method is much the same as in elementary and junior high school. The method of study most commonly used is memorization, although students are also called upon to apply memorized formulas in working problems and to make deductions in mathematical proofs. There are some exceptional high school classes, and some exceptional high schools, in which this is not so. But by and large, the perceived emphasis in secondary education is on learning facts through memorization. The secondary school teacher holds a position of authority because he has mastered factual information. Tests demand recitation of facts, papers require compilation of facts.

It is only natural, then, that the typical student sees college along these same lines. Reinforced by the relation between elementary school, junior high, and high school, the students usually believe that the relation between high school and college is the same as that between junior high school and high school. They believe that the difference between high school and college is that college courses are simply more difficult and that they are more difficult because they present more difficult factual information; they examine more difficult topics; they go over topics covered in high school but in a more detailed and painstaking way. College is taken to be different from high school *only* in being more difficult. Unfortunately this belief is reinforced by the actual content and method of presentation of typical freshman courses and programs. For example, in the first semester a freshman might takes a course in English composition, a beginning physics course, a course in a foreign language, and perhaps a lower-level survey course in social science or history. These courses are often indistinguishable from high school courses.

New Types of Intellectual Work

At the same time, college freshmen sometimes suspect or expect that college is or should be different *in kind* (not just in difficulty) from high school—that somehow intellectual activity in college is or should be of a distinctly different and higher level. And this expectation is fulfilled when the student gets beyond the introductory survey courses. There the instructors do seem to expect something different *in kind* from the student, though without telling the student explicitly and in detail what this is.

The good college teacher presents some information, in the sense of "what is currently believed." But he also spends much time talking about *the basis* on which this information is currently believed. *A large part of college work consists of discussing and examining the basis of current beliefs.*

The difference between high school and college is not that there is intellectual activity in one and not in the other. The difference is that college work requires that students engage in a *different kind* of intellectual activity, *in addition to* the activity of understanding the material that is presented. The first type of intellectual activity in both high school and college is understanding the material. Even here, though, college requires a different and higher type of understanding. Once the material is understood, the college student must perform another sort of intellectual work on the material, namely critical examination and evaluation. A main difference, then, between high school and college is that *new types of intellectual work are required at the college level.*

To see why new types of intellectual work are required, let's look again at the way in which materials are presented in high school and college. In high school, they are presented in an authoritative manner—almost as if they were absolutely and eternally true. This mode of presentation is reinforced by the fact that the content that is presented in high school is, typically, material about which people feel very, very sure. The laws of optics, the basic facts of American history, the structure of a plant, the operation of the Federal Reserve System—these are matters about which people feel great assurance, perhaps even certainty. They can be presented on the basis of authority. They are not controversial. Of course, we all know that once in a while, something about which we are very sure in this way turns out to be false—or at least subject to revised beliefs. Nevertheless, revisions of this sort are infrequent.

But in college a different attitude prevails toward the material being presented. Rather than being treated as unchanging fact, it is treated as beliefs or conclusions that have been reached on the basis of investigations.

At this point I must pause for a moment in order to talk about the kinds of statements that I'm making here. I have made, and will make, statements that assert that college work has such-and-such features or that college differs from high school in this or that way. And some of you might find that in some of your courses, or indeed in your whole college career, the work is not of this kind. In fact, some or all of your college work may seem not so different from your experience in high school. This may, of course, be due to your mistakenly approaching college work as if it were just the same as high school work. But I must admit that some college work really is no different from high school work. So how can I be justified in claiming so confidently that the two are different? My answer to this depends on first making a certain important distinction, the distinction between a *descriptive* statement and a *normative* statement. A *descriptive* statement tells how things in fact *are*. A normative statement tells how things *should be*, regardless of how they in fact are. If you say to me, "Things in my college *are not* the way you describe them," my reply is that they *should be* the way I describe them. Thus, some of my statements look like descriptive statements but they are to some extent normative statements too. My statements on this topic are intended to describe the way things are at the best colleges (not to be confused with the best-known colleges) and the way they should be in every college. I admit that some college teachers treat their materials as if they were teaching high school. And I admit that some exceptional high school teachers treat their materials in a college manner. What I am trying to do is not so much describe what actually goes on in the places called "high schools" and in the places called "colleges" as describe two different types of work and then say that the more advanced work is what ought to be going on in colleges. *Only* this more advanced work ought to count as "higher education." So my statements are partly descriptive (of the best teachers and the best colleges) and partly normative (in claiming that this is what ought to go on in college).

Now let's return to the difference between high school and college just mentioned. I said that in college materials are treated as beliefs or conclusions reached through investigation. Modern people take a certain attitude toward beliefs, namely that if a person believes something, he should have a basis for such beliefs. This can be put in the following way: it is rational to believe something only if one has a basis for that belief. One basis is what we call evidence. Most people today believe that, in secular or nonreligious matters at least, one should have evidence for one's beliefs, that it is right to believe on the basis of evidence and wrong to believe that for which there is not sufficient evidence. W. K. Clifford, a nineteenth-century English mathematician and philosopher, put this point very directly when he said: "It is wrong always, everywhere, and for anyone, to believe anything upon insufficient evidence." Clifford puts this point with perhaps greater moral fervor than most people would, but I think that no one would deny that he expresses a view that is quite widespread in contemporary thought.

Material is presented in college not as something to be believed on the basis of authority but as something to be believed because such belief is rationally justified and can be rationally defended. Thus, much work in college—and, I would say, the work that is characteristic of college—deals with the rational justification of belief. College teachers are concerned not merely with imparting information but also, and mainly, to present and examine the basis on which this information is or should be believed. They do this because they want this material to be believed on the basis of reason rather than on the basis of authority. It is a basic presupposition of the modern mind that rationally based belief is better than belief based on authority, on faith, or on some other nonrational process. Thus, much time in college is spent investigating the rationality of this or that belief.

It is important to notice that once we make this shift from authority to rational evaluation, the mode of presentation of the material—and the way in which we regard the material—also changes. Material that is presented on the basis of authority is presented as factual and is given an air of being absolutely and unchangeably true. Material that is presented on the basis of rational justification is presented as belief, as theory, as hypothesis, sometimes as conjecture—as material supported to a greater and lesser degree by argument and evidence. And this difference in mode of presentation makes an enormous difference in how the material is regarded. What is treated in high school as eternal and unchangeable fact that human beings have discovered in their continual and relentless progress toward total knowledge will be treated in college as belief that may perhaps be well supported at the present but that could turn out to be wrong. Another way of putting this is: what is fact in high school is often only theory—perhaps well-supported theory but nevertheless only theory—in college. And theories must be treated as such: one must examine the evidence to see how much support it gives the theory; and alternative theories must be examined to see which is better, that is, to see which theory should be believed.

Basis of Belief

Why do we believe that beliefs should be rationally based? Is this belief itself rationally based? Or is this belief itself merely an arbitrary presupposition or assumption? After all, someone might claim that what matters about a belief is not whether it is rational but instead whether it is true or false. If a belief is true, then it does not matter whether or not it is held on a rational basis. A true belief that is irrational will be as effective in our lives as a true belief that is totally rational. Consider the following example. Suppose that a businessman has been kidnapped and is being held for ransom. His wife has a dream in which she sees her husband being held captive in an old warehouse by the harbor, and she wakes believing that he is indeed there. At the same time, the chief of detectives has been working all night on the case, gathering evidence, tracing the car used in the kidnapping, questioning witnesses, and interviewing suspects. By daybreak the chief of detectives comes to believe that the businessman is being held captive in that very same abandoned warehouse. He and his men break into the warehouse and rescue the businessman. So it turns out that the wife's belief is true and that the detective's belief is true, even though the first is irrational and the second is rational. But what difference did the rationality or irrationality of the belief make? If the police had followed up on the wife's belief instead of the detective's belief, they would have gone to the same warehouse and rescued the businessman anyway. This seems to show that it is the truth of the belief, not its rationality, that matters.

This would be a good argument if our beliefs were always true and never false. But beliefs can be false, and our problem is to separate the true from the false. What we must do is find good reasons for believing what we believe. We think that if we base our beliefs on good reasons, our beliefs will turn out to be true more often than false. The wife does have a reason for believing that her husband is being held in the warehouse: she dreamed it was so. But we believe that this is not a good reason because many of the things that we dream turn out to be false. Dreaming does not, for most of us, provide a reliable guide to the truth. Hence the wife's belief is considered by modern persons to be unjustified, that is, irrational. But it is felt that evidence is a reliable guide to the truth, and that the more evidence we have, the more we are justified in believing what we do believe.

Since college students are expected to believe on the basis of good reasons, they are expected to know what those good reasons are. They are expected to know not only facts but also the reasons those are believed to be facts. Therefore, much time in college is spent in examining reasons to see if they are *good* reasons. For example, a high school text on American history might state that Alexander Hamilton was one of the chief architects of our

Republic, that Hamilton's ideas were extremely influential in shaping our form of government. A college teacher covering this period of American history would not let a statement like this pass without examination—he would demand to know the reasons for believing this claim to be true. This is, in part, why college courses beyond the initial survey courses usually cover a small specialized topic: it takes time to examine and evaluate reasons, to consider and discard alternative theories, to look at a theory from many sides before deciding that the reasons are good enough to accept the theory.

So one question with which college work is concerned is the question: "What are the reasons for believing this?" And the next question is: "Are these reasons good reasons for believing this?" And for any particular belief about which this second question is asked, the answer might turn out to be no. In that case, the belief is not justified—or, alternatively, we are not justified in believing that. The answer might turn out to be no in the case of the belief that Alexander Hamilton's ideas were influential in shaping this country's government. "But," someone will say, "that's ridiculous. Of course Hamilton was influential. All the books say so. Everyone believes it. And it's obvious." But is it so obvious? What are the reasons for believing it? If Hamilton was influential, then we should be able to give good reasons for believing that he was. And if we do not know of any reasons, or if the reasons are not good reasons, then we should not believe that he was influential.

My point here is that the business of college teaching and learning—namely the examination of reasons for beliefs—gives rise to, encourages, and absolutely depends on both students and teachers having an attitude of skepticism, of questioning, of not taking anything for granted. The whole project of college teaching and research—indeed, the whole project of the modern mind—is to base belief only on good reasons. Moderns feel that only this is rational and legitimate. We have banished authority, superstition, magic, and prophecy as bases for belief. We pride ourselves on rejecting these "primitive" and "emotional" reactions to the world. We exalt reason. And what this means is that we attempt to base belief only on good reasons. We are told that in the Middle Ages, people believed things because the ancient Greek philosopher Aristotle said that they were true. They believed these things on Aristotle's authority. This is now seen as illegitimate; instead, we should see for ourselves whether things are true by gathering evidence and finding good reasons for ourselves. Various tribes base some beliefs on the results of magical rites. We regard this as mere superstition. The modern mind rejects all this. And college simply reflects this view about the legitimation of belief by inquiring into the rationality of every belief to find out whether each belief is supported by good reasons.

This view has extremely important consequences. Because *every* belief ought to be based on good reasons, *every* belief must be examined. This includes even the most obvious beliefs. In fact, it is especially important to examine those claims and beliefs that are most obvious—it is precisely because something is "obvious" that people will not have examined the reasons behind it. But it may turn out that any particular belief, even an "obvious" belief, is unjustified. It may turn out that although we thought that there were good reasons for that belief, when we take a hard look at the case, there are no good reasons for it.

College as a "Subversive" Institution

This questioning of everything, including the obvious, is the mission of college in carrying out this project of modern intellectual life. And this sometimes has uncomfortable consequences for colleges, college teachers, and college students. For this mission makes the college potentially the most "subversive" institution in society. Here is an example. It has been held as "obvious" by many people in our country that the American economic system (a variety of capitalism) is superior to the Communist economic system. In college one might well investigate this belief to see if it is backed up by good reasons. However, merely raising and discussing this matter is likely to seem (and certainly has in the past seemed) to large segments of the American people as sedition, as "anti-American," as a betrayal of the trust of the American people in colleges and universities, as a lack of faith in America. And in the past, college teachers have been threatened and punished for doing just this sort of thing. College teachers have been fired from their jobs or made to sign loyalty oaths because they have investigated such topics or have come to have unorthodox views on such topics. The anti-Communist witchhunts of the 1950s, associated with the name of Sen. Joseph McCarthy (R-Wis.), included college teachers among their victims. Here is another example. College teachers who investigated and taught about Darwinian evolution were considered by powerful conservative segments of society to be undermining established religion and were persecuted for this, when in fact they were only doing their jobs, namely, inquiring into the reasons for a particular belief. Somewhat closer to our own time, several academics have been threatened because they have proposed that intelligence and social behavior are genetically determined. They have been prevented from speaking to groups and have even occasionally been physically assaulted. Their views have been condemned by liberals as politically dangerous. Thus, we find colleges under attack by both liberals and conservatives. All of this was foreshadowed by the situation of Socrates, the first person in recorded Western culture to have seriously examined the basis of common and obvious beliefs. Socrates unceasingly questioned others to find out whether they had good reasons for their beliefs about such sensitive topics as justice, piety, and virtue. He was finally accused of corrupting the youth and casting doubt on the gods, tried by the Athenian people, and put to death. Inquiry into reasons for beliefs has sometimes been a dangerous activity, from Socrates' time to the present, because the answer could always turn out to be no, in which case some favorite or important beliefs are threatened.

This phenomenon is not limited to college teachers. It extends to college students themselves. Many college students, after hearing and talking with their instructors and other students, have gone home during vacations and questioned important beliefs that they had formerly shared with their parents. They sometimes question their parents' way of life ("How can you live in this expensive house and drive several cars while people in other parts of the world are starving?"). Sometimes they question their parents' religious beliefs. Tensions develop and fierce quarrels break out between parents and students over just this kind of issue. So the basic attitude fostered by college—questioning of the reasons for beliefs—does sometimes lead to uncomfortable situations, and both students and faculty must be prepared to withstand this and to hold firm in carrying out the project of critical inquiry. College is sometimes thought of as an "ivory tower," as somehow not part of "real" life. But the strong emotions generated when favorite beliefs are questioned show that college work has a direct connection with important aspects of "real" life. If college were irrelevant to life, no one would care what was being done in colleges, and colleges would be viewed with amused tolerance rather than with sometimes heated emotion, vituperation, and outright assault.

When you inquire into the reasons for a belief, you may seem to be doubting that belief. When you raise questions about the reasons for a belief, some people may take you to be attacking that belief. We should distinguish here between two attitudes that one may take toward a belief when investigating the reasons for it: *doubting* the belief, in the sense of suspecting or believing that it is false; *suspending* the belief, in the sense of neither believing it to be true nor believing it to be false. This second attitude is a neutral attitude toward the belief and it maximizes the objectivity with which you pursue your inquiry into the reasons behind the belief. In view of this distinction, we can see that to raise questions about the reasons for a belief is not necessarily to attack it, since the questioner may have the second attitude toward the belief instead of the first attitude. When you take this attitude of suspension of belief toward a statement, you are no longer regarding that statement as an expression of fact. For example, you no longer regard it as a fact that Hamilton was influential in shaping our government. You are now investigating to see if the reasons justify your taking the statement to express a fact. The statement expresses a "claim," a "hypothesis," a "theory," or a "supposition." When this statement is found to be supported by good reasons, then it may be said to express a fact.

Why Reasons Matter

Why is it that college work is so concerned with the reasons for our beliefs? I have already briefly mentioned one reason for this: we hold that a belief that is supported by good reasons is more likely to be true than one that is not supported by good reasons. You should not, however, allow this justification of the search for good reasons to go unchallenged and unexamined. Is it true that good reasons make truth more likely? Someone may say that this connection between good reasons and likelihood of truth must exist because a reason will count as a *good* reason *only if* its presence does produce a greater likelihood of truth. This is what being a good reason *is*. But this response only shifts the problem by raising a new and equally important question: what types of reasons increase the likelihood of truth?

There is a second, very different, justification of the search for good reasons. One could form beliefs capriciously—that is, choose in an arbitrary manner to believe this or that. For example, if you wanted to believe that you are the best figure skater in the world, you would simply go ahead and believe it, ignoring all evidence. The trouble with forming one's beliefs in this way is that eventually—and probably sooner rather than later—you will come into frustrating, or even violent, contact with the real world. If you did believe that you were the greatest figure skater in the world but weren't, you might demand special privileges for yourself of the type often enjoyed by great artists. And you would be shocked and frustrated when you did not get what you wanted. Basing beliefs on good reasons has been found to aid in avoiding frustrations of this sort and to help in achieving one's goals. We might call this a "pragmatic" justification of the search for good reasons. Beliefs based on good reasons help us to get along better in the world.

A third justification is what we might call a "social" justification: basing beliefs on good reasons fits together well with our democratic way of life. In a democracy, authority is frowned upon as a basis for social decisions and social action. We do not believe in following the orders of a dictator or a tyrant. Instead, we "reason together" to decide what ought to be done. We try to persuade others that our position or view is the best; and we do this by trying to show that our position is supported by the best reasons. When a zoning dispute comes up in the city council, a new curriculum is proposed in the university, or an expansion plan is discussed by a group of businessmen and women, each side tries to show that the best reasons support its alternative. This is not to deny that other factors—personal influence, threats, emotion, bribery—sometimes weigh heavily or even determine the final decision. Nevertheless, our ideal—and often our practice—is to reason and to argue for or against one side or the other in an attempt to reach the best decision. This is the way we believe that we should relate to one another in society. Each person, we feel, ought to be treated as a rational, independent judge, interested in doing what is right and capable of being persuaded by argument. This democratic vision has nothing to do with whether beliefs supported by good reasons are likely to be true. It has nothing to do with whether beliefs supported by good reasons are more likely to be instrumental in the achievement of our goals. Instead it has to do with the way in which we think about ourselves, the kinds of persons we are or would like to become, and the ways in which we want to relate to and interact with others in society. Basing belief on good reasons discovered in cooperative discussion with others helps to make us the persons that we want to be and to produce the type of society in which we want to live.

A fourth justification is to be found in the works of the ancient Greek philosopher Plato. Plato's works take the form of dialogues between Socrates (who was Plato's teacher) and others whom Socrates encountered in Athens. These dialogues have a question-and-answer format, with Socrates asking the questions in a way that results in a critical examination and evaluation of the beliefs of others on such important topics as justice, piety, and virtue. In fact, Plato's dialogues are probably the single greatest influence in the formation of Western rationality; any critical evaluation of Western rationality should begin with an evaluation of Plato's view of the function of the intellect in living. In the *Meno*, a dialogue about the nature of virtuous action, Socrates eventually poses the question: is true belief equally as good, equally as valuable, as justified true belief (that is, true belief supported by good reasons)? In other words, he poses the question: what difference does justification, or support by good reasons, make? Isn't it enough to have true belief even if it is not supported by good reasons? It appears to many people that true belief is as useful as justified true belief, that justification by good reasons adds nothing, and so one need not bother about justification. As Socrates put it: "Then true opinion is as good a guide to correct action as knowledge . . . right opinion is not less useful than knowledge." To show that this is wrong and that good reasons are important, Socrates begins with the story of the statues of Daedalus, which are so lifelike that they need to be fastened down to prevent them from running away:

> they are not very valuable possessions if they are at liberty, for they will walk off like runaway slaves; but when fastened, they are of great value, for they are really beautiful works of art. Now this is an illustration of the nature of true opinions: while they abide with us, they are fruitful and beautiful, but they run away out of the human soul, and do not remain long, and therefore they are not of much value until they are fastened by the tie of the cause . . .

Socrates is saying here that if a person has a merely true belief without knowing the justification of that belief, then he is not likely to have that belief for very long. A true belief is of as much value as a justified true belief as long as you have the true belief. But the trouble is that you are likely to change your mind about the merely true belief because you do not know the reasons behind it. Thus, beliefs that are merely true and not also justified are of little value because these beliefs do not stay around—you do not believe them—long enough to be of value. For example, suppose you believe the maple is a deciduous tree because someone told you this. This is a true belief. But you are accepting the belief merely on the basis of authority; you do not know its justification; you do not know why you should believe it. If someone else were to come along and tell you that the maple is not a deciduous tree, you would probably not know whom to believe; you would feel that you no longer knew what the truth was, and you would give up your belief that the maple is a deciduous tree. You would no longer have this true belief, and thus this true belief could do you no good at all. This is precisely the situation you are in if you believe things because your high school or college teachers told you that they are true. Someone else might come along and tell you something different, challenging your belief, and then you would not know whom or what to believe. But if you know the grounds—the good reasons or justification—for your beliefs, then when your belief is challenged, you can defend your belief, not only to other people but to yourself too. You are therefore more likely to retain your true beliefs when you know *why* you ought to hold them. You are in a good position to evaluate and reject the justifications (if any) offered for other beliefs. Thus, justified true belief turns out to be more useful to us than merely true belief because it stays with us longer. We are more likely to continue to hold it.

Finally, there is a fifth and equally important justification of the search for good reasons. Earlier I said that in high school, students are required to do a certain kind of intellectual work, namely understanding the material presented. This is so in college, too. And the investigation of reasons and arguments for a belief assists in understanding that belief. To put this in a somewhat different way, if one does not know how to defend a belief, if one does not know what counts as good reasons for a belief, then to that extent one does not understand that belief. This is another of the lessons of the dialogues of Plato. In these dialogues, Socrates, through adroit questioning, seems to cast grave doubt on the favorite beliefs of other people. Many readers take Socrates to have shown in this way that these beliefs of others are false. But in many cases this is not so. For it is also possible, even likely, that these people do not defend their beliefs properly in the face of Socrates' probing questions. And they do not defend them properly because they do not fully understand their own beliefs. Thus, Socrates' questioning reveals others' lack of understanding rather than falsity. If these people had understood their beliefs, they would have known what to say in defense of those beliefs. Thus, one of Socrates' messages to us is this: it is as useless and as dangerous to hold beliefs that may be true but which you do not understand as it is to hold beliefs that are out-and-out false. By investigating reasons for our beliefs, we come to understand them better.

Reflective Writing: *What specific contrasts does Meiland make between academic work in high school and college? What greater demands does he see in the college curriculum? How can you best prepare yourself to succeed at this level? Taking up the author's assertion that college requires a more critical approach, what points does he make that you might disagree with or question? What counterarguments can you offer?*

On the Uses
of a Liberal Education:

As Lite Entertainment
for Bored College Students

Mark Edmundson at the University of Virginia

This essay, originally published in Harper's Magazine *in 1997, focuses its critique mainly on the consumerist impulses of the larger American society and on college students themselves. Mark Edmundson, an English professor at the University of Virginia and author of books on literary criticism, argues that today's students too often approach college courses, particularly in the humanities, as "lite entertainment" rather than as places for serious study, intense scrutiny of ideas, and personal development.*

To Consider: *As you read this essay, highlight the examples Edmundson gives that suggest students are bored and don't take their classes seriously. What do you think of his evaluation of his students? What attitude do you think he wishes more students would take to their coursework and why?*

Today is evaluation day in my Freud class, and everything has changed. The class meets twice a week, late in the afternoon, and the clientele, about fifty undergraduates, tends to drag in and slump, looking disconsolate and a little lost, waiting for a jump start. To get the discussion moving, they usually require a joke, an anecdote, an off-the-wall question—When you were a kid, were your Halloween getups ego costumes, id costumes, or superego costumes? That sort of thing. But today, as soon as I flourish the forms, a buzz rises in the room. Today they write their assessments of the course, their assessments of *me*, and they are without a doubt wide-awake. "What is your evaluation of the instructor?" asks question number eight, entreating them to circle a number between five (excellent) and one (poor, poor). Whatever interpretive subtlety they've acquired during the term is now out the window. Edmundson: one to five, stand and shoot.

And they do. As I retreat through the door—I never stay around for this phase of the ritual—I look over my shoulder and see them toiling away like the devil's auditors. They're pitched into high writing gear, even the ones who struggle to squeeze out their journal entries word by word, stoked on a procedure they have by now supremely mastered. They're playing the

115

informed consumer, letting the provider know where he's come through and where he's not quite up to snuff.

But why am I so distressed, bolting like a refugee out of my own classroom, where I usually hold easy sway? Chances are the evaluations will be much like what they've been in the past—they'll be just fine. It's likely that I'll be commended for being "interesting" (and I am commended, many times over), that I'll be cited for my relaxed and tolerant ways (that happens, too), that my sense of humor and capacity to connect the arcana of the subject matter with current culture will come in for some praise (yup). I've been hassled this term, finishing a manuscript, and so haven't given their journals the attention I should have, and for that I'm called—quite civilly, though—to account. Overall, I get off pretty well.

Yet I have to admit that I do not much like the image of myself that emerges from these forms, the image of knowledgeable, humorous detachment and bland tolerance. I do not like the forms themselves, with their number ratings, reminiscent of the sheets circulated after the TV pilot has just played to its sample audience in Burbank. Most of all I dislike the attitude of calm consumer expertise that pervades the responses. I'm disturbed by the serene belief that my function—and, more important, Freud's, or Shakespeare's, or Blake's—is to divert, entertain, and interest. Observes one respondent, not at all unrepresentative: "Edmundson has done a fantastic job of presenting this difficult, important & controversial material in an enjoyable and approachable way."

Thanks but no thanks. I don't teach to amuse, to divert, or even, for that matter, to be merely interesting. When someone says she "enjoyed" the course—and that word crops up again and again in my evaluations—somewhere at the edge of my immediate complacency I feel encroaching self-dislike. That is not at all what I had in mind. The off-the-wall questions and the sidebar jokes are meant as lead-ins to stronger stuff—in the case of the Freud course, to a complexly tragic view of life. But the affability and the one-liners often seem to be all that land with the students; their journals and evaluations leave me little doubt.

I want some of them to say that they've been changed by the course. I want them to measure themselves against what they've read. It's said that some time ago a Columbia University instructor used to issue a harsh two-part question. One: What book did you most dislike in the course? Two: What intellectual or characterological flaws in you does that dislike point to? The hand that framed that question was surely heavy. But at least it compels one to see intellectual work as a confrontation between two people, student and author, where the stakes matter. Those Columbia students were being asked to relate the quality of an *encounter,* not rate the action as though it had unfolded on the big screen.

Why are my students describing the Oedipus complex and the death drive as being interesting and enjoyable to contemplate? And why am I coming across as an urbane, mildly ironic, endlessly affable guide to this intellectual territory, operating without intensity, generous, funny, and loose?

Because that's what works. On evaluation day, I reap the rewards of my partial compliance with the culture of my students and, too, with the culture of the university as it now operates. It's a culture that's gotten little exploration. Current critics tend to think that liberal-arts education is in crisis because universities have been invaded by professors with peculiar ideas: deconstruction, Lacanianism, feminism, queer theory. They believe that genius and tradition are out and that P.C., multiculturalism, and identity politics are in because of an invasion by tribes of tenured radicals, the late millennial equivalents of the Visigoth hordes that cracked Rome's walls.

But mulling over my evaluations and then trying to take a hard, extended look at campus life both here at the University of Virginia and around the country eventually led me to some different conclusions. To me, liberal-arts education is as ineffective as it is now not chiefly because there are a lot of strange theories in the air. (Used well, those theories *can* be illuminating.) Rather, it's that university culture, like American culture writ large, is, to put it crudely, ever more devoted to consumption and entertainment, to the using and using up of goods and images. For someone growing up in America now, there are few available alternatives to the cool consumer worldview. My students didn't ask for that view, much less create it, but they bring a consumer weltanschauung to school, where it exerts a powerful, and largely unacknowledged, influence. If we want to understand current universities, with their multiple woes, we might try leaving the realms of expert debate and fine ideas and turning to the classrooms and campuses, where a new kind of weather is gathering.

From time to time I bump into a colleague in the corridor and we have what I've come to think of as a Joon Lee fest. Joon Lee is one of the best students I've taught. He's endlessly curious, has read a small library's worth, seen every movie, and knows all about showbiz and entertainment. For a class of mine he wrote an essay using Nietzsche's Apollo and Dionysus to analyze the pop group The Supremes. A trite, cultural-studies bonbon? Not at all. He said striking things about conceptions of race in America and about how they shape our ideas of beauty. When I talk with one of his other teachers, we run on about the general splendors of his work and presence. But what inevitably follows a JL fest is a mournful reprise about the divide that separates him and a few other remarkable students from their contemporaries. It's not that some aren't nearly as bright—in terms of intellectual ability, my students are all that I could ask for. Instead, it's that Joon Lee has decided to follow his interests and let them make him into a singular and rather eccentric man; in his charming way, he doesn't mind being at odds with most anyone.

It's his capacity for enthusiasm that sets Joon apart from what I've come to think of as the reigning generational style. Whether the students are sorority/fraternity types, grunge aficionados, piercer/tattooers, black or white, rich or middle class (alas, I teach almost no students from truly poor backgrounds), they are, nearly across the board, very, very self-contained. On good days they display a light, appealing glow; on bad days, shuffling disgruntlement. But there's little fire, little passion to be found.

This point came home to me a few weeks ago when I was wandering across the university grounds. There, beneath a classically cast portico, were two students, male and female, having a rip-roaring argument. They were incensed, bellowing at each other, headstrong, confident, and wild. It struck me how rarely I see this kind of full-out feeling in students anymore. Strong emotional display is forbidden. When conflicts arise, it's generally understood that one of the parties will say something sarcastically propitiating ("whatever" often does it) and slouch away.

How did my students reach this peculiar state in which all passion seems to be spent? I think that many of them have imbibed their sense of self from consumer culture in general and from the tube in particular. They're the progeny of 100 cable channels and omnipresent Blockbuster outlets. TV, Marshall McLuhan famously said, is a cool medium. Those who play best on it are low-key and nonassertive; they blend in. Enthusiasm, à la Joon Lee, quickly looks absurd. The form of character that's most appealing on TV is calmly self-interested though never greedy, attuned to the conventions, and ironic. Judicious timing is preferred to sudden self-assertion. The TV medium is inhospitable to inspiration, improvisation, failures, slipups. All must run perfectly.

Naturally, a cool youth culture is a marketing bonanza for producers of the right products, who do all they can to enlarge that culture and keep it grinding. The Internet, TV, and magazines now teem with what I call persona ads, ads for Nikes and Reeboks and Jeeps and Blazers that don't so much endorse the capacities of the product per se as show you what sort of person you will be once you've acquired it. The Jeep ad that features hip, outdoorsy kids whipping a Frisbee from mountaintop to mountaintop isn't so much about what jeeps can do as it is about the kind of people who own them. Buy a jeep and be one with them. The ad is of little consequence in itself, but expand its message exponentially and you have the central thrust of current consumer culture—buy in order to be.

Most of my students seem desperate to blend in, to look right, not to make a spectacle of themselves. (Do I have to tell you that those two students having the argument under the portico turned out to be acting in a role-playing game?) The specter of the uncool creates a subtle tyranny. It's apparently an easy standard to subscribe to, this Letterman-like, Tarantino-like cool, but once committed to it, you discover that matters are rather different. You're inhibited, except on ordained occasions, from showing emotion, stifled from trying to achieve anything original. You're made to feel that even the slightest departure from the reigning code will get you genially ostracized. This is a culture tensely committed to a laid-back norm.

Am I coming off like something of a crank here? Maybe. Oscar Wilde, who is almost never wrong, suggested that it is perilous to promiscuously contradict people who are much younger than yourself. Point taken. But one of the lessons that consumer hype tries to insinuate is that we must never rebel against the new, never even question it. If it's new—a new need, a new product, a new show, a new style, a new generation—it must be good. So maybe, even at the risk of winning the withered, brown laurels of crankdom, it pays to resist newness-worship and cast a colder eye.

Praise for my students? I have some of that too. What my students are, at their best, is decent. They are potent believers in equality. They help out at the soup kitchen and volunteer to tutor poor kids to get a stripe on their résumés, sure. But they also want other people to have a fair shot. And in their commitment to fairness they are discerning; there you see them at their intellectual best. If I were on trial and innocent, I'd want them on the jury.

What they will not generally do, though, is indict the current system. They won't talk about how the exigencies of capitalism lead to a reserve army of the unemployed and nearly inevitable misery. That would be getting too loud, too brash. For the pervading view is the cool consumer perspective, where passion and strong admiration are forbidden. "To stand in awe of nothing, Numicus, is perhaps the one and only thing that can make a man happy and keep him so," says Horace in the *Epistles,* and I fear that his lines ought to hang over the university in this era of high consumer capitalism.

It's easy to mount one's high horse and blame the students for this state of affairs. But they didn't create the present culture of consumption. (It was largely my own generation, that of the Sixties, that let the counterculture search for pleasure devolve into a quest for commodities.) And they weren't the ones responsible, when they were six and seven and eight years old, for unplugging the TV set from time to time or for hauling off and kicking a hole through it. It's my generation of parents who sheltered these students, kept them away from the hard knocks of everyday life, making them cautious and over-fragile, who demanded that their teachers, from grade school on, flatter them endlessly so that the kids are shocked if their college profs don't reflexively suck up to them.

Of course, the current generational style isn't simply derived from culture and environment. It's also about dollars. Students worry that taking too many chances with their educations will sabotage their future prospects. They're aware of the fact that a drop that looks more and more like one wall of the Grand Canyon separates the top economic tenth from the rest of the population. There's a sentiment currently abroad that if you step aside for a moment, to write, to travel, to fall too hard in love, you might lose position permanently. We may be on a conveyor belt, but it's worse down there on the filth-strewn floor. So don't sound off, don't blow your chance.

But wait. I teach at the famously conservative University of Virginia. Can I extend my view from Charlottesville to encompass the whole country, a whole generation of college students? I can only say that I hear comparable stories about classroom life from colleagues everywhere in America. When I visit other schools to lecture, I see a similar scene unfolding. There are, of course, terrific students everywhere. And they're all the better for the way they've had to strive against the existing conformity. At some of the small liberal-arts colleges, the tradition of strong engagement persists. But overall, the students strike me as being sweet and sad, hovering in a nearly suspended animation.

Too often now the pedagogical challenge is to make a lot from a little. Teaching Wordsworth's "Tintern Abbey," you ask for comments. No one responds. So you call on Stephen. Stephen: "The sound, this poem really flows." You: "Stephen seems interested in the music of the poem. We might extend his comment to ask if the poem's music coheres with its argument. Are they consistent? Or is there an emotional pain submerged here that's contrary to the poem's appealing melody?" All right, it's not usually that bad. But close. One friend describes it as rebound teaching: they proffer a weightless comment, you hit it back for all you're worth, then it comes dribbling out again. Occasionally a professor will try to explain away this intellectual timidity by describing the students as perpetrators of postmodern irony, a highly sophisticated mode. Everything's a slick counterfeit, a simulacrum, so by no means should any phenomenon be taken seriously. But the students don't have the urbane, Oscar Wilde–type demeanor that should go with this view. Oscar was cheerful, funny, confident, strange. (Wilde, mortally ill, living in a Paris flophouse: "My wallpaper and I are fighting a duel to the death. One or the other of us has to go.") This generation's style is considerate, easy to please, and a touch depressed.

Granted, you might say, the kids come to school immersed in a consumer mentality—they're good Americans, after all—but then the university and the professors do everything in their power to fight that dreary mindset in the interest of higher ideals, right? So it should be. But let us look at what is actually coming to pass.

Over the past few years, the physical layout of my university has been changing. To put it a little indecorously, the place is looking more and more like a retirement spread for the young. Our funds go to construction, into new dorms, into renovating the student union. We have a new aquatics center and ever-improving gyms, stocked with StairMasters and Nautilus machines. Engraved on the wall in the gleaming aquatics building is a line by our founder, Thomas Jefferson, declaring that everyone ought to get about two hours' exercise a day. Clearly even the author of the Declaration of Independence endorses the turning of his university into a sports-and-fitness emporium.

But such improvements shouldn't be surprising. Universities need to attract the best (that is, the smartest *and* the richest) students in order to survive in an ever more competitive market. Schools want kids whose parents can pay the full freight, not the ones who need scholarships or want to bargain down the tuition costs. If the marketing surveys say that the kids require sports centers, then, trustees willing, they shall have them. In fact, as I began looking around, I came to see that more and more of what's going on in the university is customer driven. The consumer pressures that beset me on evaluation day are only a part of an overall trend.

From the start, the contemporary university's relationship with students has a solicitous, nearly servile tone. As soon as someone enters his junior year in high school, and especially if he's living in a prosperous zip code, the informational material—the advertising—comes flooding in. Pictures, testimonials, videocassettes, and CD-ROMs (some bidden, some not) arrive at the door from colleges across the country, all trying to capture the student and his tuition cash. The freshman-to-be sees photos of well-appointed dorm rooms; of elaborate phys-ed facilities; of fine dining rooms; of expertly kept sports fields; of orchestras and drama troupes; of students working alone (no overbearing grown-ups in range), peering with high seriousness into computers and microscopes; or of students arrayed outdoors in attractive conversational garlands.

Occasionally—but only occasionally, for we usually photograph rather badly; in appearance we tend at best to be styleless—there's a professor teaching a class. (The college catalogues I received, by my request only, in the late Sixties were austere affairs full of professors' credentials and course descriptions; it was clear on whose terms the enterprise was going to unfold.) A college financial officer recently put matters to me in concise, if slightly melodramatic, terms: Colleges don't have admissions offices anymore, they have marketing departments. Is it surprising that someone who has been approached with photos and tapes, bells and whistles, might come in thinking that the Freud and Shakespeare she had signed up to study were also going to be agreeable treats?

How did we reach this point? In part the answer is a matter of demographics and (surprise) of money. Aided by the G.I. bill, the college-going population in America dramatically increased after the Second World War. Then came the baby boomers, and to accommodate them, schools continued to grow. Universities expand easily enough, but with tenure locking faculty in for lifetime jobs, and with the general reluctance of administrators to eliminate their own slots, it's not easy for a university to contract. So after the baby boomers had passed through—like a fat meal digested by a boa constrictor—the colleges turned to energetic promotional strategies to fill the empty chairs. And suddenly college became a buyer's market. What students and their parents wanted had to be taken more and more into account. That usually meant creating more comfortable, less challenging environments, places where almost no one failed, everything was enjoyable, and everyone was nice.

Just as universities must compete with one another for students, so must the individual departments. At a time of rank economic anxiety, the English and history majors have to contend for students against the more success-insuring branches, such as the sciences and the commerce school. In 1968, more than 21 percent of all the bachelor's degrees conferred in America were in the humanities; by 1993, that number had fallen to about 13 percent. The humanities now must struggle to attract students, many of whose parents devoutly wish they would study something else.

One of the ways we've tried to stay attractive is by loosening up. We grade much more softly than our colleagues in science. In English, we don't give many Ds, or Cs for that matter. (The rigors of Chem 101 create almost as many English majors per year as do the splendors of Shakespeare.) A professor at Stanford recently explained grade inflation in the humanities by observing that the undergraduates were getting smarter every year; the higher grades simply recorded how much better they were than their predecessors. Sure.

Along with softening the grades, many humanities departments have relaxed major requirements. There are some good reasons for introducing more choice into curricula and requiring fewer standard courses. But the move, like many others in the university now, jibes with a tendency to serve—and not challenge—the students. Students can also float in and out of classes during the first two weeks of each term without making any commitment. The common name for this time span—shopping period—speaks volumes about the consumer mentality that's now in play. Usually, too, the kids can drop courses up until the last month with only an innocuous "W" on their transcripts. Does a course look too challenging? No problem. Take it pass-fail. A happy consumer is, by definition, one with multiple options, one who can always have what he wants. And since a course is something the students and their parents have bought and paid for, why can't they do with it pretty much as they please?

A sure result of the university's widening elective leeway is to give students more power over their teachers. Those who don't like you can simply avoid you. If the clientele dislikes you en masse, you can be left without students, period. My first term teaching I walked into my introduction to poetry course and found it inhabited by one student, the gloriously named Bambi Lynn Dean. Bambi and I chatted amiably awhile, but for all that she and the pleasure of her name could offer, I was fast on the way to meltdown. It was all a mistake, luckily, a problem with the scheduling book. Everyone was waiting for me next door. But in a dozen years of teaching I haven't forgotten that feeling of being ignominiously marooned. For it happens to others, and not always because of scheduling glitches. I've seen older colleagues go through hot embarrassment at not having enough students sign up for their courses: they graded too hard, demanded too much, had beliefs too far out of keeping with the existing disposition. It takes only a few such instances to draw other members of the professoriat further into line.

And if what's called tenure reform—which generally just means the abolition of tenure—is broadly enacted, professors will be yet more vulnerable to the whims of their customer-students. Teach what pulls the kids in, or walk. What about entire departments that don't deliver? If the kids say no to Latin and Greek, is it time to dissolve classics? Such questions are being entertained more and more seriously by university administrators.

How does one prosper with the present clientele? Many of the most successful professors now are the ones who have "decentered" their classrooms. There's a new emphasis on group projects and on computer-generated exchanges among the students. What they seem to want most is to talk to one another. A classroom now is frequently an "environment," a place highly conducive to the exchange of existing ideas, the students' ideas. Listening to one another, students sometimes change their opinions. But what they generally can't do is acquire a new vocabulary, a new perspective, that will cast issues in a fresh light.

The Socratic method—the animated, sometimes impolite give-and-take between student and teacher—seems too jagged for current sensibilities. Students frequently come to my office to tell me how intimidated they feel in class; the thought of being embarrassed in front of the group fills them with dread. I remember a student telling me how humiliating it was to be corrected by the teacher, by me. So I asked the logical question: "Should I let a major factual error go by so as to save discomfort?" The student—a good student, smart and earnest—said that was a tough question. He'd need to think about it.

Disturbing? Sure. But I wonder, are we really getting students ready for Socratic exchange with professors when we push them off into vast lecture rooms, two and three hundred to a class, sometimes face them with only grad students until their third year, and signal in our myriad professorial ways that we often have much better things to do than sit in our offices and talk with them? How bad will the student-faculty ratios have to become, how teeming the lecture courses, before we hear students righteously complaining, as they did thirty years ago, about the impersonality of their schools, about their decline into knowledge factories? "This is a firm," said Mario Savio at Berkeley during the Free Speech protests of the Sixties, "and if the Board of Regents are the board of directors . . . then . . . the faculty are a bunch of employees and we're the raw material. But we're a bunch of raw material that don't mean . . . to be made into any product."

Teachers who really do confront students who provide significant challenges to what they believe, *can* be very successful, granted. But sometimes such professors generate more than a little trouble for themselves. A contro-versial teacher can send students hurrying to the deans and the counselors, claiming to have been offended. ("Offensive" is the preferred term of repug-nance today, just as "enjoyable" is the summit of praise.) Colleges have brought in hordes of counselors and deans to make sure that everything is smooth, serene, unflustered, that everyone has a good time. To the counselor, to the dean, and to the university legal squad, that which is normal, healthy, and prudent is best.

An air of caution and deference is everywhere. When my students come to talk with me in my office, they often exhibit a Franciscan humility. "Do you have a moment?" "I know you're busy. I won't take up much of your time." Their presences tend to be very light; they almost never change the temperature of the room. The dress is nondescript: clothes are in earth tones; shoes are practical—cross-trainers, hiking boots, work shoes, Dr. Martens, with now and then a stylish pair of raised-sole boots on one of the young women. Many, male and female both, peep from beneath the bills of monogrammed baseball caps. Quite a few wear sports, or even corporate, logos, sometimes on one piece of clothing but occasionally (and disconcert-ingly) on more. The walk is slow; speech is careful, sweet, a bit weary, and without strong inflection. (After the first lively week of the term, most seem far in debt to sleep.) They are almost unfailingly polite. They don't want to offend me; I could hurt them, savage their grades.

Naturally, there are exceptions, kids I chat animatedly with, who offer a joke, or go on about this or that new CD (almost never a book, no). But most of the traffic is genially sleepwalking. I have to admit that I'm a touch wary, too. I tend to hold back. An unguarded remark, a joke that's taken to be off-color, or simply an uncomprehended comment can lead to difficulties. I keep it literal. They scare me a little, these kind and melancholy students, who themselves seem rather frightened of their own lives.

Before they arrive, we ply the students with luscious ads, guaranteeing them a cross between summer camp and lotusland. When they get here, flat-tery and nonstop entertainment are available, if that's what they want. And when they leave? How do we send our students out into the world? More and more, our administrators call the booking agents and line up one or another celebrity to usher the graduates into the Millennium. This past spring, Kermit the Frog won himself an honorary degree at Southampton College on Long Island; Bruce Willis and Yogi Berra took credentials away at Montclair State; Arnold Schwarzenegger scored at the University of Wisconsin-Superior. At Wellesley, Oprah Winfrey gave the commencement address. (*Wellesley*—one of the most rigorous academic colleges in the nation.) At the University Vermont, Whoopi Goldberg laid down the word. But why should a worthy administrator contract the likes of Susan Sontag, Christopher Hitchens, or Robert Hughes—someone who might actually say something, something disturbing, something "offensive"—when he can get what the parents and kids apparently want and what the newspapers will softly commend—more lite entertainment, more TV?

Is it a surprise, then, that this generation of students—steeped in consumer culture before going off to school, treated as potent customers by the university well before their date of arrival, then pandered to from day one until the morning of the final kiss-off from Kermit or one of his kin—are inclined to see the books they read as a string of entertainments to be placidly enjoyed or languidly cast down? Given the way universities are now administered (which is more and more to say, given the way that they are currently marketed), is it a shock that the kids don't come to school hot to learn, unable to bear their own ignorance? For some measure of self-dislike, or self-discontent—which is much different than simple depression—seems to me to be a prerequisite for getting an education that matters. My students, alas, usually lack the confidence to acknowledge what would be their most precious asset for learning: their ignorance.

Not long ago, I asked my Freud class a question that, however hoary, never fails to solicit intriguing responses: Who are your heroes? Whom do you admire? After one remarkable answer, featuring T. S. Eliot as hero, a series of generic replies rolled in, one gray wave after the next: my father, my best friend, a doctor who lives in our town, my high school history teacher. Virtually all the heroes were people my students had known personally, people who had done something local, specific, and practical, and had done it for them. They were good people, unselfish people, these heroes, but most of all they were people who had delivered the goods.

My students' answers didn't exhibit any philosophical resistance to the idea of greatness. It's not that they had been primed by their professors with complex arguments to combat genius. For the truth is that these students don't need debunking theories. Long before college, skepticism became their habitual mode. They are the progeny of Bart Simpson and David Letterman, and the hyper-cool ethos of the box. It's inane to say that theorizing professors have created them, as many conservative critics like to do. Rather, they have substantially created a university environment in which facile skepticism can thrive without being substantially contested.

Skeptical approaches have *potential* value. If you have no all-encompassing religious faith, no faith in historical destiny, the future of the West, or anything comparably grand, you need to acquire your vision of the world somewhere. If it's from literature, then the various visions literature offers have to be inquired into skeptically. Surely it matters that women are denigrated in Milton and in Pope, that some novelistic voices assume an overbearing godlike authority, that the poor are, in this or that writer, inevitably cast as clowns. You can't buy all of literature wholesale if it's going to help draw your patterns of belief.

But demystifying theories are now overused, applied mechanically. It's all logocentrism, patriarchy, ideology. And in this the student environment—

laid-back, skeptical, knowing—is, I believe, central. Full-out debunking is what plays with this clientele. Some have been doing it nearly as long as, if more crudely than, their deconstructionist teachers. In the context of the contemporary university, and cool consumer culture, a useful intellectual skepticism has become exaggerated into a fundamentalist caricature of itself. The teachers have buckled to their students' views.

At its best, multiculturalism can be attractive as well-deployed theory. What could be more valuable than encountering the best work of far-flung cultures and becoming a citizen of the world? But in the current consumer environment, where flattery plays so well, the urge to encounter the other can devolve into the urge to find others who embody and celebrate the right ethnic origins. So we put aside the African novelist Chinua Achebe's abrasive, troubling *Things Fall Apart* and gravitate toward hymns on Africa, cradle of all civilizations.

What about the phenomenon called political correctness? Raising the standard of civility and tolerance in the university has been—who can deny it?—a very good thing. Yet this admirable impulse has expanded to the point where one is enjoined to speak well—and only well—of women, blacks, gays, the disabled, in fact of virtually everyone. And we can owe this expansion in many ways to the student culture. Students now do not wish to be criticized, not in any form. (The culture of consumption never criticizes them, at least not *overtly*.) In the current university, the movement for urbane tolerance has devolved into an imperative against critical reaction, turning much of the intellectual life into a dreary Sargasso Sea. At a certain point, professors stopped being usefully sensitive and became more like careful retailers who have it as a cardinal point of doctrine never to piss the customers off.

To some professors, the solution lies in the movement called cultural studies. What students need, they believe, is to form a critical perspective on pop culture. It's a fine idea, no doubt. Students should be able to run a critical commentary against the stream of consumer stimulations in which they're immersed. But cultural-studies programs rarely work, because no matter what you propose by way of analysis, things tend to bolt downhill toward an uncritical discussion of students' tastes, into what they like and don't like. If you want to do a Frankfurt School-style analysis of *Braveheart*, you can be pretty sure that by mid-class Adorno and Horkheimer will be consigned to the junk heap of history and you'll be collectively weighing the charms of Mel Gibson. One sometimes wonders if cultural studies hasn't prospered because, under the guise of serious intellectual analysis, it gives the customers what they most want—easy pleasure, more TV. Cultural studies becomes nothing better than what its detractors claim it is—Madonna studies—when students kick loose from the critical perspective and groove to the product, and that, in my experience teaching film and pop culture, happens plenty.

On the issue of genius, as on multiculturalism and political correctness, we professors of the humanities have, I think, also failed to press back against our students' consumer tastes. Here we tend to nurse a pair of—to put it charitably—disparate views. In one mode, we're inclined to a programmatic debunking criticism. We call the concept of genius into question. But in our professional lives per se, we aren't usually disposed against the idea of distinguished achievement. We argue animatedly about the caliber of potential colleagues. We support a star system, in which some professors are far better paid, teach less, and under better conditions than the rest. In our own profession, we are creating a system that is the mirror image of the one we're dismantling in the curriculum. Ask a professor what she thinks of the work of Stephen Greenblatt, a leading critic of Shakespeare, and you'll hear it for an hour. Ask her what her views are on Shakespeare's genius and she's likely to begin questioning the term along with the whole "discourse of evaluation." This dual sensibility may be intellectually incoherent. But in its awareness of what plays with students, it's conducive to good classroom evaluations and, in its awareness of where and how the professional bread is buttered, to self-advancement as well.

My overall point is this: It's not that a left-wing professorial coup has taken over the university. It's that at American universities, left, liberal politics have collided with the ethos of consumerism. The consumer ethos is winning.

Then how do those who at least occasionally promote genius and high literary ideals look to current students? How do we appear, those of us who take teaching to be something of a performance art and who imagine that if you give yourself over completely to your subject you'll be rewarded with insight beyond what you individually command?

I'm reminded of an old piece of newsreel footage I saw once. The speaker (perhaps it was Lenin, maybe Trotsky) was haranguing a large crowd. He was expostulating, arm waving, carrying on. Whether it was flawed technology or the man himself, I'm not sure, but the orator looked like an intricate mechanical device that had sprung into fast-forward. To my students, who mistrust enthusiasm in every form, that's me when I start riffing about Freud or Blake. But more, as my evaluations showed, I've been replacing enthusiasm and intellectual animation with stand-up routines, keeping it all at arm's length, praising under the cover of irony.

It's too bad that the idea of genius has been denigrated so far, because it actually offers a live alternative to the demoralizing culture of hip in which most of my students are mired. By embracing the works and lives of extraordinary people, you can adapt new ideals to revise those that came courtesy of your parents, your neighborhood, your clan—or the tube. The aim of a good liberal-arts education was once, to adapt an observation by the scholar Walter Jackson Bate, to see that "we need not be the passive victims of what we deterministically call 'circumstances' (social, cultural, or reductively psychological-personal), but that by linking ourselves through what Keats calls an 'immortal free-masonry' with the great we can become freer—freer to be ourselves, to be what we most want and value."

But genius isn't just a personal standard; genius can also have political effect. To me, one of the best things about democratic thinking is the conviction that genius can spring up anywhere. Walt Whitman is born into the working class and thirty-six years later we have a poetic image of America that gives a passionate dimension to the legalistic brilliance of the Constitution. A democracy needs to constantly develop, and to do so it requires the most powerful visionary minds to interpret the present and to propose possible shapes for the future. By continuing to notice and praise genius, we create a culture in which the kind of poetic gamble that Whitman made—a gamble in which failure would have entailed rank humiliation, depression, maybe suicide—still takes place. By rebelling against established ways of seeing and saying things, genius helps us to apprehend how malleable the present is and how promising and fraught with danger is the future. If we teachers do not endorse genius and self-overcoming, can we be surprised when our students find their ideal images in TV's latest persona ads?

A world uninterested in genius is a despondent place, whose sad denizens drift from coffee bar to Prozac dispensary, unfired by ideals, by the glowing image of the self that one might become. As Northrop Frye says in a beautiful and now dramatically unfashionable sentence, "The artist who uses the same energy and genius that Homer and Isaiah had will find that he not only lives in the same palace of art as Homer and Isaiah, but lives in it at the same time." We ought not to deny the existence of such a place simply because we, or those we care for, find the demands it makes intimidating, the rent too high.

What happens if we keep trudging along this bleak course? What happens if our most intelligent students never learn to strive to overcome what they are? What if genius, and the imitation of genius, become silly, outmoded ideas? What you're likely to get are more and more one-dimensional men and women. These will be people who live for easy pleasures, for comfort and prosperity, who think of money first, then second, and third, who hug the status quo; people who believe in God as a sort of insurance policy (cover your bets); people who are never surprised. They will be people so pleased with themselves (when they're not in despair at the general pointlessness of their lives) that they cannot imagine humanity could do better. They'll think it their highest duty to clone themselves as frequently as possible. They'll claim to be happy, and they'll live a long time.

It is probably time now to offer a spate of inspiring solutions. Here ought to come a list of reforms, with due notation about a core curriculum and various requirements. What the traditionalists who offer such solutions miss is that no matter what our current students are given to read, many of them will simply translate it into melodrama, with flat characters and predictable morals. (The unabated capitalist culture that conservative critics so often endorse has put students in a position to do little else.) One can't simply wave a curricular wand and reverse acculturation.

Perhaps it would be a good idea to try firing the counselors and sending half the deans back into their classrooms, dismantling the football team and making the stadium into a playground for local kids, emptying the fraternities, and boarding up the student-activities office. Such measures would convey the message that American colleges are not northern outposts of Club Med. A willingness on the part of the faculty to defy student conviction and affront them occasionally—to be usefully offensive—also might not be a bad thing. We professors talk a lot about subversion, which generally means subverting the views of people who never hear us talk or read our work. But to subvert the views of our students, our customers, that would be something else again.

Ultimately, though, it is up to individuals—and individual students in particular—to make their own way against the current sludgy tide. There's still the library, still the museum, there's still the occasional teacher who lives to find things greater than herself to admire. There are still fellow students who have not been cowed. Universities are inefficient, cluttered, archaic places, with many unguarded corners where one can open a book or gaze out onto the larger world and construe it freely. Those who do as much, trusting themselves against the weight of current opinion, will have contributed something to bringing this sad dispensation to an end. As for myself, I'm canning my low-key one-liners; when the kids' TV-based tastes come to the fore, I'll aim and shoot. And when it's time to praise genius, I'll try to do it in the right style, full-out, with faith that finer artistic spirits (maybe not Homer and Isaiah quite, but close, close), still alive somewhere in the ether, will help me out when my invention flags, the students doze, or the dean mutters into the phone. I'm getting back to a more exuberant style; I'll be expostulating and arm waving straight into the millennium, yes I will.

Reflective Writing: *What specific points in this essay might well make a student angry and why? What evidence does Edmundson provide for these provocative comments, and how convincing is this evidence to you? What do you think about his indictment of the larger society that shapes students' consumerist attitudes?*

On the Uses
of a Liberal Education:
As a Weapon in the Hands
of the Restless Poor

Earl Shorris

In the previous essay, Mark Edmundson critiques the privileged students at his elite university for the lack of seriousness and earnestness with which most approach their academic work. Here, Earl Shorris, author of many books on American culture and politics, and a believer in the importance of liberal education, discusses the powerful impact of a demanding great-books curriculum on a far less advantaged group of inner-city residents.

To Consider: *Edmundson says he wants some of his students to be "changed by the course" he teaches, in the sense that he wants them "to measure themselves against what they have read" (128). Shorris comments on Viniece Walker, "With no job and no money, a prisoner, she had undergone a radical transformation . . . She had learned to reflect" (88). For more than 2,000 years, philosophers and educators have talked about the development of reason and reflection as key goals of schooling. In reading Shorris's article, highlight the areas that suggest how and why these students learned to think and were transformed by the course. What do you think Shorris means by learning how to think? Why is it so important? How can we compare the two groups of students in these two essays?*

Next month I will publish a book about poverty in America, but not the book I intended. The world took me by surprise—not once, but again and again. The poor themselves led me in directions I could not have imagined, especially the one that came out of a conversation in a maximum-security prison for women that is set, incongruously, in a lush Westchester suburb fifty miles north of New York City.

I had been working on the book for about three years when I went to the Bedford Hills Correctional Facility for the first time. The staff and inmates had developed a program to deal with family violence, and I wanted to see how their ideas fit with what I had learned about poverty.

Numerous forces—hunger, isolation, illness, landlords, police, abuse, neighbors, drugs, criminals, and racism, among many others—exert themselves on the poor at all times and enclose them, making up a "surround of force" from which, it seems, they cannot escape. I had come to understand that this was what kept the poor from being political and that the absence of politics in their lives was what kept them poor. I don't mean "political" in the sense of voting in an election but in the way Thucydides used the word: to mean activity with other people at every level, from the family to the neighborhood to the broader community to the city-state.

By the time I got to Bedford Hills, I had listened to more than six hundred people, some of them over the course of two or three years. Although my method is that of the *bricoleur*, the tinkerer who assembles a thesis of the bric-a-brac he finds in the world, I did not think there would be any more surprises. But I had not counted on what Viniece Walker was to say.

It is considered bad form in prison to speak of a person's crime, and I will follow that precise etiquette here. I can tell you that Viniece Walker came to Bedford Hills when she was twenty years old, a high school dropout who read at the level of a college sophomore, a graduate of crackhouses, the streets of Harlem, and a long alliance with a brutal man. On the surface Viniece has remained as tough as she was on the street. She speaks bluntly, and even though she is HIV positive and the virus has progressed during her time in prison, she still swaggers as she walks down the long prison corridors. While in prison, Niecie, as she is known to her friends, completed her high school requirements and began to pursue a college degree (psychology is the only major offered at Bedford Hills, but Niecie also took a special interest in philosophy). She became a counselor to women with a history of family violence and a comforter to those with AIDS.

Only the deaths of other women cause her to stumble in the midst of her swaggering step, to spend days alone with the remorse that drives her to seek redemption. She goes through life as if she had been imagined by Dostoevsky, but even more complex than his fictions, alive, a person, a fair-skinned and freckled African-American woman, and in prison. It was she who responded to my sudden question, "Why do you think people are poor?"

We had never met before. The conversation around us focused on the abuse of women. Niecie's eyes were perfectly opaque—hostile, prison eyes. Her mouth was set in the beginning of a sneer.

"You got to begin with children," she said, speaking rapidly, clipping out the street sounds as they came into her speech.

She paused long enough to let the change of direction take effect, then resumed the rapid, rhythmless speech. "You've got to teach the moral life of downtown to the children. And the way you do that, Earl, is by taking them downtown to plays, museums, concerts, lectures, where they can learn the moral life of downtown."

I smiled at her, misunderstanding, thinking I was indulging her. "And then they won't be poor anymore?"

She read every nuance of my response, and answered angrily, "And they won't be poor *no more*."

"What you mean is—"

"What I mean is what I said—a moral alternative to the street."

She didn't speak of jobs or money. In that, she was like the others I had listened to. No one had spoken of jobs or money. But how could the "moral life of downtown" lead anyone out from the surround of force? How could a museum push poverty away? Who can dress in statues or eat the past? And what of the political life? Had Niecie skipped a step or failed to take a step? The way out of poverty was politics, not the "moral life of downtown." But to enter the public world, to practice the political life, the poor had first to learn to reflect. That was what Niecie meant by the "moral life of downtown." She did not make the error of divorcing ethics from politics. Niecie had simply said, in a kind of shorthand, that no one could step out of the panicking circumstance of poverty directly into the public world.

Although she did not say so, I was sure that when she spoke of the "moral life of downtown" she meant something that had happened to her. With no job and no money, a prisoner, she had undergone a radical transformation. She had followed the same path that led to the invention of politics in ancient Greece. She had learned to reflect. In further conversation it became clear that when she spoke of "the moral life of downtown" she meant the humanities, the study of human constructs and concerns, which has been the source of reflection for the secular world since the Greeks first stepped back from nature to experience wonder at what they beheld. If the political life was the way out of poverty, the humanities provided an entrance to reflection and the political life. The poor did not need anyone to release them; an escape route existed. But to open this avenue to reflection and politics a major distinction between the preparation for the life of the rich and the life of the poor had to be eliminated.

Once Niecie had challenged me with her theory, the comforts of tinkering came to an end; I could no longer make a homage to the happenstance world and rest. To test Niecie's theory, students, faculty, and facilities were required. Quantitative measures would have to be developed; anecdotal information would also be useful. And the ethics of the experiment had to be considered: I resolved to do no harm. There was no need for the course to have a "sink or swim" character; it could aim to keep as many afloat as possible.

When the idea for an experimental course became clear in my mind, I discussed it with Dr. Jaime Inclán, director of the Roberto Clemente Family Guidance Center in lower Manhattan, a facility that provides counseling to poor people, mainly Latinos, in their own language and in their own community. Dr. Inclán offered the center's conference room for a classroom. We would put the three metal tables end to end to approximate the boat-shaped tables used in discussion sections at the University of Chicago of the Hutchins era,[1] which I used as a model for the course. A card table in the back of the room would hold a coffeemaker and a few cookies. The setting was not elegant, but it would do. And the front wall was covered by a floor-to-ceiling blackboard.

Now the course lacked only students and teachers. With no funds and a budget that grew every time a new idea for the course crossed my mind, I would have to ask the faculty to donate its time and effort. Moreover, when Hutchins said, "The best education for the best is the best education for us all," he meant it; he insisted that full professors teach discussion sections in the college. If the Clemente Course in the Humanities was to follow the same pattern, it would require a faculty with the knowledge and prestige that students might encounter in their first year at Harvard, Yale, Princeton, or Chicago.

I turned first to the novelist Charles Simons. He had been assistant editor of *The New York Times Book Review* and had taught at Columbia University. He volunteered to teach poetry, beginning with simple poems, Housman, and ending with Latin poetry. Grace Glueck, who writes art news and criticism for the *New York Times,* planned a course that began with cave paintings and ended in the late twentieth century. Timothy Koranda, who did his graduate work at MIT, had published journal articles on mathematical logic, but he had been away from his field for some years and looked forward to getting back to it. I planned to teach the American history course through documents, beginning with the Magna Carta, moving on to the second of Locke's *Two Treatises of Government,* the Declaration of Independence, and so on through the documents of the Civil War. I would also teach the political philosophy class.

Since I was naïf in this endeavor, it did not immediately occur to me that recruiting students would present a problem. I didn't know how many I needed. All I had were criteria for selection:

Age: 18–35

Household income: Less than 150 percent of the Census Bureau's Official Poverty Threshold (though this was to change slightly).

Educational level: Ability to read a tabloid newspaper.

Educational goals: An expression of intent to complete the course.

Dr. Inclán arranged a meeting of community activists who could help recruit students. Lynette Lauretig of The Door, a program that provides medical and educational services to adolescents, and Angel Roman of the Grand Street Settlement, which offers work and training and GED programs, were both willing to give us access to prospective students. They also pointed out some practical considerations. The course had to provide bus and subway tokens, because fares ranged between three and six dollars per class per student, and the students could not afford sixty or even thirty dollars a month for transportation. We also had to offer dinner or a snack, because the classes were to be held from 6:00 to 7:30 P.M.

The first recruiting session came only a few days later. Nancy Mamis-King, associate executive director of the Neighborhood Youth & Family

Services program in the South Bronx, had identified some Clemente Course candidates and had assembled about twenty of her clients and their supervisors in a circle of chairs in a conference room. Everyone in the room was black or Latino, with the exception of one social worker and me.

After I explained the idea of the course, the white social worker was the first to ask a question: "Are you going to teach African history?"

"No. We'll be teaching a section on American history, based on documents, as I said. We want to teach the ideas of history so that—"

"You have to teach African history."

"This is America, so we'll teach American history. If we were in Africa, I would teach African history, and if we were in China, I would teach Chinese history."

"You're indoctrinating people in Western culture."

I tried to get beyond her. "We'll study African art," I said, "as it affects art in America. We'll study American history and literature; you can't do that without studying African-American culture, because culturally all Americans are black as well as white, Native American, Asian, and so on." It was no use; not one them applied for admission to the course.

A few days later Lynette Lauretig arranged a meeting with some of her staff at The Door. We disagreed about the course. They thought it should be taught at a much lower level. Although I could not change their views, they agreed to assemble a group of Door members who might be interested in the humanities.

On an early evening that same week, about twenty prospective students were scheduled to meet in a classroom at The Door. Most of them came late. Those who arrived first slumped in their chairs, staring at the floor or greeting me with sullen glances. A few ate candy or what appeared to be the remnants of a meal. The students were mostly black and Latino, one was Asian, and five were white; two of the whites were immigrants who had severe problems with English. When I introduced myself, several of the students would not shake my hand, two or three refused even to look at me, one girl giggled, and the last person to volunteer his name, a young man dressed in a Tommy Hilfiger sweatshirt and wearing a cap turned sideways, drawled, "Henry Jones, but they call me Sleepy, because I got these sleepy eyes—"

"In our class, we'll call you Mr. Jones."

He smiled and slid down in his chair so that his back was parallel to the floor.

Before I finished attempting to shake hands with the prospective students, a waiflike Asian girl with her mouth half-full of cake said, "Can we get on with it? I'm bored."

I liked the group immediately.

Having failed in the South Bronx, I resolved to approach these prospective students differently. "You've been cheated," I said. "Rich people learn the humanities; you didn't. The humanities are a foundation for getting along in the world, for thinking, for learning to reflect on the world instead of just reacting to whatever force is turned against you. I think the humanities are one of the ways to become political, and I don't mean political in the sense of voting in an election but in the broad sense." I told them Thucydides' definition of politics.

"Rich people know politics in that sense. They know how to negotiate instead of using force. They know how to use politics to get along, to get power. It doesn't mean that rich people are good and poor people are bad. It simply means that rich people know a more effective method for living in this society.

"Do all rich people, or people who are in the middle, know the humanities? Not a chance. But some do. And it helps. It helps to live better and enjoy life more. Will the humanities make you rich? Yes. Absolutely. But not in terms of money. In terms of life.

"Rich people learn the humanities in private schools and expensive universities. And that's one of the ways in which they learn the political life. I think that is the real difference between the haves and have-nots in this country. If you want real power, legitimate power, the kind that comes from the people and belongs to the people, you must understand politics. The humanities will help.

"Here's how it works: We'll pay your subway fare; take care of your children, if you have them; give you a snack or a sandwich; provide you with books and any other materials you need. But we'll make you think harder, use your mind more fully, than you ever have before. You'll have to read and think about the same kinds of ideas you would encounter in a first-year course at Harvard or Yale or Oxford.

"You'll have to come to class in the snow and rain and the cold and the dark. No one will coddle you, no one will slow down for you. There will be tests to take, papers to write. And I can't promise you anything but a certificate of completion at the end of the course. I'll be talking to colleges about giving credit for the course, but I can't promise anything. If you come to the Clemente Course, you must do it because you want to study the humanities, because you want a certain kind of life, a richness of mind and spirit. That's all I offer you: philosophy, poetry, art history, logic, rhetoric, and American history.

"Your teachers will all be people of accomplishment in their fields," I said, and I spoke a little about each teacher. "That's the course. October through May, with a two-week break at Christmas. It is generally accepted in America that liberal arts and the humanities in particular belong to the elites. I think you're the elites."

The young Asian woman said, "What are you getting out of this?"

"This is a demonstration project. I'm writing a book. This will be the proof, I hope, of my idea about the humanities. Whether it succeeds or fails will be up to the teachers and you."

All but one of the prospective students applied for admission to the course.

I repeated the new presentation at the Grand Street Settlement and at other places around the city. There were about fifty candidates for the thirty positions in the course. Personal interviews began in early September.

Meanwhile, almost all of my attempts to raise money had failed. Only the novelist Starling Lawrence, who is also editor in chief of W. W. Norton, which had contracted to publish the book; the publishing house itself; and a small, private family foundation supported the experiment. We were far short of our budgeted expenses, but my wife, Sylvia, and I agreed that the cost was still very low, and we decided to go ahead.

Of the fifty prospective students who showed up at the Clemente Center for personal interviews, a few were too rich (a postal supervisor's son, a fellow who claimed his father owned a factory in Nigeria that employed sixty people) and more than a few could not read. Two home-care workers from Local 1199 could not arrange their hours to enable them to take the course. Some of the applicants were too young: a thirteen-year-old and two who had just turned sixteen.

Lucia Medina, a woman with five children who told me that she often answered the door at the single-room occupancy hotel where she lived with a butcher knife in her hand, was the oldest person accepted to into the course. Carmen Quiñones, a recovering addict who had spent time in prison, was the next eldest. Both were in their early thirties.

The interviews went on for days.

Able Lomas[2] shared an apartment and worked part-time wrapping packages at Macy's. His father had abandoned the family when Abel was born. His mother was murdered by his stepfather when Abel was thirteen. With no one to turn to and no place to stay, he lived on the streets, first in Florida, then back in New York City. He used the tiny stipend from his mother's Social Security to keep himself alive.

After the recruiting session at The Door, I drove up Sixth Avenue from Canal Street with Abel, and we talked about ethics. He had a street tough's delivery, spitting out his ideas in crudely formed sentences of four, five, eight words, strings of blunt declarations, with never a dependent clause to qualify his thoughts. He did not clear his throat with badinage, as timidity teaches us to do, nor did he waste his breath with tact.

"What do you think about drugs?" he asked, the strangely breathless delivery further coarsened by his Dominican accent. "My cousin is a dealer."

"I've seen a lot of people hurt by drugs."

"Your family has nothing to eat. You sell drugs. What's worse? Let your family starve or sell drugs?"

"Starvation and drug addiction are both bad, aren't they?"

"Yes," he said, not "yeah" or "uh-huh" but a precise, almost formal "yes."

"So it's a question of the worse of two evils? How shall we decide?"

The question came up near Thirty-fourth Street, where Sixth Avenue remains hellishly traffic-jammed well into the night. Horns honked, people flooded into the street against the light. Buses and trucks and taxicabs threatened their way from one lane to the next where the overcrowded avenue crosses the equally crowded Broadway. As we passed Herald Square and made our way north again, I said, "There are a couple of ways to look at it. One comes from Immanuel Kant, who said that you should not do anything unless you want it to become a universal law; that is, unless you think it's what everybody should do. So Kant wouldn't agree to selling drugs *or* letting your family starve."

Again he answered with a formal "Yes."

"There's another way to look at it, which is to ask what is the greatest good for the greatest number: in this case, keeping your family from starvation or keeping tens, perhaps hundreds of people from losing their lives to drugs. So which is the greatest good for the greatest number?"

"That's what I think," he said.

"What?"

"You shouldn't sell drugs. You can always get food to eat. Welfare. Something."

"You're a Kantian."

"Yes."

"You know who Kant is?"

"I think so."

We arrived at Seventy-seventh Street, where he got out of the car to catch the subway before I turned east. As he opened the car door and the light came on, the almost military neatness of him struck me. He had the newly cropped hair of a cadet. His clothes were clean, without a wrinkle. He was an orphan, a street kid, an immaculate urchin. Within a few weeks he would be nineteen years old, the Social Security payments would end, and he would have to move into a shelter.

Some of those who came for interviews were too poor. I did not think that was possible when we began, and I would like not to believe it now, but it was true. There is a point at which level of forces that surround the poor can become unsurmountable, when there is no time or energy left to be anything but poor. Most often I could not recruit such people for the course; when I did, they soon dropped out.

Over the days of interviewing, a class slowly assembled. I could not then imagine who would last the year and who would not. One young woman submitted a neatly typed essay that said, "I was homeless once, then I lived for some time in a shelter. Right now, I have got my own space granted by the Partnership for the Homeless. Right now, I am living alone, with very limited means. Financially I am overwhelmed by debts. I cannot afford all the food I need . . ."

A brother and sister, refugees from Tashkent, lived with their parents in the farthest reaches of Queens, far beyond the end of the subway line. They had no money, and they had been refused admission by every school to which they had applied. I had not intended to accept immigrants or people who had difficulty with the English language, but I took them into the class.

I also took four who had been in prison, three who were homeless, three who were pregnant, one who lived in a drugged dream-state in which she was abused, and one whom I had known for a long time and who was dying of AIDS. As I listened to them, I wondered how the course would affect them. They had no public life, no place; they lived within the surround of force, moving as fast as they could, driven by necessity, without a moment to reflect. Why should they care about fourteenth-century Italian painting or truth tables or the death of Socrates?

Between the end of recruiting and the orientation session that would open the course, I made a visit to Bedford Hills to talk with Niecie Walker. It was hot, and the drive up from the city had been unpleasant. I didn't yet know Niecie very well. She didn't trust me, and I didn't know what to make of her. While we talked, she held a huge white pill in her hand. "For AIDS," she said.

"Are you sick?"

"My T-cell count is down. But that's neither here nor there. Tell me about the course, Earl. What are you going to teach?"

"Moral philosophy."

"And what does that include?"

She had turned the visit into an interrogation. I didn't mind. At the end of the conversation I would be going out into "the free world"; if she wanted our meeting to be an interrogation, I was not about to argue. I said, "We'll begin with Plato: the *Apology*, a little of the *Crito*, a few pages of the *Phaedo* so that they'll know what happened to Socrates. Then we'll read Aristotle's *Nicomachean Ethics*. I also want them to read Thucydides, particularly Pericles' Funeral Oration in order to make the connection between ethics and politics, to lead them in the direction I hope the course will take them. Then we'll end with *Antigone*, but read as moral and political philosophy as well as drama."

"There's something missing," she said, leaning back in her chair taking on an air of superiority.

The drive had been long, the day was hot, the air in the room was dead and damp. "Oh, yeah," I said, "and what's that?"

"Plato's Allegory of the Cave. How can you teach philosophy to poor people without the Allegory of the Cave? The ghetto is the cave. Education is the light. Poor people can understand that."

At the beginning of the orientation at the Clemente Center a week later, each teacher spoke for a minute or two. Dr. Inclán and his research assistant, Patricia Vargas, administered the questionnaire we had devised to measure, as best we could, the role of force and the amount of reflection in the lives of the students. I explained that each class was going to be videotaped as another way of documenting the project. Then I gave out the first assignment: "In preparation for our next meeting, I would like you to read a brief selection from Plato's *Republic:* the Allegory of the Cave."

I tried to guess how many students would return for the first class. I hoped for twenty, expected fifteen, and feared ten. Sylvia, who had agreed to share the administrative tasks of the course, and I prepared coffee and cookies for twenty-five. We had a plastic container filled with subway tokens. Thanks to Starling Lawrence, we had thirty copies of Bernard Knox's *Norton Book of Classical Literature,* which contained all of the texts for the philosophy section except the *Republic* and the *Nicomachean Ethics.*

At six o'clock there were only ten students seated around the long table, but by six-fifteen the number had doubled, and a few minutes later two more straggled in out of the dusk. I had written a time line on the blackboard, showing them the temporal progress of thinking—from the role of myth in Neolithic societies to *The Gilgamesh Epic* and forward to the Old Testament, Confucius, the Greeks, the New Testament, the Koran, the *Epic of Son-Jara,* and ending with Nahuatl and Maya poems, which took us up to the contact between Europe and America, where the history course began. The time line served as context and geography as well as history: no race, no major culture was ignored. "Let's agree," I told them, "that we are all human, whatever our origins. And now let's go into Plato's cave."

I told them that there would be no lectures in the philosophy section of the course; we would use the Socratic method, which is called maieutic dialogue. "'Maieutic' comes from the Greek word for midwifery. I'll take the role of midwife in your dialogue. Now what do I mean by that? What does a midwife do?"

It was the beginning of a love affair, the first moment of their infatuation with Socrates. Later, Abel Lomas would characterize that moment in his no-nonsense fashion, saying that it was the first time anyone ever paid attention to their opinions.

Grace Glueck began the art history class in a darkened room lit with slides of Lascaux caves and next turned the students' attention to Egypt, arranging for them to visit the Metropolitan Museum of Art to see the Temple of Dendur and the Egyptian Galleries. They arrived at the museum on a Friday evening. Darlene Codd brought her two-year-old son. Pearl Lau was late, as usual. One of the students, who had told me how much he was looking forward to the museum visit, didn't show up, which surprised me. Later I learned that he had been arrested for jumping a turnstile in a subway station on his way to the museum and was being held in a prison cell under the Brooklyn criminal courthouse. In the Temple of Dendur, Samantha Smoot asked questions of Felicia Blum, a museum lecturer. Samantha was the student who had burst out with the news, in one of the first sessions of the course, that people in her neighborhood believed it "was not no use goin' to school, because the white man wouldn't let you up no matter what." But in a hall where the statuary was of half-human, half-animal female figures, it was Samantha who asked what the glyphs meant, encouraging Felicia Blum to read them aloud, to translate them into English. Toward the end of evening, Grace led the students out of the halls of antiquities into the Rockefeller Wing, where she told them of the connections of culture and art in Mali, Benin, and the Pacific Islands. When the students had collected their coats and stood together near the entrance to the museum, preparing to leave, Samantha stood apart, a tall, slim young woman, dressed in a deerstalker cap and a dark blue peacoat. She made an exaggerated farewell wave at us and returned to Egypt—her ancient mirror.

Charles Simmons began the poetry class with poems as puzzles and laughs. His plan was to surprise the class, and he did. At first he read the poems aloud to them, interrupting himself with footnotes to bring them along. He showed them poems of love and of seduction, and satiric commentaries on those poems by later poets. "Let us read," the students demanded, but Charles refused. He tantalized them with the opportunity to read poems aloud. A tug-of-war began between him and the students, and the standoff was ended not by Charles directly but by Hector Anderson. When Charles asked if anyone in the class wrote poetry, Hector raised his hand.

"Can you recite one of your poems for us?" Charles said.

Until that moment, Hector had never volunteered a comment, though he had spoken well and intelligently when asked. He preferred to slouch in his chair, dressed in full camouflage gear, wearing a nylon stocking over his hair and eating slices of fresh cantaloupe or honeydew melon.

In response to Charles's question, Hector slid up to a sitting position. "If you turn that camera off," he said. "I don't want anybody using my lyrics." When he was sure the red light of the video camera was off, Hector stood and recited verse after verse of a poem that belonged somewhere in the triangle formed by Ginsberg's *Howl*, the Book of Lamentations, and hiphop. When Charles and the students finished applauding, they asked Hector to say the poem again, and he did. Later Charles told me, "That kid is the real thing." Hector's discomfort with Sylvia and me turned to ease. He came to our house for a small Christmas party and at other times. We talked on the telephone about a scholarship program and about what steps he should take next in his education. I came to know his parents. As a student, he began quietly, almost secretly, to surpass many of his classmates.

Timothy Koranda was the most professional of the professors. He arrived precisely on time, wearing a hat of many styles—part fedora, part Borsalino, part Stetson, and at least one-half World War I campaign hat. He taught logic during class hours, filling the blackboard from floor to ceiling, wall to wall, drawing the intersections of sets here and truth tables there and a great square of oppositions in the middle of it all. After class, he walked with students to the subway, chatting about Zen or logic or Heisenberg.

On one of the coldest nights of the winter, he introduced the students to logic problems stated in ordinary language that they could solve by reducing the phrases to symbols. He passed out copies of a problem, two pages long, then wrote out some of the key phrases on the blackboard. "Take this home with you," he said, "and at our next meeting we shall see who has solved it. I shall also attempt to find the answer."

By the time he finished writing out the key phrases, however, David Iskhakov raised his hand. Although they listened attentively, neither David nor his sister Susana spoke often in class. She was shy, and he was embarrassed at his inability to speak perfect English.

"May I go to blackboard?" David said. "And will see if I have found correct answer to zis problem."

Together Tim and David erased the blackboard, then David began covering it with signs and symbols. "If first man is earning this money, and second man is closer to this town . . . ," he said, carefully laying out the conditions. After five minutes or so, he said, "And the answer is: B will get first to Cleveland!"

Samantha Smoot shouted, "That's not the answer. The mistake you made is in the first part there, where it says who earns more money."

Tim folded his arms across his chest, happy. "I shall let you all take the problem home," he said.

When Sylvia and I left the Clemente Center that night, a knot of students was gathered outside, huddled against the wind. Snow had begun to fall, a slippery powder on the gray ice that covered all but a narrow space down the center of the sidewalk. Samantha and David stood in the middle of the group, still arguing over the answer to the problem. I leaned in for a moment to catch the character of the argument. It was even more polite than it had been in the classroom, because now they governed themselves.

One Saturday morning in January, David Howell telephoned me at my home. "Mr. Shores," he said, Anglicizing my name, as many of the students did.

"Mr. Howell," I responded, recognizing his voice.

"How you doin', Mr. Shores?"

"I'm fine. How are you?"

"I had a little problem at work."

Uh-oh, I thought, bad news was coming. David is a big man, generally good-humored but with a quick temper. According to his mother, he had a history of violent behavior. In the classroom he had been one of the best students, a steady man, twenty-four years old, who always did the reading assignments and who often made interesting connections between the humanities and daily life. "What happened?"

"Mr. Shores, there's a woman at my job, she said some things to me and I said some things to her. And she told my supervisor I had said things to her, and he called me in about it. She's forty years old and she don't have no social life, and I have a good social life, and she's jealous of me."

"And then what happened?" The tone of his voice and the timing of the call did not portend good news.

"Mr. Shores, she made me so mad, I wanted to smack her up against the wall. I tried to talk to some friends to calm myself down a little, but nobody was around."

"And what did you do?" I asked, fearing this was his one telephone call from the city jail.

"Mr. Shores, I asked myself, 'What would Socrates do?'"

David Howell had reasoned that his co-worker's envy was not his problem after all, and he had dropped his rage.

One evening, in the American history section, I was telling the student about Gordon Wood's ideas in *The Radicalism of the American Revolution.* We were talking about the revolt by some intellectuals against classical learning at the turn of the eighteenth century, including Benjamin Franklin's late-life change of heart, when Henry Jones raised his hand.

"If the Founders loved the humanities so much, how come they treated the natives so badly?"

I didn't know how to answer this question. There were confounding explanations to offer about changing attitudes toward Native Americans, vaguely useful references to views of Rousseau and James Fenimore Cooper. For a moment I wondered if I should tell them about Heidegger's Nazi past. Then I saw Abel Lomas's raised hand at the far end of the table. "Mr. Lomas," I said.

Abel said, "That's what Aristotle means by incontinence, when you know what's morally right but you don't do it, because you're overcome by your passions."

The other students nodded. They were all inheritors of wounds caused by the incontinence of educated men; now they had an ally in Aristotle, who had given them a way to analyze the actions of their antagonists.

Those who appreciate ancient history understand the radical character of the humanities. They know that politics did not begin in a perfect world but in a society even more flawed than ours: one that embraced slavery, denied the rights of women, practiced a form of homosexuality that verged on pedophilia, and endured the intrigues and corruption of its leaders. The genius of that society originated in man's re-creation of himself through the recognition of his humanness as expressed in art, literature, rhetoric, philosophy, and the unique notion of freedom. At that moment, the isolation of the private life ended and politics began.

The winners in the game of modern society, and even those whose fortune falls in the middle, have other means to power: they are included at birth. They know this. And they know exactly what to do to protect their place in the economic and social hierarchy. As Allan Bloom, author of the nationally best-selling tract in defense of elitism, *The Closing of the American Mind*, put it, they direct the study of the humanities exclusively at those young people who "have been raised in comfort and with the expectation of ever increasing comfort."

In the last meeting before graduation, the Clemente students answered the same set of questions they'd answered at orientation. Between October and May, students had fallen to AIDS, pregnancy, job opportunities, pernicious anemia, clinical depression, a schizophrenic child, and other forces, but of the thirty students admitted to the course, sixteen had completed it, and fourteen had earned credit from Bard College. Dr. Inclán found that the students' self-esteem and their abilities to divine and solve problems had significantly increased; their use of verbal aggression as a tactic for resolving conflicts had significantly decreased. And they all had notably more appreciation for the concepts of benevolence, spirituality, universalism, and collectivism.

It cost about $2,000 for a student to attend the Clemente Course. Compared with unemployment, welfare, or prison, the humanities are a bargain. But coming into possession of the faculty of reflection and the skills of politics leads to a choice for the poor—and whatever they choose, they will be dangerous: they may use politics to get along in a society based on the game, to escape from the surround of force into a gentler life, to behave as citizens, and nothing more; or they may choose to oppose the game itself. No one can predict the effect of politics, although we all would like to think that wisdom goes our way. That is why the poor are so often mobilized and so rarely politicized. The possibility that they will adopt a moral view other than that of their mentors can never be discounted. And who wants to run that risk?

On the night of the first Clemente Course graduation, the students and their families filled the eighty-five chairs we crammed into the conference room where classes had been held. Robert Martin, associate dean of Bard College, read the graduates' names. David Dinkins, the former mayor or New York City, handed out the diplomas. There were speeches and presentations. The students gave me a plaque on which they had misspelled my name. I offered a few words about each student, congratulated them, and said finally, "This is what I wish for you: May you never be more active than when you are doing nothing . . ." I saw their smiles of recognition at the words of Cato, which I had written on the blackboard early in the course. They could recall again too the moment when we had come to the denouement of Aristotle's brilliantly constructed thriller, the *Nicomachean Ethics*— the idea that in the contemplative man was most like God. One or two, perhaps more of the students, closed their eyes. In the momentary stillness of the room it was possible to think.

The Clemente Course in the Humanities ended a second year in June 1997. Twenty-eight new students had enrolled; fourteen graduated. Another version of the course will begin this fall in Yucatán, Mexico, using classical Maya literature in Maya.

On May 14, 1997, Viniece Walker came up for parole for the second time. She had served more than ten years of her sentence, and she had been the best of prisoners. In a version of the Clemente Course held at the prison, she had been my teaching assistant. After a brief hearing, her request for parole was denied. She will serve two more years before the parole board will reconsider her case.

A year after graduation, ten of the first sixteen Clemente Course graduates were attending four-year colleges or going to nursing school; four of them had received full scholarships to Bard College. The other graduates were attending community college or working full-time. Except for one: she had been fired from her job in a fast-food restaurant for trying to start a union.

Notes

1. Under the guidance of Robert Maynard Hutchins (1929–1951), the University of Chicago required year-long courses in the humanities, social sciences, and natural sciences for the Bachelor of Arts degree. Hutchins developed the curriculum with the help of Mortimer Adler, among others; the Hutchins courses later influenced Adler's Great Books program.
2. Not his real name.

Reflective Writing: *It might be easy to distance yourself from the low-income, unemployed students discussed in this essay. It might be easy to suggest that only their desperation to escape poverty led them to engage so deeply with the philosophy, literature, and art they studied in their special program. What else could it be that students found so compelling and empowering about their program? How might such a course of study affect you and why?*

The Allegory of the Cave

Plato

This famous Greek philosopher lived from 428 to 347 B.C., spending most of his life in Athens, where he founded and directed the Academy from the year 380 B.C., until his death. Plato was a student of Socrates, and many of his works consist of discussions or "dialogues" between Socrates and his students. Much of his work is still studied today, including such dialogues as the Apology, Crito, Phaedrus, *and* Gorgias. *His classic study of politics and society is titled the* Republic. *"The Allegory of the Cave," excerpted from the* Republic, *distinguishes between the world of the senses, which we can see, and the world of ideas or knowledge, which is much more difficult to observe.*

To Consider: *What are the main characteristics of the world of the senses and the world of knowledge? In what ways do these two worlds differ for Plato? What does Plato mean by "the idea of good"?*

Socrates: And now, I said, let me show in a figure how far our nature is enlightened or unenlightened:— Behold! human beings living in an underground den, which has a mouth open towards the light and reaching all along the den: here they have been from their childhood, and have their legs and necks chained so that they cannot move, and can only see before them, being prevented by the chains from turning round their heads. Above and behind them a fire is blazing at a distance, and between the fire and the prisoners there is a raised way; and you will see, if you look, a low wall built along the way, like the screen which marionette players have in front of them, over which they show the puppets.

Glaucon: I see.

And do you see, I said, men passing along the wall carrying all sorts of vessels, and statues and figures of animals made of wood and stone and various materials, which appear over the wall? Some of them are talking, others silent.

You have shown me a strange image, and they are strange prisoners.

Like ourselves, I replied; and they see only their own shadows, or the shadows of one another, which the fire throws on the opposite wall of cave?

145

True, he said; how could they see anything but the shadows if they were never allowed to move their heads?

And of the objects which are being carried in like manner they would only see the shadows?

Yes, he said.

And if they were able to converse with one another, would they not suppose that they were naming what was actually before them?

Very true.

And suppose further that the prison had an echo which came from the other side, would they not be sure to fancy when one of the passersby spoke that the voice which they heard came from the passing shadow?

No question, he replied.

To them, I said, the truth would be literally nothing but the shadows of the images.

That is certain.

And now look again, and see what will naturally follow if the prisoners are released and disabused of their error. At first, when any of them is liberated and compelled suddenly to stand up and turn his neck round and walk and look towards the light, he will suffer sharp pains; the glare will distress him, and he will be unable to see the realities of which in his former state he had seen the shadows; and then conceive some one saying to him, that what he saw before was an illusion, but that now, when he is approaching nearer to being and his eye is turned towards more real existence, he has a clearer vision—what will be his reply? And you may further imagine that his instructor is pointing to the objects as they pass and requiring him to name them,—will he not be perplexed? Will he not fancy that the shadows which he formerly saw are truer than the objects which are now shown to him?

Far truer.

And if he is compelled to look straight at the light, will he not have a pain in his eyes which will make him turn away to take refuge in the objects of vision which he can see, and which he will conceive to be in reality clearer than the things which are now being shown to him?

True, he said.

And suppose once more, that he is reluctantly dragged up a steep and rugged ascent, and held fast until he is forced into the presence of the sun himself, is he not likely to be pained and irritated? When he approaches the light his eyes will be dazzled, and he will not be able to see anything at all of what are now called realities.

Not all in a moment, he said.

He will require to grow accustomed to the sight of the upper world. And first he will see the shadows best, next the reflections of men and other objects in the water, and then the objects themselves; then he will gaze upon the light of the moon and the stars and the spangled heaven; and he will see the sky and the stars by night better than the sun or the light of the sun by day?

Certainly.

Last of all he will be able to see the sun, and not mere reflections of him in the water, but he will see him in his own proper place, and not in another; and he will contemplate him as he is.

Certainly.

He will then proceed to argue that this is he who gives the season and the years, and is the guardian of all that is in the visible world, and in a certain way the cause of all things which he and his fellows have been accustomed to behold?

Clearly, he said, he would first see the sun and then reason about him.

And when he remembered his old habitation, and the wisdom of the den and his fellow-prisoners, do you not suppose that he would felicitate himself on the change, and pity them?

Certainly, he would.

And if they were in the habit of conferring honours among themselves on those who were quickest to observe the passing shadows and to remark which of them went before, and which followed after, and which were together; and who were therefore best able to draw conclusions as to the future, do you think that he would care for such honours and glories, or envy the possessors of them? Would he not say with Homer, "Better to be the poor servant of a poor master," and to endure anything, rather than think as they do and live after their manner?

Yes, he said, I think that he would rather suffer anything than entertain those false notions and live in this miserable manner.

Imagine once more, I said, such an one coming suddenly out of the sun to be replaced in his old situation; would he not be certain to have his eyes full of darkness?

To be sure, he said.

And if there were a contest, and he had to compete in measuring the shadows with the prisoners who had never moved out of the den, while his sight was still weak, and before his eyes had become steady (and the time which would be needed to acquire this new habit of sight might be very considerable), would he not be ridiculous? Men would say of him that up he went and down he came without his eyes; and that it was better not even to think of ascending; and if any one tried to loose another and lead him up to the light, let them only catch the offender, and they would put him to death.

No question, he said.

This entire allegory, I said, you may not append, dear Glaucon, to the previous argument; the prisonhouse is the world of sight, the light of the fire is the sun, and you will not misapprehend me if you interpret the journey upwards to be the ascent of the soul into the intellectual world according to my poor belief, which, at your desire, I have expressed—whether rightly or wrongly God knows. But, whether true or false, my opinion is that in the world of knowledge the idea of good appears last of all, and is seen only with an effort; and when seen, is also inferred to be the universal author of all things beautiful and right, parent of light and of the lord of light in this visible world, and the immediate source of reason and truth in the intellectual; and that this is the power upon which he who would act rationally either in public or private life must have his eye fixed.

I agree, he said, as far as I am able to understand you.

Reflective Writing: *What is the thesis or main argument of Plato's allegory? How might you apply this thesis to your own life? Write about a time when your idea of reality was altered because of some knowledge you gained, such as learning what a person was really like or finding out the facts about an event or situation. How did your "ascent into the intellectual world" change you?*

Lowering the Bar:

Why We Have Such Low Expectations for Students Even Though They Could Easily Do More

Stuart Rojstaczer

This essay comes from the author's book Gone for Good, *a personal chronicle of university life by a professor of science from Duke. The book's title refers to an earlier age in which educational standards were higher. The book is intended to show how an American research university functions. In this chapter, Rojstaczer discusses his experiences teaching science classes for nonscience majors and argues that students are not sufficiently challenged in their classes.*

To Consider: *How does the author adapt his teaching methods as he gains more classroom experience? Why does he think students could do more schoolwork than they are currently asked to do?*

It was the first day of my first undergraduate class. The lecture hall had a capacity of about 150 and was a bit like a movie theater with a sloping floor that rose gradually with distance from the lectern. Although old, the room was well designed. A three-paneled chalkboard covered the front wall. Every seat was relatively close to the front of the room. There were ample windows that gave the room excellent lighting.

Sixty-five students sat in front of me ready to begin an introductory class in environmental science. They looked collectively nervous and shy, which is typical for a first day. But I wasn't nervous. I've been comfortable in front of crowds my entire adult life. I introduced myself. I'm aware that first impressions are very important and I tried to be light-hearted and energetic. I welcomed the students and then made a joke about my funny last name. I'm a bit goofy in front of a classroom, which usually helps bridge the gap between the students and myself. When I was a kid, there were two kinds of professors that I noticed in movies. There was the imposing imperious professor, à la John Houseman in the film *The Paper Chase*. Then there was the goofy one, à la Fred MacMurray in *The Absent Minded Professor*. I tended toward the absent-minded model, a kind of borscht belt version of Fred MacMurray. I hadn't taught in ten years, but my sense of humor still went over well with this generation of students. What I would learn, however, is that my expectations of student performance and approach to teaching science were no longer suitable.

149

I handed out the syllabus and laid out the structure of the class. I wasn't trying to overwhelm the students with a great deal of work. My objective was to create an attractive class that had high annual enrollments and enticed a few of the students to become majors in my department. I expected the class to study what I thought was a modest amount, about four to six hours a week. In terms of logistics, there were six homework assignments, one group project on an environmental topic of choice, and three exams. No late homework was allowed, but students were allowed to drop their lowest homework score. One of the students toward the front of the class raised her hand and asked, "Will the exams be multiple choice?" "No," I said. "They will be short essay exams." She made a face. I never saw her in class again.

I didn't know that my class structure was highly unconventional. Homework assignments, which I thought were essential, generally were not given in introductory science classes unless they were a part of the premedical or engineering curriculum. Exams with multiple-choice or fill-in-the-blank questions were the general rule for these introductory classes as well. Requiring students to write papers was not all that unusual, but requiring group projects that consisted of a jointly authored paper and a presentation was not done. My expectations were that they would think and work reasonably hard. They would feel good about the class because they would learn interesting material. Where did I get such ideas? Partly, I received them from my own education. I wanted to teach the way that I liked being taught.

As a student, the professors that I really learned from were the ones who stretched their students. Some did it with humor, and some with intimidation. Regardless of the exact method used, their major goal was intellectual discovery. They knew that most students would not go on to lead an intellectual life, but they wanted all students to be thoroughly exposed to the life of the mind while they were in college. This is the way I wanted to teach and it was the way I had taught very successfully, albeit briefly, ten years previous.

As a graduate student at the University of Illinois, I gave a weekly lecture and laboratory as part of an introductory environmental science class similar to the one I would teach at Duke. I liked the experience and it was one of the reasons that I decided to become a professor. Almost all of the students were nonscience majors and had a good work ethic. We developed a good rapport and I distinctly remember that the students felt positive about the material they learned. I also remember feeling satisfied with their level of achievement. The material I presented assumed that the students had remembered their high school math and with a little bit of review could use their high school chemistry. The homework was designed to give students a basic introduction to environmental problem solving. In a class of twenty students, I gave three As and A minuses, a lot of Bs and quite a few Cs and I didn't receive a complaint about grades.

Although I had been successful earlier, times had changed. My expectations of student performance, which were considered reasonable in 1980, were too hard nosed for the students of 1991. I was bound to scare students away from my classes. Much of the competition for students came from classes that were both easier and different in approach than mine. Ironically, the class that I had taught in 1980 represented, at the time, one of the easier ways to fulfill a science requirement. Classes in introductory chemistry and physics were much harder both in terms of workload and grading, and they still were in 1991. Over the intervening years, however, many universities had eliminated or weakened their science requirements. At Duke for example, a science requirement existed, but since 1986 it could be easily avoided, and over 10 percent of the students never enrolled in a science class. In response, professors who taught science classes that were not a part of the premedical or engineering curriculum felt compelled to make classes easier in order to maintain reasonable enrollments.

Also over the intervening time, a new wave of classes had taken hold in colleges and universities. In the social sciences and humanities, these classes focused on current events and popular culture. In the natural sciences, they focused on the broad achievements of science and abandoned the traditional assumption that in order to understand science, students had to learn by doing and solve problems. These "new wave" classes tended to be easier in terms of workload, intellectual expectation, and grading. They began to be introduced in the 1960s, and by the 1980s their number was large enough to constitute a college curriculum all its own. Students were free to mix or choose from two paths of study, the traditional and the new wave. Parents of students and conservative social critics have been more concerned about the overt leftist political advocacy of a small number of these new wave classes rather than their tendency to demand less of students.

I wasn't aware of this change in expectations and approach over the previous decade. And if I had known, I probably would have ignored it because I was confident that I could attract students with my own methods. I put the class together with loving care. I ransacked the library researching various topics. I thought long and hard about homework assignments and I included material that I thought was exciting and societally relevant. I gave the course an ambitious title, "Environment and Industrial Civilization."

Senior faculty watched me spending all this time on my course, and I felt I knew what they were thinking. If this boy spends this much time teaching there isn't a prayer that he will get tenure. But I ignored the hints that I received from senior faculty. Besides, I was doing research as well. I was putting in a good seventy to eighty hours a week to make sure that I got off to a good start. This meant, of course, that I was largely ignoring my family. Like many people, I was too caught up in my work to notice. In retrospect, I can't laugh about how caught up I was in my work, but I can laugh about how unrealistic my goals were.

During the second lecture, I handed out my first homework. I was a bit nervous about it. While it seemed a relatively easy tune-up piece requiring no more than about four hours of work, I really did not know what Duke students were capable of doing. As a check, I asked my wife to look at the homework and she thought it seemed reasonable. Then I gave it to my teaching assistant (who helped with grading the homework), who thought it was much too hard. Then again, this teaching assistant was a below average student. He was a Ph.D. candidate admitted from another country in exchange for allowing some of our faculty to do fieldwork in that country (politics are clearly a part of science just as they are in the rest of real life). So I didn't quite know what to expect.

The average grade for the first homework was 94 and I thought I was off to a good start. But the truth was that, even early on, the mood of the class was mixed. Sure, everyone could do the work I assigned. They were smart students, but many were expecting a light and easy overview that would fulfill Duke's optional science requirement. Instead I was giving them a reasonably thorough introduction to environmental problem solving. Ten years previous, my approach and expectations were part of the mainstream, but they weren't anymore.

So after a few weeks, when I looked out at the class, I saw three distinct groups. About 30 percent of them seemed to be enjoying the experience. Another 50 percent were of mixed emotions about the class. Some of them liked the material, but did not appreciate the workload. Others liked my teaching style, but did not like the material. Finally, another 20 percent were highly negative. This group either hated science or hated the amount of work or hated me. They, by and large, dutifully attended and took notes because they wanted to do well on the exams, but they were not enthused. A few were fearful of the prospect of taking an essay test in a science class. I saw the pain on some of their faces while I lectured.

I was not, however, like Bill Clinton. I did not feel their pain. I wasn't going to make the class easier to appease those who were disinterested. I wanted to give the motivated students their money's worth. So I focused on those who were really enjoying the class. In any given lecture (attendance was typically about 80 percent) there were about a dozen of them sprinkled throughout the lecture hall. When I asked questions of the class, they were the ones who participated in the give and take. As someone trained in the sciences, I was used to classes where the tendency was to gear the class to the scientifically talented. Mine was a kinder, gentler version of this approach. You didn't have to be talented in the sciences, but I lectured with the assumption that you were motivated to learn.

I mentioned to my colleagues that I was gearing my class to the motivated students. They were not supportive of this approach. But to my way of thinking at the time, what I was doing was the right thing. Nowadays, I still feel this way, but from a practical matter (my enrollments would be negligible if I followed my feelings), I have to spend more time appeasing the slackers.

I should say that I was (naively) surprised by the large number of slackers I had to teach in this class. I came to one of the better universities in the country and expected to teach bright, strongly motivated students. Most were very bright, but quite a few were not motivated. They were clearly here principally for the social aspect of college rather than for an education. Thinking about my own undergraduate years, there were also many students who were slackers. They went to school to earn their credentials so that they could go on in life. Educationally, they went through the motions, and focused on the parties and alcohol at night.

But I'm dwelling far too much on the poor students. There were many students in this class who were clearly interested in more than a grade. Having some slackers in this class was simply the price of teaching in a not so perfect world.

While not everyone liked my class, the students were almost always attentive and polite. Initially, I took this aspect of my class for granted. But then I gave a guest lecture in another introductory science class. The professor had not made much of an attempt to be serious about educating, and during my guest lecture the attention level was barely perceptible. People were reading the newspaper. They engaged in side conversations like I wasn't even there. I felt like a minor musician playing in a bar and not being listened to. I tried to get them to listen, but was unsuccessful. After the lecture, two students came up to the front of the class to talk to me.

"Professor R.," one of them said, "we want to apologize for the rudeness of this class."

"Is it always this bad, or is it just because I am a guest lecturer?" I asked.

"No. It's pretty much this way all of the time." After talking to them, I didn't feel so bad about having to lecture to this class. I felt much worse about these two students who wanted to learn something, but had to do so under compromising conditions.

My first class continued onward with the same mixture of enthusiasm and grimacing faces. The average homework grades continued to be high for all but the true slackers. The exam grades varied more widely. The average class grade on the short essay exams was about a B to B minus. I thought that this was pretty good for grades, but remember I had not taught for ten years. What was an acceptable average grade in 1980 was not acceptable in 1991 (or today). At my university, the average grade for students rose from 3.0 to 3.4 from 1986 through 1994 before it stabilized. Similar changes had taken place across the country in the 1970s to 1980s. In the eleven years since my first teaching experience, professors were grading easier almost everywhere.

There are at least a few reasons why grades have risen. One is that professors long ago figured out lowering expectations and giving high grades meant less time dealing with students and more time for research. In essence, there is an unspoken contract between the professor and the student. The professor agrees to provide an easy class in order to be left alone. The student "benefits" in having more time for social activities.

Second, it also doesn't hurt that easily graded classes attract more students. (I don't think students are behaving inappropriately by preferring classes with high grades. They would be foolish not to.) Departments with large student enrollments tend to get larger budgets and stand a much better chance of getting permission to hire new faculty. These incentives often drive professors to institute lax grading policies.

Third, the full emergence of new wave classes across the university has created a significant new source of grade inflation. The reasons why these classes tend to grade generously vary. Some of the professors of new wave classes find grades to be an antiquated standard, and that unbiased judgment of student performance is impossible. Most faculty do not agree with this "post-modern" view, but in order not to lose students to the new wave classes, they feel compelled to keep pace and raise their grades.

Probably a more subtle reason for the elevation in grades (at least at private universities) is the dramatic increase in tuition over the last twenty years. For example in 1976, tuition (including fees) at Duke, Harvard, and Chicago was $3330, $4090, and $3517, respectively. Over the following two decades tuition at most private universities rose at roughly double the rate of inflation. In 1997, tuition at the three institutions noted above was in the range of $21,000 to $23,000. When a student represents $22,000 in revenue, that student has a fair degree of economic clout. There is a tendency to want to reward that student in some way for choosing that university. One way of doing this is to give the student easy grades and an easy sense of achievement. It could be said that the student is inadvertently bribing the university. Also, parents like to receive good news from their children, and by inflating grades, universities assure that most students will be able to inform their parents that they are doing well in school.

Regardless of the causes, grade inflation has proven difficult to reverse. At Stanford since the mid-1990s, faculty have been trying to find a way to reduce their average GPA from a truly outlandish 3.6 to a modestly outlandish 3.4. Since my university's average GPA is already at the 3.4 level, I guess I should feel proud of our relatively stringent grading standards. Our attempts at reversing grade inflation, however, have not been successful. A 1997 effort at Duke to institute a rating of students that rewarded those who enrolled in difficult classes was defeated overwhelmingly by the faculty.

As is typical of elite private universities today, almost all of the departments at Duke give As and Bs to more than 90 percent of the students. Taken at face value, this indicates that the performance of students is almost always good to excellent. Relative to these standards, my grading was too tough. When I handed back exams, I caused some disappointment and anger.

Halfway through the class, I ran into a senior who had taken a graduate level class with me during the previous semester. He was a friend of five of the students in the undergraduate class, and they had enrolled on his recommendation.

"My friends are angry with me," he said. "Couldn't you lighten up for my sake?" I made a joke and told him that lightening up wasn't in my future plan. In restrospect, I should have taken his advice seriously.

The capstone experience for the class was a group project on an environmental topic. The class broke into groups of three and four students. Although I had written a list of suggested topics, I encouraged students to come up with their own topic. But out of the fifteen groups in the class not one of them did so. I was disappointed by this lack of academic independence. In retrospect, I think that they were simply trying to play it safe. There was always a certain risk that I would think poorly of a topic that wasn't already on my list.

Each group was also allotted fifteen minutes of class time to present their material, with no restrictions on presentation format. There was an incentive beyond the grade (at least I thought it was an incentive) to the project and presentation: The group with the best overall project and presentation was invited to my home for dinner.

Early on, a few of the students complained about the group nature of the project. There were worries about potential personality conflicts and the possibility of one person screwing it up for everyone else. But I thought that they would learn more by working together. To make sure that the groups were working effectively, I asked the students to write progress reports along the way. The reports I received suggested that the students' fears about the project were not materializing.

There was one strange twist, however. The night before the project was due, at about 10:30 P.M., someone knocked on my door at home. I was already in bed reading, so I put on my bathrobe to answer it. I thought it might be a neighbor. Instead, it was a student who wanted to talk about the length of his section of his group report. Each student was supposed to contribute a five to seven-page section in addition to a five to seven page group synthesis. The student standing in front of me had a question about these guidelines.

"Is it OK if my section is longer than five to seven pages?" he asked.

"How much longer is it, Craig?" I asked. Craig was a senior, short and muscular with a lot of nervous energy. A few weeks before, I had run into him on the quad and we had discussed what he was going to do after he graduated. He had told me that he had lined up a job on the currency futures market in Chicago. I thought that Craig's intense nature would serve him well in a fast-paced job.

Standing in front of me that night, Craig seemed to be in somewhat of a panic that he had gone overboard on his assignment and that I might dock him for not following the rules. I thought that this was kind of odd, but I also thought that I probably couldn't understand the mind of a twenty-one year old college student. I, of course, had been twenty-one years old at one time, but being panicky about assignments never was in my repertoire. As an undergraduate, I didn't care about grades. I wasn't concerned about getting ahead. Any sense that I had about achievement and recognition of achievement didn't come until my mid-twenties.

"About twelve pages, professor."

"Twelve pages? That sounds fine. Just hand it in tomorrow." Craig thanked me and left on his moped.

The next week I began to read the group projects. When I got to Craig's group, I read with more curiosity than usual. Craig's group had put together one of the better projects and it was generally well thought out and very impressive. All except for the portion written by Craig. His twelve-page portion was well written and well researched, but it had hardly anything to do with the other sections or the main topic of the project. There were a few sentences that seemed to be related to the project, but they were out of context in relation to the rest of the twelve pages. Even more strange, these sentences were highlighted in bold print in an unsuccessful and meager attempt to relate his portion to the rest of the project. Why write so much about something that was almost completely unrelated to the assignment? I thought about this for a little while and then it came to me. He had probably taken a report (hopefully his own) written for another class and slightly doctored it for his group project.

Now it all made a little sense. He had come to my home perhaps out of some fear that he was cheating and would get caught. Alternatively he had come in order to make me think that he had worked extensively on this project. If he wrote this paper for another course, then I wanted to find out what course it was. I went to the registrar's office and looked at his transcript.

He had taken a botany course two semesters previous and had received an A. The paper he gave me would have fit perfectly in a botany class. I called up the professor of that class.

"Did Craig X write a paper on the topic of Y?" I asked.

"Oh, yes," the professor said. "I remember that he wrote a very fine paper on that topic."

"Yes, I know it's a fine paper," I said. "I have a copy of it submitted for an assignment in my own class."

I thought about the situation. He had apparently written the paper himself. Of course, this paper was written for another course and he was trying to get credit twice for one piece of work. But technically, it was unclear to me that if this paper really was appropriate for both classes it could not be used for both classes. The problem was, however, that it was not appropriate for my class. It wasn't completely unrelated, but it was far from what I had asked for.

I decided to give Craig a grade of D. On his section I wrote, "well written and researched but not appropriate for the assignment." Craig never came to me afterwards to complain about his grade on the project. He just took the bad grade and moved on with the rest of his life.

I should note that I have had to deal with very few cheating incidents. It is true that I allow most of my classes to bring a crib sheet to exams. In these classes about the only way you can cheat is to copy from a neighbor. This has happened very rarely. Overall, my experiences suggest that college students are a pretty honest bunch.

My class continued on its path toward the final exam. The final phase of the class was the oral presentation portion of the projects. These were a mixed bag, but there were a few excellent pieces of work that seemed to make the experience worthwhile. I awarded my home-cooked meal at my house to one of the groups. We had a pleasant time together and I felt that I had ended my class on a good note.

I graded the final exam and handed out final grades. I decided to be generous in grading the final. By including the generally high homework scores, the average grade point in the class moved up to 3.1, but was still below my university's average for a class. Ten percent of the class received As. A key problem in my grading was that I wasn't aware that the "gentleman's C" of a decade ago had been inflated to a "gentleman's B." I received several calls and visits from people complaining about their grade.

I didn't mind the calls and visits. The students weren't too huffy and they generally took my comments in stride. The only unusual incident was when a student came into my office in a tank top with no bra, and said as she leaned over my desk, "I would do anything to get a better grade." It was easy to see what the "anything" was and I felt like I was caught in a B grade movie. I didn't know this at the time, but there is a joke that begins almost with the exact same scenario. The professor responds to the come-on by asking, "Anything?" The student leans closer and whispers in his ear, "Yes, anything." The teacher then whispers back, "Well then, why don't you try studying?"

Unlike the professor in the joke, I felt too awkward to come up with a witty response. It's not that I was worried about a future sexual harassment suit. I just can't stand corruption, an aversion that I developed in my teens and twenties while working in the inherently corrupt business of construction. At any rate, the student took the news well that I wouldn't change her grade. This was the only time anyone tried to bribe me, either with sex or money, in my first seven years of teaching. So much for rampant sleazy intrigue between students and professors.

When I got back the student reviews for my class, they were more positive than I expected. Twenty percent did hate the class, but their comments generally were above the belt. The group of people who I thought had mixed emotions was not as large as I thought. I think that I was misinterpreting some students' reticence to participate during lecture as a sign that they had misgivings about the class. Many of my friends and colleagues have noted the relative passivity of students in the 1980s and 1990s. Fortunately, I've found that there are almost always a few students who are outspoken and liven up class atmosphere.

In the reviews, there were complaints about the boring and technical nature of science, the grading, and the workload. The number of complaints that related to a dislike of science broke down into two camps. There were those who did not like the problem-solving aspects of the class. The homework involved use of high school math, which turned off a lot of students. Problem solving involved examining details, and they weren't interested in the details. As noted earlier, there are many other classes in the sciences that do not focus on problem solving, and these students clearly would have preferred such a class.

The other camp would have hated any science class, details or no details. I know that, in general, American students think science is boring. Many books have been written on this topic and I have read some of them. The bottom line is that students feel negative about science in high school, and by the time they go to college, this view of science has hardened. So if someone thinks that science is boring before they get to college, I'm going to let myself off the hook and say that there is little I can do about this. I cannot, in one class, erase the effects of negative feelings toward science obtained from society and in high school biology, chemistry, or physics.

In terms of the complaint that the course demanded too much work, the student evaluations were fairly interesting. The students that complained about the workload reported that they spent an average of five hours per week studying outside of class. This meant that there was a significant disparity between what those students and I thought was a reasonable level of commitment to class study. It also probably meant that many university classes required scant outside work.

Many of the review comments were positive and some were enthusiastic, but overall the students gave the class average marks. Whatever the level of the ratings, students did not recommend this class to their friends. The next time I taught the class there were 30 percent less students. In fact, over the next six years each successive class brought significantly lower enrollment. I tried to counter the slide in enrollment by tinkering extensively with the class. I changed its title, changed homework, removed the group project and changed texts. But nothing worked. I was losing badly to the competition of other introductory science classes.

In the sixth and final year I added a required laboratory section. In doing so, I thought that the class would benefit because we could run experiments and do some fieldwork. The change may have improved class content, but it made the class even less attractive because having a lab meant that students would have to spend an extra hour in the classroom.

Enrollment plummeted to nine students. I had big ideas, but their implementation was not practical. In making most of my changes, I was foolishly trying to increase enrollment by improving the class content. I was avoiding the obvious. If I wanted reasonable enrollment in my undergraduate classes, I had to lower my standards.

Finally, after six years, I decided that I had to completely revamp my teaching approach for undergraduates. I didn't want to teach to nearly empty classrooms and neither did Duke. At about this time, my university came to the realization that the era of exponential growth in higher education had ended. In response, the administration began to examine its balance sheets more carefully. They began a serious accounting of anything that could be quantified. One facet of a university that can be quantified easily is student enrollment. In its accounting of student enrollment, our administration found my department lacking. We were teaching half as many students per faculty member as a typical department. We were under the gun to increase our numbers.

So I made a bold retreat. I would now recognize the changes that had taken place over the years and instead of teaching students how to perform science, I would teach them how to appreciate science. I would now largely ignore detail, focus almost entirely on the big picture, reduce the workload, and grade easier. In upper-division courses, I would give up the notion of training students for jobs or research in science. In introductory science courses, I would drop homework assignments and material that assumed knowledge of high school science and math. My major goal had become less ambitious and more pragmatic. I wanted my students to be well-informed citizens who could think somewhat critically about scientific issues that affected society.

I employed this approach for the first time in an upper-division science class in which almost all students were science majors. All through the semester, I kept it easy and relatively light. To keep myself from feeling too bad about selling out my educational principles, I kept reciting the phrase "informed citizen" to myself like a mantra. I hoped that none of these students would go on to graduate school in the sciences. I felt that I had abrogated my responsibility to train them to be scientists.

The reaction to this new approach was enthusiastic. I gave lots of As (to about 30 percent of the class), which I'm sure helped matters. I reduced the workload by about half and reduced the amount of material by about a third relative to previous classes. I did not completely cave in. I still required them to write short essay exams. I still required them to think about what they had heard in class and read in the text, but a lot less thoughtfully than before. Basically, I decided to stretch them only a tiny bit. If my classes were a track and field high jump, what I did was lower the bar a good meter. To do well, they did not have to work as hard or be as talented. Instead of having to work the "onerous" five to ten hours per week I previously expected in an upper-division class, they worked an average of three hours a week.

In reading the student evaluations of this class, it was clear that I was now much more in line with other classes at my university. The students noted that the class made them think and that it wasn't the usual memorize and spit it out science class. These students were science majors so I didn't have to get over the barrier of convincing them that science was interesting.

They also noted that they enjoyed the dynamics of the class. This seemed odd to me. I didn't ask for or receive much participation from this particular class. There were jokes that went back and forth between myself and the students about class logistics (tests, field trips, etc.) and issues of the day that had nothing to do with the class material. But little substantive interaction was going on. I think what they were saying was that they appreciated the lightheartedness with which I approached the class. I think that they also appreciated the dynamics associated with a "sit back and learn" approach to education.

After I read the reviews, I remembered a performance evaluation that I received the year previous from the committee that approved my tenure. They noted that I was considered demanding in the classroom, and characterized my teaching performance as "average." They, however, expressed "confidence that he will learn the skills necessary to become an excellent teacher." I laughed to myself thinking about this comment. The committee was right. I was a ridiculously slow learner, but I had learned the value of changing with the times and teaching easier.

So I'll play devil's advocate here and say what is wrong with having a happy classroom full of students? Sure, I only give them half to two-thirds of what I would like to give them. Sure, the material I've dropped is the most difficult. But the students learn something, don't they? And they like learning it, don't they? Won't they retain more of what they have learned this way? Isn't this better than having a classroom with too few students?

My answer to the devil is that yes, given the generally low expectations we have for our students, this is the better way to teach. But if we raised our standards, the students could do the work. With high standards present across the university, they would not think twice about putting in five hours a week outside of class or ten hours a week for that matter. They might be able to enjoy a well-taught class that required them to work hard because that class would represent the expectation of the university at large. This would not be a novel approach. We expected more of our students in the recent past.

And what about the trend of teaching science appreciation instead of science methods? Over the years, I've warmed to this approach for non-science majors. These students tend to come to college with such negative feelings about science that we are pretending if we think that they will retain anything of value from a traditional science class. Classes that focus on scientific literacy, however, need to establish high academic standards. Also, this approach has spread to the teaching of science majors, and we are now producing, in small but worrisome numbers, a breed of science student that can't solve science problems.

At a place like my university, we get bright students and probably more than a third of them are also motivated and mature when they arrive. Another third, in the context of a university with high standards, would get up to speed and develop their motivation and maturity. But we are generally not challenging students at most universities, including my own. We let them coast if they choose to do so.

I feel bad that I cannot challenge the best. Imagine having an Olympics where the standards for gold medals are easily attained. For example, imagine a high jump competition where we grant a gold medal to every participant who can jump over the bar when it is at a height of one meter. The best get a gold medal along with many others, but they never find out just how much they can achieve.

At my university, a significant number of students are self-motivated and set their own high standards. Many of them set standards much higher than my own. But intellectual achievement should not be a self-service operation, particularly given the cost of higher education today. The American university could easily be a place where all students are expected to enhance their intellectual talents.

Reflective Writing: *Professor Rojstaczer seems rather unhappy with the attitude and performance of students in his science classes at Duke University. What are the reasons for his unhappiness? What suggestions does he have for improving the situation? He argues that "we are generally not challenging students at most universities, including my own. We let them coast if they choose to do so." How would you, as a student, respond to this argument with reasoned, well-supported arguments of your own?*

Too Many Students Are Holding Jobs for Too Many Hours

Jacqueline E. King

This essay was originally an opinion piece in the weekly Chronicle of Higher Education *in 1998. The* Chronicle *is the leading publication for news and analysis on American colleges and universities. It is widely read by educators. The essay's author, Jacqueline E. King, is director of federal-policy analysis at the American Council on Education. In this reading, King does more than just state her view that college students spend too much time working at low-level outside jobs. She presents evidence of various kinds supporting her position on the negative effects of a demanding work schedule on student learning in college.*

To Consider: *Why, in King's view, do so many college students work 25 hours or more at outside jobs? How does this work detract from the demands of a college education? What exactly is it that the author feels can be lost when a student invests so much time on the job?*

Most undergraduates work while they are enrolled in college, to avoid acquiring student-loan debt or to lessen the amount that they must borrow. This is one of the many reasons that the current debate about lowering the interest rate on student loans is so crucial. If Congress, as part of the reauthorization of the Higher Education Act, can reduce substantially the interest rate that students must pay, it may encourage some to cut back on work and to borrow to make up the difference. Because many of the financial benefits of going to college hinge on receiving a degree, borrowing at a low interest rate would be a better strategy for students than working so many hours that they either never manage to graduate or don't have enough time to study to make good grades.

Lowering the cost of student loans is just one method of helping students to balance work and borrowing. Understanding the amount of time that students spend working, and the characteristics of student workers, can help policy makers and campus officials find other ways to help students pay for college without hindering their academic progress.

Eight out of 10 students work while pursuing an undergraduate degree. In financing their college education, they are more likely to use

162

earnings from jobs held during the academic year than they are any other type funds, including student aid or parental support, although dollar amounts from these other categories may be larger.

Policy makers need to realize, however, that there are two types of working students: employees who study, and students who work.

Full-time employees who also attend college make up about a third of working undergraduates. They are usually older and attend part time. The other two-thirds of working undergraduates are students who have jobs to meet their college expenses. Most of the latter group are full-time students, under 24, and financially dependent on their parents. Over half of them attend four-year institutions. As one of my colleagues quipped, these are "blue-jeans-wearing, backpack-toting, bicycle-riding, traditional American college students." Yet, on average, they work 25 hours per week.

Clearly, these two groups of working students have different needs and would benefit from different governmental and institutional policies. On the federal level, for example, employees who attend college part time would benefit most from tax exemptions for the tuition benefits provided by employers. At the campus level, these students need convenient class times and the opportunity to take classes on line, as well as after-hours access to services such as academic advising and child care. These full-time workers are the students whom institutions such as the University of Phoenix were designed to serve, and whom traditional universities have long tried to serve through their evening-extension divisions.

In contrast, full-time students, the ones working an average of 25 hours per week, have their own problems and needs. Much has been said and written about student indebtedness, yet the more serious problem may be that students are working long hours to eliminate or at least lessen their need to borrow—and, in the process, imperiling their ability to succeed academically. We have focused so much of our attention on students who borrow that we have tended to ignore the difficulties of those who do not.

Longitudinal research, by the Department of Education's National Center for Education Statistics, on students who began college in 1989 has shown that, although working fewer than 15 hours per week can have a positive effect on students' likelihood of staying in college, working more than that has a negative effect.

According to the department's "1995–96 National Postsecondary Student Aid Study," only about 20 percent of students at public four-year institutions were able to avoid both borrowing *and* working during that academic year. Fewer than 15 percent took out loans and either did not work or worked fewer than 15 hours per week. Conversely, more than 40 percent did not borrow any money at all but worked 15 or more hours per week. The remaining 25 percent took out loans and worked 15 hours or more.

As opposed to working long hours, borrowing does not seem to harm students' persistence in college or their academic success. Recent results from the Department of Education's longitudinal study show that students who borrow are just as likely to graduate as those who don't. Of course, we don't want students to borrow more money than they can reasonably afford to repay. Nonetheless, working long hours to avoid borrowing is equally inadvisable.

Increasing the amount of money available for grants to students seems the most logical step that policy makers and college administrators could take. The recent increase in the maximum Pell Grant, from $2,700 to $3,000, is a step in the right direction. But such a relatively small increase is unlikely to change students' work patterns substantially. Interestingly, full-time undergraduates who borrow are more likely to receive grants than their peers who choose not to borrow. In part, this is because many students who don't take out loans do not apply for financial aid of any kind.

Of the students who worked but did not borrow in academic 1995–96, about half did not apply for aid. Stories about students' "drowning in debt," combined with the common misperception that grant aid is available only for those who are very poor, may have discouraged some students from applying for aid. The complexity of the application process also may have deterred some students.

At any rate, campus officials must help students understand that it may be in their best interest to borrow, so that they can work fewer hours. At the very least, students should understand that it is always worth their time and effort to apply for student aid.

Helping students to make decisions about working and borrowing is not a task for financial-aid administrators alone. Because taking on too much work can have a negative effect on whether students graduate, and on how well they do while they are enrolled, it is incumbent upon such people as directors of orientation programs, faculty academic advisers, and residence-hall counselors to help students find a reasonable balance between working and borrowing. Based on the research cited above, a good rule of thumb would be that full-time students ideally should work no more than 15 hours per week.

Of course, any hope of reducing students' reliance on work also hinges on institutions' success in keeping tuition increases as small as possible. Certainly, we have made much progress on that front since 1995, with the lowest percentage increases in 30 years. Given the public pressure on institutions to rein in further increases in the cost of providing an education and the prices charged to students, it seems likely that smaller-than-average increases will continue for the immediate future. This will be especially good news to the 25 percent of full-time undergraduates who borrow and still work more than 15 hours per week.

As we try to reduce the amount of time that students spend working, colleges should do more to help those students cope. Time-management and study skills are particularly important for students who have limited time to devote to their course work. Even for undergraduates who live on or near their campus, distance-learning classes that give students access to faculty members and course materials at their convenience can be beneficial. Students also need help dealing with the personal consequences of juggling many competing demands. Stressed-out students too often turn to drugs or binge drinking to "blow off steam," with negative consequences for individual students as well as others on the campus. Some of these problems might be avoided or reduced if colleges offered students early and regular assistance in managing stress.

These are just a few of the policies and practices—besides lowering the interest rate on student loans—that might make life easier for students who work many hours each week. This, in turn, would improve their chances of academic success. The first step, however, is to convince campus officials and policy makers that too many students are working too many hours, and that they need our help.

Jacqueline E. King is director of federal policy analysis at the American Council on Education.

Reflective Writing: *List the arguments that author King makes against students working more than a small number of hours while attending school full-time, and give a response to those arguments. Your response need not be fully in support of or in opposition to King's views; it can be a mix, as people's views on controversial topics often are. Think about ways in which you agree and/or disagree with the author.*

Introduction to *Beer and Circus*:

How Big-Time College Sports Is Crippling Undergraduate Education

Murray Sperber

This essay comes from the 2000 book Beer and Circus: How Big-Time College Sports Is Crippling Undergraduate Education. *The author is an English professor at Indiana University and a prominent critic of college sports. Though a sports fan himself, he believes that big-time intercollegiate athletics are corrupting American universities and compromising undergraduate study. In this chapter, Sperber draws on a well-known sociological study to place college students into four categories based on how they approach school and social activities.*

To Consider: *What are the specific attributes of the four types of college students Sperber discusses? As you read, consider whether or not the author's assessment seems accurate and if there might be other categories that he is missing.*

This "introduction" provides definitions of the four major student subcultures that have long existed in American higher education: the collegiate, the academic, the vocational, and the rebel. An early-1960s study by sociologists Burton Clark and Martin Trow outlined the main characteristics of these subcultures and noted that "an individual student may well participate in several of the subcultures available on his [or her] campus, though in most cases one will embody his [or her] dominant orientation."

Almost forty years later, although more students than ever before participate in several campus subcultures, and sometimes move from one dominant one to another, Clark and Trow's description of the subcultures—with major emendations and additions—still applies to undergraduate life in America. However, as they stressed and it is important to repeat: These "are types of subcultures and not types of students," and stereotyping undergraduates serves no purpose; in fact, it obscures the study of them.

Past college student life is prologue to the present, and the past reveals the depth and continuity of the undergraduate subcultures. Therefore, this introduction adds necessary historical material to the basic definitions.

166

Collegiate Culture

The collegiate culture [is] a world of football, fraternities and sororities, dates, drinking, and campus fun. A good deal of student life on many campuses revolves around this culture. . . . Teachers and courses and grades are in this picture but somewhat dimly and in the background. The fraternities have to make their grade-point-average, [other collegiate] students have to hit the books periodically if they are to get their diplomas, some gestures have to be made to the adult world of courses and grades which provides the justification for the collegiate round . . . the busy round of social activities. . . .

It [the collegiate culture] is, however, indifferent and resistant to serious demands from the faculty for an involvement with ideas and issues.

—Burton Clark and Martin Trow, sociologists

The undergraduates who participate in this subculture are usually termed *collegians* or *collegiates*. The subculture began in the eighteenth century when the sons of the rich came to college for four years of pleasure and social contacts. They considered academic work an intrusion on their fun, and they were content to pass their courses with a "gentleman's C" grade. As higher education expanded in the nineteenth century, many sons and some daughters of the middle class entered universities, and the new collegians started the fraternity and sorority system, as well as the first intercollegiate athletic teams. The collegiate subculture remained antieducational, and this characteristic continued into and through the twentieth century, with student social activities, particularly the campus party scene, taking precedence over academic endeavors.

From their founding in the nineteenth century, college fraternities became bastions of the collegiate subculture and its mores. Adopting Greek letter names and elaborate ceremonies (in imitation of the Masonic order), Greeks used high-minded rhetoric to justify their traditions and customs, but, then as now, their main purpose was fellowship and partying. In the first half of the twentieth century, they so dictated the terms of student life that the Gamma Delta Iota movement began.

Some undergraduates, either not invited to join a fraternity or sorority or unable to afford the expenses of Greek life, remained independent and lived in university dormitories or off-campus rooming houses. But these students wanted to participate in the collegiate subculture—particularly its partying and support of intercollegiate athletics—and they banded together, calling themselves Gamma Delta Iotas (God Damn Independents), turning their housing units into versions of Greek houses. As their name indicates, the GDIs took pride in not being Greek, but they so imitated the originals that they canceled the meaning of the term *independent*. Most important, they extended the boundaries of the collegiate subculture to include large numbers of non-Greek undergraduates.

In the second half of the twentieth century, the size and influence of the collegiate subculture varied from school to school and from decade to decade. In the 1950s, particularly at state universities, the collegiate subculture was large and powerful (the movie *Animal House* attempts to portray Greek life in this era), but, in the politically turbulent 1960s, the subculture shrank, even at Big-time U's. In subsequent decades, the collegiate population increased considerably, and, at the beginning of the twenty-first century, at some public universities with residential campuses, a large percentage of undergraduates belong to Greek organizations, or live in highly collegiate dorms, or in off-campus mini-versions of Greek houses. On the other hand, at many urban schools and small private colleges, the collegiate subculture has never been an important factor in student life and shows no signs of becoming one. No matter what its size or influence at an individual institution, this subculture has always retained its antiacademic bias and formed the core of the campus and off-campus party scene.

Academic Culture

Present on every college campus, although dominant on some and marginal on others, is the [undergraduate student] subculture of serious academic effort. The essence of this system of values is its identification with the intellectual concerns of the serious faculty members. These students . . . work hard, get the best grades, and let the world of ideas and knowledge reach them.

—Burton Clark and Martin Trow, sociologists

At the beginning of American higher education, the first teachers were ministers, and the first students were the sons of the rich—except for a small number of clergymen's sons and some young men hoping to join that profession. These latter students refused to participate in the fun and games of the collegiate subculture; moreover, unlike the collegians, they did not regard the minister teachers with hostility—quite the opposite, they considered them role models, and they emulated their seriousness. The ministers responded by paying special attention to this small group of students, rewarding some, upon graduation, with academic positions, and helping others acquire church pulpits. In this way, the ministers perpetuated themselves and their vocations. Similarly, in the nineteenth century, when colleges evolved into universities, and minister teachers gave way to professional faculty members, these men and women also chose their successors—the minority of students with academic ambitions—and this tradition continues to this day.

From the eighteenth century on, the collegians scorned their academically inclined classmates, regarding them with suspicion and as fair game for pranks and insults. One historian of American higher education terms the serious undergraduates *the outsiders:* on many campuses they were, and still are, outside the mainstream of student life—the collegiate subculture.

Unlike the collegians who mainly exist in a world of immediate gratification, the outsiders practice deferred gratification. They accept the curriculum and the discipline imposed by the faculty because they believe that, after four years, they will enter graduate or professional school and have a professional, often an academic, career. As a result, they are the undergraduates who do all the reading assignments, who turn in their papers on time, who prepare for exams and perform excellently on them, and who attend the professor's office hours.

In the nineteenth century, the collegians called serious students, among other derogatory names, "grubs," "polers," "bootlicks," and "toadies." In the twentieth century, the jibes persisted, only the terms changed: "grinds," "geeks," "dweebs," as well as expressions referencing the more overt sexuality of the age, "brown-noses," "ass-lickers," and "throats." Academic students have always tried to ignore the insults, and have continued to raise their hands in class. Outside of class, the young academics sought one anothers' company, often living together in on- and off-campus housing units. If a university contained a sizable number of serious students, they created their own subculture within the larger undergraduate world; however, if only a few attended the school, they usually became isolated and lonely.

As Clark and Trow indicated, the academic subculture is "present on every college campus, although dominant on some and marginal on others." Today, at some private colleges and universities, a large percentage of undergraduates belong to it; such institutions as the University of Chicago and Brandeis University send a large percentage of their students on to graduate and professional schools. However, at many public universities, academically inclined students constitute a single digit minority, and this translates into a very low percentage of the school's graduates going on for advanced degrees.

Some men and women who began their university careers within the academic ethos of a private institution end up teaching at Big-time U's with huge collegiate subcultures and small academic ones. As a result, these faculty members have minimal understanding of, and sympathy for, the majority of their undergraduate students. In addition, even those professors who attended public universities as undergraduates, because usually they belonged to the academic subculture and disliked the collegiate one, often exhibit an animus toward the collegians in their classrooms. They were outsiders as undergraduates, and they remain outsiders as professors.

Vocational Culture

For [vocational students], there is simply not enough time or money to support the extensive play of the collegiate culture. To these students, many of them married, most of them working anywhere from twenty to forty hours a week, college is largely off-the-job training, an organization of courses and credits leading to a diploma and a better job than they could otherwise command. . . .

But, like participants in the collegiate culture, these students are also resistant to intellectual demands on them beyond what is required to pass the courses. To many of these hard-driven students, ideas and scholarship are as much a luxury and distraction as are sports and fraternities.

—Burton Clark and Martin Trow, sociologists

Vocational students have long existed in American higher education (today, they constitute over half of all college students). Traditionally, vocationals were characterized as students "working their way through college," and they neither participated in collegiate life nor, unlike academic students, attracted special attention from the faculty.

The first wave of vocational students entered American higher education at the beginning of the twentieth century. Often the children of recent immigrants, they mainly attended urban colleges and universities, and usually lived at home, lacking the money or inclination to reside in a dormitory or a Greek house.

Unlike collegians at residential schools, vocationals did not regard college as a "fun interval" between adolescence and adulthood; for vocationals, attending university was another job, similar to their part-time or full-time occupations. As a result, most vocational students lacked the time and energy to intellectually engage their schoolwork, and they considered their classes as obstacle courses with hurdles to be jumped as efficiently as possible.

Vocationals were more conscientious students than the collegians—the casual "gentleman's C" was alien to them—but they tended to do their homework quickly and often achieved what was called the "plebian C." Most of all, they wanted their C's to add up to a college degree. However, unlike the collegians, who viewed a sheepskin as an excellent trophy of the good times at Ol' Siwash, or the academic students, who considered a diploma as proof of attaining a high level of knowledge and culture, the vocationals saw a degree as an entrance fee into the middle class.

After World War II, an enormous wave of vocational students permanently changed America's colleges and universities. As a result of the legislation popularly known as the GI Bill, more than a million ex-service personnel entered higher education, many of whom were the first persons in their families to attend college. The vets regarded going to college as a job, and often took "extra loads" of courses to finish as quickly as possible.

To accommodate these students, and to gain their government-paid tuition dollars, many private colleges, small and sleepy domains of class privilege before the war, transformed themselves into large, bustling, and democratic facilities; public universities grew exponentially, also expanding their clientele from the children of the middle class to multiclass and multiage students; and municipal schools benefited greatly, their long-standing vocational orientation fitting the vets well.

In the post–WWII period, the undergraduate population on most campuses doubled or tripled from prewar levels, and the number of college graduates increased accordingly. In 1939–40, around two hundred thousand Americans received college degrees; ten years later, the first graduating class that included WWII vets pushed the degree total to close to five hundred thousand, and, in the 1950s, the total continued to grow as increasing numbers of nonvets entered higher education. The GIs, who pioneered so much of modern consumer America in the 1950s, including the necessity of owning a car and a house, turned a college degree into a required consumer product, mandatory for all classes of Americans. Henceforth, for a person to succeed in the United States, he or she needed a college diploma.

America's colleges and universities welcomed this new public attitude—it helped reposition them from their historic place on the periphery of American society to the center of postwar commerce and prosperity. Once a college degree became an indispensable consumer item, it guaranteed schools a large and continuous stream of students. It also convinced legislators and taxpayers to support higher education with much more public money than ever before.

Previous to 1945, in the entire history of American higher education, change had occurred at a relatively slow pace. At the end of WWII, higher education entered a phone booth as mild-mannered Clark Kent and came out as Superman, bursting with muscles and money, ready to take on the world. The postwar university soon became, in the words of the president of the fastest-growing school in the country, the University of California, "a multiversity," enrolling many more students than previously. Yet, the traditional student subcultures continued, the vocational one competing for pride of place on some campuses with the collegiate and academic ones.

Not all undergraduates liked this configuration, and, in the 1950s, the rebel subculture, long in existence but marginal at almost every school, began to grow in numbers and importance. Then, in the 1960s—to the bewilderment and distaste of the majority of Americans—the rebels became the largest student group at many institutions, permanently influencing the future of higher education and American society.

Rebel Culture

Some kind of self-consciously nonconformist [rebel] exists in many of the best small liberal arts colleges and among the undergraduates in the leading universities. These students are often deeply involved with ideas, both the ideas they encounter in their classrooms and those that are current in the wider society of adult art, literature, and politics. . . .

The distinctive quality of this student style is a rather aggressive nonconformism, a critical detachment from the college they attend and from its faculty.

—Burton Clark and Martin Trow, sociologists

The goal of rebel students in all eras has been self-development, finding their own way through the maze of higher education and into the complexity of adult society. As part of their search for identity, rebel students exhibit a selective studiousness. Unlike the collegians and vocationals, they are not anti-intellectual. When rebel students enjoy a college course, they do the required work in it and much more, usually attaining a top grade; however, when they dislike a course's content, they dismiss it as irrelevant to their personal interests, and often disappear from class, accepting a low grade, even an F. Rebels differ from academic students who pursue an A in every class, whether they like the material or not, and who always try to please their faculty parents.

Rebel students often do not relate to their professors, even in the courses in which they work hard. Rebels see their "nonconformist" values in conflict with "straight" academic ones, and, as Clark and Trow indicate, "To a much greater degree than their academically oriented classmates, these students use off-campus groups and currents of thought as points of reference . . . in their strategy of independence and criticism" of university and all other authorities. The connection of rebel students to vital parts of the wider culture, notably the political and artistic avant-gardes, occurred throughout the twentieth century and became this subculture's most important contribution to higher education.

More than any other group of undergraduates, the rebels helped destroy the real and imaginary walls that, historically, had detached colleges and universities from their surrounding communities (the concept of a university as an "ivory tower"). The rebels also led the fight against the artificial *in loco parentis* (in place of parents) rules that enabled schools to confine their students to campus housing and to restrict their off-campus movements. Equally significant, the rebels created viable off-campus areas for themselves and other undergraduates.

From the 1950s on, after their college days ended, either through graduation or, more often, after dropping out, some rebels remained near their schools and established the prototypes of the off-campus districts that now border almost every college and university in America. In the 1950s, enclaves of ex-student rebels lived near the University of California at Berkeley, Harvard, the universities of Chicago, Michigan, Wisconsin, and a few other schools. They started alternative bookstores, coffee houses, and other establishments, transforming the off-campus streets into areas that accommodated political and cultural dissidents as well as members of the university community. These off-campus sections also became magnets for rebels in the region who had no affiliation with the school but wanted to live in a congenial place.

The rebels and their off-campus areas flourished in the 1960s, and, during this period of political protest and lifestyle experimentation, more undergraduates belonged to the rebel subculture than at any other time in the history of higher education. At some schools, the rebels formed a majority of the student body and, in alliance with off-campus rebels, led large demonstrations in favor of civil rights and against the war in Vietnam, and they also started communes and other housing experiments.

But, as the protests of the 1960s waned, so did the number of rebel students. Today, they comprise a small minority at most colleges and universities. Rebels continue to search for personal identity, and some participate in current political protests while others welcome the newest manifestations of avant-garde art and music. Undergraduates in other subcultures watch and sometimes join them, and, even though the rebel subculture may never again attain its 1960s size and importance, rebel students will always have a place in higher education.

In surveying the long history of America's colleges and universities, the persistence and continuity of the student subcultures amaze the observer. The world outside the university changes radically, but the preoccupations of undergraduates remain remarkably similar. In their early-1960s study of student subcultures, Clark and Trow noted that, above all, rebel students "pursue an identity"; collegians "pursue fun"; academic students seek "knowledge"; and vocationals fix on "a diploma."

At the beginning of the twenty-first century, the necessity of university certification—a diploma—is more important than ever before for almost all students. Nevertheless, the vocationals remain the undergraduates most preoccupied with this credential, and the rebels the least concerned. The academics need to receive a diploma—preferably one "with honors"—on their way to advanced degrees; and the collegians consider it a "large ticket" consumer item, a purchase akin to an expensive automobile, but something that should not obstruct college fun and beer-and-circus.

Reflective Writing: *Murray Sperber discusses four categories of college student, drawing on the work of sociologists Clark and Trow. While declaring that these categories are not mutually exclusive and that students may move between one category and another, Sperber talks about the collegian, the rebel, the academic, and the vocational student. What are the main characteristics of these subcultures? What other student subcultures might you add to the list, and what would be some of their main features?*

The University Serving the Community

Thomas Ehrlich

A former president of Indiana University, the author believes that college students should have ample opportunities to perform community service. Active himself in such work, he developed numerous service programs while working as a university administrator. In this essay, Ehrlich argues that service, always part of the American university's mission, should become more central, and he gives examples of schools that are attempting to do so.

To Consider: *Dr. Ehrlich uses numerous anecdotes and personal examples to make his point. How effective is this strategy in helping to convince you to accept the author's argument?*

A few years ago I read a report by an Indiana University sophomore, written for a course that required the students to engage in volunteer service. For his service project the student had returned to his junior high school to talk to students there about the value of education. This young man had been a star football player in high school, recruited by many colleges. But in his senior year a serious injury ended his athletic career, a loss he still had not accepted.

"All the way there," he wrote, "I wondered how I was going to convince those kids I was sincere when really I was still so bitter. But I talked to them about the importance of an education, and the message seemed to sink in. I was someone they knew had been injured and had it all taken away, so I felt my speech was helpful to them.

"But just as important," he went on, "this assignment has helped me more than you can know. I was able to look into their eyes and see how lucky I am to have experienced all that I have, and that my education is something I can be proud of."

This student's words highlight the power of volunteer service: A commitment to the well-being of others is an electric force for good—for ourselves as well as for those we serve. It is often hard for young people to believe that what we do as individuals can make a real and lasting difference, but I am convinced that engaging in service to others brings home that truth in ways that nothing else can. At Indiana University and at other colleges throughout the country, I have talked with hundreds of student volunteers such as the young man whose report I just quoted. Over and over they say they have found, through volunteer service, experiences they would never trade.

My father was my role model for community service as I was growing up. His deep sense of obligation to help others led him to be active in scores of civic groups. This was an aspect of his character that impressed me strongly as a child, and I tried to follow his lead in whatever ways I could— not always with success. On one occasion, during World War II when my father was working in Washington for the Office of Price Administration, a local movie theater held a drive for scrap metal. The theater promised a free movie ticket for those who contributed ten pounds. I brought my mother's iron and enjoyed the movie enormously. Returning home, I told my mother I had been trying to help serve the war effort, like my father. The effect of my donation on the war effort was certainly minimal, but the same cannot be said about the effect on my mother's temper when she learned she had lost her only means of ironing clothes.

Pro Bono Publico

I did not begin to think seriously about service in a university context until I became a law school dean at Stanford. As a law teacher, I had been involved in several faculty committees and served on the board of a national organization in international law. But as dean I felt compelled to look hard at how well and in what ways law schools serve society.

I found myself troubled by what I saw. Most law teachers were disengaged from the profession for which they were training students; indeed, some seemed to harbor a disdain for law practitioners. I understood the matter because I myself had left law practice after two years; I had no interest in continuing to serve private clients—precisely what most of my students would be doing. Yet as a law dean I became convinced that law schools and their faculties have an important obligation to help the legal profession. In the years that followed, Stanford significantly expanded its efforts in this direction.

I became troubled also about the legal landscape in the country, especially in regard to the lack of legal representation for poor people in America. Our country's law schools were doing little to address that widespread problem. I often spoke out on the matter and, as a result, in 1975 I was given the opportunity to put the rest of my anatomy where my mouth was. Congress had just established the Legal Services Corporation to provide civic legal help to poor people—almost thirty million men and women living below subsistence level. For a decade, federal support for civil legal services had been provided through an office in the Executive Branch. But politics had so embroiled the effort that a new organization, independent of the Executive Branch, was needed. After difficult partisan wrangling, a board of directors for the new corporation had been selected and was seeking its first president. I had the good fortune to be chosen for the job.

My experiences over the next three and a half years as president of a rapidly expanding program of legal services for poor people helped to underscore that law schools can play a major role in this arena. A number of schools agreed to provide training for legal services lawyers; others were recruited to serve as centers of expertise in particular areas of poverty law. And law schools throughout the country, with support from the Legal Services Corporation, rapidly expanded their programs of service to the poor in their communities. At Legal Services I also promoted mandatory *pro bono* work for all lawyers. I did this because I am convinced that our legal system works as it should only when lawyers are willing to give their time in public service.

On a personal level, I gained enormously from my time in Legal Services and from the experience of listening to and working with men and women in the most difficult economic circumstances. I came to understand how much one can learn from those one is trying to serve, and gathered new insights about myself as well. I felt some reluctance, therefore, when President Carter asked me to turn to the international arena as the first director of the International Development Cooperation Agency, charged with coordinating all U.S. bilateral and multilateral assistance for third world countries.

I was persuaded to take this new assignment because I believe one should not say no to the President of the United States, and because it was an opportunity I might never have again to lead a new federal agency. In fact, the last two years of the Carter administration were difficult ones, and it was particularly tough trying to establish a federal organization in the face of fierce resistance from established bureaucracies. I often thought that the only real supporter of foreign aid—and of me—was the President, who was extremely supportive. The experience was frustrating, though I grew in my understanding of third world poverty and the struggle for survival of so many peoples around the globe. Perhaps most important, the experience reinforced my conviction, when I returned to the world of higher education as provost at the University of Pennsylvania, that public service should be an integral part of my commitment as a university administrator.

The Tradition of Serving Society

Looking back to an earlier era in American higher education, we find service clearly at center stage. Harvard College, the nation's first institution of higher education, was established in 1636 to ensure that a sufficient number of clergy would be available to minister to the citizens of Massachusetts. In words carved on Harvard's gates, the College was "To advance learning and perpetuate it to posterity, dreading to leave an illiterate ministry to the churches when our present ministers shall lie in the dust."

Serving God and helping lay people in that service was the reason Harvard came into existence. But soon thereafter, along with breeding ministers, Harvard College—in the words of President Charles W. Eliot—"began early to breed and prepare for public functions men [no women then] who served as magistrates, teachers, social and military leaders, and heads of the communities in which they lived."

A later example of focus on community service is the University of Pennsylvania, founded in 1740 by Benjamin Franklin to give expression to Franklin's secular vision of service. Penn's first provost, William Smith, came to Franklin's attention through an essay Smith wrote describing a mythical utopian community, called Mirania, that contained a college to train citizens for their civic responsibilities. At colonial colleges of the time, the classics were taught almost to the exclusion of other disciplines. With brilliant foresight, Smith devised for Penn a curriculum of studies that addressed the practical problems of living, working, and governing in Pennsylvania. Civic service was an expected opportunity and obligation for the first graduates of Penn—as today it should be for all higher education graduates.

Unlike Penn, Indiana University is a public institution, but the founding fathers of the Hoosier state were no less committed to the principle that service and education are linked—not least because, as Indiana's Constitution of 1816 declares, "Knowledge and learning [are] . . . essential to the preservation of a free government." In 1820, when IU was founded, every college graduate was expected to give substantial time and effort to public service. This concept was reinforced by President David Starr Jordan in a baccalaureate address given in 1886 to the IU graduating class: "You are to be good citizens, of course," Jordan told the new graduates, "to break no laws, to deal justly, to support your families, to keep out of jail, but all this we expect of every citizen, educated or not. The State has a right to ask more of you. It asks not only that you should break none of its laws, but that you should help to make and to sustain wise laws: that you should stand for good, for right living, for right thinking, and for right acting in the community."

Service was also the dominant purpose of the public institutions supported through the Morrill Act of 1862. Under the terms of the act—which set the precedent for federal aid to education—the government allocated public land in each state to provide for public institutions of higher education. In these "land grant institutions," as they came to be called, the "leading object" was to teach subjects "related to agriculture and the mechanic arts," though not excluding general science, classical studies, and military science.

At the founding of many public and private universities, therefore, service was the ultimate goal, with teaching and scholarship the means of achieving that goal. The institutions had a coherence of vision and a sense of shared purpose. In the course of time, however, the three primary activities of faculty—teaching, research, and service—have drifted apart and service has been drained of its original drive. Faculty are reviewed for compensation, promotion, and tenure on the basis of their efforts in all three categories, but service is rarely considered as important as the other two. At Indiana University, for example, I heard recently that a faculty member, when asked about his service, replied in all seriousness that he viewed his letters of complaint to his dean as his service to the University.

Service at Center Stage

I am convinced that it is time to rethink the concept of service, to move it back to center stage in higher education, and to unify service with teaching and research. Education should nurture the heart as well as the head, and educational institutions bear a special responsibility to encourage the values that support public service. The past years have seen a rising tide of concern about our colleges and universities. Critics say that institutions of higher education see themselves as privileged enclaves, that they focus on research at the expense of teaching, that they seek only to prepare graduates for the job market—and are even doing poorly at that task. But if those of us in education do our job, the school years, from kindergarten through college and beyond, can be a time to develop a personal sense of responsibility. We want our students to be educated citizens. It is no less important that they also be thoughtful individuals who contribute their time and their talents in their communities. Voluntary action reflects distinctly American values, values that are fundamental to the strength of our society, and these values must be fundamental in education.

Increasing numbers of young people today, certainly more than at any time since the 1960s, want to engage in volunteer service. They see a need and reach out to help. In recent decades young people have often been pictured as self-involved and alienated. But the Civil Rights movement, the Peace Corps, Job Corps, Vista, and many other programs have been powerful engines for change, putting values into action and inspiring millions of Americans, young and old, to do their part to make the world a better place.

What are the obstacles to a more central role for service in the university's mission? The obstacles are easier to diagnose than to cure, but certainly a key stumbling block is the lack of a strong sense of community on most university campuses. This is particularly true at urban institutions serving mainly commuting students, for the primary allegiance of those students is to their families and jobs, not to the institution. But a lack of community is also common at large research universities, where the first allegiance for many—perhaps most—faculty members is to their disciplines, not to their campuses. Faculty most often view recognition by peers, at their own and other universities, as the principal currency of the academic realm.

What steps can we take to restore the role of service in universities? The first and most important step is to integrate service into the curriculum. In this enterprise, professional schools at the graduate level are already in the lead. Professional schools combine service with classroom work because their students need to practice what—at least at schools of theology—they will one day preach and—at other schools—what they will later perform. It is common today in law schools for students to devote considerable time to helping clients, often indigent clients, under the supervision of faculty, just as in medical schools students learn their profession while serving patients in hospitals and clinics. Indianapolis civic leader Michael Maurer highlighted the importance of service as a component in professional education when he recently established a prestigious merit scholarship for the IU School of Law at Bloomington. The scholarship requires the recipient to participate in a public service project during each semester.

Incorporating service into the curriculum is particularly important at the undergraduate level, and here much remains to be done. As students progress through their education, linking service with academic work helps them understand the human dimensions of academic disciplines and develop a conceptual framework for their service. To cite examples from Indiana University, an undergraduate degree program in the School of Health, Physical Education and Recreation requires students majoring in the program to give a total of 320 hours of volunteer work in senior citizen centers, youth agencies, and other public service organizations that relate to their future careers. In the IU School of Public and Environmental Affairs, undergraduates studying public management work with county agencies in a variety of areas that include waste management, tourism, and the court system.

I particularly encourage service learning, as it has come to be called, for undergraduates because it offers opportunities to reflect, in an academic context, on the experiences of service. The result of this reflection is that the subject taught—history, literature, or sociology, for example—and the service experience are mutually enriched for the students.

Extracurricular, non-academically related service programs are also of great value for students. One of many illustrations is a volunteer program at the Indiana University School of Business, in which more than 250 undergraduates participate every year. I saw a report by one of these students, Chris Pollock, on his volunteer experiences. Pollock worked with Junior Achievement, teaching a course in business fundamentals to sixth graders, and also participated as a volunteer in Boys Club, Habitat for Humanity, and the Red Cross. "I firmly believe that anyone's simple interest in helping the community confirms the fact that people care about people," he wrote. "When kids see you care, they tend to care more as well. When you make a friend, you become a friend. These gestures may not bring about world peace, but they do add positively and constructively to the community."

The University and National Service

In recent years, politicians from every point on the political spectrum have championed volunteer community service. President Carter, since leaving office, has spent time each year helping build homes for poor families. George Bush, during his presidency, sponsored the Points of Light Foundation because of his belief that, in his own words, "any definition of a successful life must include serving others." Also during the Bush administration, Congress adopted the National and Community Service Act to encourage volunteer service, particularly among young people.

I recall during the early days of the Commission on National and Community Service a day-long passionate discussion on "Why Service?" A leading member of the Commission, George Romney, himself a presidential candidate in an earlier era, said in essence that service was needed because the problems facing this country were so great that government could not grapple with them. Without service, Romney suggested, the crises of crime, drugs, urban decay, and so forth would overcome us. I agree, but I am convinced that service is important, particularly for young people, for still stronger reasons. Volunteer service shapes our personal values—our sense of responsibility and self-esteem, our leadership abilities, our appreciation for diversity, and our sense of community. The enduring measure of success, therefore, is not the impact on society's ills, though that impact can be substantial, but rather the impact on the character of those who serve. From this perspective, community service goes beyond charity—doing good for the sake of doing good—and is a civic act in the highest sense.

As evidence of this, a Gallup survey done in 1992 for an organization called Independent Sector reveals that those who are active in volunteer service are much more likely to vote than those who are not. Similarly, individuals who give their time and talents in service generally involve themselves in the world around them through other avenues as well—civic groups, alumni associations, and service organizations such as Junior Achievement—creating a network of citizenship in their communities and in their own lives. But more research is needed on these and other correlations to understand cause and effect, and more research can and will be done as community service becomes increasingly integrated into educational programs.

President Clinton also has voluntary action close to his heart. Early in his presidency he described his idea of national community service in a speech at Rutgers University. Service, he said, is rooted "in the concept of community—the simple idea that none of us on our own will ever have as much to cherish about our own lives if we are out here all alone, as we will if we work together." Clinton proposed and Congress adopted new legislation to establish a national network to help forge the common bonds of citizenship. His plan called for thousands of community service opportunities for young people, all with a particular emphasis on health care, the environment, crime control, and education.

The act looks to the expansion of service opportunities from about 20,000 at the outset to at least 100,000. These will include part-time as well as full-time positions in programs developed on many different models throughout the country. Criteria have been established to ensure that the programs have measurable performance goals, that they meet real educational, environmental, public safety, or human services needs, provide positive experiences to participants, and do not displace existing workers. The act specifies that all participants receive a stipend, without regard to need, just as do volunteers in Vista and the Peace Corps. In addition, a post-service benefit is provided to be used for education.

In the 1970s and 1980s, service opportunities offered by universities were a cottage industry. Individual mentors helped individual students on a path of service. Now, in the remaining years of this decade, universities have extraordinary opportunities to help the service movement shift from a cottage industry to a real profession. Currently, we have no schools of public service that are the counterpart of schools of public health. More fundamental, we have no real infrastructure to support a rapidly expanding network of service opportunities on the scale proposed by the Clinton administration. In an era when higher education is often battered and certainly bruised, what higher ground could be taken than for universities to help build the needed infrastructure for training, technical support, monitoring, and research?

Only a few isolated training opportunities exist for those who want a career, or at least a period of years, in service. Leadership is key to successful community service programs, and training is key to leadership. Currently, most training is on-the-job. Ad hoc arrangements have been crafted by individual service programs, but even universities that emphasize student service have no organized training except on a program-by-program basis.

Now that a national service network is being established, training must shift to a larger scale. Goals will need to be defined. For example, interpersonal skills such as leadership and conflict resolution are vital to leaders of service programs. Service leaders also need to understand the workings of local, state, and national government, interaction with the private sector, and the philosophy and practice of philanthropy and public service.

A spectrum of other issues might well be included in a service curriculum, ranging from the most abstract, such as readings on altruism, to the most operational, such as materials on tax-exempt status. Technical assistance for service programs across the country, and monitoring of their operations, are no less needed, and universities could help provide that assistance and support. In the process, students engaged in training could practice what they learn, much as those in schools of education and social work have practical experience built into their education. As such arrangements become more widespread, opportunities for all students to engage in service in an academic context can become possible.

Service Learning

Community service in the context of academic courses and seminars—often termed "service learning"—is important for two fundamental and interrelated reasons: (1) Service as a form of practical experience enhances learning in all arenas of a university's curriculum; and (2) the experiences involved in community service provide unique enrichment opportunities by reinforcing the moral and civic values inherent in serving others.

Many faculty members, however, question integrating community service into the undergraduate curriculum, and want proof that service enhances academic objectives. Does a student learn more political science, sociology, or English literature if a course in that discipline includes a community service component? The answer depends on the substance of the course and its academic objectives, but I am convinced that service will enhance academic learning in many courses.

Last year, three political science professors reported on a course they taught, "Contemporary Political Problems," at the University of Michigan. Out of a class of eighty-nine students, they randomly selected one group to be involved in community service, along with readings and written assignments, while the other sections did some added traditional assignments. On three scales, they found that the students in the community-service section succeeded more than did their classmates: Their grades were higher (by blind grading), they reported higher satisfaction in the course evaluations, and their awareness of societal problems was greater. The effort was repeated, with students being allowed to choose to work in a political or social-service organization, and the results were equally positive. The faculty members emphasized that a key factor in these results was time spent integrating community service into the curriculum by regular discussion sessions.

Few comparable studies have been done with the same care, and no data exist on the long-term impact of service in terms of learning. But the few reports that have been prepared not only underscore the need for more studies, but also give strong evidence in favor of expanding service learning in the undergraduate curriculum. One can imagine results similar to those in the Michigan study in a sociology course on welfare, for example, and in a wide variety of courses in public policy. In such disciplines, if regular reflection on community service is integrated into written assignments and discussions of readings, the service should enrich the other course work.

In professional disciplines, clinical work has long been considered essential for the educated practitioner. In law and medicine, for example, academic learning in the classroom, library, and laboratory initially came as a supplement to apprentice programs. One learned how to be a lawyer by serving as an apprentice to a seasoned attorney, studying in a law office while assisting the attorney with clients and in court. That is how Thomas Jefferson learned; he was an apprentice to George Wythe, who subsequently became our country's first professor of law at William and Mary College. In the course of the nineteenth century, the study of law in a law school was allowed by the gatekeepers of the profession—the organized bar—to substitute for time spent in a law office. Apprenticeship was still the customary route to the bar until law schools became well established toward the end of the nineteenth century.

Ironically, the revolution that transformed legal education into an academic discipline eliminated all clinical dimensions for a time. It was not until the 1960s that clinical legal education returned. It came with a strong push from the organized bar and with the help of a private foundation. It also came because a group of faculty members at Harvard Law School developed an extensive clinical program for law students in their third year, and other schools followed suit, using the framework for clinical legal education developed at Harvard.

In the health professions and in other fields such as social work and public administration, practical experience has also long been seen as essential for students. The challenge has been to integrate experience with the theoretical learning that goes on in the classroom. Ideally, a constantly iterative process occurs—a student learns anatomy from textbooks and lectures, the student practices with a cadaver, and then learns more in the classroom and the laboratory. No one seriously questions the need for medical students and students in other professions to spend time in practicing what they will later perform. The importance of clinical training is apparent.

But how does clinical training serve to enrich learning in the arts and sciences, which are at center stage in undergraduate education? The answer in the sciences is clear. No one today would teach chemistry without requiring students to have experience in a laboratory doing actual experiments. One can know that two parts of hydrogen and one part of oxygen, when mixed properly together, explode into water, but until one has seen the process in the laboratory, the knowledge is only an abstraction. More important, laboratory experience enables students to come to know the scientific method firsthand, by developing an hypothesis, testing it, and reaching judgments based on evidence.

The usual counterpart of the chemistry lab is the library for students in the liberal arts, and a research paper is the usual product that results. Empirical studies are sometimes required of students in the social sciences, but rarely of those in the humanities. For disciplines in all fields of the liberal arts, however, service can enrich study by connecting academic abstractions, often remote from the experience of students, with human experiences involving others. Service enables students to learn about themselves and their values as they help those in need. Service connects thought and feeling in a deliberate way, creating a context in which students can explore how they feel about what they are thinking, and what they think about how they feel.

The humanities present a special challenge in linking to service because the humanities' palette is the widest and most diffuse. The proposition that service enriches learning in all arenas of the university finds its test case in literature. How can one "experience" *Middlemarch* as well as read it?

Answers to that question became clearer to me during a course I taught on "Altruism, Philanthropy, and Public Service" in my last year at Indiana University and again at Duke University. The answers relate to my point that the experiences involved in community service help to strengthen moral and civic values. One explicit aim of the course was to help undergraduate students understand their own value systems and the extent of their personal commitment to help their neighbors. Each student was expected not only to participate in class and write several papers, but also to serve in a community service agency for at least three hours each week. Students were required to keep a journal describing their service experiences and the ways in which those experiences enriched their readings for the class.

Class sessions early in the course focused on altruism in literature. Among the assigned readings was "The Snow Image," a short story by Nathaniel Hawthorne. In the story, two children playing in the snow create "an image out of snow" and call it their "snow sister." The image is so lifelike that the children's father is convinced it is a real child. Despite his children's strong objections, he brings it inside the house to warm it at the stove. Soon a puddle of water is all that is left of the snow image.

This story triggered lively class discussions about whether altruistic behavior must actually help the recipient, or whether good intentions are sufficient. Those discussions were immeasurably enhanced because the students were themselves engaged in community service projects. Some of those projects provided assistance without much regard to whether the assistance was requested by the recipients. Comparing their experiences to ideas in the Hawthorne story, the students gained new perspectives on their own attitudes and actions.

Each of the other readings in the course—excerpts from the Old and New Testaments, Thomas Aquinas, and contemporary philosophers and social scientists—was similarly reinforced by the interaction of insights from the texts and from the service experiences. I finished the course convinced that community service provides a particularly powerful means to link theory and practice for students in the humanities. By enriching the life experiences students bring into the classroom, service helps them to read literature or history or philosophy with greater insight, and to experience in their own lives issues that are at the heart of those disciplines. When readings are examined closely against a background of actual experiences in community service—through class discussions, journals, and essays—students share experiences in ways that deepen their analyses of texts and the frameworks within which they think about their service.

Carefully linked to intellectual inquiry, service enables students to relate more personally to, for example, Dorothea Brooke and Dr. Lydgate in *Middlemarch* and the sharecroppers in James Agee's *Let Us Now Praise Famous Men*. In the process of relating to those characters and the problems they face, students can gain greater understanding of themselves. The result is to enrich both the readings and the service.

My experience in teaching this course reinforces points stressed by John Dewey, who spent a lifetime elaborating the thesis that theory and practice must work together. Dewey believed that individuals should not be trained for narrow professions alone but for life, and that learning in the classroom and in practical arenas should constantly interact—lest we be unable to learn from our experiences or link those experiences to our intellectual inquiries.

Enhancing learning is not the only rationale for including a community service component in academic courses, though I think it is the primary one. Two other reasons have been articulated at some length by strong advocates of service learning. Robert Coles of Harvard urges that community service be included in humanities and social sciences courses to enrich the moral character of students. He puts the matter this way:

> For a number of years I have taught undergraduates a course titled "The Literature of Social Reflection." Several discussion sections are reserved for students doing community service, who can use the assigned readings as a basis for reflection upon what they are experiencing in their work as volunteers. . . . They connect the intellectual and moral issues posed by the readings to the students' everyday struggles to figure out what they are trying to do and to what effect; how they are to learn about people who are different from themselves; and not least, how those people regard them and their purposes.

To educational theorist Benjamin Barber of Rutgers University, the primary rationale for linking community service to the classroom is civic education. In his words in *An Aristocracy of Everyone:*

> Where students use experience in the community as a basis for critical reflection in the classroom, and turn classroom reflection into a tool to examine the nature of democratic communities and the role of the citizen in them, there is an opportunity to teach liberty, to uncover the interdependence of self and others, to expose the intimate linkage between rights and responsibilities. . . .

These two perspectives, one emphasizing moral issues and the other emphasizing civic concerns, are closely related to each other and to a third perspective: that community service as a regular part of an undergraduate course in the humanities or social sciences can link classroom learning to the professional and personal lives of students after graduation. Community service ties together elements of both vocation and avocation.

Overall, service learning is expanding rapidly in higher education, fueled by increased student interest in community service and by renewed attention to enhancing student learning. This expansion of service learning is one of five broad and related trends I see in undergraduate teaching, trends that I believe will mark a revolution in pedagogy. The other four trends are increased attention to problem areas, as opposed to academic disciplines; collaborative learning, as opposed to isolated learning; technology, as opposed to chalkboards; and assessment, as opposed to ignorance about student learning.

A few words may serve to illuminate these trends in the context of one institution—Portland State University in Portland, Oregon—which is now revising its entire curriculum under the able leadership of its president, Judith A. Ramaley. In the first phase of the revision, centering on general education, all freshmen are required to take one of several "freshman experience" courses, each of which focuses on an issue cluster. The initial clusters are the city, conflict resolution, the home, pluralism, and Einstein. A team of faculty members from different disciplines designs the curriculum for each course, and each team member teaches a section of the course, with other team members helping out in their areas of expertise. The Einstein team, for example, includes professors of computer science, English, physics, and sociology. The students also work in teams, and their collaborative learning helps them teach each other and build on their differing abilities. In addition to enhancing the learning process, collaborative learning promotes the skills of teamwork that are needed in workplaces, community organizations, and other realms of life.

All of the freshman experience courses are technology intensive. Students learn about the course material at computer workstations, and in the process they learn a good deal about computer technology as well. Each course has a carefully articulated set of objectives, and student learning is assessed to determine the extent to which the course is meeting those objectives. Finally, all students are involved in community service that is integrated into their classroom experiences. In the Einstein course, for example, students in one section teach about Einstein in high-school classes, and the high-school students in those classes subsequently teach about Einstein in elementary-school classes. Learning is enhanced at each level by opportunities to serve and to reflect on the service. Correspondingly, service experiences are strengthened by linking them to course readings, papers, and other assignments.

Portland State is among the leaders in service learning and in other dimensions of the coming higher-education revolution in pedagogy. Another fine example is the new California State University campus at Monterey, which is working to establish a total learning environment where all students will be engaged in service integrated into the curriculum.

Education should not be value-free, as Peter Smith, the president at Monterey, stresses. It should serve to deepen our sense of connectedness and responsibility to others. Incorporating volunteer service into undergraduate education, as an integral part of that education, emphasizes for students that serving others is part of being an educated person. In much the same way that clinical practice arises out of education in medicine, in law, in religion, and in other fields, service should arise out of values learned though education.

For all these reasons, the time has come to unify service with teaching and research. Community service by students is a particularly powerful means to promote this objective. Integrated into the curriculum and under the guidance of faculty, it can be a catalyst for new strengths in higher education with far-reaching benefits for our society.

Reflective Writing: *"Education should not be value-free," Ehrlich says in this essay. What specifically does he mean by this quote? Looking over the examples of service learning that he provides, what values does he want a college education to transmit? How might service learning experience contribute to your own education?*

A Guide to Good Teaching:
Be Slow and Inefficient

Michael Randall

Efficiency in education is all the rage these days and for lots of good reasons. Technological advances have made it possible for teachers to reach larger and larger groups of students in disparate locations. Financial considerations have made it essential for colleges to cut costs wherever possible, and small, seminar-type classes have been a frequent casualty. An emphasis on preprofessional education has shifted students' attention away from developing "the life of the mind" and toward studies more relevant to their chosen career paths. Jogging along (at a leisurely pace) in the opposite direction of all of these trends is Mark Randall, professor of French. In the following essay, he argues the value of a more traditional kind of teaching, one that is often slow and inefficient. Such an approach, he suggests, is crucial if students are to turn information into knowledge—his definition of learning. Professor Randall teaches French at Brandeis University.

To Consider: *As you read, consider just what the author sees as the value of "slow and inefficient" teaching. Try taking your time with this essay, not only summarizing its main points but also making whatever connections you can with some of the other essays from this unit.*

I have the rather dubious honor of writing as a representative of a dying breed, like an Atlantic salmon, a spotted owl, or a cod. Soon distance learning will have rendered the professor obsolete, and translation devices will have made language courses redundant. In fact, English will probably be the world's only language, and modern American popular culture will have completely washed away the historical past. Appreciation of literature will enjoy the same nostalgic status as book or LP collecting, and interactive PlayStations will have replaced books themselves. Professors of Renaissance French literature will, or perhaps already do, seem as quaint as the milkman who, in the days before the strip mall, delivered those heavy glass bottles to your doorstep before dawn.

Perhaps it is inevitable that those whose business it is to flog Rabelais, Montaigne, and Neo-Platonic poetics to technology-savvy, career-conscious, and heavily indebted students should begin to wonder whether their role as teachers is superfluous. After all, teachers, in general, are the apotheosis of human inefficiency. We get sick, we make mistakes, we don't always get along with our colleagues, and sometimes we even give lousy grades to our clients (the students), thereby upsetting the company directors, who see their market share imperiled as customers flee to more user-friendly competitors.

Professors of old foreign literatures, in particular, do not represent what a friend of mine once called "efficient asset allocation." I think he meant that money could be better spent on professors teaching more immediately useful courses than literature. I've mulled over his comment during the last several months, and I've come to think that perhaps teaching often needs to be inefficient. In fact, the value of literary studies, especially of literature like that of the Renaissance and the Middle Ages—at least in my classes—is in their very inefficiency.

As in the case of fast food or artificial insemination, the fastest and most efficient process is not always the most enjoyable. "Slow" food and the tried and true method of reproduction are ultimately less efficient than their speedier alternatives, but not without their own peculiar pleasures. I would like to extend that somewhat inappropriate metaphor to the act of teaching, and to make a case for slow teaching.

In my classes, it is at those moments when the information flow slows to a trickle and even comes to a stop that teaching begins to take place. Learning starts when the essay by Montaigne or the passage by Rabelais ceases to be information and takes root in the student's mind.

Those moments, which we have all experienced, occur in different ways: Sometimes there is a "eureka" yell, and the sudden babble about how a student's life has been changed forever. (This is rare, and should be avoided, since the post-eureka depression that sets in when life goes on as before can be difficult to handle for both student and professor.) Sometimes a smaller charge goes off, when a concept, idea, or image settles into a student's psyche and ceases to be simply words on the page. Sometimes a stillness descends, when it seems that an idea is absorbed and promises to become something greater when it is cross-pollinated with another idea, concept, or image. Sometimes you don't even realize that anything has happened at all.

Such moments form the core of slow, inefficient teaching. A good, inefficient teacher strives to lead students to texts that are not "information" and that cannot be "translated" into a more readily understandable language. These texts, in fact, demand that students drop their understanding of the world based on the present and become part of a reality not their own. In this way, that foreign reality becomes a part of their new and expanded present. As the students' awareness is broadened to include the foreignness of the past, their present becomes more inclusive and their sense of the new ever sharper.

Often the texts that are most effective in slowing down the flow of information are the most enigmatic: The prologues to Rabelais's *Gargantua* or just about any essay by Montaigne often bring students to a halt, since the meaning of those works is not, and never will be, fully self-evident. I am sure that such texts and problems exist in every subject, from phys. ed. to physics.

My role as a teacher is to bring those texts to the students and hope that they snag something in their minds so that the information flow slows or even comes to a momentary stop. If I can draw students into the literary world of 400 to 500 years ago—even briefly—their present can become richer and more complex, if not more efficient. A student who has come to grips with a text from another culture from many centuries ago no longer perceives the present in quite the same way. The awareness of the complexity of a difficult text from a foreign culture leads to an awareness of the complexity that marks our present culture. That makes for a less-efficient consumer of facile marketing and political spin; but that inefficiency makes for a richer individual and a more responsible citizen.

I am rarely even partially successful, but my own efficiency as a teacher can be measured by those moments when students enter into a dialogue with the text, when the text ceases to be part of the seemingly endless flow of information whizzing by us all, and the students step briefly into a world very different from their own.

This sort of learning is perhaps even more valuable today, when intellectual worth increasingly is understood in terms of how much information one can process. We might do well to remember that knowledge consists of more than information; rather, it is the ability to understand and to appreciate the difficult and complex products of the human imagination. That type of knowledge is common to all of our subjects and is the meat and potatoes of education. Teaching that supports that kind of understanding is by nature slow and labor-intensive. In a word, inefficient.

I would like to propose the lowly piece of chalk as a symbol of slow teaching. Highly unglamorous and prone to creating clouds of dust and teeth-gritting noise, chalk enjoys the advantage of being slow; it takes time to write with it, and you need to get up and go to the blackboard to use it. It can also be used to create an interactive classroom when given to students to write with, in groups, alone, or both. And it can be used over and over again with little chance of crashing. When it does finally crumble, it can be readily and inexpensively replaced. Chalk, hopelessly old-fashioned, by its very inefficiency helps to slow down the information flow and allows learning to take place.

I hope this has not come across as some lunatic Luddite's litany against modernity. I know how lucky I am to be teaching at a modern university, spending days and evenings reading rare editions of obscure authors in the library; writing articles and conference papers; and preparing for class by reading poems, essays, and novels by writers such as Louise Labé, Michel de

Montaigne, and François Rabelais. But I cannot help but think that Huck Finn's remark that he "didn't take no stock in dead people," referring to Moses, could apply to much of modern culture, university and otherwise. In light of society's increasing obsession with the present and with speed, it is important to remember that some forms of knowledge are best served by slowness and by an awareness of the transience of the present.

Future generations might well thank us for emphasizing the importance of slow teaching. Without our efforts to valorize the seemingly inefficient, by training our students' eyes and minds on the foreign and on the past, the future might be characterized by a limitless present in which difference has disappeared, and in which intellectual worth is calculated merely in terms of ever-greater speed. Fast and efficient, such a world might not be worth living in.

Reflective Writing: *This essay uses humor and irony to discuss its subject: the nature of good teaching. But in its main argument, the author seems to be very serious. At a time when education is more and more dominated by the goals of speed and efficiency, he advocates that teachers slow down. Specifically, he urges teachers to take their time in class when imparting new knowledge and to work at a slower pace when helping students savor and digest that knowledge. What, in his view, are the benefits of this more leisurely approach? Can you think of particular learning experiences, in school or outside of school, that support or counter his position?*

Possible Essay Topics

For this assignment, choose one of the following topics and write a three- to four-page essay. In your essay, be sure to draw significantly on readings from this unit of the anthology. But rather than merely summarizing or restating ideas from the essays, you will also want to add your own discussion and analysis of the readings and how they relate to your own ideas and experiences. Make sure your ideas are well developed and your prose carefully edited and proofread.

1. In "On the Uses of a Liberal Education" Edmundson critiques the idea that students should be casual "consumers" of the college experience. He argues instead that true higher learning demands a more serious kind of critical engagement on the part of students. He suggests that it also requires some unsettling, tough-minded, no-nonsense instruction from one's professors. In the next reading, Shorris describes an educational program for low-income, college-age students that is very rigorous and that he claims the students find not only interesting but also liberating, empowering, and life changing.

   For the purposes of this essay, try to place yourself in both educational contexts and consider what your experience might be in each. From your own perspective, what are the advantages and disadvantages of the students' approach to college that Edmundson examines? Why does there seem to be so much more genuine motivation and engagement in learning at the less prestigious, elite educational setting? Draw substantially on at least one other reading from the unit in writing your own essay. The Ehrlich essay may be particularly relevant here for its discussion of the moral and ethical dimension of a college education.

2. In his essay from Unit Four, Neusner lists criteria for defining average, good, and exceptional teaching. Rojstaczer from his perspective as a teacher critiques what he views as his students' lack of true engagement in their education. Write an essay in response to both readings from your own perspective as a student with many years of experience in school. Using what you have learned in class about the structure of argumentative writing, examine carefully the authors' arguments. Draw on some of the other readings in the unit, as well as your own background

and opinions, in developing an argument about the qualities necessary to be a "good" college student and/or professor. Also consider how our culture, including the college environment, supports or does not support those qualities.

3. Think about your own experiences and goals as a student, and consider yourself as a learner. What, to you, is the essence of "being in college"? What do you mean by learning, and what role does it play in your college experience? Consider, Sperber's categories of college student subcultures. Zoom in on a school experience of your own, from any level of schooling, and consider the relation of this experience to your developing notion of the nature of learning. In reflecting on these questions and in writing this essay, draw in some significant way on at least three of the readings from this unit, in addition to previous readings if you wish.

4. Jack Meiland discusses differences between thinking and learning in college and in high school. He constructs an argument based on his own knowledge as a long-time college philosophy instructor. At the forefront of college requirements, he suggests, is the expectation that students will think critically and actively about their subject matter, rather than simply accept and repeat what the teacher and textbooks say.

   For this assignment, write an essay using the specific kinds of critical thinking the author discusses (and be clear about what he says). Think back on your high school education, what you were expected to learn, how you were expected to think, and how you did actually carry out your schoolwork. Relate these high school experiences to what you are now being asked to do in college. How are they similar? How are they different? What are the advantages and disadvantages of the various kinds of thinking and learning discussed? How do you see yourself, at this point in your education, as a thinker and learner?

5. Former Indiana University president Thomas Ehrlich believes that college students should be given ample opportunities to serve their communities and that such work can be an integral part of a college education. In light of Ehrlich's discussion, consider your own ideas, experiences, and expectations regarding community service. What specifically does Ehrlich argue regarding what has come to be known as "service learning"? How does such work relate to the other aspects of a college education? Why should or should not the university be involved in organizing and promoting these sorts of activities? In answering these questions, you might consider the portraits of bored, apathetic, and self-absorbed college students discussed in some of the other readings in this unit.

UNIT THREE

The Purposes of College

The headline from a recent *Chronicle of Higher Education* article reads as follows: "More Freshmen Than Ever Appear Disengaged from Their Studies, Survey Finds." This article discusses a comprehensive survey of more than 250,000 first-year, full-time college students from around the country. For more than 30 years, the survey has examined the backgrounds, habits, and aspirations of a representative sample of the nation's first-year college students, who currently number about 1.6 million. Commenting on the data, Linda J. Sax, the survey's director and an education professor at UCLA, makes this assessment: "Students do what they have to do to get into college and graduate school, but their intrinsic interest in what they're learning seems to be down."

Current students' reasons for attending college appear to center primarily on the development of marketable skills and the potential for economic gain, not on specific academic interests. These motivations perhaps help explain why many students often seem less than fully engaged with the subject matter of their courses, particularly when that coursework is outside their area of specialization. In the survey, when asked to select from a list of objectives the ones they considered essential or very important, students' most popular choice was "being very well-off financially," at 75 percent. By comparison, just 41 percent chose "developing a meaningful philosophy of life," 19 percent picked "becoming involved in programs to clean up the environment," and 27 percent selected "keeping up to date with political affairs." Only 34 percent of students said they had spent at least six hours a week on schoolwork in the past year, down from 44 percent 10 years ago. By far the most popular majors were in business, engineering, and professional fields, with corresponding declines in arts and humanities and social sciences. From this general statistical profile of U.S. first-year college students, one could argue that a great many students choose higher education for a very specific—and perhaps narrow—purpose.

College professors and administrators tend to have a different perspective on the value and purpose of a college education. The University of Cincinnati's official mission statement lists the following as its overall institutional goals, and these goals, it should be noted, are comparable to those found at other similar institutions:

> The University of Cincinnati has as its primary mission making the world a better place through excellence in research, teaching, and public service. Integral to the mission of the University is a commitment to academic freedom, the spirit of inquiry, respect for human dignity and tolerance of diverse beliefs.
>
> Valuing teaching, research, creativity, and service within our educational goals, the University accomplishes its mission by:
> - Transmitting and critiquing the wisdom of previous generations;
> - Fostering exploration of natural phenomena, the arts, and human experience to build new knowledge;
> - Providing avenues that facilitate access to higher education;
> - Providing leadership in the learned and professional societies and in our communities;
> - Maintaining a commitment to excellence in each of our programs.
>
> The oldest Colleges of the University of Cincinnati were formed to meet the needs of a growing frontier community for doctors, lawyers, engineers, teachers, and artists. The spirit of close cooperation with the city and surrounding area has remained a hallmark of the University as it surpassed its local and regional significance to become a University which serves the state, the nation, and the world.
>
> Today, each of our colleges continues to play a unique role by attracting a distinguished and diversified faculty and student body whose interaction stimulates intellectual and creative activity. In this synergistic environment, students of the University of Cincinnati are prepared to enhance both their chosen fields of endeavor and the communities in which they live. Graduates of our programs share a commitment to a lifetime of learning, personal and professional accomplishments, and service.

As you can see, the university mission statement is a broad and ambitious one. It includes but is not limited to the acquisition of job and career skills. Therefore, by seeking out a university education, students enter an environment in which intellectual development and a commitment to serving their community are just as much fundamental expectations as is acquiring professional competence. But what many do not understand is that even the career qualifications students hope to develop are not limited to those emphasized in the major. In carrying out its educational mission, the university asks students to take courses not simply in a narrow area of specialization but also in a variety of fields. From educators' perspectives, such courses make up an important part of the undergraduate course of study. According to the 1997 University of Cincinnati *Viewbook* publication, "If you think a liberal arts education is not very practical, think again. The CEOs of most major corporations value highly the skills you'll gain—being able to think critically and solve problems effectively. 'These are the well-rounded and practical skills business executives want . . . They perceive a liberal arts education . . . to be excellent practical preparation' *(Change Magazine)*."

The readings in this unit investigate the wide range of purposes for college, the reasons for the existence of higher education, and the potential benefits of postsecondary study. One essay questions American society's emphasis on college and argues that many students might be better off not attending. Many students entering college focus exclusively or primarily on career preparation goals but in the process may be ignoring other valuable aspects of a college education. In addition, a narrow focus on the major field of study may prevent students from taking full advantage of coursework outside the major, even though this coursework could itself help sharpen intellectual abilities useful in the professional world. The following essays are designed to introduce you to ideas about education that will help you gain a better understanding of what college has to offer and make the most of your college experience.

The first author, philosopher of education Steven Cahn, explains the value of college study for the society as a whole, not simply for the individual, and provides a rationale for coursework in the liberal arts and sciences. Next, student Mark Jackson argues in favor of career-based education supplemented by humanities courses that he feels also play a role in preparing students for the work world. The following two essays each look at the major field of study. Professor Jacob Neusner analyzes the intellectual and institutional makeup of the major and offers suggestions to students on how best to choose an area of specialization. Ernest Boyer, a leading expert on higher education, surveys the role of the major in student learning and argues for an "enriched" major that places the field of study in a cultural, political, and historical context. Former Secretary of Labor Robert Reich describes the types of jobs—and the skills required for them—that will increasingly dominate the U.S. labor market. Distinguished seventeenth-century philosopher and jurist Francis Bacon, one of the originators of the English essay, weighs in with a brief description of the reasons for studying and learning. Although Bacon does not specifically address the question of university study, his essay is very relevant to a consideration of the purposes of college.

The remaining chapters in this unit concern the contemporary university. Professors (and brothers) Robert and Jon Solomon consider the many disparate missions of universities today, and the difficulties students can have in navigating their way through the college experience. Author and activist Paul Rogat Loeb explores—and deplores—the popularity of becoming wealthy as a primary motivation for attending college. Northeastern University President Richard M. Freeland argues that career-based education can be as intellectually challenging and academically rich as traditional study in the arts and sciences. Finally, an essay by writer Zachary Karabell argues that far too many students are attending college these days, and that college can be the wrong choice for many.

The Democratic Framework

Steven Cahn

What is college for? Why do states, for example, spend billions of dollars on higher education? Is college exclusively for the student? Many students these days seem to think college exists so that interested and qualified people willing to work hard can earn a degree and go on to lucrative careers. But is it also about the acquisition of knowledge and personal growth? Are there other, larger purposes, reasons why college benefits us not just as individuals but as a society? What is the role of liberal arts courses in a student's education? Steven Cahn addresses such questions in the following excerpt from his 1979 book Education and the Democratic Ideal. *Cahn is a professor of philosophy and author of more than a dozen books.*

To Consider: *Cahn argues that our democratic form of government in this country requires a certain type of educational system. As you read, pay careful attention to the development of his argument. Where does he convince you? Where do you find yourself questioning his reasoning? What is the basis for your judgments?*

Education is the acquisition of knowledge, skills, and values. But what knowledge, skills, and values ought to be acquired? Who ought to acquire them? And how should they be acquired? These questions highlight the three central concerns of any philosophy of education: the subject matter, the student, and the instructional method. And primary among these is the student, for what is to be learned and how it is to be learned ultimately depend upon who is to do the learning.

Here is where our educational philosophy rests on our political philosophy, for a commitment to the democratic system of government implies a concern for the education of every citizen. In a democracy our own welfare depends heavily upon the wisdom of our neighbors. To some this claim may appear no more than naïve sentimentality, but dismissing it would be a fundamental error, a misunderstanding of the processes of decision-making within a democratic society.

Perhaps no setting better exemplifies the essence of democracy than a polling place on election day. There, waiting to cast ballots, are the various members of the community—the carpenter, the waitress, the lawyer, the bus driver, the street cleaner, the businessman, the piano tuner, the nurse. Each is given one vote, and the will of the majority prevails.

Standing in line right behind one another, we might imagine, are Archie Bunker and a professor of political science. If asked about his preferences, Archie might reply that he doesn't have any idea who's running in this election, but that it doesn't make any difference anyway, since he has voted for the same party all his life and has no intention of ever switching. As for the bond issue that appears in the upper-right-hand corner of the voting machine, he hadn't realized it was there, but now that you've mentioned it, he will be sure to vote against it, since he votes against all bond issues on the grounds that he prefers things just as they are and doesn't care for any changes. (If Archie seems too much a caricature, consider how important a candidate deems the exact position of his name on the ballot. Politicians are well aware that the top spot is preferable, since a sizable number of voters select whichever is the first name on the list, apparently believing that higher is better.)

Standing behind Archie is a university professor who has devoted his life to an intense study of the American political system. He may be familiar with the views of every candidate on the ballot and may even have helped formulate the exact wording of the bond issue. He, like Archie, receives one and only one vote. His erudition entitles him to nothing more.

Does this system make any sense? After all, if you visited a physician and sought advice as to whether to undergo an operation, you would be appalled if he explained that his policy in such cases was to poll a random sampling of passersby and act in accordance with the will of the majority. A community would be similarly dismayed if it hired an engineer to build a bridge, and he appeared one day to announce that he could not decide how deeply to lay the foundations and would like to be guided by a vote of the townspeople. To solve medical or engineering problems, we seek expert judgment, not the uninformed opinions of the populace. Why, then, faced with political problems, do we take the issue to all the people, rather than to a specialist?

Plato asked this question in his *Republic,* and, believing there to be no reasonable answer, he proceeded to construct a system of government based on the view that issues of public policy, being complex, technical matters, ought to be placed in the hands of experts. The Platonic utopia was to be directed and controlled by a small group of philosopher-kings, chosen on the basis of their natural aptitudes and specially educated for their role. Most members of that society were to be mere tradesmen; the farmer was expected only to farm, the cobbler only to cobble. They were to play no role in the governance of the state, and their education, therefore, was to be in the narrowest sense a trade education. Indeed, from Plato's point of view, it would have been a grave mistake even to suggest to a farmer or cobbler that he participate in the affairs of government, for the farmer was naturally fitted only to farm, the cobbler naturally fitted only to cobble. The philosopher-kings were the individuals naturally fitted to rule, and they would do so most effectively if not interfered with by those ill-suited to deliberate about the important decisions affecting the future of their society.

Plato compared the working of a democratic society to the situation aboard a ship on which the sailors are arguing over the control of the helm, while none of them has ever learnt navigation. And if someone on board happens to possess the needed skills, his qualifications are disregarded on the grounds that steering a ship requires no special competence. Plato scornfully observed that ". . . with a magnificent indifference to the sort of life a man has led before he enters politics . . . [a democracy] will promote to honour anyone who merely calls himself the people's friend."

Even the most ardent supporter of the democratic form of government must recognize the force of Plato's trenchant criticisms. But an intelligent commitment to democracy is not based upon a belief in the system's perfection, for no human institution is infallible. The question is not whether democracy has weaknesses; the question is whether democracy has fewer weaknesses than any of the alternatives. And here, I believe, is where Plato's analysis went awry.

By whatever procedures the rulers of an oligarchy are selected, mistakes are possible, and, as the events of history have so often demonstrated, once unrestrained authority is placed in the wrong hands, the results are calamitous. In a democracy the foolish decision made on one occasion can be undone on another, but when all control has been transferred to the oligarchs, second chances are no longer possible. Members of a democracy avoid having to make the difficult, dangerous, and unalterable decision of whom to entrust with absolute power.

Furthermore, however kindhearted the rulers may initially appear, in time they tend to lose touch with those they rule, and even the best-intentioned of sovereigns find it difficult to remain sensitive to the needs and desires of those under their control. Lord Acton's aphorism remains applicable: "Power tends to corrupt; absolute power corrupts absolutely." Faced with debased leadership, citizens of a democracy can vote improvement, but citizens of an oligarchy must either shed their own blood in attempted revolution or else suffer in silence.

Although oligarchs may possess greater expertise in certain technical matters than do other individuals, each member of a society possesses special insight into his own problems, interests, and goals. John Dewey pointed out that "the individuals of the submerged mass may not be very wise. But there is one thing they are wiser about than anybody else can be, and that is where the shoe pinches, the troubles they suffer from." Only the democratic system ensures that this self-knowledge is taken into account in the governmental process.

A democratic society is distinguished, moreover, by the quality of life inherent in its procedures. Competitive elections require the expression of opposing points of view, the protection of the right of citizens to speak freely, to write freely, to assemble freely. The open air of a democracy invites individuality and variety, thereby enhancing the opportunity for increased self-consciousness and self-fulfillment. Conflicting ideas and attitudes produce a vitality that enriches the experience of all.

However, now having made the case for democracy, we should consider the potential weaknesses of the system. It is fine to have faith in the common man, but anyone who realizes the tragic mistakes and gross injustices that have been carried out in accordance with the will of the majority knows how foolish or immoral popularly supported policies can be. And the responsibility for such failures must ultimately be borne by the members of a democracy themselves. No matter how angrily they may denounce their political leaders, the people originally chose them and can by the very same process replace them. Every elected official is aware that in order to retain his position he must be sensitive to the desires of his constituents; if he is out of touch with their wishes, he will soon be forced to seek other employment.

But this power of the people presents democracy with its most crucial problem, for what defense is there against a narrow-minded or gullible citizenry? If the public cannot distinguish reason from demagogy, integrity from duplicity, wisdom from folly, then all is lost. For not only is an open society susceptible to a misguided majority, but by its very nature it offers avenues to power for potential tyrants who, having availed themselves of freedom, would at the first opportunity deny it to others.

So the crucial question is: how can the members of a democracy be provided with the necessary understanding and capability to reap the greatest possible benefits from the democratic process while at the same time protecting that process from those who would seek its destruction? The answer is to be found in the enterprise of education.

Now it becomes clear why in a democracy every individual's education should be of such vital concern. For the ignorance of some is a threat to all. If a person should complain that his democracy is providing too much education for too many people, he thereby reveals his misunderstanding of the nature of a democratic society. How can the electorate be too educated, how can they know too much, how can they be too astute? Too little education, however, and there may soon be no democracy.

The Content of a Liberal Education

Having recognized the need for education within a democracy, we need to determine the appropriate content of that education. In addition to an understanding and appreciation of the democratic system itself, what knowledge, skills, and values are necessary to enable individuals to live intelligently and responsibly as free persons in a free society?

We may begin by noting the obvious fact that all members of a democracy should be able to read, write, and speak effectively. An individual who is unable to understand others or make himself understood is both hindered in his personal growth and unable to participate fully in the free exchange of opinions so vital to the democratic process. A command of language is indispensable in the marketplace of ideas, and hence it is of vital importance for members of a democracy to acquire linguistic facility.

Also essential is an understanding of public issues. How can a citizen sensibly enter into discussion of matters he does not understand? How can he reasonably evaluate the judgment of his representatives if he is unable to comprehend the complexities of the questions they are deciding? In a democracy public issues cover an enormous range of topics, for every action of a government is an appropriate subject for open discussion, and such actions typically involve social, political, economic, scientific, and historical factors. Consider some of the critical issues confronting the world today: poverty, overpopulation, pollution, ideological conflict, the dangers of nuclear warfare, and the possible benefits of space research. How can these matters be intelligently discussed or even understood by those ignorant of the physical structure of the world, the forces that shape society, or the ideas and events that form the background of present crises? Thus substantial knowledge of natural science, social science, world history, and national history is required for all those called upon to think about public issues, and in a democracy such participation is required of everyone. Granted, elected representatives must carry the major burden of formulating and implementing governmental policies. Still, each citizen has both the right and the duty to evaluate and try to influence the decisions of his government.

The study of science requires familiarity with the fundamental concepts and techniques of mathematics, since such notions play a critical role in the natural sciences and an ever increasing role in the social sciences. Furthermore, apart from its use in other inquiries, mathematics is itself an invaluable aid in the handling of everyday affairs, for, as Alfred North Whitehead noted: "Through and through the world is infected with quantity. To talk sense, is to talk in quantities. It is no use saying the nation is large,—How large? It is no use saying that radium is scarce,—How scarce? You cannot evade quantity."

But to know the results of scientific and historical investigations is not sufficient; one must also understand the methods of inquiry that have produced those results. No amount of knowledge brings intellectual sophistication, unless one also possesses the power of critical thinking. To think critically is to think in accord with the canons of logic and scientific method, and such thinking provides needed protection against the lure of simplistic dogmas that appear attractive, yet threaten to cut the lifeline of reason and stifle the intellect. A member of a democracy who cannot spot a fallacious argument or recognize relevant evidence for a hypothesis is defenseless against those who would twist facts to suit their own purpose.

Still another characteristic should be possessed by all members of a democracy: sensitivity to aesthetic experience. An appreciation and understanding of the literature, art, and music of various cultures enriches the imagination, refines the sensibilities, deepens feelings, and provides increased awareness of the world in which we live. In a society of aesthetic illiterates not only the quality of art suffers but also the quality of life.

In connection with the study of literature it should be noted that significant value is derived from reading some foreign literature in its original language. Not only does great literature lose some of its richness in translation, but learning another language increases linguistic sensitivity and makes one more conscious of the unique potentialities and limitations of any particular tongue. Such study is also a most effective means of widening cultural horizons, for understanding another language is a key to understanding another culture.

Another indispensable element of education for members of a democracy is a knowledge of human values. Aristotle long ago recognized that virtue is of two kinds, what he termed "moral virtue" and "intellectual virtue." Moral virtue, which we might call "character," is formed by habit. One becomes good by doing good. Repeated acts of justice and self-control result in a just, self-controlled person who not only performs such acts but does so from an unshakeable disposition.

Intellectual virtue is what we might refer to as "wisdom." In a narrow sense, a wise person is one who is a good judge of value. He can distinguish worth from cost. He is blessed with discernment, discretion, and an abundance of that most precious of qualities, common sense.

But in a broader sense, a wise person is one with intellectual perspective, who is familiar with both the foundations of knowledge and its heights, who can scrutinize the fundamental principles of thought and action while maintaining a view of the world that encompasses both what is and what ought to be. The path to wisdom in this sense lies in the study of those subtle analyses and grand visions that comprise philosophy. Such understanding affords a defense against intimidation by dogmatism while providing a framework for the operation of intelligence.

Clearly, education within a democracy must not be limited to training individuals in occupational techniques, for regardless of a citizen's mode of employment, he is expected to make judgments about sundry matters of public policy, and his education must be broad enough to enable him to do so wisely. Among the Romans such an education was permitted only to freemen (in Latin: liberi), and we thus refer to it as a "liberal education."

It would be a serious error, however, to separate liberal and vocational education. If the members of a democracy are to be not only knowledgeable participants in the political arena but also effective contributors in the social sphere, each should be provided with the necessary skills, social orientation, and intellectual perspective to succeed in some wide field of occupational endeavor. But such vocational education must not be confused with narrow job-training. Animals are broken in and trained; human beings ought to be enlightened and educated. An individual ignorant of the aims of his actions is unable to adjust in the face of changing conditions and is thus stymied by a world in flux. Sidney Hook has observed: "There is a paradox connected with vocational training. The more vocational it is, the narrower it is; the narrower it is, the less likely it is to serve usefully in earning a living . . . there is no reason—except unfamiliarity with the idea—why vocational education should not be liberalized to include the study of social, economic, historical, and ethical questions. . . ." Such broadened vocational preparation is not only of use to the future worker himself; its benefit to society is apparent to anyone who has ever been forced to deal with the mechanized mind of a bureaucrat.

As a means of further clarifying the content of a liberal education, consider the oft-repeated objection that such an education is not relevant. What is the appropriate reply?

Sometimes "relevant" is taken to mean "topical." In this sense a subject is relevant if it deals with current happenings. Thus a Greek tragedy or the history of the United States would not be relevant, whereas productions by avant-garde dramatists or racial conflicts in America today would be. But to use the word "relevant" in this way confuses what is topical with what is timely. The plays of Sophocles were topical only during the golden age of Athens, but they are timely in every age, for they never lose their power to enrich personal experience and deepen our response to the human condition. Slaves in America were freed by 1865, but an understanding of their lives prior to then provides important insights into current social tensions. To confine a liberal education to what is topical would exclude much material of value to all members of a democracy, and so, given that meaning of the term, a liberal education need not be relevant.

On occasion, however, "relevant" is used to refer to any subject concerned with the nature, origin, or solution of the fundamental social, political, intellectual, or moral problems of our time. In this sense a liberal education is indeed relevant, since its very purpose is to enable citizens to make wise decisions about the issues confronting them.

But to avoid distorting this notion of relevance, certain precautions are in order. Not every problem is a fundamental one. A liberal education should, for example, shed light on the nature of capitalism, not merely devise plans to increase sales in a local store. Whatever the heuristic value of such case studies, intellectual perspective involves the power of abstraction.

It must also be emphasized that certain knowledge and skills not explicitly related to any specific contemporary problems are nevertheless crucial to a liberal education, since they form the basis for an intelligent approach to all problems. As we have seen, without linguistic and mathematical facility, without the power of critical thinking, without philosophical sophistication, it would be impossible to deal adequately with the crises of the age.

In addition, concentration upon contemporary events may result in a failure to recognize how inextricably they are tied to the past and how much can be learned about them through a study of the past. The urgencies of present problems should not mislead us into overlooking their historical background, for in order to know where you are going, it is advantageous to know where you have been.

One final note. I have described the content of a liberal education without providing particulars, for they necessarily vary within a changing world. We face difficulties unknown to our ancestors and likely to be forgotten by our descendants. The strength of a liberal education lies in its adaptability to each generation's problems, whether they be long-standing or of recent vintage. What we need to learn depends upon what we need to do, and while some needs remain constant, others are mutable. How easy it is to forget that the intellectual giants who contributed to the making of the modern mind were themselves breakers of tradition, impelled to forge new tools in an effort to handle what were for them the issues of the day.

Reflective Writing: *Steven Cahn begins his argument with a definition: "Education is the acquisition of skills, knowledge, and values" (179). What are the skills, knowledge, and values he believes are most important in education? Make a list based on your own educational priorities and compare the two. What are the differences and how do you account for them?*

The Liberal Arts:
A Practical View

Mark Jackson

*Mark Jackson wrote this essay as a first-year business major committed to a prepro-
fessional education but beginning to consider other possibilities. Looking back on the
essay a year later, he wrote the following:*

> *I entered Freshman English 102 with a number of rigid beliefs about why a college edu-
> cation is valuable. My reasons for attending college were practical. I wanted a higher
> education so that I could get a better job and make more money. College was not going
> to be a time of intrinsic exploration, discovery, and maturation. My roommate and I
> jokingly called that approach the "neo-hippie" mentality. Naturally, the professor who
> taught my Freshman English class disagreed with my narrow view of a higher educa-
> tion. When my English class began to study a number of essays by prominent authors
> on the value of a liberal arts education, I was afforded an excellent opportunity to attack
> this "neo-hippie" view of the college experience. I knew that I held a minority opinion
> on this issue, so I wrote this essay with the specific intention of provoking a response
> from the rest of the class and the professor. I had intended only to challenge their views
> on this subject. As I wrote the essay, however, I started to question my own perspective
> on the value of a liberal arts education. Now, over a year later, some of my opinions are
> quite different.*

To Consider: *Like Steven Cahn in the previous essay, Mark Jackson discusses the
value of a liberal arts education. While reading, consider ways in which Jackson's
essay is similar to and different from Cahn's. Which piece do you find more convincing and why?*

Many students question the reasoning behind a liberal arts education. But
even though they may have been forced to swallow liberal arts propaganda
since junior high, students seldom receive a good explanation for why they
should strive to be "well-rounded." They are told that they should value the
accumulation of knowledge for its own sake, yet this argument does not convince those, like myself, who believe that knowledge must have some practical value or material benefit to be worth seeking.

In "What Is an Idea," Wayne Booth and Marshall Gregory argue con-
vincingly that "a liberal education is an education in ideas—not merely

206

memorizing them, but learning to move among them, balancing one against the other, negotiating relationships, accommodating new arguments, and returning for a closer look" (17). These writers propose that a liberal arts education is valuable to students because it helps to develop their analytical-thinking skills and writing skills. This is, perhaps, one of the best arguments for taking a broad range of classes in many different subjects.

Other more radical arguments in favor of the liberal arts are less appealing. Lewis Thomas, a prominent scientist and physician, believes that classical Greek should form the backbone of a college student's education. This suggestion seems extreme. It is more reasonable to concentrate on the English language, since many students do not have a firm grasp of basic reading and writing skills. Freshman English and other English courses serve as a better foundation for higher education than classical Greek could.

The opposition to a liberal arts curriculum grows out of the values that college-bound students learn from their parents and peers: they place an immeasurable value on success and disregard anything that is not pertinent to material achievements. Students often have trouble seeing what practical value studying a particular discipline can have for them. Teenagers who are headed for the world of nine-to-five employment tend to ignore certain studies in their haste to succeed.

My parents started discussing the possibility of college with me when I was in the sixth grade. They didn't think that it was important for me to go to college to become a more fulfilled human being. My mom and dad wanted me to go to college so that I might not have to live from paycheck to paycheck like they do. Their reason for wanting me to go to college has become my primary motivation for pursuing a college degree.

I remember getting into an argument with my high school counselor because I didn't want to take a third year of Spanish. I was an A student in Spanish II, but I hated every minute of the class. My counselor noticed that I didn't sign up for Spanish III, so he called me into his office to hassle me. I told him that I took two years of a foreign language so that I would be accepted to college, but that I did not want to take a third year. Mr. Gallivan told me that I needed a third year of foreign language to be a "well-rounded" student. My immediate response was "So what?!" I hated foreign languages, and no counselor was going to make me take something that I didn't want or need. I felt Spanish was a waste of time.

I frequently asked my high school counselor why I needed to take subjects like foreign languages and art. He never really gave me an answer (except for the lame idea about being "well-rounded"). Instead, Mr. Gallivan always directed my attention to a sign on the wall of his office which read, There's No Reason for It. It's Just Our Policy! I never found that a satisfactory explanation.

Norman Cousins, however, does offer a more reasonable explanation for the necessity of a liberal education. In his essay "How to Make People Smaller Than They Are," Cousins points out how valuable the humanities are for career-minded people. He says, "The irony of the emphasis being placed on careers is that nothing is more valuable for anyone who has had a professional or vocational education than to be able to deal with abstractions or complexities, or to feel comfortable with subtleties of thought or language, or to think sequentially" (31). Cousins reminds us that technical or vocational knowledge alone will not make one successful in a chosen profession: unique problems and situations may arise daily in the context of one's job, so an employee must be able to think creatively and deal with events that no textbook ever discussed. The workers who get the promotions and advance to high positions are the ones who can "think on their feet" when they are faced with a complex problem.

Cousins also suggests that the liberal arts teach students communication skills that are critical for success. A shy, introverted person who was a straight A student in college would not make a very good public relations consultant, no matter how keen his or her intellectual abilities. Employees who cannot adequately articulate their ideas to a client or an employer will soon find themselves unemployed, even if they have brilliant ideas. Social integration into a particular work environment would be difficult without good communication skills and a wide range of interests and general knowledge. The broader a person's interests, the more compatible he or she will be with other workers.

Though it is obvious that liberal arts courses do have considerable practical value, a college education would not be complete without some job training. The liberal arts should be given equal billing in the college curriculum, but by no means should they become the focal point of higher education. If specialization is outlawed in our institutions of higher learning, then college students might lose their competitive edge. Maxim Gorky has written that "any kind of knowledge is useful" (264), and, of course, most knowledge *is* useful; but it would be insane to structure the college curriculum around an overview of all disciplines instead of allowing a student to master one subject or profession. Universities must seek to maintain an equilibrium between liberal and specialized education. A liberal arts degree without specialization or intended future specialization (such as a master's degree in a specific field) is useless unless one wants to be a professional game show contestant.

Students who want to make the most of their college years should pursue a major course of study while choosing electives or a few minor courses of study from the liberal arts. In this way, scholars can become experts in a profession and still have a broad enough background to insure versatility, both within and outside the field. In a university's quest to produce "well-rounded" students, specialization must not come to be viewed as an evil practice.

If educators really want to increase the number of liberal arts courses that each student takes, they must first increase the popularity of such studies. It is futile to try to get students to learn something just for the sake of knowing it. They must be given examples, such as those already mentioned, of how a liberal education will further their own interests. Instead of telling students that they need to be "well-rounded" and feeding them meaningless propaganda, counselors and professors should point out the practical value and applications of a broad education in the liberal arts. It is difficult to persuade some college students that becoming a better person is an important goal of higher education. Many students want a college education so that they can make more money and have more power. This is the perceived value of a higher education in their world.

Works Cited

Booth, Wayne, and Marshall Gregory, eds. *The Harper and Row Reader.* 2nd ed. New York: Harper, 1988.
_____. "What Is an Idea?" Booth and Gregory 15–18.
Cousins, Norman. "How to Make People Smaller Than They Are." Booth and Gregory 30–32.
Gorky, Maxim. "On Books." Booth and Gregory 255–66.
Thomas, Lewis. "Debating the Unknowable." Booth and Gregory 797–803.

Reflective Writing: *Mark Jackson quotes various authorities in presenting his own views on the role of liberal arts courses in higher education. Examine the quotations from three sources: Wayne Booth and Marshall Gregory, Mr. Gallivan, and Norman Cousins. What are each of these authorities saying, why does Jackson employ them in his discussion, and what is your own response to each?*

What People Learn in College:

The Major

Jacob Neusner

This essay places the academic major in an intellectual and institutional context. The author explains how the major fits into the larger university framework and into a student's overall course of study. He also offers suggestions for deciding on a major, based on a quarter-century experience as a college professor. The essay is by Jacob Neusner, whose piece on criteria for students to grade professors appears in Unit Four.

To Consider: _Before reading, list on paper your own reasons for choosing or being interested in a particular major. Compare these with the suggestions Neusner makes. What differences appear, and what do these differences suggest about your original motives for pursuing a specific course of study?_

The most prominent feature of college, in most people's minds and in fact, is the major or the field of concentration. When you meet a college student, you ask first, Where do you go to college? Then you ask, What's your major? What people say about the major dominates discussion—not what people learn in it, not how people benefit from it. And since college education costs a lot of money, people want to know how they can make a living with what they learn—hence, with what they learn in their major. Who can blame them? But they really are wrong. In later life your major matters very little, and after college few will ask you about it. What you study matters less than what happens to you because of what you study. And you may grow intellectually and emotionally in chemistry as much as in applied math, in the study of religion or of music or of history as much as in political science or sociology, let alone business administration, journalism, nursing, and home economics. Every subject may contribute to your growth in mind and heart and spirit, and any subject may be turned into mind-numbing and soul-killing technicalities.

Well, just what is a major? Who defines and controls a major? Who sells it? Who benefits by having college education organized around the major?

First, "major" or "field of concentration" is that area in which a student takes about a quarter to a third or even half of the courses required for the degree, and in which the level of courses generally proceeds from elementary to advanced. The major thus defines the subject or area the student learns with special emphasis. It is the one field, among many, about which students are supposed to be well informed. Accordingly, the challenge of the junior and senior years reflects the rewards of sustained learning, or the major. Here, it is clear, students focus their attention and time; they progress onward and upward, and they move from being passive recipients of facts to being active participants in the quest for learning. They rise to those mature levels of intellect—in some one, specific subject, to be sure—to which, in coming to college, they aspire. What stands behind the idea of a major? First, the theory, then, the politics. And then the strategy for developing a major.

Theory

The theory is that the human sciences organize themselves in one of two ways. They seek general rules, applicable in a broad range of human worlds ("cultures," "societies," and other historical entities). These rules form such disciplines as psychology, history, sociology, anthropology, or the historical study of religion; they come from anywhere and apply everywhere. For these rules, specific human worlds serve as exemplary materials, that is, we see how history or sociology or the science of politics works in one country or another. The other mode of organization—when rightly done it will complement the first—focuses upon the distinctive traits of a particular human world. You study one small subject and seek to interpret that subject in such a way as to make it tell you about the broader human condition. You study, for instance, American history or French literature or the experience of women through history. In those specific subjects, you learn about what it means to be a human being in America, what it means to use your imagination in France, how a particular sex encounters the issues of life common to both.

In theory, universities organize work in the human sciences in both of these ways, with disciplinary departments, such as political science, sociology, and history, in which the same methods apply to a diversity of problems and settings, and with interdisciplinary departments, such as classics, Egyptology, religious studies (involving both history and philosophy of religion), and American, Slavic, black, women's, or Judaic studies. In these departments, people bring a broad range of questions to a particular human world. Both modes of organizing learning prove their worth every day. No student's education is complete without a systematic acquaintance with each. In the one the student learns to see things whole and all together; in the other, the student learns to see things in detail and with respect for difference, specificity, and even the imponderable of what seems private and particular, yet addresses the human condition as everyone knows it. The hard sciences, for their part, focus upon the natural world—its biology, its chemistry, for instance—and through that one thing teach method about how to study everything. So much for the theory. Now to the politics.

Politics

The major reflects the power of the department and the politics of the university. If professors are influential, then the subject they teach will attract attention and financial support; if they are not, then their subject will be labeled trivial or unimportant. Both subjects may prove equally significant, but politics will dictate which set of courses thrives and which one perishes. When, for example, a university faculty decides which subjects form the "core" of the curriculum (that is, the group of courses to be required), these chosen subjects are frequently those taught by the professors in the room the day they voted on a new curriculum. When choosing a college or a major, take this fact into account. If you want to study foreign languages, and the budgets of the departments that teach foreign languages are being cut back, then that is not the college for you. If the major you wish to pursue is taught by a department not held in high esteem, then go to a college in which it is.

Departments usually define majors. Given what we claim a major is, we should expect that the nature and structure of a discipline or subject should define the rules of mastering that subject or discipline. If a major is supposed to present a well-organized and systematic process of learning a given subject, then a major should emerge logically from the definition and structure of that subject, first things first, second things second, unimportant things never. But too often that is not how it works.

The program of courses required by a major is haphazard. Rarely do departments define the purpose of the major; or if they do, rarely do they define it in terms of what students actually do and how courses really lead students from level to level. The well-organized and logically structured majors usually come from the natural sciences and mathematics, engineering and computer science departments, rarely from the social sciences, and never from the humanities. In fields in which knowledge is factual and set, rather than a function of taste and judgment, a major can be constructed as a composition of logical progression from fact to fact, skill to skill, method to method. Try learning calculus without algebra and you'll see what I mean.

In the humanities and in most of the social sciences, the major often presents a mishmash of what professors happen to be teaching that year. True, many departments will offer what they call a methods course, by which they mean a course in the basic approaches, questions, and problem-solving techniques of the subject. Or, at the very least, they will present a course bearing the lowest possible number, for example, 1, and let people assume that that course introduces the subject. After all, it stands before No. 2, No. 20, or No. 200. But if you look into that introductory course in English, history, religious studies, and the like, you see, for good or ill, nothing either less, or more, elementary than what you see in courses that allegedly rest upon and build upon that introductory course. These second and third level courses will strike you as more specific and limited in focus. They will be, for example, not about Europe in the twentieth century, but about the causes of World War I; not about the formation of the American nation, but about theories of the American revolution. The description of the subject explains only what is covered. It rarely indicates that the methods or disciplines, the intellectual challenge of the course, stand upon a foundation already laid down. The upper level course may not even take for granted information already mastered in an earlier course. For the truth is that, in general, the humanities and a fair part of the social sciences do not present subjects that allow for system, for the logical unfolding of methods or techniques. When we deal with issues of taste and judgment, experience in reflection and wisdom, what orderly sequence leads step by step from the ignorant to the wise person?

A major is meant to balance the diffuse and diverse curriculum, within which a student makes choices, by setting up a cogent and coherent segment of the curriculum for a student's close attention. But the major may well present diffusion and diversity on a small scale. Rather than redefine the subject and how it is taught, a department will set requirements that will give the appearance of order, structure, and logic, in order to validate its existence as a department, as a coherent field of study. You must keep this in mind when you begin to develop your major.

The great educator, Jonathan Z. Smith, who served as dean of the college at the University of Chicago, phrases the matter succinctly in *Choice:*

> In most cases, departments and majors lack coherence because they are neither subject matters nor disciplines. Rather than the principled stipulation of a domain of inquiry (a perfectly legitimate endeavor), they are the result of a series of gentlemen's agreements. Take, as an example, a department or a major in English literature—frequently one of the larger and most politically self-conscious units on campus. Scholars in English employ a host of methods, not one of which is unique to their field of inquiry, most of which are shared with the majority of other departments in the humanities and, increasingly, with the social sciences as well. Nor is there any coherent limit, any modesty, to their domain. Almost anything printed from left to right in Roman type may be taught: from Greek tragedies to world literature; from myth to mysticism; psychoanalytic theory, social anthropology, popular literature, technical texts.

Smith sees the first course in the major as a well-organized survey. The last course provides for individual research of some kind. But he says, "What comes in between is political rather than substance: a course with each of the major professors." He further argues that when people plan degrees, majors, and courses, they make choices. Since no one can, or would want to, learn everything about everything, all of education begins in a set of choices. He therefore holds that whatever we do requires justification and rationalization:

> I take as a corollary to this that each thing taught or studied is taught or studied not because it is "there," but because it is an example, an *exempli gratia* of something fundamental that may serve as a precedent for further interpretation and understanding. By providing an arsenal of skills and paradigms from which to reason, that which may first appear to be strange or novel can become intelligible.
>
> Given this: that each thing which is taught is taught by way of an example and that the curriculum is an occasion for institutional choice, then the primary choice is: What shall the things taught exemplify? This ought to be explicit in every academic endeavor, at every level of the curriculum.

He further concedes explicitly:

> To these matters of choice and exemplification, no single answer can be given. These must remain institutional choices which fit each institution's peculiar ecology. But we may demand that they be articulated, and tested for, and that the goals be explicitly built into every course of study and not left for accidental discovery by a student. Students ought not to be asked to organize and integrate what the faculty will not. Distribution requirements—whether at the level of general education or the middle-range of the major, violate these two injunctions at will.

Once we recognize that the curriculum, the major, the department, come to us because of a combination of political and intellectual circumstances, we face a new set of tasks. We must make up our minds about issues on which "the experts" cannot help us. Departments do not usually exhibit intellectual coherence. It follows that human knowledge—"everything about everything"—will not reach us when considerations other than intellectual ones intervene in how that knowledge finds definition and categorization. If the bulk of what we know as true constitutes the outcome of processes of taste and judgment, as much as weighing and measuring, then the individual's power to exercise that taste, that judgment, should predominate. And this is the premise to follow in defining your major.

Choosing a Major

Exactly how, then, should you choose your major? Precisely the way you choose your courses—but much more carefully. Here are the criteria that seem to me decisive:

1. The major should be offered by a strong department and be made up of courses taught by first-rate professors. Do not choose a major merely because the subject interests you. If the professors who give the courses that make up the major are boring or trivial, they will rapidly persuade you that the subject of the

major is not so interesting. The department should offer lectures by guests and other extracurricular programs.

2. The major should take up a subject that interests you. Even the greatest professor of mathematics could not turn me into a mathematician, though I loved the subject. At some point, at about stage three of any theorem, I always end up asking myself why I have to know all this. You too should know in your heart why you must know the subject at hand, the major you have chosen.

3. The major should concern a subject or discipline that you think you would like to continue to study after college. It should bear so immediately and in such an important way upon your long-term plans that you can imagine continuing the study twenty years after college.

4. The major should not direct you, the month after college, into a particular job. It should not provide those skills that will permit you to make your living right away. If it does, you may find those skills obsolete, as knowledge grows and technology changes. What is relevant today to how you make a living may prove irrelevant to making a living tomorrow.

If you think Number 1 contradicts Number 2 and Number 3 contradicts Number 4, you are not totally wrong. What I am suggesting is that you balance your decisions so that your education turns out to be both intellectually stimulating and personally interesting, long-lasting, and in some ways useful.

Still, what matters most is the intellectual strength, the scholarly commitment and vitality, the academic authenticity of the professors in the department you choose. Take as an example a field I know well: the academic study of religion. The field attracts students because of the intrinsic interest of the subject of religion, to which most people, in this country, are exposed as they grow up. When you consider the issues addressed in the study of religion, you cover the whole range of human knowledge and experience: culture, society, literature, art, music, dance, how we feel and how we think, all in relationship to God, history, and eternity. Yet the field of religion as an academic subject has yet to define for itself high standards of learning, even appropriate subject matter and an ongoing curriculum. So people can teach anything they want and call it "religion," because religion is anything people say it is. And anyone can declare himself or herself not just a person who professes a religion but a professor of religion. So here I find Numbers 1 and 2 in serious conflict, since you can study a great subject with frauds and know-nothings.

The conflict of Numbers 3 and 4 is more obvious. Prelaw students used to think they should study Latin, because the law books use Latin phrases. These days that notion seems out of date. But today prelaw students imagine they should study political science or government, just as prebusiness students take for granted they should study economics, and premedical students biology. And the engineers-to-be take a lot of engineering courses. And why not? These students are not wrong, but they often limit themselves too early in life to subjects they will learn better and more currently later on.

Worse, they close doors they should leave open. Later on they may feel a sense of inadequacy about such subjects as literature, art, music, history, and philosophy and not read related books or go to plays *they* would enjoy. More important, they may discover that what they think does not matter to lawyers, doctors, engineers, and women and men in business because they are not well-rounded enough to speak of critical issues and concerns to people in all those professions. So choose your major with those same considerations of balance and proportion that go into the selection of your courses.

One final thought: In choosing your major, don't forget that after college you're allowed to read books. In the four years of college you don't have to learn everything you're ever going to know. So in choosing your major, you might even leave something for later.

Reflective Writing: *What, according to Neusner, is a major, and what is its role in the university? Evaluate his criteria for choosing a major. How do these criteria relate to the author's assertion in another publication that "we in universities have a single purpose: to open minds to new ideas"?*

Specialization:

The Enriched Major

Ernest Boyer

Much of the coursework you undertake in college will be devoted to your major. But what exactly is a major? What knowledge and skills should it impart? Ernest Boyer is former president of the Carnegie Foundation for the Advancement of Teaching and author of numerous books and reports on higher education. He takes up these questions in this essay from his 1987 book, College: The Undergraduate Experience in America. *Boyer advances the idea of an "enriched" major that goes beyond narrow job training. For Boyer, the enriched major encourages students "not only to explore a field in depth, but also to help them put their field of special study in perspective" (110).*

To Consider: *As you read, think about the major you are considering. What are Boyer's main arguments about how and why a major should be "enriched"? What are the advantages of such enrichment? Are there any disadvantages, from your own perspective? How does this notion of an enriched major relate to your own reasons for choosing a particular area of study?*

What's your major?

If there were a contest for the most popular question on the American campus, that would be the winner. The latest edition of the *College Blue Book* lists more than six thousand different majors and the number is rapidly expanding. From Sun Belt colleges to universities in the Ivy League, careerism dominates the campus.

At most colleges in our study, we found the baccalaureate degree sharply divided between general and specialized education. Students overwhelmingly have come to view general education as an irritating interruption—an annoying detour on their way to their degree. They all too often do not see how such requirements will help them get a job or live a life.

This unhealthy separation between the liberal and useful arts, which the curriculum and the faculty too often reinforce, tends to leave students poorly served and the college a weak and divided institution. We take the position that if the undergraduate experience is to be renewed, general and specialized education must be viewed as contributing to common, not competing, ends.

Most students agree that pursuing a special field of study, one that leads to a career, is the main reason for going to college—and for staying, too. Over a third of the undergraduates at public institutions and slightly fewer of those at private ones say that if college did not increase their prospects for employment they would drop out.

The push toward career-related education has come to dominate most campuses and, during the past fifteen years, it has dramatically increased. At almost all colleges in our study, new vocational majors have been added and old ones have been split up into smaller pieces. One East Coast university had just one major in forestry in 1965. By 1975, forestry had become a separate college offering four different majors. By 1985, when we visited the institution, the college had seven majors in this division, including three specialties in horticulture alone: fruit and vegetable horticulture, ornamental horticulture, and turf-grass horticulture.

Another university we visited offered only one major in business administration in 1965. The faculty, in response to marketplace demand, dramatically expanded the program. Last year we found not one, but twenty-one, business-related majors. Here's the list: administrative office management; business and office education; domestic public administration; employee services and industrial recreation; fashion merchandising; finance; foods and nutrition in business; general business; health services administration; international public administration; labor relations; management; management information systems; marketing; marketing and distributive education; occupational safety and health; operations management; organizational and mass communications; personnel management; professional accounting; and societal relations in business and industry.

These examples reflect the pattern nationwide. Between 1968 and 1984, the percentage of baccalaureate degrees awarded in business, computer science, engineering, and the health professions increased, while the percentage of degrees awarded in traditional liberal arts fields, especially foreign languages and the physical and social sciences, went down along with education degrees, reflecting, among other things, changes in the job market and new career options for women (Table 1).

The shift toward business and away from the liberal arts has been described as the new vocationalism in higher education and, based on the preferences of today's students, it seems likely that, in the short term, this pattern will persist. In 1970, when entering freshmen were asked about their preferred majors, the largest percentage chose "arts and humanities." In 1985, the percentage choosing this field had declined by more than half. During the same period, physical science showed a similar decline. In

TABLE 1   Baccalaureate Degrees in Selected Disciplines as a Percentage of Total
Baccalaureate Degrees Conferred

	1968	1973	1978	1981	1984	Change 1968 to 1984
Biological sciences	5	5	6	5	4	−1
Business	13	14	18	22	24	11
Computer science*	0	0	1	2	3	3
Education	21	20	15	12	10	−11
Engineering	6	6	6	8	10	4
Fine arts	4	4	4	4	4	0
Foreign languages	3	2	1	1	1	−2
Health professions	3	4	7	7	7	4
Physical sciences	3	2	3	3	2	−1
Social sciences	19	17	12	11	10	−9

*Degrees in computer science were less than 1 percent of all baccalaureate degrees awarded in 1968 and 1973.

SOURCE: U.S. Department of Education, National Center for Education Statistics, *Digest of Education* statistics, 1970, p. 89; Ibid., 1976, pp. 111–16; Ibid., 1980, pp. 120–24; Ibid., 1983–84, pp. 113–17; data for 1984, U.S. Department of Education, Center for Statistics, unpublished surveys of "Earned Degrees Conferred."

contrast, the percentage of freshmen who identified business as their intended major increased from 16 to 27 percent. Today, business is the most popular field of undergraduate study (Table 2).

For years, "specialization" has been the watchword for employers, too. In spite of impressive speeches by corporate leaders, when it is recruitment time on campus, business and engineering majors are often chosen first. The director of career development at one college told us she had talked with an executive at the local manufacturing plant about placing a bright English major. The executive said he would not even talk to the woman until she had taken some business courses.

Students, in their search for a secure future, have read the signals all too literally, and the liberal arts have taken a back seat to the more practical, career-related training. But there are signals that the pendulum may be swinging back. "I sense a shift in interest toward people with more generalist backgrounds and less practical, specialized, technical training," said Christopher Shinkman, the former director of Stanford University's placement office. "Employers recently have begun looking harder for liberal arts people."

A survey of 2,813 businessmen who require computer skills in their operations revealed that reading ability, reasoning skills, and personal enthusiasm rank far more importantly than technical training for new employees. A study by Northwestern University shows that many major companies plan to increase their hiring of liberal arts graduates by some 20 percent.

TABLE 2   Percentage of Entering Freshmen Intending to Major in Selected Fields of Study, 1970–85

Intended Major	1970	1975	1983	1984	1985	Change 1970 to 1985
Arts and humanities	21	13	8	8	8	−13
Biological sciences	4	6	4	4	3	−1
Business	16	19	24	26	27	+11
Education	12	10	6	7	7	−5
Engineering	9	8	12	11	11	+2
Physical science	6	4	3	3	2	−4
Professional occupations*	X	X	14	14	13	−1
Social science	9	6	6	7	8	−1

*Includes architecture, home economics, library science, nursing, and related health professions.

X: Professional occupations category not comparable in years 1970 and 1975 with years later than 1980.

SOURCE: Alexander Astin and Associates, *The American Freshman: National Norms for Fall 1970* and other selected years (Los Angeles: Cooperative Institutional Research Program), 1970, p. 41; 1975, p. 44; 1983, pp. 46–47; 1984, pp. 48–49; 1985, pp. 48–49.

Caught in the crossfire of competing interests, many campuses still are torn between careerism and the goals of liberal learning. At one college we visited, members of the faculty complained bitterly about the way the baccalaureate degree, as one professor put it, "is now the property of the professional schools and controlled by accrediting committees." In contrast, a professor of marketing said, "I have nothing at all against students taking courses in literature and the arts. But those things they can pick up on their own later in life if they're interested. My students tell me what they're here for is to get a good practical education that will serve them in the working world."

A history professor told us he was "deeply offended" by his college's policy of adding majors at "the whim" of local business interests. He said, "The administration is destroying any hope that this will become a respected educational institution. They are trying to create a multiversity, all things to all people, and when you do that, quality education suffers." In response, the president said "the college risks losing political support if it does not respond to community needs. If financial leaders want more business courses, we'll have more business courses."

At another college an English professor described the conflict this way: "There really is the 'two cultures' phenomenon on this campus. The two sides have a hard time talking to each other. Today there is some superiority emanating from the technical side. They feel confident these days. And you hear it from students, too, who say their professors are continually speaking disparagingly about the humanities, degrading the people who teach it."

The head of the faculty senate spoke still more bluntly: "It seems obvious that someone should bring together the humanities and technical faculty for a 'peace conference.' Everyone should be checked for weapons at the door. The amount of misunderstanding and hostility crackling between the 'two cultures' is amazing and, considering our liberal arts mission, probably destructive. Each side needs somehow to be convinced that they are working for similar objectives."

In our national survey of faculty we found attitudes about specialized and general education split almost down the middle. On one hand, 45 percent of the faculty reported that they would prefer teaching courses that focused on "limited specialties," rather than those that covered a wide variety of material. On the other hand, about half the faculty said that undergraduate education in America would be improved if there were *less* emphasis on specialized training and more on liberal education. About 40 percent agreed that the typical undergraduate curriculum has suffered from the specialization of faculty members. Then again, about half the faculty said they prefer teaching students who have a clear idea of the career they will be taking (Table 3).

This ambivalence reflects, we suspect, a deeper conflict among faculty over goals. We found, for example, that on some campuses, faculty opposed new career-related majors because they were considered "too novel" or "too new." Overlooked in such debates was the fact that most disciplines that now have status within the academy—modern languages, laboratory sciences, for example—were themselves once considered too novel for the academy to embrace. Professor Frederick Rudolph reminds us that at the turn of the century, "At [the University of] Chicago chemists fought zoologists over disputed scientific territory, and economists fought sociologists as both laid claim to statistics. History and classics fought for control of ancient history at Harvard." We conclude that the "newness" of a proposed field of study is not a sufficient reason for its rejection, nor should tradition alone be used to justify holding to an existing major.

We also found a resistance to new majors not just because of newness, but because the graduates would work in less prestigious fields. We heard it

TABLE 3 Faculty Attitudes Toward Specialized Education

	Percent Who Agree
I prefer teaching courses which focus on limited specialties to those which cover a wide variety of materials.	45
Undergraduate education in America would be improved if there were less emphasis on specialized training and more on broad liberal education.	53
The typical undergraduate curriculum has suffered from the specialization of faculty members.	41
In my undergraduate courses I prefer teaching students with a clear idea of the career they will be taking.	47

SOURCE: The Carnegie Foundation for the Advancement of Teaching. National Survey of Faculty, 1984.

argued, for example, that it is all right to prepare students to be doctors, but not nurses. To educate future college teachers is applauded, but to prepare students to teach in elementary school is considered a less worthy task. To dig ruins of the past as an archeologist is considered a respectable career objective, but to work with ruined lives in an urban jungle as a social worker is a less well-regarded field of study. Lost in these debates was the recognition that college graduates, instead of being demeaned by all but the prestigious professions, can, in fact, lift up a job and give it meaning.

But the most heated curriculum debates we encountered focused not on the newness or the status of a major, but on whether the proposed program was too "job-related." Here the battle lines were most sharply drawn. Many faculty members, especially those at liberal arts colleges, voiced the opinion that it is inappropriate for colleges to offer majors that are primarily "vocational." At one faculty meeting we attended, a science professor declared that the college would be "demeaned" if it offered programs that lead directly to a job. At a small college in the Northwest, the faculty recently voted down a proposed major in computer science. "It doesn't belong in the curriculum in the liberal arts. It's tied too closely to a job," we were told.

Again, what we found missing in these discussions was the recognition that a university education has always been considered "useful." Samuel Eliot Morison reminds us that the first formal universities were "distinctly purposeful." There was a utility to learning and students enrolled to prepare themselves for what was considered worthy work. The University of Salerno was a medical school and the universities that followed in its wake— Bologna, Paris, Oxford, Cambridge—offered only four courses of study— law, medicine, theology, and the arts. The first three were explicitly vocational, and law was the most popular of all the medieval studies.

The practical nature of the medieval university was portrayed vividly by C. P. Snow in a short narrative history of Cambridge University. Students, he wrote, studied a curriculum that would seem to us "arid, valueless, just word chopping." They attended classes in "cold, comfortless, straw-strewn rooms," some "in bitter poverty and half starved." They did this for one motive; "if they could get their degree, jobs lay ahead. Jobs in the royal administration, the courts, the church; jobs teaching in the schools—the fees were not light, and the teachers made a good living. The training was in fact vocational, and jobs lay at the end."

The point is that all students, regardless of their major, are preparing for productive work. As with engineering and business and computer science, a student who majors in English or biology or history will, it is assumed, someday become employed and use what he or she has learned for some useful end. Even the most traditional colleges expect their graduates to move on to careers. And a great embarrassment for a department occurs when its graduates "cannot get placed."

This is not to suggest that colleges become vocational schools; nor does it mean that every kind of career preparation is appropriate for the baccalaureate degree. In response to marketplace demands, many institutions are offering narrow technical training and providing credentialing for occupations, devoid of rich intellectual content. Therefore, in judging the merits of a major, the issue is not the newness, or status, or even the utility of the program. Rather, the basic test of a proposed major is this: Does the field of study have a legitimate intellectual content of its own and does it have the capacity to enlarge, rather than narrow, the vision of the student?

We conclude that career preparation in the undergraduate experience means more than a job. At its best, such an education will help students not only to be technically prepared but also to discover the personal and social significance of work. Thomas F. Green puts the challenge this way:

> . . . if we are to understand the relationship between education and work we need to make a *sharp distinction between work and job.* There is an enormous difference between the person who understands his career as a succession of jobs and a person who understands the succession of jobs he has held as all contributing to the accomplishment of some work . . . Work is basically the way that people seek to redeem their lives from futility. It, therefore, requires the kind of world in which hope is possible, which is to say, the kind of world that yields to human effort.

The challenge then is to enlarge lives by bringing meaning to the world of work. And the special task of the undergraduate college is to relate the values of liberal learning to vocation. Therefore, what we propose, as a centerpiece of the undergraduate experience, is the *enriched major.* By an *enriched major* we mean encouraging students not only to explore a field in depth, but also to help them put their field of special study in perspective. The major, as it is enriched, will respond to three essential questions: What is the history and tradition of the field to be examined? What are the social and economic implications to be understood? What are the ethical and moral issues to be confronted?

Here then is the heart of our curriculum proposal: Rather than view the major as competing with general education, we are convinced that these two essential parts of the baccalaureate program should be intertwined. Through such a curriculum the student can move from depth to breadth as departments put the specialty in larger context. If a major is so narrow and so technical that it *cannot* be discussed in terms of its historical and social implications, if the work in the proposed field of study cannot be a broadening experience, then the department is offering mere technical training that belongs in a trade school, not on a college campus, where the goal is liberal learning.

And yet we found that in many fields, skills have become ends. Scholars are busy sorting, counting, and decoding. We are turning out technicians. But the crisis of our time relates not to technical competence, but to a loss of social and historical perspective, to the disastrous divorce of competence from conscience. Alfred North Whitehead wrote about "the unimportance—indeed, the evil—of barren knowledge." Knowledge, Whitehead argued, becomes important only when we *use* it, and, we might add, apply it to humane ends.

Professionals in almost every field—doctors, journalists, lawyers, businessmen, computer specialists, biochemists, stockbrokers—once they begin to practice their craft, must respond to questions that relate not just to the "what" and "how" of the field, but to the "why" as well. Specialists must make judgments that are not only technically correct but also include ethical and social considerations. And the values professionals bring to their work are every bit as crucial as the particularities of the work itself.

But the foundation of an advanced service society is quality, not quantity. A television set is a complex instrument, but producing high-quality sets in large numbers is much easier than producing high-quality programming. Designing high-powered automobiles, fast trains, and supersonic airplanes requires technological skills, but we are far from designing environments and transportation systems that effectively serve human needs. And, given the escalating rates of divorces compared to happy, solid marriages, it looks as though putting a microwave oven in every kitchen is easier than having a congenial dinner.

In an editorial titled "How to Make People Smaller Than They Are," Norman Cousins wrote:

> The doctor who knows only disease is at a disadvantage alongside the doctor who knows at least as much about people as he does about pathological organisms. The lawyer who argues in court from a narrow legal base is no match for the lawyer who can connect legal precedents to historical experience and who employs wide-ranging intellectual resources. The business executive whose competence in general management is bolstered by an artistic ability to deal with people is of prime value to his company. For the technologist, the engineering of consent can be just as important as the engineering of moving parts.

Can the undergraduate experience be viewed as an integrated whole? Again, it was Whitehead, in his famous essay "The Aims of Education," who declared that "there can be no adequate technical education which is not liberal, and no liberal education which is not technical . . . Education should turn out the pupil with something he knows well and something he can do well." We are confident that the goals of general education, when properly defined, can be accomplished through the major. The liberal and the useful arts can be brought together in the curriculum just as they inevitably must be brought together during life. Such linkage should be cultivated in all disciplines, and be exemplified in the lives of those who teach them.

Consider these examples: Students specializing in computer science might be introduced to the history of technology and the social impact of the information revolution. English majors could be asked to explore the roots of language and consider how symbol systems can be creatively used or dangerously abused. Those in architecture, genetics, industrial chemistry, and television production might be asked to examine the social and ethical implications of their work. The pre-engineering student would understand that beyond technical skills there are concerns for the physical environment to be considered.

During our study we found both good and bad examples. One college, for example, has a textile management major in which fifty-four semester hours of textile courses—"Yarn Structures and Form," "Textile Costing Inventory Control," and "Fabric Structure"—were required. Courses such as these consume about 40 percent of a student's time; business courses take another 16 percent. A total of 56 percent of the student's program is devoted to this major.

It is difficult to believe that this laundry list of courses represents a legitimate discipline. Much of this can be better learned on the job, and specialized information is too often imparted without an intellectual framework. Course descriptions speak only of "skills"—the sort of statement one finds in trade school pamphlets and brochures. Nowhere is the student encouraged to view the specialty in larger context. As now organized and taught, the program does not make the grade as an enriched major.

In contrast, we found at a large state university a journalism major in which students are being offered breadth in a field that is often considered narrow. In this program there are courses on the history of communication and the ethics of journalism. The dean said, "I feel strongly that an undergraduate program is for people who are not experienced enough to be sure of what they want. Not all of the students here are primarily interested in journalism as a career. We have at least fifteen a year who go to law school. We do not owe a student just a ready-made formula for career training."

Like this journalism major, the business major at another university is also known for its enrichment. "It's a big part of our reputation," says the Director of Undergraduate Programs. "As a faculty, we have decided, several times, to keep the undergraduate program very general, to look at the larger context, and not get down to the technical aspects of management. We don't want narrowly trained undergraduates—we think we're honing minds here. They should see business as a social enterprise."

At Northeastern University, both humanities and professional school faculty have long been concerned with the narrow orientation of their students. The colleges of Pharmacy, Business Administration, and Criminal Justice have now each hired at least one humanist, and the social science departments have increased offerings in policy areas relevant to the professional schools. Communication between traditionally isolated colleges of the university has increased, and faculty research has developed out of themes presented in these new courses.

Stanford University has a program in human biology that introduces students to policy problems, such as population and hunger, pollution, conservation of natural resources, and the costs and delivery of health care. In addition to traditional requirements in biology and statistics, students take either health or environmental policy courses and complete a supervised project that involves them in a community service agency. Faculty are drawn from the medical school and traditional departments of the university.

Worcester Polytechnic Institute in Massachusetts has completely revised its undergraduate engineering program. The new "WPI Plan" is designed to educate "technological humanists." The institute states its educational philosophy as follows:

> The learning of facts without values can no longer be acceptable. Scientists and engineers must be able to evaluate the consequences of modern technology and of their own decisions in the world we live in. Social scientists and humanists, on the other hand, must develop a greater understanding of the basic forces of technology.
>
> We need people today who can understand both technology and its social implications, who understand their machines and also have an awareness of their place in the human spectrum. Specialization must be tempered with interdisciplinary breadth, for the solutions to the problems of our technological world demand minds of wide scope.

Sir Eric Ashby, the noted British educator, wrote: "The path to culture should be through a man's specialism, not by by-passing it . . . A student who can weave his technology into the fabric of society can claim to have a liberal education; a student who cannot weave his technology into the fabric of society cannot claim even to be a good technologist."

As the major begins to intersect with the themes of common learning, students can return, time and time again, to considerations of language, heritage, social institutions, and the rest. At a college of quality when a major is so enriched, it leads the student from depth to breadth and focuses not on mere training, but on liberal learning at its best.

In the end, integrating the liberal and the useful arts depends every bit as much on people as on programs. Courses alone do not bring coherence. Faculty must provide the enlightening and integrative foundation so essential to a successful undergraduate experience. They should not only be devoted to their disciplines but also embody and exemplify in the classroom the spirit of a liberal education.

Reflective Writing: *What exactly does Boyer mean by an enriched major, and why does he feel a major should be enriched? What would your own intended field of study need to include in order to fit Dr. Boyer's definition? How would you personally benefit (or not) from an enriched major?*

Hire Education:

The Secretary of Labor Tells You Where the Jobs Will Be in the New Economy

Robert B. Reich

This 1994 essay by then United States Secretary of Labor Robert Reich was published in Rolling Stone *and, unlike many of the readings in this book, was therefore intended to be read by an audience of young people. In this article, Reich lays out his view of where the national (and international) economy is going and what education and skills students will need to prosper in the years to come. Reich lists four rules or guidelines, emphasizing flexibility, collaboration, technology, and a long-term commitment to learning.*

To Consider: *Secretary Reich describes certain characteristics of the working world where your generation will be looking for employment. Highlight these features as you read. What conclusions can you draw from his comments about the world of work as it exists now and as he suggests it will exist in the future?*

When historians chronicle the 20th century's final decade, they will tell the story of a generation of young Americans who came of age at the moment our economy underwent its most dramatic transformation. The first rumbles of this change began several years ago, and its tremors have already shaken the lives of many older people. But the women and men now in their 20s—the workers who will track their way through the new economy—will have to learn which of these seismic shifts will open opportunities and which will produce pitfalls. This, more than any other factor, will determine what kinds of lives they lead.

Who are we talking about? Numbers narrate the tale most vividly. This generation is small. In 1973, people in their 20s made up 27 percent of the work force; in 1993, they made up 23 percent. In theory, fewer people in the work force ought to reduce the competition for jobs, along with the anxiety this competition sparks. But the reverse is happening; something else is going on.

Young people actually are earning less than their parents. In 1973, the typical man between the ages of 25 and 34 earned nearly $30,000 a year. In 1993, he earned only $21,604 (in inflation-adjusted dollars). Young women's earnings did increase—but far more slowly than earnings for women of other ages. Today, the median income of households headed by people under 30 is 15 percent lower than it was two decades earlier. This explains why so many members of the generation boomerang back home to live with their parents. They're not too lazy or too timid to live on their own, as some of the media have suggested—they can't afford it.

This decline is just the most visible feature of the new economy's landscape, but it's a slippage that hints at the tectonic shift going on beneath us: the radical divergence of earning power between those with marketable skills and those without. Last year, the average college-educated 25-to-34-year-old man earned $40,035. For women it was $30,542. Compare that with the earnings of Americans of the same age who had not received a high-school diploma. Men earned an average of $18,187; women, $14,500. It's a notable set of statistics: one college graduate earns more than two people who didn't graduate from high school. This is the largest gulf between high earners and low earners in our nation's history.

The main reason for this gap is the demise of steady mass-production jobs. In the past 20 years, the proportion of 25-to-34-year-old workers in traditional blue-collar work dropped from 36 percent to 28 percent, while the share in white-collar positions rose from 52 percent to 57 percent. This is the first generation to hold a "McJob," the first for which a clothing store (called, ironically enough, the Gap) has become both an arbiter of fashion trends and a significant employer of job-hungry youth.

It's even worse in the inner cities for a growing number of young people who lack the education, job networks and transportation links necessary to obtain any job in the legitimate economy. According to the 1990 census, during any given week, more than one-half of all males 16 and older who live in high-poverty areas are not working. More than one in three men in high-poverty areas reported not working even a single day during the entire year.

For those who do work—whether it's behind a fast-food counter or behind a trading desk—the person beside you is more likely than ever to be a woman. In 1973, 57 percent of women in their 20s were in the work force. Twenty years later, the figure had climbed to 73 percent.

All of these trends tangle above the surface, but they grow from common roots. During the lifetime of this generation, America has moved from an economy founded on companies making more and more of the same product at lower and lower prices to an economy founded on companies quickly providing customized products that meet the tailored needs of smaller groups of customers.

To succeed in the old economy, many workers merely had to follow orders and perform the same routine tasks day after day. But in the new economy, success will hinge on the ability to quickly identify and solve problems. And an economy where these skills determine who wins and who loses is an economy that operates by a new set of rules.

Rule 1. Be Prepared to Change Collars

For years the picture of American prosperity was the man in the gray flannel suit, the relatively content 9-to-5 white-collar commuter. But it has become painfully obvious that this middle-class icon is fading. Companies are routinely slicing through layers of management, laying off thousands of midlevel executives and paring their work forces to an essential core. New technologies and fierce international competition forced this change on us.

So where are the jobs for the next middle class? That's a question that provokes anxiety in parents and young people alike. But it's a question with an answer, one that lurks in a little-noticed but absolutely critical trend just beginning to emerge. The Bureau of Labor Statistics projects that between 1990 and 2005, there will be a 37 percent increase in demand for "technicians."

This job classification defies the traditional color scheme of the old economy, in which white-collar managers supervised blue-collar employees. Technicians often wear dresses or ties (like white-collar types), but they also often work with their hands and use tools (like the blue-collar types). They blur the old categories.

Technicians operate computers monitoring robots that assemble electronic equipment. They run tests on breakthrough drugs in the laboratories of biotechnology companies. They drive trucks equipped with modems and make just-in-time deliveries. They assist lawyers by going on line to research cases and statutes. They manage sections of retail stores, periodically tapping PCs to determine which items are selling well and which may need a price cut. They install office machines and link them together in complex communications networks.

This new work usually required education beyond high school, but these jobs don't always demand a four-year college degree. They offer challenges and opportunities for women and men willing to keep pace with new technology.

Rule 2. Learn to Love the Web

For many people who came of age after World War II, work-force achievement often meant climbing the corporate ladder—stepping from one level of hierarchy to the next. Following this path now—or even expecting to—would be foolish. The ladder is gone.

The new jobs—the ones that will dominate the future workplace—will demand constant creativity and autonomy, even within individual companies. In these jobs, compensation won't be based on seniority, title or age, but on how innovative an employee can be in devising solutions, delivering new services or developing new ideas. Often they'll work in teams. (And whatever their own race or gender, their teammates will include more women and people of color than any generation in history.) At the end of a project, these teams will often disband, and people will move to the next team—whether in the same company or between firms.

The ladder will be replaced by a web. Webs have a center but not a "top." And webs offer an almost infinite number of paths as each point connects with all others. Rather than trudge from one rung to another in a rigid course, this generation will work in webs that are created for specific purposes—to develop software, design an advertising campaign, fashion a new financial instrument or find a cure to a disease—and then dissolve when the purpose has been fulfilled.

Consider the $6 billion a year video-game industry, in which the most popular products often spring from webs: A producer at a game company in Palo Alto, Calif., might have an idea for "edutainment" software based on a well-known children's story. She'll pull together computer programmers, designers and artists to begin developing the product, each person's skill adding to and reinforcing the skills of the others. Now suppose they decide their product would be even better with full-motion video to allow consumers to choose different endings to the story. They'll add a screenwriter and actors—expanding their web from Silicon Valley to Hollywood. As this aspect of the project nears completion, marketers—some in house, some in New York or even overseas—are added to the web. Next come the people who add value through their expertise in distribution. The distributors talk to the designers, the marketers talk to the writers. The web mates prize collaboration—if for no other reason than that their individual compensation is linked to the eventual sales of the game. And if their product does well, the web will add technicians who can rewrite the computer codes so the software will operate on other game machines. Eventually, the web will disappear. Some of the web mates will work together again. Others may not. But what matters is that each person's experience gives him or her an edge for the next project.

Employment Growth by Major Occupational Group 1990 to 2005

Occupation	Percent Change
Technicians	37
Professional	33
Service	28
Managerial	27
Sales	24
Administrative Support	13
Precision Production	12.5
Agriculture Related	4
Operators, Laborers	3.5

In organizations arranged like the video-game company, slavishly pleasing hierarchical superiors becomes less crucial, while networking with peers assumes new importance. Success will depend on one's ability to find webs and navigate through them. And whoever can spin the webs—and locate talented workers to populate them—will really prosper.

Rule 3. It's a Wired World. Get Used to It

The ultimate web, of course, is the thicket of computer networks that allows people to instantly zap text, data, video and sound to anyone else on the planet. Much of the collaboration this generation will do will take place over networks. Going to work might eventually mean turning on your PC and riding the info highway to your destination.

That shouldn't be a problem for the first generation to be raised on computers. Micro-processors have crept into every corner of our lives. They're in wristwatches, even musical greeting cards. Computer gurus call this proliferation Moore's Law, after a founder of the Intel Corporation. Moore's Law holds that every 18 months, micro-processors double in power and thus halve in cost—a development that has placed the massive power of mainframe computers on the desks (and soon in the palms) of millions.

Even automobile manufacturing, perhaps the quintessential Industrial Age operation, has succumbed to the computer. In 1990, 18 percent of the typical functions in a Ford automobile were controlled by computer. In 1994, the proportion is 82 percent.

In a wired world, fewer Americans will directly manufacture products. But more of us will devise better methods for making products or will add value through design, marketing or engineering. In all these endeavors, whether developing a prototype of a new car, charting customer demographics or regulating the temperature of a building, computers are essential partners. And as computers are used as much for communications as for computation, enormous sums of money and vast amounts of information can zip around the globe with the tap of a computer key. A nation's only long-term competitive advantage, therefore, comes from the one resource that stays put: its workers—their skills, their abilities, their capacity to work together. Which brings us to Rule 4, the most important one on the list.

**Rule 4. What You Earn Depends Even More
on What You Learn**

You've heard it. I've heard it. Our parents even heard it from their parents. Get a good education. That has always been wise counsel, but today, unlike the days when young people could walk out of high school directly into steady mass-production jobs, those who disregard this advice do so at their increasing peril. Every economic reality that confronts the young is linked to education and skills.

Not surprisingly, a majority of America's top earners hold college degrees. What's striking is the 30 million of the highest-paid Americans who did not graduate from traditional four-year colleges, although nearly all received additional education beyond high school—post-secondary training from a technical school, perhaps, or training on the job. And in the next highest-paid group, populated by platoons of technicians, even larger portions received employer training or additional education. By contrast, nearly all those who made up the bottom half of the earnings distribution received only a high-school education. For high-school dropouts the picture is even grimmer. Among 16- to 24-year-olds who lack a high-school diploma, half are unemployed.

This connection between earning and learning explains the surge in enrollment in America's community colleges. In the bellwether state of California, home to a robust community-college system, enrollment in these institutions has jumped 300 percent in the last three decades. Most community colleges there and elsewhere offer a traditional program of academics, but many have also teamed with local businesses to provide job training; programs for such trail-blazing fields as computer-aided design, registered-nurse certification, hazardous-waste management and statistical-process control. And in one true test of their value, community colleges are producing results. On average, a woman with a community-college degree earns 33 percent more than her counterpart with only a high-school diploma; for men, it's 26 percent more.

A corollary to the earning-learning rule is that security no longer comes from sticking with a single company for 30 years but from maintaining a portfolio of flexible skills. President Clinton calls this lifelong learning—and it's the driving force behind his efforts to expand student loans, create a national-service program and build a nationwide system to move young people smoothly from the classroom to a job via apprenticeships.

These are the new rules of the road. Failure (or the inability) to heed them will have severe consequences for a country that is slowly splitting apart into distinct groups bounded by the quality of their skills and their ability to keep them sharp. Reversing this drift—in an economy powered by a new set of rules—is the challenge all of us have been handed.

Generations inherit their burdens, but they chart their own destinies.

Reflective Writing: *Secretary Reich makes a strong claim when discussing the mobility and rapidly changing nature of the new global economy. He says, "A nation's only long-term competitive advantage, therefore, comes from the one resource that stays put: its workers, their skills, their abilities, their capacity to work together" (231). What kind of college education is needed for the world Reich describes? How do Reich's description and his education proposals match your own sense of the work world and the knowledge and skills necessary to succeed in it?*

Of Studies

Francis Bacon

Bacon lived in London, England, from 1561 to 1626. He was a distinguished lawyer in the courts of Queen Elizabeth and King James. He was also a famous author, a leading thinker of his day, and one of the originators of the essay, or brief discussion of an idea or issue, in English. His works include Novum Organum *(1620), a discussion of the scientific method and inductive reasoning;* The Advancement of Learning *(1605), a sweeping study of human knowledge; and* The Essays *(1601), from which the present reading is taken. Bacon's essays tend to be short examinations of an idea. In this essay, he uses his considerable powers of intellect to consider different aspects of—and reasons for—reading and learning.*

To Consider: *In this essay consisting of one long paragraph, the author lists three purposes for study and learning. From your own experience and observation, think of as many examples of each purpose as you can. How do these three purposes relate to one another? How do they relate to what you are doing as a college student?*

Studies serve for delight, for ornament, and for ability. Their chief use for delight is in privateness and retiring; for ornament, is in discourse; and for ability, is in the judgment and disposition of business. For expert men can execute and perhaps judge of particulars, one by one, but the general counsels and the plots and marshalling of affairs come best from those that are learned. To spend too much time in studies is sloth; to use them too much for ornament is affectation; to make judgment wholly by their rules is the humour of a scholar. They perfect nature, and are perfected by experience, for natural abilities are like natural plants that need pruning by study; and studies themselves do give forth directions too much at large, except they be bounded in by experience. Crafty men condemn studies; simple men admire them; and wise men use them, for they teach not their own use, but that is a wisdom without them and above them, won by observation. Read not to contradict and confute, nor to believe and take for granted, nor to find talk and discourse, but to weigh and consider. Some books are to be tasted, others to be swallowed, and some few to be chewed and digested; that is, some books are to be read only in parts; others to be read, but not curiously, and some few to be read wholly and with diligence and attention. Some books also may be read by deputy, and extracts made of them by others, but that would be only in the less important arguments and the meaner sort of books; else distilled books are like common distilled waters, flashy things. Reading maketh a full man, conference a ready man, and writing an exact man. And therefore, if a man write little, he had need have a great memory; if he confer little, he had need have a present wit; and if he read little, he had need have much cunning, to seem to know that he doth not. Histories make men wise, poets witty, the mathematics subtile, natural philosophy deep, moral grave, logic and rhetoric able to contend.

Reflective Writing: *Why, according to Francis Bacon, should one read and study? What does he say are not good reasons for studying? What other reasons can you add for and against studying? Can you translate the reasons Bacon provides for and against studying in terms of modern society and the business world?*

The Mission
of the University

Robert Solomon and Jon Solomon

This reading comes from the authors' 1993 book, Up the University: Recreating Higher Education in America. *Robert Solomon is a philosophy professor at the University of Texas, and his brother Jon Solomon is a professor of classics at the University of Arizona. Both have published extensively in their scholarly fields, authoring over a dozen books. In the reading, the authors discuss what a university attempts to do, give some historical background on contemporary higher education in this country, and suggest the qualities students should supply in order to have a successful college education.*

To Consider: *Foremost among the qualities the authors recommend for college students is what they describe as "the right kind of attitude." How do they define this attitude, and how does it compare with your own attitude? Finally, how does it relate to the other aspects of the university discussed by the authors, such as the faculty research mission and the emphasis on intercollegiate sports?*

The "Multiversity"

What is a university? It is an educational community, a place for teaching and learning. Everything else is secondary, irrelevant, or out of place. Of course, an education includes learning about life, and life is not learned in a vacuum. And so it is essential that the life of the university be as rich and varied as possible. The university should provide a rich social life, filled with friendship, romance, and diversity. A university education should assist students in the pursuit of a career or profession. The university should be an intrinsic part of the surrounding community. And because students learn best in an enlightened learning environment, faculty research, whatever other aims it may serve, is essential to the university as well. It provides the atmosphere in which learning is inspired by example and not imposed by authority.

The problem is that these essential but still secondary features of the university have become ends in themselves. For most American high school students, acceptance into one or another university is the definitive event of

235

their adult social lives and careers, a place to establish lifelong friendships, enter society, find business associates, and form political alliances. Not surprisingly, many students (with the blessing of their parents) choose a university primarily on the basis of the "contacts" it will provide or view the university primarily as a dating service. The university has become, in the minds of many, a training center, whose primary if not sole aim is to prepare students for a career. Doctors, lawyers, engineers, nurses, and architects are tested, trained, and accredited or eliminated from the career path they seek to follow. It is no longer a well-kept secret that the purpose of our best MBA programs is to act as super-employment agencies for corporations rather than to "teach business skills" as such, which are, for the most part, learned better on the job, in the particular context, and according to the particular demands and expectations of a particular industry or company. The university sets the standards, carries on the traditions, defines the quality, and excludes the quacks, but in the pursuit of professional credentials, the idea of education is often laid by the wayside.

So, too, the university is a training and testing ground for America's multibillion-dollar obsession with sports. Of course, sports bring a beneficial unity to campus life and provide an outlet for youthful enthusiasm as well as "school spirit" and a golden opportunity for a few talented young athletes. But as sports have become the most visible attribute of a school, pre-professional sports eclipse intramural and honestly amateur sports in importance, and athletes who have utterly inadequate training for academics are recruited with a vigor unknown to even the country's top Merit Scholars. They are not "students" but candidates for the pros, and many of them fail to make the grade both academically and athletically. Enormous amounts of money are involved, and aside from frequent charges of hypocrisy and criminality, it is obvious that, for many athletes, the purpose of the university has nothing to do with education.

A university cannot be a "great" university without a dynamic research program and an industrious, productive professoriat. But much of the research on campus today is only secondarily the pursuit of knowledge. It is the search for status, for notoriety. Much of it is sheer junk, although we know that everyone thinks of their own interests as utterly important and essential to the future of the world. Or research is primarily a business, often hidden off campus and irrelevant to the education that has already been paid for by the taxpayers and the students' tuition. Much of the budget and resources as well as the energy of university administrators and many professors is increasingly structured around research and devoted to the pursuit of prestigious research grants, which are said to help finance the operation and growth of the university. The university has become a major corporation, its eye on the bottom line, its ambition to grow and grow and grow.

The American university is also an important instrument of foreign policy and international relations. In any international crisis, the television networks and cable channels are filled with faces of university professors offering explanations, suggestions, and solutions. And the campuses are filled with foreign faces and accents, the sons and daughters of refugee families from Cambodia, Vietnam, and Latin America, students from China, Iran, and India who have every intention of returning home at the end of their studies. The university is no longer a domestic or local concern. The university is, by its very nature, "politicized." Not only are courses and whole programs concerned with geopolitics, but at any given time the future leaders of more than half the nations of the world are being educated in American universities. The state of the world twenty years from now is already being settled, as Churchill said of the "public" schools of England, on the playing fields and in the coffee lounges of our universities and colleges. The university, already a political entity, is then abused by professors who turn their classes into a political soapbox and the campus into a political battleground. Education gets sacrificed to ideology, and the students become pawns in the process.

> "What is the task of all higher education?" To turn men into machines.
> "What are the means?" Man must learn to be bored.
>
> —Friedrich Nietzsche, *Twilight of the Idols*

In the tumultuous sixties, the then vice-chancellor of the University of California at Berkeley Clark Kerr introduced the word *multiversity* to capture this complexity and confusion. Kerr used the word to refer to the gigantic conglomerates that were rapidly developing from his California universities. Buffered by competing political and economic interests, universities were filled with tens of thousands of undergraduates who were falling into the cracks because they were no longer considered an essential substance. Universities had become giant corporations and served global corporate and political interests. Enormous amounts of money from federal grants and high-powered research dwarfed and eclipsed the more spiritual life of the university. Sports were no longer physical exercise and local entertainment but big business, and many universities were no longer mere citizens of communities but the economic backbone of them. "Multiversity" was an administrative shrug of the shoulders, an admission of defeat, an excuse for neglecting undergraduate education and reducing it to cost-benefit analysis.

It was about that time, in the midst of an unpopular and unsuccessful war, that the university came to think of itself as primarily a research institution. And it was about that time, when the students were not only more numerous but better and smarter than they had ever been, that the very role of students within the university came into question. They began to be treated as irritations and mere obstacles to the real business of the university, and consequently, they quickly learned to act like irritations and obstacles, too. Thirty years later, the problem of the university is still that education has been pushed to the back shelf. In the face of numerous competing interests, the students are neglected and even ignored by the university.

> By the late nineteenth century, the advancement of knowledge through *research* had taken firm root in American higher education, and colonial college values, which emphasized teaching undergraduates, began to lose ground. . . . Indeed, the founders of Johns Hopkins University considered restricting study on that campus to the graduate level only. In the end, undergraduate education proved to be necessary, but the compromise was reluctantly made, and for many professors, class and lecture work became almost incidental.
>
> —Ernest L. Boyer, *The Carnegie Report: Scholarship Reconsidered*

"The Marketplace of Ideas"

Money and Metaphors

> Our concepts structure what we perceive, how we get around the world, and how we relate to other people.
>
> —George Lakoff and Mark Johnson, *Metaphors We Live By*

The concepts through which the university is defined and the metaphors through which it is perceived inevitably reflect the larger culture within which it is situated. The "ivory tower" metaphor was appropriate for the medieval university, with its religious virtues of devotion, fidelity, and pure-mindedness. During the Renaissance, as a secularized society became entranced with the classics, the universities became more like museums, with scholars collecting and preserving old pagan manuscripts, studying them, and sometimes translating them into the contemporary idiom. In the nineteenth century, as Europe asserted its superiority, the university became one of the instruments of that superiority, celebrating and exaggerating the virtues of "European" civilization. As the world's wealthiest civilizations converged in the international marketplace, so too, there came to be a much-celebrated "marketplace of ideas," a place where ideas, as well as money and goods, could be negotiated, examined, and exchanged. Today in America we live in a capital-intensive, consumer-driven, "postindustrial" corporate society. Thus it should not be surprising that most students have never heard of Borges or Thucydides or Marquez or Joyce or Mishima or Mao or Mecca or Angkor War.

It may be a bit perverse to measure the university's mission by its conditions for failure, as it is to measure an investment solely by the potential loss. But what becomes obvious in this now-standard litany is that a distinctive mission for the university is presupposed even by those who most vehemently attack the university today. Critics may complain about ethnocentrism and male chauvinism and cultural imperialism, but you can bet that they would rather die than be found to be *ignorant* of one of the figures they are demeaning. One can legitimately attack Shakespeare in today's university community, even dismiss or ridicule him—but it is expected that in any case one will have read him.

The university is an investment in a culture, in continuity and intelligence. It is not primarily a financial investment, and the rewards are not necessarily financial either. There is more than one way for a community to become "rich."

What Is an Education?

The Japanese word for *teacher* means roughly "he who pours," but if that sounds offensive to students, we should think of some of our own metaphors of passivity, of students as empty vessels, sponges, and raw materials. But the real problem here is not only the reduction of the active, grasping mind and restless personality of the student to a static, passive receptacle. It is also the misunderstanding about what it is that gets learned.

For a few thousand years, philosophers and sages have distinguished between information, knowledge, and wisdom. Information has simply to do with input and output, with memory and recognition. One does not get an education by memorizing the Denver telephone directory, even if it is filled with useful information. It would not be much different if the book were Gray's *Anatomy* or the chronology of English kings. Nor would information become an education if one were to memorize the definitions and details of E. D. Hirsch's now-infamous list of "things that a literate person should know." Education is not just information, nor is it the processing of information, as popular as that phrase has become since the computer revolution. If it were, we would not need teachers or, for that matter, students. A good computer can hold more information—and retrieve it more quickly—than even the most brilliant student or teacher.

Of course, a considerable amount of information is necessary just to provide the skeletal framework within which further research and understanding can take place. But information alone does not provide understanding nor carry with it instructions for its use or about its significance. It is knowing how to handle information and what to do with it to understand the world and oneself that counts as an education. "Just the facts" may have been good enough for Sergeant Joe Friday, but it is not good enough for us. We do not want students to learn just facts; we want them to acquire knowledge as well.

Students are not information processors, although information and its digestion are, of course, part of the educational process. They are, first of all, seekers after meaning. They want to be excited by ideas. They want something that they can use, or something that intrigues them, something that answers questions, including the questions that a talented teacher has only recently planted in their minds. Students, unlike computers, require motivation. Knowledge, ultimately, is that motivation. Knowledge is not a discipline but a passion. In order to succeed, knowledge acquires what discipline it requires. Allan Bloom was right, although most of his critics simply ignored this part of his message, when he compared education to an act of love (*eros*). He was returning to what was the very best in the ancient Platonic model of education—the education and inspiration of souls and not merely the transmission of information.

But education is not primarily concerned with knowledge either. Here we have to disagree with John Searle, who identifies the university as a "knowledge institution." To be sure, it is that, but it is something more besides. Knowledge is still too impersonal, too specialized, just as the idea of the professor as an "expert" is too narrow to explain his or her importance to the education of a student. Education is also an enriching, a deepening of the personality, a stimulated curiosity, and a certain love, even reverence, for learning. What the university does in its dealings with particularly impressionable and vulnerable eighteen-year-olds and older students is to open up their minds. That is not, as the current insult has it, to let their brains fall out. It is rather to give them the freedom and the knowledge to gain wisdom. That presupposes a great deal of information and curiosity, and it requires a great deal of knowledge and its accompanying skills. But we all know how information can eclipse common sense and how knowledge can lead to great pretense and foolishness. Wisdom, on the other hand, is the passion for living well.

> Without virtue, without the education of the heart, expertise and ambition easily become demonic. How can society survive if education does not attend to those qualities it requires for its perpetuation?
>
> —James T. Lancy, president, Emory University, "The education of the heart"

Wisdom is, in modern terms, having one's priorities straight. Young professionals fresh out of college work seventy-hour weeks in order to afford a Porsche, forgetting about the virtually costless pleasures of a good book or a deep conversation. With a little wisdom, the smart ones will see their way through it, and the point of an education is to show them the way. A wise friend once said that the most important decision a person ever makes in this society is how *little* money one needs to live on. The wisdom behind that homey bit of advice was, of course, that money is a mere means, and if you do not understand what it is you really want, the means may readily eclipse the end. It has also been said that "You can never get enough of what you didn't really want in the first place," and this seems to be all too true of a great many people in our society. Wisdom is knowing what one wants, what is important, what is really worth working and living for, and why. Wisdom means understanding oneself and other people, having a deep appreciation of emotions and the calamities that can befall a human being. One cannot be both insensitive and wise.

One of the most important sources of wisdom can be found in the professor who actually exemplifies wisdom as well as teaches it. Very few people actually "have" wisdom; even Socrates insisted he was just in love with and in search of it. But in the love of teaching and learning, in that rare satisfaction with life, the professor has always been a potentially inspiring figure for those who seek something more than the fads and fallacies of our consumer society.

As for the students, growing up, acquiring wisdom, and "finding oneself" as the expression goes, are essential to university life even if they seem like a continuation of adolescence and irresponsibility. (For some graduate students and professors, the continuation of irresponsibility seems to be a lifelong project.) But the idea of growing up, corralled into its proper university context, is an important supplement to the usual too-restricted emphasis on the passing down of information and the acquisition of knowledge. Great literature, for example, is not just a source of knowledge, much less a source of information, and philosophy is not just protolegal training in argumentative techniques. The classics are not just a vocabulary lesson in preparation for the more arcane jargon of medicine and the law. These subjects and the rest of the world "humanities" are profound mirrors of the soul, the source of the most basic understanding of ourselves. They may provide only minimal information and little by way of knowledge as such. But they are the source of wisdom, which for every student, no matter what his or her career or professional objectives, is the ultimate goal of a university education.

For the students, then, the most important prerequisite for higher education is positive motivation, the right kind of attitude. This is much more important than the usual "requirements" for college entry—professional ambitions, higher-than-average SAT scores, and an impressive grade point average. The ideal student is one who really wants to learn, who has a thirst for knowledge and—a desire for wisdom, no matter what his or her IQ, test-taking ability, or accomplishments in high school. What good is a 1300 SAT if a student is bored and only wants to sit in the frat house and drink beer? Admissions officers take note, but there is no way to quantify or test such attitudes with computer-graded examinations.

And as for the faculty, teaching should be challenging and inspiring, even (dare we say it again?)—*fun*. For what we teach is not "the facts," nor do we just impart knowledge or display our own wisdom. What we do is inspire wisdom in our students to learn and keep on learning.

Reflective Writing: *Solomon and Solomon ask, What is an education? This is a very important question, with obvious implications concerning how one would choose to approach college. How do the authors answer the question, and how might you answer it? How would you explain the similarities and differences between the two responses?*

You Make Your Own Chances:

Wealth as an Educational Goal

Paul Rogat Loeb

The author is a longtime political activist and writer who speaks and works regularly with college students around the country. This essay comes from his book Generation at the Crossroads: Apathy and Action on the American Campus, *published in 1994. The book examines college students representing political positions across the spectrum, from the very active to the inactive. In this essay, Loeb profiles a group of East Coast students, most of whom believe their purpose in attending college is to gain skills that will help them make as much money as possible. Although these students do feel an obligation to help their families and friends, they ridicule the idea that one should commit to helping the disadvantaged or making the world a better place. Rather than simply condemn these students or dismiss their ideas out of hand, Loeb attempts to understand the nature of their views.*

To Consider: *As a political activist committed to helping the disadvantaged, the author's views differ greatly from those of the apathetic and self-interested students he profiles. Yet he depicts the students rather objectively and not without some sympathy. How might you characterize the political philosophy of these career-oriented students? What beliefs motivate them? Where do you catch glimpses of the author's differing views?*

At Fairfield University, a Catholic school on the Connecticut gold coast an hour north of New York City, a group of sophomore men were teasing their friend Rick Vincent, the dorm liberal. "You want to be a teacher?" they asked. "Do you think your parents are paying fourteen thousand dollars a year for you to go into the Peace Corps and become a teacher?"

"What's wrong with wanting to help people?" Rick responded earnestly.

"Nothing," answered Tim Lovejoy, a premed major. "Your goal," he said, "is to teach and maybe go into the Peace Corps. Vigna over there just wants to be a writer. My goal is to make over fifty thousand a year. And George Lipson's is the same."

"Hey, don't sell me short," Lipson broke in with a laugh. "I want six figures at least."

Fairfield's campus is lush and wealthy; the surrounding community is wealthier. But a few miles away, in the city of Bridgeport, crumbling houses and boarded up storefronts line the streets. Unemployment soars. I asked the group whether their six-figure dreams could offer any hope to its residents. Scott, whose dad was a partner in a Wall Street brokerage firm, suggested that improved local education might help: "Starting kids off right is really important." Then he backpedaled: "But that's not my objective. It's not my job to do it."

"God helps those who help themselves," said Tim, whose dad was a doctor and whose mother was a nurse. "I feel sorry for those who get tough breaks, but we'll always have the poor. We gave the blacks a lot. Is it my fault if me or my parents make the bucks and they don't?"

"You make your own chances," Scott added.

These responses seem callous, bluntly so. Yet these students were hardly fervent New Rightists. They consistently mocked a skinny dorm-mate in Vuarnet sunglasses who idolized William F. Buckley and treated the *National Review* as the revealed word of God. Half were too unconcerned even to vote Republican. But they considered the world inherently harsh and unequal. They intended to do what they considered necessary to get their share.

Consequently, they dismissed the Bridgeport residents as regrettably expendable, perhaps even deserving their fate. And they hammered their own lives and dreams into whatever shape they hoped would spark approving corporate responses. "It would be great if we could come here to learn, and if grades were a real measure," said George Lipson, a salesman's son. "They aren't, and unfortunately the business world just isn't going to care how much I know about Plato. They're going to care whether I show them how hard I can work by getting the best grades I possibly can."

I talked with the group in a dorm lounge that overlooked rolling hills, the trees a fall palette of red, gold, and brown. They wore tailored slacks, expensive sweaters, ragged sweats, worn jeans. They sprawled on couches and chairs, coming and going as the conversation circled from midmorning till night.

Ambition to rise, they believed, was a virtue. Wealth would allow them to "send money to Rick in the Peace Corps. Or maybe give something to cancer." "I feel I owe my parents for sending me here," explained George Lipson. "My dad always says 'I want you kids to do better than I have.' I want to make good and make him proud."

"Rick and I will be living in the Bowery," remarked Paul Vigna, the aspiring writer. "Lipson will drive by in his BMW and flip us some change."

The others razzed him for this, yet for the most part agreed that the world was carnivorous and always would be. "I'm a heavy church goer," said Tim. "The priests say we should help others. But no one's gone out of their way for me."

"College has given me lots of different ideas and thoughts," observed Jim, the one blue-collar student. His dad was a railroad worker and his mom a secretary. "But I'm in school to get a good-paying job. First I want to reward my parents so they don't have to scrimp and save in the future. They both hate their work. They only do it so I can be here. I study to get good grades and to not have to live like they do."

The group's belief that you repay familial affection through economic mobility echoed narratives fundamental to America's history. These students described grandparents who came from Germany, Italy, or Poland with nothing but a willingness to bake bread, pump gas, sew clothes, or do whatever else would allow the family to claw its way up, generation by generation, to middle-class comfort. They believed anyone sufficiently motivated could replicate their passages.

You Don't Have a Life

Nevertheless, they also feared they might lose out in the race for success. For all their talk of six-figure dreams, they worried about the economic ground beneath them eroding, and wondered how long they'd keep the comforts they grew up with. "When I get money . . ." they'd casually state, as if wealth would surely come. "If you work hard, you're going to make a buck." Then they'd repeat, "I don't want to end up poor." "I don't want to end up at the bottom." They dismissed peers who voiced modest social concerns as dangerously impractical.

These Fairfield students were not alone in choosing pragmatic careerism over broader commitment or reflection. In the earlier generation of the late 1960s, more than 80 percent of entering freshmen cited "developing a meaningful philosophy of life" as a prime college goal, compared with 40 percent who selected "being very well off financially." By the late 1980s the figures had reversed. Seventy-five percent picked financial security, while only 40 percent hoped to better understand themselves in the world. Most students viewed college as just a means to material success.[1]

Students with such beliefs don't obsess constantly over their futures. They party, talk, and relax much like their counterparts in other historical times. But most feel their lives have room for only one "serious" concern: preparing to make it in the material world. They believe in a meritocracy—that the wealthy are the most deserving. But they view the success of those who make it to the top as a product, not of intrinsic worth or actual contribution to society, but of how well they manipulate appearances to those who call the shots and make the deals. They worry less about what they'll actually do than about whether they can learn to adapt.

Having grown up during a time when fortunes were built—not by producing railroads, steel mills, or houses, but by the alchemy of junk bonds and corporate takeovers—students in this group remain vague about what they hope to produce, what human needs they wish to serve. They talk mostly of what corporations will require of them, or in vague terms of wanting "an entrepreneur kind of deal." As a student from Texas explained, "I'd really like to get rich. If you have that, everything else pretty much follows."

George Lipson described how his father had spent thirty-five years traveling from store to store selling eighteenth-century furniture reproductions. His dad didn't particularly like the job and felt little excitement about the merchandise he sold. But it enabled him to give their family a comfortable Long Island home, "to buy us things, take us out to dinner, show us how much he cares. He works so hard"—George gestured toward his heart—"to look after us."

"I've got some of that as well," he continued. "When I'm out for dinner with girls or with friends of mine, I want to be able to do that. Not because I'm rich, because sometimes I'm not. Or because I want people to think I'm rich, like this guy from our dorm who drives around in a Lincoln. I just want to be able to do something for the people I care about."

"Helping people is great," Tim added, "and good teachers are great. But you can't help everyone else and throw away Number One. I want to make enough to buy a place of my own, where I can go and if someone's bothering me I can say 'Buddy, buzz off, this is mine. This is what I've paid for.' "

Tim's words portrayed a world without broader claims or attachments, a world full of predators who might seize or disrupt the comfort he intended to work so hard for. He sought a private sanctuary, safe and secure.

"Without money," added Scott, the stockbroker's son, "you have no life."

No one in the group suggested the possibility of redeeming familial love and support with other than material dreams. No one considered using school as a time to learn to think critically, to act on their beliefs, to better understand their world. They considered it wildly unrealistic to even consider trading material success for a larger common good.[2]

They also felt unequivocally hostile to attempts at social change. When I suggested Vietnam-era efforts had made a difference, they called them selfindulgent, misguided, and ineffective. The protestors, they said, made the war longer and spat on innocent soldiers caught in the middle. All but Rick and the ambivalent Paul Vigna, the aspiring writer, condemned the campus political involvements of that time.

In the same vein, the group mistrusted students who currently took political stands. "They're just a bunch of losers," Tim remarked when I mentioned Fairfield students who had protested Reagan's Central America interventions. "They have an unprofessional quality," added a friend named Bob. He called those who'd protested a local nuclear plant "just a bunch of morons." Although Rick's most radical act was to say he might want to become a teacher or to join the Peace Corps, George Lipson wrote off even this as "just trying to get noticed."

The Fairfield students differed from some others in the virulence of their individualism and in the material wealth that fueled it. They allowed no common claims to interfere with their personal chances. But they were wholly representative in denying responsibility for the ills of the world and in disdaining anyone who did speak out.

Campus activists, in the view of one Columbia student, just "protested for the sake of protesting." "They're only in it for a fad and a trend," a University of Washington woman stated, "to jump on a bandwagon, like everyone else." She used to go to Colorado College, "where there was a certain group who put up their little shanties and did their little demonstrations about divestment. They were all just imitative of the sixties. They never drew many people, and no one paid them any attention in any case."

I asked how the same activists could simultaneously be marginal and trendy. Wasn't there a contradiction? "There actually were a lot of the antiapartheid people," she admitted, "but we just called them 'the granolas.' The guys wore grass skirts and beads to go back to nature, and they built their shanties, and to me that's a trend. Because then they got in their new Saabs and drove away."

Did the guys really wear skirts, I asked? Well, just two of them, and that was once at a party. She guessed not all of them had cars, and some who did drove old clunkers. But if they really wanted to be consistent, they'd sell their possessions, give their money to Africa, and know a lot more about what they were fighting for.

Hostile students levied equally condescending charges during the height of the Vietnam era. Had the 1980s been a wholly quiescent decade, there would have been no campus activists to disparage. But when some did take committed stands, they were outnumbered by their far more numerous critics, like students who complained at the height of Columbia's successful antiapartheid blockade about people "who just sit on the steps and try to feel moral." Time and again I saw even the most thoughtful and effective political students cavalierly dismissed along with all the questions they raised.

The same stereotypes were invoked, irrespective of the cause. A Dartmouth student called those who worked on campus racial issues "just marchers with their marcher face on, swept up in their emotions, chants, the attitude they take." Some, he said, were even his friends, but they talked before thinking, constantly demanded attention, weren't nearly as knowledgeable as they ought to be. "Of course, it does seem ironic," he said, after a pause, "that we seem to feel that the people who are marching for one side or another of an issue never understand things as well as those of us who watch from the sidelines."

The mistrustful students included some who shared apparent philosophical bonds with the activists. A Dartmouth student wrote his senior thesis on ways America's military buildup has destroyed the technological and economic base of sectors like the machine tool industry. This seemed precisely the kind of question students should address, not because his judgments mirrored my own, but because Americans so rarely examine the interconnected consequences of our national choices. The student and I discussed his project and conclusions. He mentioned seeing a poster for a lecture on the arms race that I'd given the previous evening. When I excused myself to address a fundraising walkathon for Central America, he was taken aback. "Why would you involve yourself with *that?*" he asked. "Aren't they just a bunch of radicals?"

They Aren't My Neighbors

Not all the apolitical students are materially greedy. Most just want to get by. But they share a mistrust of those who act. They believe individuals succeed or fail on their own. They view personal futures as having little to do with broad political choices, but rather with individual skill, persistence, the ability to adapt. They share a sense of a world increasingly harsh, in which conscience is a luxury.

A Florida student said he knew the Central Intelligence Agency (CIA) did some dirty business in South America. But so did the Russians. If some people got hurt, they probably deserved it. A young woman at a Seattle-area community college agreed. She described, with a sense of betrayal, how her father's silence regarding his work on MX missile components echoed that of atomic weapons workers I'd interviewed for a previous book. She wanted to confront him, to work to stop the arms race, to found a campus peace group. Then she hesitated. "But isn't it good if we're warlike and frighten other nations?" she asked. "That way no one will mess with us."

In a later conversation, I asked the Fairfield group if they'd ever worried about the nuclear threat. Tim and Scott hadn't. They were Christians and knew they'd be saved to go to "a better place." Switching the conversation to his recent trip to Jamaica, Tim asked, "Why does everyone there hate the U.S. so much?"

"Because we ream people," said Vigna, bluntly. Rick mentioned El Salvador and Iran.

"So stop driving your car," said Tim. "Grow your own cotton and make your own shirt. I like how I live. Are you going to decide what's right or wrong?"

"Then what about all that Christian 'love thy neighbor' stuff?" asked Vigna, who himself was an agnostic. "What about the Jamaicans, or the people in Bridgeport?"

"They aren't my neighbors," said Scott. "Who cares if they hate us? I know my neighbors, and they live in Long Island. No way are those people my neighbors."

The phrase evokes the separations at the heart of the era these students grew up in, separations between individuals across America's widening class divisions, between past and present, and present and future, between notions that citizens have a responsibility to a broader common good, and the judgment that, as Margaret Thatcher pronounced, "There is no such thing as society—there are only individual families." Students with such beliefs hope to do well in their personal lives, even if this means averting their eyes while the world crumbles. They settle for what educator Arthur Levine once called "going first class on the *Titanic*."[3]

Exemption and Silence

Students diverge over how much those at the bottom really do make their own chances. In a sociology class at the University of South Alabama, the professor described "driving by a man with a sign that said 'I'll work for food.' It outraged me that to be able to eat, someone in this country should have to sit on a bench holding that sign. The next day, when I drove by again, I didn't feel nearly so upset. It shocked me that I was already getting used to it."

"At first I'd feel sorry for them, too," said a woman in the class. "They're all over Mobile now. But then you feel like, if they wanted a job, they could get one. They could clean houses or something. They don't have to beg."

"But their sign says that," I responded. "It says, 'I'll work for food.'"

She held her ground. "It's not our fault. Why should it be our fault if it's their problem, if they're the ones not trying to do anything for themselves? Why should we make it our problem and do something for them?"

This wasn't the callousness of the elite, but of someone who'd scraped, struggled, and wanted no claims on what she earned. Her dad, she explained, supported five kids on less than $20,000 a year. Her mom, now divorced, lived in a trailer. "I've been working since I was fifteen to put myself through college. Don't y'all tell me you can't get a job."

Other students, from backgrounds equally hard pressed, argued back. One mentioned a businessman friend, "who became homeless along with his family, five years ago. He couldn't find work because he didn't have an address."

We talked of factories leaving town, of the barriers of education and race. "They should be able to see that something's going wrong at their work," a woman commented, "instead of waiting around until things fall apart." "It's easy to say 'He hasn't tried,'" said another student. "Who are we to pass judgment? We don't even know what people are going through."

While the class generally condemned extreme social Darwinism, they blamed the situation of the man who wanted to work for food on poor luck and misfortune. They never mentioned institutional choices that might have left him on the street—a factory shutting down, a landlord raising the rent, a social welfare system that lets people go hungry.

Separation from responsibility builds on a notion of exemption, on a belief that while others might stumble, individuals by their own efforts can keep human tragedy at a distance. Writer Wendell Berry described how this sense played out in commencement exercises of a major California university:

> The graduates of the school of business wore "For Sale" signs around their necks. It was done as a joke, of course, a display of youthful high spirits, and yet it was inescapably a cynical joke, of the sort by which an embarrassing truth is flaunted. For, in fact, these graduates were for sale, they knew that they were, and they intended to be. They had just spent four years at a university to increase their "marketability." . . . But what most astonished and alarmed me was that a number of these graduates for sale were black. Had their forebearers served and suffered and struggled in America for 368 years in order for these now certified and privileged few to sell themselves? Did they not know that only 122 years, two lifetimes, ago, their forebearers had worn in effect that very sign? It seemed to me that I was witnessing the tragedy of history that the forgetfulness of history always is.

The African-American graduates, Berry suggested, could only have worn their signs, "by assuming, in very dangerous innocence, that their graduation into privilege exempted them from history. The danger is that there is no safety, no *dependable* safety, in privilege that is founded on greed, ignorance, and waste."[4]

Strong words, from one of America's strongest critical voices. As I will explore, more whites than blacks believe in this notion of exemption. My Fairfield group lived in a particularly insulating cocoon of privilege, as do Williams students who perform the half-joking football cheer "That's all right! That's OK! You're going to work for us someday!" Or students at Harvard, with a nearly identical version. They could afford to dismiss grave national and global problems as immutable.[5]

Yet even financially pressed students hope that if they can just learn the right moves, they can slide by. They turn college into what Queens College political scientist Michael Krasner calls "survival training . . . preparation so they'll do OK in a lousy world." By the mid-eighties, national surveys of high school seniors found that 90 percent expected things to get better for themselves, but only 47 percent of young men and 34 percent of young women believed the situation of the country as a whole would improve. The split in expectations leads them to prepare themselves for sale to the highest bidder, while keeping larger ideals buried in the remote closets of their souls. Whatever troubles might come, they hope to ride them out through skill, perseverance, and hard work.[6]

Their perspective isn't wholly foolish. America has always let a few individuals rise to the top, even as it becomes more economically polarized than any other advanced industrial nation. With enough money, citizens can avoid immediate crises. They can drink bottled water, live in guarded suburbs with monitored alarm systems, even pay for clean air, as people do who buy inflated real estate on the West Side of Los Angeles. Yet these separations only allow national ills to fester.

More than anything, students' individualism involves a judgment that they can not be the makers of history, but only its recipients. Broad political forces continually frame their opportunities and beliefs, but they see no chance to control them. Real choice, they insist, comes only in private life. As in Tim's dream of saying "Buddy, buzz off," they trade the freedom to shape their communities and their historical times for the right to be left alone.[7]

Notes

1. The figure for "a meaningful philosophy of life" dropped to 50 percent by 1980 and to barely 40 percent by 1989, before rebounding slightly to 44.6 percent by 1993. "Being very well off financially" began at 39 percent in 1970, hit 63 percent in 1980, and continued climbing steadily to 76 percent in 1987; it leveled off to 74.5 percent in 1993. See Astin et al., *Twenty Year Trends*, p. 97; Astin et al., *The American Freshman, 1987*, p. 60; Astin et al., *The American Freshman, 1989*, p. 56; and Astin et al., *The American Freshman, 1993*, p. 24.
2. For excellent discussions on the fears and realities of middle-class downward mobility, see Barbara Ehrenreich, *Fear of Falling* (New York: Pantheon, 1989), and Katherine S. Newman, *Falling from Grace* (New York: Vintage Books, 1989).
3. Thatcher quoted in Greil Marcus, "Obituary: The 60s," *Cake*, issue no. 4 (1991); Levine quote from Arthur Levine, *When Dreams and Heroes Died* (San Francisco: Jossey-Bass, 1980), p. 103.
4. Wendell Berry, *The Hidden Wound* (San Francisco: North Point Press, 1989), p. 128.
5. Williams cheer from Williams student Hal Hermiston, personal interview, April 1989. The Harvard cheer, identical except for the phrase "You'll work for us someday" (instead of "You're going to work for us someday"), noted in John Trumpbour, *How Harvard Rules* (Boston: South End Press, 1989), p. 5.
6. Krasner quote from phone conversation, Sept. 1988.
   See *Monitoring the Future: A Continuing Study of the Lifestyles and Values of Youth* (Ann Arbor, Mich.: Survey Research Center, Institute for Social Research, University of Michigan), volumes from 1980 through 1992. The data for these annual national surveys of high school seniors are collected under the direction of Jerald G. Bachman, Lloyd D. Johnston, and Patrick M. O'Malley. Bachman is the lead author in even-numbered years, Johnston second, and O'Malley third, with Bachman and Johnston switching positions as lead and second author in odd-numbered years. Hereafter, this body of work is cited as Bachman et al., *Monitoring the Future* (for even-numbered years), and Johnston et al., *Monitoring the Future* (for odd-numbered years). Gaps in high school seniors' expectations that things will get better for themselves but worse for the country, from *Monitoring the Future*, 1984 survey, form 4, questions A02 and A04.
7. On the notion of private liberty in American life, see Bob Blanchard and Susan Watrous, "An Interview with Frances Moore Lappé," *The Progressive*, Feb. 1990, and Richard Flacks, *Making History: The American Left and the American Mind* (New York: Columbia University Press, 1989).

Reflective Writing: *The majority of the students author Loeb quotes and discusses in this reading see little chance of influencing broader social and political developments around the country and appear far more concerned with preparing for their own future successes. Evaluate the primary reasons students provide for these views. In what ways do you agree or disagree?*

The $10,000 Hoop:

Has Higher Education Become an Exercise in Futility for Most Americans?

Zachary Karabell

The author examines the belief so common in our society today that high school graduates should go on to college. He wonders why a college degree is so often required for a variety of types of employment, at least some of which demanded far less education in the past. He suggests that "Wondering if universal higher education is really such a good thing is likely to get the wonderer charged with reckless elitism and carrying a concealed conservative weapon." Risking these charges, he questions what he feels has become an attitude not easily challenged in the United States. The author of a 1998 book, What's College For? *Karabell is a writer living in New York.*

To Consider: *Most likely, you have grown up with the attitude that college is a necessary part of one's education. How does the author try to counter that view? What opposing views, in support of higher education, come to mind?*

Americans don't agree on much. We fight about social spending, health care, sex, the military, parenting, religion, sex, the size of the federal government, taxes, sex, but there is one thing we seem to agree on: Education is a good thing, and more education is a better thing. We all know we're in a time of political paralysis, when the most active thing official Washington does is shut down the government. Yet in the past two years, below the radar screen of scandal, the president and Congress have crafted legislation to support higher education to the tune of more than $40 billion a year. President Clinton spoke of making two years of college just as universal as high school is now. Earlier this year, Clinton, in his State of the Union address, announced that higher education is an American birthright.

Apparently, most of us don't dispute such ideas. The Department of Education says that enrollment in college will surpass an all-time high of just under 15 million students this academic year, and well over half of high school seniors now go to college. Each year, we spend more than $175 billion on colleges and universities. States allocate vast amounts of tax revenue, the federal government subsidizes research and individuals go

252

tens of thousands of dollars into debt to send either themselves or their children to college.

Conventional wisdom on the issue is clear and unequivocal: College is a necessary prerequisite for skilled jobs. That piece of paper embossed with the words "graduated from" is universally believed to be a ticket to a better life, a better job, a more affluent and rewarding future. Just think of all the Hollywood images of college: pensive, clean young people—usually white—watching as charming Professor X lectures them about deep philosophical questions that will give them the keys to the universe. After several years of these experiences, the graduate emerges ready to land that first job and take that first step on a professional ladder of success and citizenship.

Oh, come on. Today's college student is more likely to be a woman in her 30s attending night school at one of those cinder-block community colleges designed by the same people who build prisons. Halls of Ivy? Not for 95 percent of the American college students today.

Higher education has been romanticized past the point of reasonable discussion. We spend all this money, expend all this energy, go into debt and exhaust an ever-rising portion of national resources. Yet few of us ask what college is supposed to provide that leads to better jobs and a better life. What are we supposed to learn in college? Politicians and educators extol the power of college to create a competitive, highly skilled work force that can hold its own in the international economy. But how does college bring that about? How does sitting in a lecture on Plato make our superconductors more competitive? How do gendered interpretations of Shakespeare make the American college graduate a good citizen? How does Accounting 101 teach you to deal with real people in a real job? In what way does learning calculus make you thrive in your job as a Blockbuster store manager, which, incidentally, the Bureau of Labor Statistics defines as a college-level job?

How did we get to this point? How is it that anyone who wants a halfway decent job now has no choice but to go to college, whether or not he did well in high school, whether or not it has been 10 years since she last entered a classroom? What if you're a single mother with two children already working a full-time job who has no money for health care or child care but has to go $5,000 into debt to get a two-year associate degree at the local community college in order to get that $3,000 pay raise? What if you're an 18-year-old guy who wants to set up a trucking business but who can't get a loan from the bank because without the degree you're seen as a high credit risk? Should you be compelled to go to college? Will anything you learn at college truly prepare you for the life of an insurance claims adjuster, or a bank teller, or a paralegal, or even an editorial assistant at a hip Internet magazine that emphasizes creativity and initiative but has little use for formal credentials?

These questions rarely get asked, and when they do, the stock response is to attack the questioner rather than to answer the question.

Wondering if universal higher education is really such a good thing is likely to get the wonderer charged with reckless elitism and carrying a concealed conservative weapon. If advanced degrees are now required for any job of substance, then suggesting that advanced degrees are not for everyone is tantamount to consigning the un-colleged to lives as second-class citizens forever stuck in the ranks of the working poor. If degrees are totems that signify the bearer as competent, intelligent and job worthy, then questioning whether everyone needs degrees is equivalent to asking if everyone needs 2,000 calories a day.

Fair enough, but aren't we forgetting something? Who ever said that college degrees signify competence? Who said that universal higher education makes for a better-prepared work force? Shouldn't we be taking a hard look at those assumptions?

We could say that a college degree signifies that the student has thought deep thoughts and learned critical analysis by reading the Great Books. But less than 20 percent of today's students take liberal arts courses, and even fewer major in a liberal arts discipline. We could say that college should be a timeout, a time of growth, a time for self-knowledge, but only a privileged few can afford that timeout, unless public funding for higher education approached, oh, $1 trillion a year. The fact is that we get pretty fuzzy when we think about college. We like the idea that college is about liberal arts, and we like to believe that college also serves some utilitarian purpose preparing students for jobs. But no one can say with any certainty that reading Plato does anything to improve the competitiveness of the American work force, and what's more, most people in college don't read Plato or any other Great Book.

The fact is that the liberal arts ideal is not what lies behind the massive growth of higher education in the past 20 years, and it is not why most of those 15 million students will go to college, or why their parents will go into debt, or why state legislators will reluctantly allocate even more money to the cause of college-educated masses.

Universal higher education is a response to the failings (real or imagined) of high school. Students routinely graduate high school barely able to write, barely able to read and not at all able to think critically. The situation is especially dire in urban public schools. Colleges now spend an inordinate amount of time on remedial education, on the teaching of basic skills that students in the rest of the developed world learn in high school. To a large extent, we've simply extended the period of basic education into college because our primary and secondary schools are not doing what they ought to be.

Universal higher education also stems from a long-held immigrant belief that education is a vehicle of social advancement. In inextricably linking jobs, mobility, individual success and economic competitiveness to college, we've bought the dubious notion that a college education is necessary for any skilled job. But it's a self-fulfilling prophecy. Faced with a choice between two applicants, one with a college degree and one without, almost any employer will choose the one with a college degree, even if the degree doesn't relate at all to the job at hand. College graduates are presumed to be better qualified, whether they have learned anything in college classrooms that make them better qualified.

For instance, a 29-year-old divorced mother who barely finished high school and who lives in a marginal urban neighborhood may have a hard-earned savvy about families, children and the streets. That may make her a superb youth counselor. But faced with a choice between her and a 21-year-old college graduate with a degree in sociology, many state agencies will hire the college graduate over the divorced mother. The college graduate may come from a more affluent background, and she may have never set foot in a ghetto until that point, but heck, she's read Durkheim and done intensive case studies, and she even interned at the local hospital for six weeks during her junior year, and more to the point, she has a college degree.

To be fair, the college graduate may end up doing a brilliant job, but there's nothing about her background that suggests that she will do even a competent job, and she clearly lacks those intangible skills that the divorced, degree-less mother has. The classroom can teach many things, but it ain't the real world. Skill-oriented classes like accounting and management don't necessarily teach someone how to deal with life in all its messiness any more than reading Hegel does. We used to draw a distinction between actual experience and book knowledge, and we used to laugh at people who thought that book knowledge was a substitute for learning by doing.

OK, some of that could be chalked up to American anti-intellectualism, but there's such a thing as too much intellectualism, and privileging book and classroom knowledge to the extent we now do often violates common sense.

Even more disturbing is that universal higher education is clothed in the rhetoric of democracy. Universal higher education is said to open doors, but in reality, it narrows our options and leaves us with less freedom to chart our lives and careers. That's because universal higher education is actually mandatory higher education. Democracy is about choice, but the trend toward universal higher education has become perversely coercive. It's one thing to insist that children have a certain amount of education, but to require adults to attend college or face dire economic consequences flies in the face of individual choice. What if someone just doesn't want to attend college? What if they believe that their skills and education are better served by volunteering for the National Park Service and learning about wildlife by living in the wild? Why should they have to go and study the microbiology of plants in a classroom setting when they'll probably decide to learn such things as their lives and careers advance?

But for now, people don't have that choice, or at least exercising that choice comes with, as some government commission might say, high social negatives. It's now presumed that someone without a college degree is stupid, because it's now so easy to go to college that only the dim, dense and unmotivated are thought to steer clear of it. And so, millions of people end up going to college not because they want to, not because they're interested in liberal arts (and by the way, given the jargon-filled academic culture today, a love of literature is not always well-served by taking an English course) and not because they have either the time, money or inclination, but simply because they must. It's as if we've decided to charge every American a tax of tens of thousands of dollars and years of time in order to join the club of the gainfully employed.

It goes without question that higher education can be a wonderful experience; it even occasionally matches the romantic notions we have of it. But for most of the 15 million students at the 3,500 institutions of higher learning, college is an anarchic place. The requirements for a degree are confusing, and no one takes the time to explain why you need to take the courses you have to take. A surprisingly high percentage of students emerge from the classroom convinced that the whole thing is a waste of time and money that could have been better spent.

We seem to have forgotten that classroom learning is only one form of knowledge, and for millions of us, not knowledge that is particularly desirable, much less necessary. As it stands, we're on the verge of consigning ourselves to mandatory higher education. Before we reach the point of no return, we should remember that universal higher education is a development that began after World War II, and is only now becoming a reality. The vast majority of our parents and grandparents, many of whom we admire for their wisdom, intelligence and business acumen, didn't go to college. Now, given the current ethos, either they were stupid . . . or we are.

Reflective Writing: *A controversial point Zachary Karabell makes is that "Universal higher education is said to open doors, but in reality, it narrows our options and leaves us with less freedom to chart our lives and careers." The fact that you are in college suggests that you disagree with this view. However, for the sake of argument, play devil's advocate against yourself and write a short piece supporting Karabell. Feel free to draw on his own points as well as whatever other good arguments you can think of.*

The Practical Path, Too, Can Be High-Minded

Richard M. Freeland

The author is president of Northeastern University, a national leader in cooperative education, which offers students regular opportunities to work full-time in their chosen fields while still pursuing their undergraduate studies. Since assuming the presidency in 1996, he has worked to strengthen links between co-op and classroom for all students. A historian by training, he has published work on the history of American higher education. In this essay, Freeland argues that professional education can and should be intellectually rich and conceptually challenging. He critiques the notion that a liberal education in the arts and sciences is the only way to promote critical thinking and intellectual growth in college students.

To Consider: *As you read this essay, think about the sort of professional education President Freeland promotes here. What are its main overall characteristics? He provides a broad, overarching perspective. Consider how his ideas might apply to one particular area of study.*

Last year, the American Academy of Arts and Sciences devoted an edition of its journal, *Daedalus*, to an exploration of the challenges faced by liberal-arts colleges. The topic appears to have hit a nerve; the journal sold out of its 19,000-copy run. Central among the challenges discussed was what one contributor called "the pressure of purpose" that such colleges face as more and more students see undergraduate education primarily as a chance to prepare for lucrative careers rather than to develop a philosophy of life.

In an article summarizing the *Daedalus* issue, *The New York Times* stated the problem sharply: Should liberal-arts colleges "shift their focus from . . . [an] education-for-its-own-sake approach to a more down to earth, job-oriented curriculum . . . ?" Colleges were being forced to choose, according to the *Times*, between the "high-minded route" and "the practical path."

The idea that preparing students for the world of work is not only different from nurturing the life of the mind, but intrinsically unworthy, has a long history within elite academic circles. I remember my surprise when I first encountered that notion as an undergraduate at one of the nation's top liberal-arts colleges during the 1960's. Although my reasons for attending

257

that college were at best poorly formulated at the time, I would certainly have put preparing myself for adult employment high on the list.

I quickly realized, however, that such priorities were more likely to be ridiculed than respected by the professors in the rarefied world I had entered. I learned to keep such thoughts to myself. Over time, I came to share the fashionable undergraduate contempt for the bourgeois world of working, and of earning to support a decent standard of living.

In recent years, the historic tension between the values of liberal education and the world of work has taken on an even greater prominence in academic discourse, as the idea has taken hold among educators that today's youth are more materialistic, less idealistic, and more self-interested than their predecessors. How often do we open the pages of one of our academic trade magazines, or scan an op-ed by a college president in the daily newspapers, to encounter some variation on the theme of the *Daedalus* issue?

The line of discussion varies. Sometimes the writer is patronizing, pointing out that a liberal education really is the best way to prepare for practical work. Sometimes the tone is moralistic, condemning as shallow the careerism of the young. But the central message tends to remain the same: The best and highest form of education is the liberal arts and sciences in the form they have traditionally been offered, and those who question that precept are either uninformed or misguided.

I believe that the endless rehashing of those tired arguments reveals a serious failure of imagination on the part of academics and an abrogation of our responsibilities to students. It is time to listen to young people about their job concerns rather than to lecture them. We should stop denigrating their entirely sensible yearning to find their places in the non-academic world and to prepare themselves for adult responsibilities.

At a time when 60 percent of young Americans attend college, we should recognize that curricular models created when higher education was reserved for social and economic elites need to be rethought. We should move beyond the shopworn opposition of liberal and professional education and seek ways to nurture in our students both the impulse to grow intellectually and the desire to prepare for the practical and material challenges of adulthood. It is time for academe to recognize that occupations apart from primarily intellectual pursuits can be, and are for many people, a rich source of meaning in their lives.

A critical first step in rethinking traditional academic views of work is to recognize the externalities that today's students face. They understand, perhaps in a way that their elders do not, that a college education has become an indispensable precondition of economic opportunity. That is a relatively new phenomenon in American culture. It was not true when my parents were growing up in the 1920's and 30's, and it was not true for me to anything like the degree it is for students today.

Contemporary students also see a far-less-settled, far-less-secure world than did I at their age. The United States may dominate the globe economically, but many young people have seen one or both of their parents restructured or downsized out of jobs. They know in their bones that economic life is unpredictable and dangerous. Should we really be surprised, against that background, that many students come to college eager to arm themselves for survival in an uncertain professional world? And what right do we have, given the realities they confront, to declare that impulse base?

Our goal must always be to empower students to lead the fullest and most rewarding lives they can. The high value we claim for liberal education derives directly from these fundamental purposes: that we free the mind from bias, that we cultivate rigorous thought, that we teach not only tolerance of difference but appreciation of diversity, and that we give our students the tools they need for a lifetime of intellectual adventure and social contribution. Let us affirm those purposes, but let us recognize that necessary to them is a student's economic independence. That's the first condition of personal freedom and therefore must be a fundamental goal of liberal education.

But the discussion must cut deeper than an acknowledgment that today's students face a different world than did their parents and grandparents, or that personal freedom requires economic independence. We need to confront an apparent bias among academics against the practical world as somehow less full of meaning and creative possibility than academic life. Writes the *Daedalus* essayist: "Call it vocationalism, credentialism, or even dollarizing—students and their families have defined undergraduate education in starkly utilitarian terms. Young people do not go to college to become fuller persons, better citizens or more lively intellects. In postwar America, college education is justified by the additional lifetime income it will produce."

Why must we assume that to be concerned with preparing for the world of work is to lack interest in becoming "fuller persons, better citizens, or more lively intellects"? The practical and the cerebral are not in opposition, at least they needn't be. For most of us, the workplace is much more than a place to make a living. It is often at work that our lives take on value beyond ourselves and our families, where we are able to make a broader contribution to society. It is also the place where intellectual ideas are honed for, and through, their application.

Instead of disparaging students' interest in their careers, we should help them see how the work they do can be an arena for personal growth, intellectual adventure, social purpose, and moral development. We should help students see how the values of intellectual honesty, personal integrity, and tolerance can strengthen the institutions in which they will work.

We should help students build bridges between the intellectual concerns they encounter in our courses of philosophy, literature, and history and the decisions they will have to make as business people, lawyers, or government officials. We should, in the end, celebrate their determination to find a niche in the turbulent and competitive contemporary economy.

We may romanticize the days when graduates could focus on a calling and not worry about an income. But it would be more realistic, and certainly more helpful, to awaken students to the callings they can find within their work.

Reflective Writing: *In this essay, Northeastern University President Freeland puts forward a broad, overarching argument in favor of a professional education that is intellectually challenging in addition to helping prepare students for the work world. In this argument, he attempts to counter the views of those who would say that only a liberal education emphasizing the arts and sciences has sufficient academic rigor. Consider more specifically how Freeland's ideas might apply to one particular field of study.*

Possible Essay Topics

For this assignment, choose one of the following topics and write a timed, in-class essay. In your essay, be sure to draw significantly on readings from this unit of the anthology. But rather than merely summarizing or restating ideas from the essays, you will also want to add your own discussion and analysis of the readings and how they relate to your own ideas and experiences. Make sure your ideas are well developed and your prose carefully edited and proofread.

1. The readings in this unit all deal in one way or another with the question of what college is for. Cahn and Jackson make different kinds of arguments in favor of broad, liberal arts study as a necessary part of higher education. Neusner and Boyer consider the role of the major in students' overall education, while Reich focuses on the relationship between higher learning and career prospects. Examine in depth two of these different arguments for being in college, in light of, and in explicit relation to, what you've read, talked about, and worked on in this course and in light of your own motivations and experiences.

2. Read over the "official" discussion of learning and curriculum provided by the department you plan to major in, and consider the relationships among your own motivations for being in college, the department's statement, and notions of learning and intellectual development discussed by several of the authors in this unit. Relate the statement as specifically as you can to points raised by Neusner and Boyer in this unit, and use your own perspective as a college student to frame your discussion.

3. Steven Cahn discusses the importance of a broad-based education in a democratic society. In Unit One, de Toqueville also mentions American democracy as a strong influence on our nineteenth-century educational system. Consider both of these interpretations in writing your own essay about relationships between education and democracy. See if any of the other readings might be relevant to your discussion as well.

4. Zachary Karabell argues that far too many students attend college who are really not cut out for higher education and would be better off—that is, happier and

more successful—pursuing other options. How would you, as a first-year college student, respond to this author about the advantages of pursuing a college education? Feel free to draw on other readings from this unit in your response.

5. Northeastern University President Richard M. Freeland has written an essay examining not so much the career potential but rather the intellectual benefits and challenges of an education in a technical field. If you are currently majoring in a technical area such as engineering, architecture, or business, write an essay in which you (a) consider what Freeland has to say and (b) examine the academic and intellectual rigors of your own technical education. What is—and what do you think should be—the role of a liberal education in your technical field? In discussing this last question, you may want to consider what such authors as Cahn, Solomon and Solomon, and Boyer have to say.

6. Many of the readings in this unit highlight the idea of college as a place to gain academic knowledge and professional expertise. Yet college also has an important social dimension as a place to make friends, have fun, and experience life in a new way. Write an essay in which you discuss the relationship between the social and academic aspects of life in college. You may wish to defend the social value of college against the more academic focus of the readings.

UNIT FOUR

Education and Assessment

Testing, testing, testing. In many different ways, it affects virtually all aspects of education. Students are assessed constantly in classes and then must pass proficiency exams and achievement tests to move from one level of education to another. Standardized tests play a large role in determining which students are admitted to which colleges. Graduate and professional schools rely heavily on such tests in admissions decisions. Even upon completing school, graduates in fields such as education, law, medicine, and accounting must pass a comprehensive exam before beginning their careers. Districtwide, statewide, and even nationwide tests face students at every turn. A huge, multibillion-dollar assessment industry has developed, and this industry is constantly expanding as testing becomes a more and more integral part of education and career training. In fact, a key issue in the 2000 U.S. presidential election concerned which candidate was proposing the larger increases in proficiency testing at the national level—both candidates argued that their plan was the more extensive.

Indeed, educational assessment is so much a part of the landscape of schooling that it may almost seem invisible, taken for granted, inevitable. For students tested throughout their entire school careers, it may be hard even to imagine schooling without such extensive assessment. But not all believe this burgeoning role of educational assessment is such a good thing. Many educators argue that the emphasis on assessment has become excessive. Critics suggest that small- and large-scale testing takes up a disproportionate amount of class time, limiting the amount of material that can be covered; that too often testing drives the curriculum, determining what material will be studied; and that standardized college entrance exams play too large a role in admissions decisions. Many educators worry that an overemphasis on testing and grades has helped make students less interested in learning for its own sake and too concerned about the bottom line. Testing proponents counter that assessments keep the educational process on track, provide useful motivation, and help educators make important distinctions regarding student performance. These are just some of the issues surrounding educational assessment, a subject that, by this point, unless you were home-schooled, you are almost certain to be intimately familiar with.

The readings in this unit focus on important aspects of educational assessment, from college admissions testing, to the role of grading, to the prevalence of cheating. The first three essays all concern standardized tests for getting into college, focusing particularly on the largest and most influential of those tests, the SAT. This topic may not seem especially relevant now that you are actually in college. But perhaps you will think otherwise after reading these pieces, which detail the significant role the SAT often plays in determining entrance to the social, political, economic, and educational elite in American society. In the first essay, Peter Sacks examines the origins of standardized testing in Britain and the United States. He looks at the beliefs and prejudices of the founders of modern testing and suggests that some of those prejudices remain a part of standardized testing today. Next, Brian Doherty critiques the SAT, questioning the test's fairness and also its accuracy in determining potential for success in college. Finally, William Dowling defends the accuracy of the verbal portion of the test in measuring students' academic abilities and supports his argument with evidence and examples from actual test questions.

Essays in this next subsection focus more on classroom assessment issues. College student Patrick O'Malley argues that instructors should give frequent exams and quizzes, as a way of forcing students to study more often and, therefore, increasing student learning. Journalist Mark Clayton discusses the question of academic dishonesty, its pervasiveness, the methods students use, and the attitudes students, faculty, and administrators have about cheating in school. Physician and learning specialist Patricia O. Quinn investigates the problems and coping strategies of learning disabled students, who struggle with traditional assessment measures, in succeeding in college. In contrast, a professor and specialist on education and the law, Perry Zirkel, examines the tests used to determine whether or not particular students really do have a learning disability and are, therefore, entitled to extra time, special tutoring, and other special considerations in their classes. The closing essay, by Professor Jacob Neusner, urges students to grade their professors and provides a set of criteria by which students can make their judgments.

Inventing Intelligence:
The Origins of Mental Measurement

Peter Sacks

Peter Sacks is a writer and critic of educational assessment. This reading comes from the author's 1999 book Standardized Minds: The High Price of America's Testing Culture and What We Can Do to Change It. *Sacks relates some of the history of intelligence testing, from its origins in nineteenth-century England to its development and large-scale implementation in the twentieth century in this country. In providing a chronology of developments in aptitude testing, the author also puts forward a definite point of view regarding such tests.*

To Consider: *What are some of the aspects of the history of mental measurement that seem to concern Sacks most? How does he relate the focus of intelligence testing in the nineteenth and early twentieth centuries to the present-day emphasis on such testing? Why does he find it significant that the originators of these tests came from privileged, upper-class backgrounds?*

It's imperative to remind ourselves of how mental testing got its start in the United States. Modern mental testing, and its principal prescription to allocate opportunity based on the designation of the cognitively deserving and undeserving, is hardly a recent invention.

Recall the eugenics movement earlier this century, when state and national policymakers passed laws to stem the flow of such intellectually and morally "inferior breeds" as Italians, Jews, Poles, and other foreigners who came to America during the waves of European immigration. The nation's pioneers of intelligence testing provided lawmakers with the scientific rationale they needed for policies that are now roundly condemned as cruel and misguided: Tens of thousands of army recruits, including recent immigrants, were subjected to IQ tests; bizarre but supposedly scientific conclusions about the natural laws of intelligence were drawn; and eugenically appropriate public policies were enacted in several states.

"An accurate measurement of everyone's intelligence would seem to herald the feasibility of selecting the better endowed persons for admission into citizenship—and even for the right of having offspring," wrote Charles

Spearman, among the fathers of modern intelligence testing, in his 1927 treatise, *The Abilities of Man*. So allocating individuals to their proper role in society, based on their intelligence, would render "perfect justice" with "maximum efficiency," Spearman told us. (1)

Gone, of course, are the unenlightened days when influential scholars and policymakers referred to people as social defectives, calling them "idiots," "morons," "imbeciles," or "degenerates" because of an intelligence test. Or are they? In 1998, when a number of prospective teachers didn't pass a controversial new teacher certification test in Massachusetts, a leading state politician labeled the teachers "idiots." Too, intelligence tests and their ilk continue to be used widely in the United States as a sorting and screening device. Although the eugenics movement as such is defunct and roundly condemned, its spirit persists in powerfully subtle ways that most Americans would barely blink an eye at. The eugenics movement may have faltered, but it nevertheless formed certain habits of mind that have been institutionalized in the American belief system.

Well represented on the fast tracks of academic ability are children of the well educated and well off, whereas children designated to the slow tracks are often poor, members of a minority group, or both. Clearly, the continued use of standardized mental tests in both public and private schools to screen the fast and slow, the bright and not bright, exacerbate already disturbing differences in wealth and opportunity in the United States.

No, it is not called eugenics any more; that's a bad word. Nowadays, except for the politicians' occasional misspoken word or two, people are rather more progressive and urbane about such matters, preferring to call this state of affairs a "meritocracy." That's a good word, one that few Americans would take issue at.

To be sure, the roots of modern mental testing are far more complex than what this chapter shows. But the aim of this chapter is to present a distillation of the main ideas of the paradigm's principal thinkers and show how their ideas remain intimately connected to the standardized mental testing of schoolchildren and adults nowadays, practices that are plagued by the same old mystifications and popular confusions. At bottom is confusion about the most basic of questions: Exactly what is intelligence, and what is it that intelligence tests really measure?

British Roots

The British mental measurement duo of Francis Galton and Charles Spearman are good people to begin with. Galton may well be considered the father of modern mental measurement. Having an obsessive tendency to count things, he invented many of the statistical techniques mental testers routinely employ to measure cognitive ability. Profoundly influenced by Charles Darwin and the role that natural selection of superior genes played in the evolution of species, Galton was an early advocate of the modern meritocratic view that the finest genetic material be permitted to rise to the top of the human heap. He was a rabideugenicist.

Like virtually all of Britain's most influential mental measurement pioneers, Galton was born into the upper social crust in 1822. His maternal grandfather was Erasmus Darwin, a well-known biologist and poet; Galton's cousin was Charles Darwin himself. When Galton's father died, Francis was provided with a fortune that permitted him a lifelong supply of independent wealth, world travel, and the means to pursue his compulsion to quantify the human mind.

Galton was an inveterate measurer and counter. His favorite saying was, "Wherever you can, count," and he applied that motto to the study of meteorology and psychology. In fact, one finds in the early mental measurement theorists like Galton, himself so influenced by Darwin, a blinding desire to place the study of human behavior into the constellation of the rigorous natural sciences. Measurement, sorting, and counting alone for Galton and his successors gave any endeavor the imprimatur of a hard science, whatever it might lack in other attributes that distinguishes real science from pseudo-science.

Galton invented many pathbreaking statistical methods for measuring intelligence, but his most indelible legacy to the way moderns think about intelligence was conceptual and ideological. After studying abilities in twins raised apart, Galton posited that intelligence is constituted by an overarching, general mental ability, as opposed to a quite distinct set of various special abilities. Also, individual differences in general mental ability were naturally selected, in a Darwinian sense. In other words, intelligence was largely an inherited trait. Galton coined the "eugenics" term, and founded the Eugenics Society (recently renamed the politically corrected Galton Institute). Galton once said: "The most merciful form of what I ventured to call 'eugenics' would consist in natality for the indications of superior strains or races, and in so favouring them that their progeny shall outnumber and gradually replace that of the old one." (2)

It would be too easy to dismiss Galton because of views that sound so similar to Nazi Germany's genocidal project to achieve racial purity. More important for our purpose is to recognize the significant connection Galton made between eugenics and meritocracy.

In Galton, the spheres of meritocracy, mental measurement, and eugenics converged into a single, simple narrative. This member of the British aristocracy might, indeed, be considered the father of modern views of meritocracy, in which one succeeds (or not) on the basis of intelligence and wit rather than one's inheritance. Society's role, therefore, was to promote policies and methods that would provide enlightened assistance to nature for selecting the best and brightest for society's most important roles.

For all Galton's influence on modern IQ mythology, Charles Spearman may have been the more important of the British mental testers in terms of setting the stage for the practical applications and interpretations of intelligence testing. Spearman gave quantitative precision to Galton's hypothesis that human intelligence was governed by a general ability that connected the dots among all other specific intellectual abilities. In doing so, Spearman harbored the conceit that his discovery of the universal principles of intelligence was akin to the monumental discoveries of the natural sciences, such as Newton's laws of motion or the laws of thermodynamics.

A fellow member of the British upper class, Spearman was a great admirer of Galton, particularly Galton's concept of "a general mental ability," passed on from generation to generation as part of an evolutionary process of natural selection of the fittest. "The notion of a general ability," says Spearman admirer Arthur Jensen, "seemed far more compelling to Spearman" than the view that humans might be "intelligent" in one or more of several ways, such as creativity, perception, memory, and so on. (3)

In his landmark 1904 paper in the *American Journal of Psychology,* " 'General Intelligence,' Objectively Determined and Measured," Spearman reported his discovery of the "general factor" of intelligence that he simply called "*g*." He likened the discovery to the grand theoretical breakthroughs of astronomy and physics, thereby providing experimental psychology with the "missing link in its theoretical justification," and produced "a practical fruit of almost illimitable promise." (4)

Spearman provided the missing link with a series of experiments involving children at a village school in Berkshire, taking measurements of their abilities in the classics, French, English, mathematics, sensory discrimination (responsiveness to light, sound, and so on), and music. Spearman analyzed his data by means of the recently invented statistical techniques of correlation analysis to determine how the schoolchildren's different abilities varied with each other. He also determined the statistical association between various abilities and several independent measures of intelligence, as indicated by rank in school, teachers' ratings, the opinion of the school rector's wife, and so on.

Before proceeding, a brief note about correlation analysis is in order for nonstatisticians. A zero correlation suggests no relationship between one variable and another, whereas a correlation of one (1.0) means that a variable rises or falls in perfect proportion to another. Generally, correlations of greater than 0.5 are considered fairly substantial degrees of association. Another thing to keep in mind: A correlation is typically designated simply as "r," and is calculated from a fairly arcane mathematical formula. Nonspecialists, however, might well be advised to routinely square that simple correlation to arrive at what's known as the "*r-squared,*" which gives a truer picture of the proportion of change in one variable that's associated with independent changes in another variable. Thus, a simple r of 0.5 squares to 0.25, meaning that 25 percent of the variance in one factor is associated with change in another one. Thus, nonstatisticians should beware that unsquared correlations leave the impression of a greater association between variables than actually exists.

Now, back to Spearman. As it turned out, most of the abilities he measured at the village school were not just highly associated with one another but also with his independent measures of intelligence. Achievement in the classics, for instance, was strongly associated with performance in French ($r = .83$) and English (.78); lesser relationships held between classics and mathematics (.70), classics and sensory discrimination (.66), and classics and music (.63). Oddly, Spearman found the lowest correlations between music and sensory discrimination and mathematics and musical talent (.40).

Based on these correlations, Spearman ranked the abilities into a hierarchy with the classics at the top, followed by French, English, mathematics, sensory discrimination, and music at the bottom. These relationships prompted Spearman to forge his grand theorem, "The Universal Unity of the Intellective Function," which stated that some "general factor," or g, was the engine driving the high association among the abilities. The classics were "loaded" with a lot of this g, French and English somewhat less, and music less still. His theorem was seemingly proven beyond doubt when he showed correlations between his measures of intelligence and the several abilities. Greek and Latin classics, being most highly saturated with the common factor g, were almost perfectly correlated with intelligence at 0.99.

Spearman was clearly enthused with this discovery of his law of Universal Unity of the Intellective Function, common to all cognitive abilities—based as it was upon on a small study of a few dozen schoolchildren. Spearman liked to believe his law was "both theoretically and practically" a "momentous" occasion for psychology. His cautions about what the finding might portend for the measurement of minds were of the boilerplate variety, as he suggested in an afterthought that further corroboration of his result would, of course, be needed. (5)

Still, Spearman's dutiful cautions about his general law didn't dissuade him from suggesting that public examinations on school subjects would be a useful proxy for objectively measuring one's overall intelligence, and therefore determine one's place in the social hierarchy. "Here would seem to lie the long wanted rational basis for public examinations," he wrote, objecting to protests that high test scores on, say, Greek syntax were surely not indicative of the "capacity of men to command troops or to administer provinces." At long last, Spearman told us, "precise accuracy" of measuring human intelligence was at hand. (6) In what's considered his greatest work, Spearman's *Abilities of Man* further refined and qualified the contours of g, and he proclaimed the scientific import of the discovery of "a system of ultimate mental laws" as being equivalent to the "Copernican Revolution." (7)

There's No There There

That Spearman elevated his finding to that of a universal natural law remains all the more startling considering the flimsy methodological foundation on which his grand theory stood—flaws that would not pass muster in genuine modern science.

What was the explanatory science behind Spearman's *g?* What he gave us was a quite particular statistical pattern that he fairly arbitrarily characterized as being imbued with a profound scientific meaning, when in fact, *there's no there there.* Other than speculating that some kind of mental energy explained the existence of *g,* Spearman's *g* lacked then and continues to endure without having the most fundamental element of science: a plausible explanation of cause and effect that might account for the observed data.

Harvard astronomer David Layzer took to task Spearman and his mental measurement progeny of recent times, including Arthur Jensen, on this point. The view that the discovery of *g* was a product of real science, simply because it appeared supported by statistical evidence, Layzer observed, is unfounded. "The first and most crucial step toward an understanding of any natural phenomenon is not measurement," he says. "One must begin by deciding which aspects of the phenomenon are worth examining. To do this intelligently, one needs to have, at the very onset, some kind of explanatory or interpretive framework." (8)

Behind the seemingly elegant statistics, the most glaring problem with Spearman's experiments on abilities was this: His independent measures of intelligence were in fact proxies for the very same abilities he was assessing. In other words, his intelligence measures—tied as they were to performance in the school subjects and teachers' opinions—were by definition dependent on changes in his chosen abilities. They amounted to the very same thing, and so of course, they would seem to correlate highly with each other.

That problem alone would suggest that Spearman's seemingly profound results were trivial and spurious. At best, one might conclude that his data demonstrated some relationship between a specific verbal or language ability and performance in Greek, Latin, French, and English. As British observers Brian Evans and Bernard Waites suggest, Spearman built his tests of *g* with "scrupulous selection of the items," rendering *g* meaningless beyond the simple arithmetical correlation that arose among Spearman's craftily engineered choice of test items. (9)

Spearman's legacy, then, is forging the indelible interpretation that persists to this day, that intelligence and performance in certain academic subjects are virtually synonymous. The entire edifice of *g* was constructed on the basis of performance on particular school subjects.

Hence, one arrives on the central flaw of Spearman's g that continues to plague mental testing's entire house of cards. Spearman's g is a general factor of what, exactly? By whose set of cultural rules are test items that capture this g included? Is g really a general ability or a spurious result of the common characteristics of very similar, specific abilities?

Alfred Binet's Pragmatism

Although Spearman was developing his pseudo-scientific explanation around his empirical observations of the intelligence of schoolchildren, Alfred Binet of France was actually creating the first practical intelligence test. Under marching orders from the French minister of public instruction in 1904 to create a reliable means for identifying mentally "defective" children, a test that would justify their being kept out of regular classrooms, Binet and his young collaborator, a physician named Simon, developed their so-called Binet-Simon Scale. That test established many of the principles and practices that continue to serve as the model for contemporary IQ testing of young children. Indeed, the Binet-Simon Scale is the original version of an intelligence test known nowadays as the Stanford-Binet Intelligence Scale, a commercially produced test that continues to be among the most popular IQ tests in the United States.

The name of the Binet-Simon Scale itself suggests its creators' principal innovation. With a series of small tests progressing from easy tasks to difficult ones, the Binet-Simon measured a child's level of intelligence according to the most difficult items he or she was able to perform. In turn, the highest level performed was equivalent to the child's so-called mental age. Thus, for instance, a four-year old who successfully performed the tasks of which most six-year-olds were capable, and no more, was said to have a mental age of six.

Binet's original, 1905 scale consisted of thirty tasks, or subtests, including many items that we might find familiar on present-day intelligence tests, such as naming objects in pictures, repeating number sequences and sentences, and comparing two weights. Children were examined individually, in a quiet room, in about forty minutes. The quiet room scenario, one-on-one with the examiner, persists as well with the modern Stanford-Binet, although the latest version now takes more than an hour to administer.

According to a series of updates of the Binet-Simon Scale published in the United States in 1916, its creators appeared to grapple from the onset over exactly what their scale measured, influenced as it was by cultural effects such as the social and economic backgrounds of the children. There's much to suggest in the scales themselves that they were powerfully influenced by such cultural factors and that differences in background culture, in turn, were associated with significant differences in children's performances.

When one examines the cultural sensitivity of the Binet-Simon Scale in detail it is evident that the very problems Binet encountered continue to plague modern uses of IQ tests.

In addition to the Binet-Simon Scale being heavily slanted toward verbal and language skills, the "right" answers preferred by Binet and Simon were suggestive of the culturally arbitrary nature of the scale itself. For instance, one question asked, *When the house is on fire, what must one do?* Binet and Simon provided the following three sets of answers given by the children:

- Set 1: *Call the fireman.—Telephone.*
- Set 2: *Save oneself.—Run into the street—One must run so as not to be burned.*
- Set 3: *One must get away.—One must put out the fire.* (10)

I invite readers to guess how Binet and Simon ranked the three sets in terms of the "right" and "wrong" answers. If you replied, as I did, that one should, first and foremost, get out of a burning house, you'd be wrong, according to Simon and Binet. The best answer, in their view, was to call the fireman. But their answer appears to be completely subjective, depending on one's background and experiences. Several questions come to mind: Would children from all the various social classes in Paris of the early 1900s have a telephone in the home? Would children of landowners be more likely than those of the poor to place high value on real property during a fire? Are fire-fighting services equally distributed between wealthy and poor neighbor-hoods, such that all children would even consider calling the fireman? Are the poor who live without reliable firefighting services more likely to attempt to douse the fire on their own?

Each of Simon and Binet's "right" and "wrong" answers to the twenty-five abstract questions can be dissected the same way. Consider question 8, which asks: *When one finds that one's copy book has been stolen, what must one do?* I asked my wife, Kathleen, who's a physician, what her answer might be. "I'd try to find the thief," she answered. Wrong answer. In general, Simon and Binet preferred answers that a child first tell his teacher. The test makers clearly frowned on replies that one either try to find the copybook, try to replace it, or try to find the thief on one's own.

Again, the valued replies appear to have nothing to do with intelli-gence—however that might be defined—and almost everything to do with subjective cultural values of the test makers and distinct cultural attitudes of their own upper-middle-class social milieu, one that perhaps rewards defer-ence to authority figures such as teachers. On the other hand, a tattletale going to the teacher first over a lost copybook might well be considered taboo for other children.

Simon and Binet had little to say on these questions of cultural con-text and "right" and "wrong" answers. In trying to account for some star-tling differences in children's performance on the scale, depending on their social and economic class, the authors acknowledged that much of the scale was laden with language and vocabulary skills learned at home in early childhood.

"Consequently," they write, "we have felt justified in supposing that language played an important part in a good many of the tests. . . . Many others seem to us to depend upon home training. It is not at school that the children are taught the days of the week, the months or colors; it is at home, or at least, it seems to us." The authors conceded, too, that their language-intensive tests provided many advantages to the highly verbal children from the upper social classes. "This verbal superiority must certainly come from the family life; the children of the rich are in a superior environment from the point of view of language; they hear a more correct language and one that is more expressive." (11)

Indeed, Binet and Simon observed that children of well-to-do parents performed consistently better on their scale than children from poor families. The authors cite the work of two independent researchers, Decroly and Degand, who administered the scale to the children of an upper-class private school in Brussels, later publishing their results in the *Archives de Psychologie* in 1910. Binet and Simon compared those results with their public school pupils in Paris's Tenth Ward, whom they describe as generally "poor without being indigent." On average, the Brussels children were measured on the scale as a year and a half advanced over those in Paris. "It is to be supposed," Binet and Simon tell us:

> that the school conducted by M. Decroly and Mlle. Degand is differently recruited. At our request M. Decroly and Mlle. Degand informed us that their pupils belong to a social class in easy circumstances; they have parents who are particularly gifted and understand education in a broad sense; they are renowned physicians, university professors, well known lawyers, etc. (12)

Despite the cultural influences on the Binet-Simon Scale, which the authors themselves more or less acknowledge, they ultimately did not deviate from their contention that the scale was a measure of general intelligence and was independent of whatever abilities a child might acquire at home or school. Their notion of untrained ability, a "natural intelligence," as they called it, was at the philosophical core of the Binet-Simon method, and it continues to hold sway in the intelligence testing of young children.

In the end, Binet and Simon's development of their pathbreaking scale had come from a far different purpose and perspective than Spearman's search for a general factor for intelligence. Still, their end result was reminiscent of Spearman's "g," that unseen and unaccounted-for force of general intelligence that mathematically titrated out of Spearman's tests on academic subjects. Like Spearman, Binet and Simon remained rather mystical about exactly what they were measuring, variously involving the abilities of "judgment, otherwise called good sense, practical sense, initiative, the faculty of adapting one's self to circumstances." (13)

Whatever their version of intelligence might be or however the Binet-Simon Scale accounted for it, what really mattered in their view was having as many tests as possible by which to discover it. "One might also say, 'It matters very little what the tests are so long as they are numerous,'" Binet famously intoned.

Further, Binet and Simon did virtually nothing to clear up the fundamental question in Spearman's work: whether, in fact, it's possible in practice to achieve such a clear conceptual separation between trained and untrained mental power, untainted by cultural forces. Such conceptual difficulties, however, were of no hindrance to the American promoters of intelligence testing, who steamrolled their version of the Binet-Simon Scale onto the American landscape.

Importing the IQ Test to America

For all the uncertainty surrounding what the Binet-Simon Scale was actually measuring—whether it was intelligence as such or some artifact of the authors' own upper-middle-class culture—observers have since speculated that Binet would have been horrified at the way his scale has been used since its importation to the United States.

Binet intended the scales as no more than a diagnostic tool for assessing the developmental progress of children, and he refrained from interpreting the scores on the examinations as the result of some fixed and unchangeable quantity of mental ability endowed at birth. In fact, he believed that one's intelligence measured with his scale could be improved, and he prescribed certain "mental orthopedics" for doing so. To those "recent philosophers" who were arguing otherwise, Binet replied, "We must protest and react against this brutal pessimism." (14)

"Binet would have resisted vigorously the hereditary-environment controversy of the next research generation," says Joseph D. Matarazzo, in a biographical sketch, "considering it as a pseudo-problem, born of an incomplete understanding of the nature of psychosocial assessment, on the one hand, and the crudity of his early test forms, on the other." (15)

We'll never know exactly how Binet would have reacted to the use of his scale in the United States. He died in 1911, five years before his creation was imported and Americanized by Lewis M. Terman of Stanford University in 1916. Under Terman's guidance and promotional skills, his Stanford-Binet Scales would become a commercial star as well as the standard for all intelligence tests to come.

Considering the human toll that ensued from mass intelligence testing of Americans after the Stanford-Binet's arrival, one could say that Binet's simple creation would become to the measurement of human minds what Einstein's famous expression about energy, matter, and the speed of light would become to human warfare. In both cases, the technology itself far outstripped larger understandings and the requisite social institutions needed to control the technology. In the case of IQ testing, the technology itself and its enthusiastic promotion often seemed to create its own set of social needs and justifications. In essence, promoters of testing in the United States had announced their magic bullet, a simple test that once and for all would measure the intelligence of human beings. Terman and his followers invited Americans to partake in all the various and wonderful ways to which the new technology could be put to use.

Indeed, one might speculate that quintessentially American commercial motivations may have driven interest and growth of the early Stanford-Binet as much as any social or scholarly motivations of its promoters. In Terman's 1916 book that unveiled Stanford-Binet to the public, *The Measurement of Intelligence,* his first task was to enumerate dozens of potential uses for the tests. The "feeble-minded," delinquents, criminals, schoolchildren, and job-seekers would all be ideal subjects for intelligence tests. Like a simple blood test, Terman's editor, Elwood P. Cubberly predicted, the intelligence test's stamp of scientific precision would unambiguously confirm any suspected defects in a person.

Although Terman's Stanford-Binet retained its predecessor's fundamental ambiguities about the nature of intelligence, Terman was not hesitant to attach exceedingly high stakes to these "blood tests." Of the "feeble-minded," Terman wrote: "It is safe to predict that in the near future intelligence tests will bring tens of thousands of these high-grade defectives under the surveillance and protection of society. This will ultimately result in curtailing the reproduction of feeble-mindedness and the elimination of an enormous amount of crime, pauperism, and industrial inefficiency." (16)

To be sure, those eugenicist views can be seen as historically interesting and unfortunate but, one might object, Terman's views then have little relevance to Americans now. Whether that's true or not, however, is irrelevant to a more important point: Besides his role in creating several new uses for intelligence tests, Terman can be credited as the inventor of a certain lingua franca, a philosophical structure for thinking about intelligence that continues to thrive in meritocratic culture today, however one might feel about the eugenics wrapper that covered his views.

Among his practical innovations, Terman may deserve substantial credit for linking intelligence and early achievement tests with the modern practice of tracking young children into various academic streams. Although educators typically no longer call the practice "tracking" per se, its essence lives on routinely and largely unchallenged as schoolchildren are segregated into various levels of classes, often depending on test scores.

Says Terman, "We are beginning to realize that school must take into account, more seriously than it has yet done, the existence and significance of these differences in (mental) endowment" which naturally lead to different courses of study. (17)

Another of Terman's gifts to our testing culture is the very American notion of "potential" ability—measured via intelligence and aptitude tests—versus actual performance or achievement as indicated in course grades, years of schooling attained, and other indicators of real-life accomplishments. Terman and other promoters of the IQ test succeeded in convincing policymakers and the public that the intelligence test amounted to a final, indisputable measuring stick of human performance. Mysteriously, such tests of innate ability came to be viewed as a better indicator of human potential than actual performance on the very sorts of things IQ tests were supposed to predict for in the first place.

Indeed, this mode of thinking has become institutionalized in the United States. As just one example, consider Public Law 94-142, the Individuals with Disabilities Education Act. Under that law, a child cannot be designated as having a specific learning disability unless his or her IQ scores are significantly higher than his scores on reading tests. Interestingly, children having this gap between IQ-measured potential and reading scores are eligible for special education services; those children having no such discrepancy are simply considered slow learners, and are not eligible for special services. According to a recent National Research Council report, there's little empirical evidence to support this longtime practice of preferential treatment of those whose potential exceeds their actual performance. (18)

The Great Equalizer

Terman graded one's intelligence according to an intelligence quotient classification system, consisting of the following categories:

- IQ above 140: "Near genius or genius."
- 120–140: "Very superior intelligence."
- 110–120: "Superior intelligence."
- 90–110: "Normal or average intelligence."
- 80–90: "Dullness, rarely classifiable as feeble-mindedness."
- 70–80: "Border-line deficiency, sometimes classifiable as dullness, often as feeble-mindedness."
- Below 70: "Definite feeble-mindedness."

To estimate the number of American children who fell into each category, Terman had to establish American norms, based on the results of giving the revised test to 2,300 subjects, including: 1,700 "normal" children, 200 "defective and superior" children, and more than 400 adults. In addition, he performed various types of analysis on 1,000 IQ scores.

Just as Binet had found on his intelligence test given to schoolchildren in Paris and Brussels, Terman discovered in his data a strong positive association between IQ scores and social class. Of the children, some 492 were categorized by their teachers as belonging to one of five social classes that Terman labeled *very inferior, inferior, average, superior, and very superior.*

Terman's data showed that a child's social class conveyed either significant IQ advantages or disadvantages, depending on whether his family was rich or poor. Belonging to the "superior" social class gave a child a full seven-point advantage in IQ score over the average of all children, whereas being from the "inferior" class provided a child with a seven-point *disadvantage.* (19)

The higher Terman climbed up the IQ scale, the more children he found in the upper rungs of the social and economic ladder. In his "superior" intelligence range of 110 to 120 IQ, Terman found children of well-to-do backgrounds at a rate five times that of children from poorer circumstances: 24 percent of this "superior" IQ group were the wealthier kids—children "of the fairly successful mercantile or professional classes," while just 5 percent of that IQ group consisted of poor children. (20) What's more, at the highest levels of measured intelligence, the numbers of poor and even moderately poor children fell to zero in Terman's data.

Among the intellectually superior, the frequency of university professor dads in Terman's examples was startling. In fact, among fathers of children having "very superior intelligence," there were five university or college professors; a lawyer; a school principal; two whose occupations were not identified; and one house painter—who so happened to be related to John Wesley. (21)

And what model children! Typical of Terman's descriptions was that of a twelve-year-old girl he called J. R., with a "mental age" of sixteen, who was the daughter of a university professor. J. R., says Terman, "was a wonderfully charming, delightful girl in every respect."

How, then, to account for this amazingly strong association between a child's social class and her performance on a mental test? Wasn't the very credibility of his newly imported and revised test of intelligence rendered highly questionable given these results? Not in the least, Terman responded to such questions. Interpreting his results through the hereditarian lens, Terman discounted the differences of home and school environments among social classes as merely run of the mill and inconsequential. Findings from his study on the new intelligence scale, Terman observed, "agree in supporting the conclusion that the children of successful and cultured parents test higher than children from wretched and ignorant homes for the simple reason that their heredity is better." (22)

The public school system, Terman suggested, was the Great Equalizer of the social classes, obviating the influences of family class background and home environment, leaving, for Terman, the cause of IQ differences almost strictly dependent on heredity. He tells us:

> It would, of course, be going too far to deny all possibility of environmental conditions affecting the result of an intelligence test. Clearly no one would expect that a child reared in a cage and denied all intercourse with other human beings could by any system of mental measurement test up to the level of normal children. There is, however, no reason to believe that ordinary differences in social environment (apart from heredity), differences such as those obtaining among (randomly selected) children attending approximately the same general type of school in a civilized community, affects to any great extent the validity of the scale. (23)

The Army Tests

And so Terman's Stanford-Binet Scale would stand, unaffected by yawning differences in economic and social opportunity. Before long, Terman's new device would be detonated among the ranks of U.S. Army recruits during World War I, in an unprecedented, massive application of standardized intelligence tests.

Working under the rather reluctant direction of Robert M. Yerkes, whom the army had appointed as head psychologist, was Carl C. Brigham, a Princeton professor who gave us the most complete public account of those infamous tests of army recruits in his 1923 book, *A Study of American Intelligence*. It is worth reexamining some of Brigham's more absurd conclusions, as perhaps the most historically vivid and explosive example of the cultural dependency of all IQ testing that persists to this day.

Brigham described the army tests as "a national inventory of our own mental capacity." The testing was massive indeed, including 81,000 "native born" Americans, 12,000 foreign-born immigrants, and 23,000 black Americans. Three mental tests were given: American-born recruits competent in English took a paper-and-pencil "Alpha" test; immigrants who didn't speak English were given the so-called "Beta" test, consisting of items thought not to depend on language skills; and each recruit was individually tested either on the Stanford-Binet Scale or on a different "performance scale," depending on competence in English.

Cut to Brigham's notorious conclusions about the intelligence of the foreign-born versus native-born Americans. Virtually all his conclusions were based on the simple comparison of the intelligence scores of the native-born white draftees relative to those of foreign-born white draftees. At high levels of intelligence, Brigham found, were higher proportions of native-borns; and at lower levels of intelligence, according to his combined measures, were greater percentages of foreign immigrants. His results "show clearly that the foreign born are intellectually inferior to the native born," Brigham pronounced. (24)

Although American-born whites were the smartest, according to Brigham, the results also demonstrated a hierarchy of intelligence among the foreign-borns. Draftees from England were easily the most intelligent of the immigrants, as some two in three were more intelligent than the average native-born American. In terms of the percentage who scored higher than the average American, England was followed by (25):

Scotland	58.8 percent	Belgium	35.3 percent
Holland	58.1 percent	Austria	28.0 percent
Germany	48.7 percent	Ireland	26.2 percent
Denmark	47.8 percent	Turkey	25.3 percent
Canada	47.3 percent	Greece	21.3 percent
Sweden	41.7 percent	Russia	18.9 percent
Norway	37.3 percent	Italy	14.4 percent
		Poland	12.2 percent

Following Brigham's analytical logic, he first noted the rather remarkable fact that measured intelligence was significantly related to the number of years one had lived in the United States. Among the foreign-born, scores on the intelligence scale rose sharply with time lived in the States—and indeed, at about twenty years' residence, measured intelligence of the foreign-born draftees were virtually identical to the natives.

The simplest and far more scientifically elegant hypothesis from these data would be that the army mental exams may have been culturally loaded to a profound degree. Therefore, immigrants with more time spent in American culture would clearly be in a position to outperform more recent arrivals to the United States.

Although a complete content analysis of the army mental exams is not my purpose, a few examples from the supposedly culture-free Beta test are illustrative. Like its Alpha counterpart, the Beta version consisted of tightly timed tests of mental gymnastics on meaningless tasks. The boredom factor alone would be enough to nix one's prospects of performing well. Beyond that, the Beta version's supposed culture-blindness was dubious, even laughable in some instances. For example, consider Beta Test 6, the picture completion test, in which examinees were shown twenty pictures, each having some flaw or element left out. According to Brigham's description, the test proctor would point to each picture and instruct the examinees to "fix it." Remember, these recruits didn't understand English; they had three minutes to finish the test.

Presuming the draftees understood the directions, some items were straightforward enough, like putting a nose on a noseless face. But other implicit cultural assumptions in the Beta test are eye-opening. One picture, for instance, shows an envelope with a postmark and the address of the recipient. The picture's supposed flaw, whether it's the lack of a stamp or even the absence of a return address, is ambiguous at best. Immigrants not accustomed to U.S. postal rules would certainly be hard-pressed to know the answer. Another drawing shows two bowlers at a bowling alley, but a test taker would have to know that—and know what bowling is—in order to see that each bowler has no bowling ball. Still another frame is of two tennis players playing on a court—without a net. This, at the turn of the century when tennis was still a sport for elites. One can only speculate how many poor immigrants from Czarist Russia had ever seen a tennis court.

For his part, Brigham did not seriously entertain the possibility that cultural factors could simply account for differences in measured intelligence among the immigrant groups. Indeed, if the tests were representative of the "typically American" experience, all the better. "It is sometimes stated," he snapped, "that the examining methods stressed too much the hurry-up attitude frequently called typically American. . . . If the tests used included some mysterious type of situation that was 'typically American,' we are indeed fortunate, for this is America, and the purpose of our inquiry is that of obtaining a measure of the character of our immigration. Inability to respond to a 'typically American' situation is obviously an undesirable trait." (26)

Thus while the army tests probably were every bit as much culturally loaded as they were stacked with Spearman's mystical *g* factor of general intelligence, Brigham preferred to interpret the measured differences among the immigrants as reflecting superior or inferior breeds of people. He went on to "prove" the race theory by means of a rather bizarre analysis of the supposed blood content of the foreign-born whites. Specifically, he tried to estimate the relative quantities of allegedly superior "Nordic blood" relative to "Alpine blood" and "Mediterranean blood" among the immigrants.

Alas, Brigham tells us, the percentage of "Nordic blood" coming into the United States had declined from 40.5 percent for the decade ending in 1850 to just 22.6 percent for the decade ending in 1920. That immigrants from countries such as England, Germany and Denmark had the highest percentages of "Nordic blood" is testament to their superior results on the intelligence scale.

Further, there was the matter of intelligence and the Jews. Although saying it was "unfortunate" that the army test data didn't provide finer grains of ethnicity among the immigrant countries, Brigham noted that many Jews had immigrated to America from the largely feeble-minded country of Russia. That, for Brigham, amounted to scientific proof in the inferior intelligence of the Jews, contrary to "popular belief." Wrote Brigham: "The able Jew is popularly recognized not only because of his ability, but because he is able and a Jew." (27)

Brigham hammers home his conclusions about race and IQ by defeating yet another straw man, one he called the "typically Nordic" hypothesis. Doing so, he continued to discount the most simple explanation—mere exposure to American culture and language—as the most likely cause of the "intelligence" differences among immigrants. Brigham tells us the only "possible escape" from the conclusion of Nordic god-given intellectual superiority is that the Alpha and Beta tests were biased in their favor, or "typically Nordic." But, refusing to go down the path of a possible cultural explanation for the score differences, Brigham simply states, dismissively, "Perhaps it would be easier to say that the Nordic is intelligent." (28)

Like Terman's Stanford-Binet Scale before, then, the army intelligence tests stood as an unassailable Rock of Gibraltar. Critics of the army tests should abandon their "feeble hypotheses," he said, and "recognize the fact that we are dealing with real differences in the intelligence of immigrants coming to our shores." (29)

Before going on, a final note about Brigham: If Terman had the vision of the widespread and remunerative applications for the new intelligence tests, Brigham had the practical genius to actually make it happen on an unprecedented scale. After Brigham's stint as an army psychologist, he returned to Princeton University, working in the admissions office, where he extended his work on intelligence tests to the sorting and selection of young men for college. That, in turn, resulted in his creation of the Scholastic Aptitude Test, the first large-scale college standardized admission exam, and he became secretary of the College Entrance Examination Board. That test, of course, lives on, known to everybody as the SAT.

Same as It Ever Was

In one form or another, we can hear echoes of Brigham's arguments even today. Whether an intelligence test, an aptitude test for college admissions, or achievement tests on school subjects, the refrain begins to sound familiar. Don't blame the messenger, proponents of mental testing have been telling Americans for decades now. Standardized tests of academic or mental ability are merely snapshots of the often unpleasant, sometimes brutal realities in real differences in human potential, firmly grounded in scientific understandings.

It's worth remembering that the eugenics practices earlier this century were products of their times, ill-considered results of unprecedented social and economic conflict that came with the expansion of industrial capitalism in the early twentieth century. As Charles Spearman suggested, Western capitalism's holy grail was to achieve maximum efficiency with perfect justice. It is still looking, and it is still using standardized tests as the answer.

With the rise of middle-class professionals, bureaucrats, shop owners, and others who shared the worldviews of the emerging bourgeoisie, Western societies at the turn of the century were in search of new rules for allocating opportunity based on merit and ability instead of blood lines. At the same time, these nations were growing enamored with science and modern technology as the answers to difficult public problems. Measuring minds to determine one's intellectual capacity and therefore one's place in a new kind of society appeared to be the perfect technological solution.

Though the science backing it up was woefully lacking, prompting many legitimate scientists to condemn the early mental testers as practitioners of a pseudo-science, mental testing was embraced by a society that saw it as a socially necessary tool of enlightened public policy. Intelligence testing had all the outward appearances of genuine science, and, more important, it provided cannon fodder for beliefs in the genetic inferiority of immigrants who would desire their own piece of the American Dream.

After World War II, economic and social conditions dramatically improved over those at century's turn, and the fortunes of the American middle class rose to unprecedented levels. Class conflict among owners of capital and workers was ameliorated by an evolving industrial capitalism tempered by government programs designed to even out its inherent inequalities, including unemployment compensation, labor protections, and efforts to democratize access to higher education.

However, that smooth postwar narrative has been shattered in recent years with the onset of several profound changes in the structure of the U.S. economy. Basic manufacturing has withered in influence and as a source of jobs, giving way to an economy increasingly driven by consumer services, high technology, and information. This "new" economy has provided exceedingly rich rewards to the highly educated and skilled and has punished scores of others who are without skills and education. As a result, the United States maintains the most highly skewed distribution of wealth between the rich and the poor of any industrial society, rivaling that of many developing nations. Thus, with the increasingly high value the new economy has placed on educational attainment and job skills, the American public has put its education system under unprecedented pressure to remain "accountable," and ensure that their children know what they need to know to survive and thrive in this brave new economy.

Further, the new economy has been accompanied by new ideology. Recent decades have wrought a sustained neoconservative movement of politicians, educational reformers, Washington think-tanks, and others who have succeeded in mounting a rear-guard action questioning the scope of federal programs. There has been a resurgence in the classical belief in the "natural order" of things, a belief grounded in a new sort of social Darwinism. Like the eugenics movement of the past, proponents of this new natural order are in need of new theories of inequality, properly updated to the sensibilities of polite society, to justify vastly unequal allocation of the nation's economic spoils.

These powerful ideological and economic trends have laid a fresh foundation for a resurgence of mental measurement in the United States. Just as the technology of mental testing performed its desired social function in the past to legitimize beliefs in genetic inferiority and exclude the new immigrants from U.S. enterprise, Americans are witnessing a reinvigorated role for mental measurement as the gatekeeper to the new economy, including testing for intelligence and ability, personality, academic achievement, and scores of other traits.

Indeed, the arguments contained in the infamous work, *The Bell Curve* by Richard Herrnstein and Charles Murray, are nothing new. The work was merely the most recent installment of a long intellectual tradition begun by the eugenicists and their mental measurement brethren. The Murray-Herrnstein book touched a nerve with an increasingly neoconservative audience receptive to its basic message: Inequality of class and race in America was simply the result of the natural order of things, arising from profound, heritable differences in the cognitive abilities of individuals. By now, that pessimistic refrain should sound familiar to readers.

And so, in this new struggle for opportunity and privilege, the nature of "defective" persons has changed from the days of Spearman, Terman, and Brigham. But the basic principle and means by which to identify these new defective persons has not changed. Polite society nowadays has its own "defectives" who don't measure up on standardized tests of so-called intelligence. Once upon a time, they were Italian and Jewish immigrants. Now, they are the poor, the uneducated, African Americans, American Indians, people with learning "disabilities," those for whom English is a second language, and others.

In the past, the designated defectives were said to be genetically inferior. Now it is simply said that, according to this snapshot on this objective test, they lack requisite abilities, cognitive development, or aptitude. Curiously, the outcome has remained eerily similar in both eras, punishing those not born to the right parents and attending the right schools, while propping open the doors of opportunity for the well-to-do. You could call it "perfect justice."

Indeed, the very same kinds of measures that sorted individuals by some correlate of intelligence in America's past remain a steady fact of institutional and social policy today, however abhorrent one may find eugenics views of history.

Notes

1. "An accurate measurement of everyone's. . . ." Charles Spearman, *The Abilities of Man* (New York: Macmillan, 1927), p. 8.
2. Galton once said. . . . quoted in Brian Evans and Bernard Waites, *IQ and Mental Testing: An Unnatural Science and its Social History* (London: Macmillan, 1981), p. 41.
3. A fellow member of the British upper class, Spearman was a great admirer of Galton . . . *Encyclopedia of Human Intelligence*, s.v. "Francis Galton, Robert J. Sternberg, editor (New York: Macmillan Publishing, 1994), p. 1009.
4. In his landmark 1904 paper . . . Charles Spearman, " 'General Intelligence,' Objectively Defined and Measured," *American Journal of Psychology* 15 (1904), p. 206.
5. Whenever branches of intellectual activity are at all dissimilar, ibid., p. 273.
6. ". . . here would seem to lie the long wanted rational basis for public examinations . . ." ibid., p. 277.
7. In what's considered his greatest work . . . Charles Spearman, *The Abilities of Man* (New York: Macmillan, 1927), p. 411.

8. Harvard astronomer David Layzer. . . . David Layzer, "Science or Superstition? A Physical Scientist Looks at the IQ Controversy," *The IQ Controversy: Critical Readings*, edited by N. J. Block and Gerald Dworkin (New York, N.Y.: Pantheon Books, 1976), pp. 194–241.

9. That problem alone would suggest. . . . ibid., p. 58.

10. In addition to the Binet-Simon Scale being heavily slanted toward verbal and language . . . Alfred Binet and Th. Simon, *The Development of Intelligence in Children* (Baltimore: Williams and Wilkins Co., 1916), p. 124.

11. "Consequently," they write, "we have felt justified in supposing. . . ." ibid., p. 320.

12. "It is to be supposed," Binet and Simon tell us. . . . ibid., p. 317.

13. Reminiscent of Spearman's "*g*," the unseen and. . . . ibid., p. 42.

14. Binet intended the Scales. . . . quoted in Leon J. Kamin, *The Science and Politics of IQ* (Potomac, Md.: Lawrence Erlbaum Associates, 1974), p. 5.

15. "Binet would have resisted vigorously. . . ." *Encyclopedia of Human Intelligence*, s.v. "Alfred Binet," Robert J. Sternberg, editor (New York: Macmillan Publishing, 1994), p. 188.

16. Of the "feeble-minded," Terman wrote. . . . Lewis M. Terman, *The Measurement of Intelligence* (Boston: Houghton Mifflin, 1916), pp. 6–7.

17. Among his practical innovations. . . . ibid., p. 4.

18. Indeed, this mode of thinking has become institutionalized. . . . National Research Council, Board of Testing and Assessment, *The Use of IQ Tests in Special Education Decision Making and Planning* (Washington, D.C.: National Academy Press, 1996), pp. 20–21.

19. Terman's data showed. . . . Lewis M. Terman, *The Measurement of Intelligence* (Boston: Houghton Mifflin, 1916), ibid., p. 115.

20. The higher Terman climbed. . . . ibid., p. 94.

21. Among the intellectually superior. . . . ibid., p. 97.

22. Findings from his study on the new intelligence scale. . . . ibid., p. 115.

23. "It would, of course, be going too far. . . ." ibid., p. 116.

24. Those results "show clearly that the foreign born are intellectually inferior. . . . Carl C. Brigham, *A Study of American Intelligence* (Princeton: Princeton University Press, 1923), p. 87.

25. In terms of the percentage who scored higher than the average American. . . . ibid., p. 119.

26. "It is sometimes stated," he snapped, "that the examining methods. . . ." ibid., p. 96.

27. Further, there was the matter. . . . ibid., p. 190.

28. Brigham hammers home his conclusions. . . . ibid.

29. Like Terman's Stanford-Binet Scale. . . . ibid., p. 180.

Reflective Writing: *After reading this essay carefully, provide a brief chronological sketch of the ideas and events leading up to the development of the modern educational testing movement. What do you think is the author's attitude toward such testing? Where and how do you see this attitude revealed? What is your own view of the author's conclusion that standardized testing today is as unfair and elitist as it was in the early twentieth century?*

Those Who Can't, Test

Brian Doherty

In this essay, the author presents an argument against college entrance examinations such as the SAT, which is administered by the large and powerful Educational Testing Service. The essay was originally published in Mother Jones Magazine *in 1998. Doherty coedited* Democracy and Green Political Thought, *with Marius de Geus (1996) and served as assistant editor for* Reason Magazine. *His title is a pun on the old saying, "Those who can, do. Those who can't, teach."*

To Consider: *Doherty criticizes the SAT from a number of different angles, arguing, for example, that the test favors students from wealthy and privileged backgrounds. Make a list of the different arguments the author makes against the widespread influence of the SAT and describe the support he provides for his arguments.*

"What does 'ETS' stand for?" asks the instructor. A beat for comic timing, then the answer: "Evil Test Society." It's not all that funny, really—ETS actually stands for Educational Testing Service—but it breaks the tension gripping this room full of college-bound high school students, and a wave of chuckles washes over the Sunday morning Princeton Review SAT prep class in west Los Angeles. The instructor, a comedian and actress by trade, seems pleased to have won over her audience. Though the kids are here by choice—and their parents are paying $745 for the privilege—most of them seem as loath to answer her prompts as any batch of ennui-haunted teenagers. They are peaceful enough, even drowsy. Still, the handful of kids here on a summer morning is at the front lines of a battleground in the war against standardized testing.

America ruptures along fault lines of ethnicity and class, and the SAT, which is written and administered by ETS, is a potential earthquake. Not surprisingly, California feels the strains of the SAT more than most.

In the wake of the passage of California's controversial Proposition 209 (which ended the use of ethnicity and gender consideration in college admissions), the University of California system is seeing a substantial decline in African American and Latino admissions to its twin flagships, UC-Los Angeles and UC-Berkeley. Some groups suggest that eliminating

285

SAT scores as an admissions criterion might remedy that disparity, but that proposal is unlikely to get far. A more realistic option is the "4 percent plan": Any student graduating in the top 4 percent of a class would be automatically eligible for admission to the UC system—though not necessarily to the campus of his or her choice.

What California could be stumbling toward, Texas has already fallen into. In 1996, the 5th U.S. Circuit Court of Appeals' *Hopwood* decision meant an end to affirmative action at the University of Texas system as well. This fall, in response to the decision, Texas enacted a 10 percent rule, admitting the top 10 percent of every Texas high school graduating class regardless of SAT scores. Thus, no big changes in minority admissions are expected in Texas' state universities.

Down in Texas, faltering in California—could the SAT really be on the ropes? Princeton Review devoutly hopes so, despite the fact that last year 35,000 kids paid the nationwide coaching service almost $26 million to learn how to beat the standardized test.

"People ask me if I'm being disingenuous: 'How can we believe you when you say you think SATs should be abolished?'" says Jay Rosner, executive director of the Princeton Review Foundation, the nonprofit wing of the Princeton Review empire that offers reduced-fee courses to minority students. "Don't you think doctors who make their living treating disease would be happy if disease disappeared?"

A lawyer, Rosner has been tilting at ETS for more than a decade, serving as an attorney in various lawsuits against the testing giant, mostly representing kids whose scores have been challenged by ETS in court. (If ETS thinks your scores are suspiciously high, it will go to mighty efforts to prove you're a cheater.)

Princeton Review's founder and president, John Katzman, says that before starting the company in 1981, he was a fan of the test. "I loved the SAT," he says. "The SAT had been very, very good to me." But the SAT didn't love him back. According to Katzman, in 1985, ETS sent spies to some of Princeton Review's courses and found 13 questions on its practice exams that ETS thought were suspiciously close to actual SAT questions, which are ETS's intellectual property. ETS sued Princeton Review and ended up settling out of court for $50,000, though Katzman says his legal fees were at least 10 times that. (ETS says it found at least 100 of its questions on the practice tests, and denies using "spies.")

"It's like I was walking through India munching a burger and had no idea what I was doing," Katzman remembers. "You find yourself in the middle of a holy war and you don't know what hit you. The whole concept of prepping for the SAT was much more controversial than I realized."

For a nonprofit corporation, ETS makes a lot of money from its tests (it had $41 million in cash reserves as of June 1997). ETS is responsible not only for the SAT but also for the Graduate Record Exam (GRE), the Advanced Placement (AP) tests, and the Test of English as a Foreign Language (TOEFL), among many others. ETS sells its standardized wares to the College Board, ostensibly responsible for the SAT, but The Chauncey Group, ETS's for-profit arm, also sells ETS tests to companies such as Microsoft, Oracle, and the American Society of Plumbing Engineers, all for use in testing and placing potential employees and members.

When ETS started in 1947, it began administering an aptitude-measurement test meant to forge order from the chaos of the nation's youngsters and some not-so-youngsters (World War II soldiers returning to school on the GI Bill) by quantifying their academic capacities through a precise, controlled exam. In the minds of the psychometrically obsessed early ETS bureaucrats, the SAT was to be the ultimate expression of the art of mental testing.

In a 1959 booklet, the company claimed the SAT "tells you how fast and how far you can go." Since then, the official line has changed. Now, according to ETS spokesman Kevin Gonzalez, the SAT measures a student's "developed reasoning skills in math and verbal [areas]." The strong correlation between a student's SAT scores and his or her scores on other standardized tests, however, suggests otherwise: What the SAT really tests is how well you do on tests.

So, in addition to trying to teach the very limited body of knowledge the SAT covers (a smattering of vocabulary, and some ninth-grade algebra and geometry), Princeton Review's instructors mostly teach their students test-taking strategies and tricks.

"ETS wants you to feel rushed," explains Victoria De Paoli, the Princeton Review instructor in west Los Angeles. "That's why the test is timed." She scrawls a chart on the chalkboard to show the students two simple things about the test that can work wonders for their scores: (1) questions in each section get progressively harder, and (2) you lose no points for questions left blank and lose only one-fourth of a point for a wrong answer. If you rush through the easy questions under the belief that you ought to answer each one, you're apt to make dumb mistakes on problems you could have gotten right. "Don't go so fast," she says. She can't say it enough.

One kid is hesitant about guessing. The odds seem bad—five choices, and only one is right. But guessers can prosper if they can eliminate even one answer as wrong. Keep in mind, the teacher tells the class, the way the test is scored. Nodding their heads, the students are starting to get it: The SAT isn't about knowledge; it's about beating the test.

Some high school teachers criticize Princeton Review because its training favors stunts over skills. Today's Princeton Review class seems to exemplify this tendency. De Paoli demonstrates to an incredulous class that you needn't read all of a reading comprehension selection to answer most of the questions—go to the questions first, she says, and they will often guide you right to the line or paragraph you need. And for "PC" authors and subjects—

and there is generally at least one of those—the answer is unlikely to be anything that sounds negative.

She tells them that for the algebra questions, if the multiple-choice answers are given in ascending order, as they often are, just start plugging in the number at "C" for all of them—if it's wrong she says, you've still instantly eliminated three potential answers.

One teenager who's skilled in algebra complains that plugging in the random numbers takes too long. "I like algebra," she says. De Paoli tells her: "Algebra is where careless errors come in."

In the next part of the lesson, De Paoli brings up "Joe Bloggs"—the mythical average student that Princeton Review uses to illustrate how ETS designs the SAT to trick its takers. After all, she says, a test everyone does well on is no good as a screening device. So for questions that are supposed to be hard—ones toward the end of a section, remember—any answer that seems obvious is probably wrong. "We're being manipulated," laments the young woman who likes algebra. She's learning Princeton Review's lesson well.

For the vocabulary section, the instructor gets the kids laughing with verbal tricks that seem so contorted it's hard to imagine they're easier to learn than simply memorizing the meaning of the words themselves. The word under discussion is "cogent." How to remember it? "Picture Tom Cruise in the movie *Jerry Maguire*," De Paoli tells the kids. "Remember that movie? Wasn't Tom Cruise COnvincing as an aGENT in that movie?" Oh, of course. Someone who's read a lot won't need these stunts—and also probably won't need Princeton Review at all. The very fact that these techniques actually work is a powerful blow to the idea that the SAT is truly a test of "aptitude," as ETS used to swear.

"Take me through the test, question by question—show me where it tests aptitude," says Katzman. He riffles through a sample test. "That question is asking you the opposite of the word 'pedestrian,' and that one's a geometry question. . . . It seems very unlikely that this is testing anything deep and meaningful." ETS seems to have all but admitted this lack of rigor: SAT used to stand for Scholastic Aptitude Test, but in 1994, ETS changed it to the Scholastic Assessment Test.

Although the Princeton Review is the bad boy of test preparation, its older and more staid competitor, the Kaplan Educational Centers, also stresses in its courses that the SAT is by no means an aptitude test. The SAT, say Kaplan's instructors, tests acquired skills—ones that their 36-hour program can help inculcate. They're proud that ETS has been forced to admit over the years that coaching *can* help. Kaplan's students average a 120-point gain (out of 1,600), with 28 percent achieving a gain of 170 points or more.

ETS will not be quick to let go of the SAT. Even the move toward eliminating the SAT on the part of big state university systems such as in Texas or

California—or the fact that highly desirable, highly competitive liberal arts colleges such as Bowdoin don't even require it anymore—isn't any real skin off ETS's nose. Most prospective students still have to take the test and kick their $22.50 fee to the company. (In 1997, 2.3 million students took the test; ETS grosses close to $50 million a year on this test alone.) And even if UC's board of regents adopts the 4 percent plan, the state will still insist that students take the test, so it can provide a body of data that UC can use to analyze the academic progress of those who were admitted with lower scores. And flawed as it may be, say admissions officials, they have nothing better to rely on. High school grades can vary wildly, and if college admission depended on grades alone, they say, they worry that grade inflation would leap even higher.

But Katzman sees trouble for ETS: "What's happening in Texas and California is the biggest threat to the SAT ever. People have been confronted with [their] inability to work around the test's flaws anymore and are saying, 'It sucks—let's just get rid of it.'"

In the academic community, those who oppose the SAT don't want to get rid of national standardized testing. Instead, they suggest switching to a test that's less flawed, arguing that tests such as the Advanced Placement exams or the SAT-II tests (formerly known as the Achievement Tests) test bodies of knowledge that are both wider and more specific, and might thus encourage high schools to improve their curricula.

In the end, the SAT is still really a problem of elites. All correlations between SAT scores and college grades suffer from the problem of "restricted range"—that is, of being a limited, selective sample. Most people going to college are doing better than the mean. (To understand the concept of restricted range, consider this example: A study of professional basketball players might not find any clear correlation between height and success in basketball—that's because the players are all pretty tall already.) It's true that having a college degree is growing in importance in America. In 1980, among 25- to 34-year-old males, those who had a bachelor's degree averaged 19 percent more income than those without one; by 1996, that same figure had shot up to 54 percent. For black people, a bachelor's degree can mean an even more astounding difference: a 77 percent rise in expected income. For women the rise is even greater still: 88 percent. Yet only 67 percent of high school graduates enter a two- or four-year college, and only around 50 percent of those earn a bachelor's degree within five years. (For blacks, the figures are 60 percent and 34 percent, respectively.)

The meritocracy that the SAT supposedly represents has a powerful emotional grip on Americans—we like to believe in essential fairness, thinking that our society gives each person an equal chance. But supporters of affirmative action maintain that everyone isn't on the same starting line in the United States because the opportunities for advancement, including getting into college, have historically been rigged in favor of whites. And public institutions such as state universities and public schools are inherently creatures of politics, so the issues that concern them, such as the SAT, are doomed to be perpetual political battlegrounds.

The debate about standardized testing is usually argued in numbers; it is really about values. ETS, with its belief that quantification can give clear answers to questions of intellectual stratification, has successfully obscured this point. As college graduation rates begin to hit 50 percent, it's hard to remember that, until 1940, most Americans didn't even finish high school. It may be too late to turn back the clock to the days when a bachelor's degree was a necessary totem for the upper class. (To judge by one of the SAT's strongest correlations, the ability to reason develops in lockstep with family income: the higher your family's income, the higher your score.)

But the children of elites know how important the right college can be. In west Los Angeles—and across America—they are going to classes like the Princeton Review's. Most of the students here have taken the SAT before—some more than once. For them, it isn't a matter of just getting into college, but of making it into UC-Berkeley or UCLA or MIT. Did the price of their summer mornings and their parents' money seem prohibitive, I asked?

Answered one young woman, "My parents said, 'We work to make sure you have the best in life . . . and you *will* go.'"

Reflective Writing: *Doherty makes a strong case against using standardized test scores in college admissions, but he also hints at the case in favor of them. Based on reading Doherty, what positive effects do the standardized tests seem to cause? What of value would be lost if standardized testing were entirely eliminated from the college admissions process? How does presenting some of the opposing points of view affect the persuasiveness of Doherty's overall argument?*

The SAT:

A New Defense

William C. Dowling

Mr. Dowling is a professor of English at Rutgers University in New Jersey and the author of numerous books and articles of literary criticism. This essay comes from the July 2000 issue of the magazine Current. *It is excerpted from his longer essay, "Enemies of Promise: Why America Needs the SAT," from the journal* Academic Questions *(Winter 1999–2000). In this essay, the author argues, against opponents of such testing, that standardized college admission tests such as the SAT legitimately distinguish between qualified and unqualified applicants and do not discriminate based on such factors as race, class, and gender.*

To Consider: *What factors, in the author's view, make the SAT a fair measure of academic ability? What arguments does Mr. Dowling make in attempting to refute the views of critics of the SAT? What assumptions does he make about the value of and need for such tests?*

In March 1998 UCLA Chancellor Albert Carnesale, a cab driver's son who had earlier risen through faculty ranks to become Provost of Harvard, announced to California taxpayers what he thought was a bit of good news. UCLA had just enrolled its most academically outstanding class in history, with freshmen SAT scores putting it among the most selective public universities in the nation. The response, from UCLA's Affirmative Action Coalition, African Student Union, and other campus groups, was outraged, leading to "days of action" at which Mr. Carnesale was accused of wanting to turn UCLA into the "Harvard of the West." These protesters wanted to concentrate not on SAT scores but on a different set of statistics they saw as being an intolerable consequence of Proposition 209, the constitutional amendment that had abolished many affirmative action policies. Since 1997, the number of black, Hispanic, and American Indian freshmen admitted to UCLA had fallen from 2,066 to 1,327, a decline of 36 percent.

On the face of it, the opposition between Chancellor Carnesale and his opponents looks like a simple battle of statistics. Yet for critics of the SAT, the verbal and mathematical reasoning test annually administered to over a million high school seniors by the Educational Testing Service (ETS), the real truth about the confrontation lay in their conviction that Carnesale's statistics constituted an unrecognized public fraud. To the Affirmative Action Coalition, citing a drop in minority enrollments is simply to use a convenient numerical idiom to talk about real 18-year-olds born into poverty or culturally deprived circumstances, actual minority youngsters being denied their rightful place in a public university system. To cite SAT scores is, on the other hand, to parade numbers that are quite literally meaningless, a sort of statistical mumbo jumbo devised by a dominant social class to keep the less fortunate in their place.

Anyone familiar with the rhetoric of FairTest, the Cambridge, Massachusetts organization that has led the national assault on the SATs, will be aware that I am not exaggerating for effect. FairTest's widely-circulated "SAT Fact Sheet," for instance, darkly warns readers that the SAT is "a direct descendant of the racist anti-immigrant Army Mental Tests of the 1920s." An only slightly less inflammatory rhetoric is used by John Katzman, one of the founders of Princeton Review, an SAT-coaching outfit that makes no secret of its contempt for the test. "It's an arbitrary, biased, somewhat pointless exam," says Katzman, "that doesn't test anything important." But criticism of the SAT is not restricted to a few strident critics of ETS and standardized testing. Here is Larry Stedman, a respected researcher on tests and educational policy: "The SAT is a speed endurance test, made up of 200 problems in 3 hours, or more than one problem per minute. And much of it is made up of what can, at best, be charitably called verbal conundrums and math puzzles."

Yet there is a paradox here. Whatever the ultimate verdict on the SAT, its recent role as a scapegoat in the Affirmative Action debate turns the story of the test's actual origins inside out. For the authorizing presence behind national-level standardized testing in America was James Bryant Conant, who, having in 1933 risen to the presidency of Harvard from humble origins, was determined to open the university to intellectually promising students from throughout the United States, regardless of social or economic background. The SAT was developed—largely by Charles Chauncey, then an assistant dean at Harvard under Conant—as part of the Harvard National Scholarship program, through which Conant hoped to break the hold on Harvard of a wealthy, eastern, prep-school-educated elite, and with it a pernicious mind-set including (as Nicholas Lemann says) a "casual and unearned assumption of superiority" and an "inability to see immigrants, Catholics, Jews, and the poor as fully human."

My own interest in the SAT controversy arose initially from my experience as an English professor at Rutgers University—particularly as a regular teacher of English 219, a course in the "close reading" of poetry—and then, as I did more research, from a growing sense that several hidden elements in the controversy have never been gotten across by ETS or others sincerely wishing to defend the test in terms of Conant's original vision, as a common yardstick permitting bright youngsters from disparate backgrounds to aspire to top colleges and universities. (I should say that everything that follows concerns the test's *verbal* section, normally abbreviated as SATV. This test, which is an improved version of the original SAT, has borne the burden of opponents' attacks. The more specialized mathematical section was added only belatedly, in an attempt to improve the SAT's predictive power.)

Verbal Scores

I began to suspect that the SATV measures something real and important several years ago, when one of my Rutgers students came by my office to ask for a recommendation to English graduate programs at Harvard, Yale, Berkeley, and Chicago. At this point, like most English professors, I was fluent in the idiom of SAT verbal scores—and scores on the Graduate Record Examination (GRE), the next-higher-level version of the SAT—and, like university professors generally, had always been disposed to discount them more as badges of socio-economic status than a measure of verbal aptitude or cognitive ability. This particular student, who was from a working-class New Jersey family, had done brilliant work for me as a freshman in English 219 three years before. As is customary, she had brought me her grade transcript—it showed all A's—but being abnormally conscientious, she had also brought a complete packet including her high school SAT and recent GRE scores. In both, she had scored 800 on the verbal section.

As anyone familiar with the ETS scoring system will be aware—the scale on both the SAT and GRE runs from 200 points at the bottom to 800 points at the top—these were spectacular scores. Since this student had done superb work in an English course concentrating on such difficult poets as Donne and Shakespeare and Milton, I began to wonder if the SATV, which I had so often heard debunked as a measure of verbal or cognitive ability, was meaningless after all. When a departmental task shortly thereafter gave me an opportunity to compare the grades of my English 219 students over several years with their incoming SATV scores, I compiled a simple statistical chart. What I found was that the SATV scores had an extraordinarily high correlation with final grades, and that neither, in the many cases where I had come to know my students' personal backgrounds, seemed to correlate very well with socio-economic status.

Nonetheless, I make no claims as a statistician. I mention these correlations only because they led me to several years' research into the SAT controversy. My point in what follows, based on a great deal of reading about the SAT and its implications for educational policy, plus an extensive analysis of actual SAT tests, will simply be that the intuitive sense of most high school and university teachers that some students are verbally brighter than others, and that this bears in a direct and crucial way on their ability to do college-level work, seems to me to match up very well with verbal and cognitive levels as measured by the SATV. The way to understand why this is so, I have come to believe, is not to argue about scores and demographic statistics, but to go inside an actual SAT verbal test to try to get a feel for how it works. That is what I will undertake to do below. Before doing so, however, I want to address one important preliminary issue, which is the mistaken or misleading notion that the SAT, if it is to have any validity as a test of cognitive ability, should be a successful predictor of college grades. For this is a point on which ETS has done as much as opponents of the SAT to encourage widespread confusion.

Almost every attack on the SAT begins by asserting that ETS has fraudulently promoted the test as a predictor of student performance. As usual, FairTest leads the chorus. "What is the SAT Used For?" asks FairTest's "fact sheet." Answer: "The SAT is validated for just one purpose: predicting first-year college grades. It does not do even this very well. Testmakers acknowledge that high school grade-point average (GPA) or class rank are the best predictors of first-year grades, despite the huge variation among high schools and courses." ETS has never been able to counter such charges satisfactorily, not least because in the early days of the SAT it did, in fact, promote the test as a grade predictor. The result has been endless puzzlement about what the SAT is and means.

To understand why the originators of the SAT were disposed to think of the test as a grade predictor, it helps to recall Conant's vision of a common yardstick in relation to the Harvard National Scholarships. Suppose, for instance, that it is 1935. You are a bright high school student from a rural community in Iowa or Oregon, to which the rumor of Harvard has barely penetrated. No one in your family has ever gone to college. The education given by your grammar school and high school is rudimentary. But you have read your way through the local public library—the amount you read is a source of constant amazement to your parents and neighbors—and gotten good grades in your classes. I, on the other hand, simply represent the latest generation of my wealthy Massachusetts family to attend Groton, where, more through sheer tenacity than any outstanding intellectual gifts, I have also managed to compile a good grade point average.

When the SATs appeared on the national scene, there was an element of romance and even suspense in this scenario, a combination of what might be called its prince-and-the-pauper and gunfight-at-the-OK-Corral aspects, that appealed to those who, like James Bryant Conant, had risen from obscure origins through sheer intellectual ability. For if, in the scenario we are imagining, you and I walk into geographically distant rooms on the same day to answer an identical set of questions, and you emerge with a 780 verbal score to my 610, it seems entirely reasonable to suppose that your endless hours of reading have served better to educate you than my six years at Groton. The notion of the SAT as a predictor of grades was originally meant simply as a validation of this point. Were you and I to enter Harvard in the same freshman class, you would have the capacity to outperform me academically—that is, in once-conventional terms, to get better grades—despite the incontestable superiority of my Groton education.

Grade Inflation

Today, as is admitted by virtually everyone except FairTest, this sort of rationale has been blown out of the water by runaway grade inflation at both the high school and college levels. In some high schools, it is now not unusual for more than a third of the senior class to graduate with an A average, and the percentages of A's given out at colleges and universities are endlessly reported in the national press: Georgetown, 42 percent, Harvard, Yale, and Williams all over 35 percent, most public universities 30 percent or higher. Nor do the grades given out even at elite institutions seem to have much relation to student ability or performance. As reported by his lawyer, an impostor who in the early 1990s gained admission to Yale with a fake transcript earned a B average in the two years before he was caught, even though his GPA at the community college he previously attended had been only 2.1. In this climate, predicting grades is a little like predicting the price of potatoes during the Weimar inflation of the early 1920s, a pointless and erratic enterprise.

Still, there is a more important reason why the notion of the SAT as a grade predictor has always been meaningless. It turns on the distinction, still taught in introductory logic courses, between necessary and sufficient conditions. Breathing oxygen is, for instance, a necessary but not a sufficient condition of your remaining alive over the next six months. To specify *sufficient* conditions, one would have to list all the other things—food, water, a certain minimum body temperature—that permit you to function as a physical organism. This is why the notion of the SAT as a predictor of grades made no sense even in the days when grades bore a genuine relation to student performance. For grades involve not just intellectual ability but such factors as discipline, mental concentration, and efficient use of time. In no era could a freshman who chose to get drunk every night rather than to study be predicted to do well in his English classes, whether or not he had entered college with a 780 SAT verbal.

Character

In reality, a high SATV score has always been a measure not of whether a student would perform well in college courses demanding verbal ability, but only of a *sine qua non*—that is, a necessary condition—for doing so. The other factors explain why admissions officers at selective colleges and universities spend so many hours poring over supplementary materials for clues to what in a more innocent age could be called personal and moral character—letters from teachers, employers, and counselors, reports from alumni interviews, the winning of a Westinghouse Science Award or a national violin competition. A 780 verbal assures, in short, that this student can do the work, even if the college is as competitive as Williams or Harvard. But only the other materials in the packet are able to suggest whether this is also a student who, under the pressures of an Ivy League freshman year, might wind up throwing in the towel. On these matters the SAT necessarily remains silent, nor has anyone ever really pretended otherwise.

ETS has never chosen to dwell on this obvious point, one suspects, because in America the very notion of the SAT as a *sine qua non* is a political powder keg. We find it easy enough to admit that a student with a 780 SAT verbal score is not going to do well at Harvard if he spends his evenings getting drunk. It is very difficult to face the fact that a student with a 480 SAT verbal, no matter how disciplined or hard working, simply could not do well there. The popularity of professional sports in American society, it is sometimes said, is due to their being the one domain in which we have somehow come to terms with the idea of natural ability. No American male is offended at being told that, no matter how hard he practiced, he could never be Michael Jordan or, indeed, a starting player in the NBA. Yet the thought that many students with good study habits and high aspirations do not have what it takes to do the work at Harvard or Berkeley remains a source of deep discomfort. It is ETS's quite understandable reluctance to come out and say this that has left it open to attack from organizations like FairTest.

The greatest source of confusion about the SATV is that it purports to measure something—"developed verbal ability," as it is called in the psychometric literature—that can be made to look mysterious, to the point that, like powers of augury or mental telepathy, one may be led to doubt that it exists at all. Yet verbal aptitude isn't mysterious. If you were able to read the first sentence of this paragraph with perfect comprehension, for instance, you were demonstrating a high level of what ETS means by developed verbal ability. Partly, this just means that your vocabulary is large enough to let you understand the English used by educated speakers. (Consider, in that first sentence, *purports, psychometric, augury, telepathy*.) But it also means that you've done enough reading to be able to follow complex sentences, as a violinist or pianist, after years of lessons and practice, is able to sight-read a musical score. That's what people who use the SAT to evaluate student aptitude mean by "developed" verbal ability.

Pragmatics

Now take a moment to think about what was happening as you were reading the preceding paragraph. One feature of your comprehension is especially helpful in understanding how the SATV works. Notice that, although the paragraph consisted of several sentences, you had to understand those sentences not simply as isolated combinations of words, but as adding up to a whole greater than its parts. This is to say that higher-level reading comprehension includes a set of logical, syntactic, and semantic relations so complex that modern linguistic theory has barely begun to see how they work. This is especially true in the area of "pragmatics," which deals with the rules of relevance by which we get from one sentence to the next even in ordinary conversation. The most important thing the SATV tests is the student's grasp of these relations.

To see how it does so, let's look at the verbal sections of an actual SAT, taken by students nationwide in November 1996. (One of the major consequences of the so-called truth in testing law passed by the state of New York in 1979 is that ETS now releases "used" SATs for students who want to gain some familiarity with the test before taking it. This test is taken from *10 Real SATs*, published by the College Board in 1997.) Like every other SATV, this one poses questions in three categories: *sentence-completion items,* in which the test-taker is asked to fill in blanks from a list of words or word pairs; *analogy items,* which test a grasp of logical relationships through matched word pairs; and *reading comprehension items,* which ask students to read one or more passages of prose and then to answer a series of analytic questions. The format is standard: the first two verbal sections, containing items of each kind, are timed to take 30 minutes. The final section, reading comprehension only, is timed at 15 minutes.

Let's look at each category in turn. The point of the SAT's sentence-completion questions is to measure vocabulary and powers of syntactic analysis. To see how they do so, consider two sentences with blanks representing the missing words. I am going to make them extremely simple—though no simpler than many items ETS designates as difficulty level I—to give the clearest possible idea of the principle involved:

a) Seeing that his right _____ had come unlaced, George bent down and laced it back up.
b) Feeling intensely _____ after her hot afternoon working in the garden, Susan went to the refrigerator and got a cold _____.

At this very elementary level, the SATV sentence-completion format suggests why critics like Larry Stedman have been led to say that it involves little more than verbal conundrums. Who could not see that a word like *shoe* is needed to complete (a), or that only some pair like *thirsty . . . drink* will do in (b)? The point that tends to get lost in discussions of the SATV is that, with verbally competent test-takers, the format works in just the same way up to a very high level of complexity. That is, a student with high verbal aptitude will treat *every* item in the sentence-completion sections in the way readers on all levels treat items like (a) and (b), seeing what words are needed to complete the blanks even before looking down to examine the available choices offered.

Let's see how the same principle works on the sample SATV I've chosen. The first item in the test is, as it happens, a sentence completion. Let me begin by giving the sentence in isolation:

> 1) Many cultural historians believe that language has a _____ purpose: it serves not only as a means of communication but as a means of defining culture.

This is what the SAT calls a difficulty level 1 item—since I'm going to be talking about difficulty levels quite a bit in what follows, I'll abbreviate this as *dl* from now on—and, like the elementary examples I offered a moment ago, it suggests in very clear terms what sort of word is needed. To answer (a) above, we surmised that whatever George bent down towards had to be something with laces that could come untied, hence *shoe*. Here, the part of the sentence following the blank makes it obvious that the word we need is going to have to specify two purposes that language can serve, namely (1) as a *means of communication,* and (2) as a *means of defining culture.* So what is needed is an adjective meaning "two." Here are the answers offered by the test:

> (A) foreign   (B) literary   (C) false   (D) dual   (E) direct

The answer, of course, is (D). But it's essential to see, before dismissing items like this as too elementary to warrant discussion, that students at a low level of reading comprehension will find even this question difficult. For the sentence in which the blank occurs contains vocabulary—*cultural, communication, defining*—that will be over the heads of some test-takers, and the syntax that permits one to see that an adjective meaning "two" is necessary will have been impenetrable to many remedial-level students. Suppose, for instance, that a test taker has grasped that a *purpose* is being talked about, but has not understood that the sentence then goes on to specify exactly two purposes. Suddenly, other answers on the list seem plausible. We are talking about language, after all, and language can be used with a *literary* purpose (writing a poem), or a *direct* purpose (ordering someone to perform an action), or a *false* purpose (lying to a grand jury). Where some students see a single answer standing out with crystalline clarity, in short, many others will see a bewildering thicket of possibilities.

With the same principle in mind, let's look at a two-blank item. As before, I'll give the sentence first, letting you project possible answers before looking at the actual list of choices:

> 4) Born _____, children will follow their natural inclination to explore their surroundings with a _____ that belies the random appearance of their play.

Range of Possibilities

The first blank, one sees, permits only a very narrow range of possibilities. The word, whatever it turns out to be, will have to be an adjective modifying *children,* and this adjective will have to describe the *natural inclination* of children *to explore their surroundings.* The key to the second blank, just as obviously, is the term *belies,* which means to give the lie to or be inconsistent with—e.g., "George's outgoing manner belies his actual shyness." Here, what is *belied* is the apparent *randomness* of children's play: they look like they're playing randomly; but what they're really doing, says the sentence, is *exploring their surroundings.* Here are the choices offered the test-taker.

    (A) innocent . . . deviousness
    (B) serious . . . merriment
    (C) curious . . . purposefulness
    (D) eager . . . moderation
    (E) aware . . . casualness

The answer is (C). This is a *dl2* item, which means that, although most students taking this particular SATV got it right, some got it wrong. Nor is it hard to guess what reduced those students to puzzlement: a test-taker who doesn't know what *belies* means also won't see the logic that leads to (C). At higher levels of difficulty—*dl4* and *dl5,* which is the range, roughly speaking, in which students who get over 700 on the SATV operate comfortably—it is the relations of vocabulary to reading comprehension that matters most. Still, it is the *relation,* and not merely the vocabulary, that SAT sentence-completion items test at this more advanced level. Consider, for instance, this *dl4* question:

> 9. The traditional process of producing an oil painting requires so many steps that it seems _____ to artists who prefer to work quickly.

Notice that, as in earlier examples, it is still the syntax of the sentence that is doing the work. Painting in oil *requires many steps,* so that it is demanding, laborious, time-consuming. And *artists who prefer to work quickly* don't want to spend this kind of time. To such artists, therefore, the process of producing an oil painting would inevitably seem _____. Now in this case, we can't predict exactly what is going to go in the blank, but a reader with moderately good verbal comprehension will nonetheless have seen readily enough what sort of meaning is wanted: *tedious, pointlessly time-consuming, so tedious that it seems like it will never end,* etc. So we look at the list of choices offered by the test:

    (A) provocative   (B) consummate   (C) interminable   (D) facile   (E) prolific

Vocabulary

The answer is (C), obviously, but this will not be obvious to someone who has no idea what *interminable* means. To such a person, by the same token, the other choices will look like a welter of wholly opaque terms: someone who can't recognize *interminable* when it occurs in a sentence is not going to have much better luck with *provocative, consummate, facile,* or *prolific.* Critics very often try, when talking about the way the SAT measures vocabulary, to imply that it involves little more than an arbitrary word-list of useless terms. But in fact the test operates on principles that seem entirely reasonable. Someone able to describe his wait at the doctor's office as *interminable* is also likely to know what you mean if you describe a dress or a remark as *provocative.* Someone who has no idea what *interminable* means, on the other hand, is going to find a great deal of intellectually demanding writing impenetrable.

In a moment I want to look at the SAT's analogy and reading comprehension sections, but let us pause a moment to take stock. From David Owen's *None of the Above: Behind the Myth of Scholastic Aptitude,* published in 1985, to the latest fulminations of FairTest, critics of the SAT have worked hard to suggest that the test's verbal portion consists of pointless conundrums followed by arbitrary and meaningless lists of answers from which the hapless student is compelled to choose while the clock ticks remorselessly away in the background. Yet (critics say) there is no particular logic involved in choosing "right" answers. They may be answered "correctly" only if one is privy to a secret code issued by ETS to students lucky enough to be born into wealthy families.

Even the few actual SATV questions we've looked at, however, will suggest a far different picture. For in every case it has clearly not been ETS but the *sentence* that is choosing one item from the ABCDE list. More importantly, the way in which it does so exactly mirrors a process central to reading comprehension at any but the most elementary level. The same, as we've seen, goes for the vocabulary demanded by $dl4$ and $dl5$ questions: the way to grasp the meaning of *interminable* or *provocative* or *consummate* is not to be born into a wealthy family but to get to the public library and begin reading. So far, in short, the SAT may simply be seen to be testing the cognitive powers that come into play when one is reading Aristotle or Thoreau or Henry James. On a test meant to measure students' readiness for college-level reading and thinking, this does not seem unreasonable.

Analogy Questions

To get a line on the SATV's analogy questions, it's only necessary to see that college-level reading involves a grasp of logical as well as syntactic relations. At the simplest level, the analogies test elementary part-whole and part-part relations of a sort that would have been familiar to a schoolchild in ancient Greece. At a somewhat higher level, the SAT's analogy sections also test a complex sort of logical relation that derives from semantic entailment, the precise nature of which is a matter of considerable debate in contemporary linguistic theory. But this sort of entailment is something every competent speaker of a language deals with intuitively and, in ordinary cases, unerringly. Thus, for instance, any native speaker of English will agree that the sentence *George had a nightmare* must "logically imply" *George had a dream.* To see why and how such entailments work, it is necessary only to subject them to what Kant called the law of contradiction. Suppose someone told you—meaning it in absolutely literal terms—that *Harry killed Sally,* but then failed to understand that Sally was dead. You would have every right to assume that this speaker doesn't wholly grasp the meaning of at least some English sentences.

When they simply test such matters as the part-whole relation, the SATV's analogy items tend to be pretty elementary, with any difficulty coming not from the logical relation but from the vocabulary. Here, for instance, is a *dl*3 question from our test's analogy section:

Preamble: Statute

Notice that, as with the sentence-completion items we looked at earlier, the question even in isolation sets up a purely formal expectation: since a *preamble* is something that comes before a *statute* or law to explain its meaning or purpose, whatever satisfies the analogy is going to have to display the "coming before" and also the "declaring purpose" features of a preamble. We could even think up, before looking down to see what choices are offered, various pairs that satisfied the analogy: *introduction: manual,* for instance, or *prologue: play,* either of which gives us written texts in a relation to each other analogous to *preamble: statute.* Here is the list of choices actually offered:

(A) interlude: musical
(B) conclusion: argument
(C) foreword: novel
(D) epilogue: address
(E) premier: performance

The answer is, of course, (C). The difficulty that makes this a *dl*3 item must be coming, clearly, from the vocabulary: a student who does not know what an *epilogue* is will not know that it comes *after* a preceding text or speech or performance, and therefore cannot be seen as analogous to a *preamble.* In the same way, a test-taker who has no idea that an *interlude* is something that comes in the *middle* of a performance will be at a loss about what is supposed to be analogous to what in this case. (Such examples suggest why, as has been widely reported in recent years, students who take Latin in high school tend to improve their SAT scores. Even a first-year Latin student will know that the *pre-* of *preamble* signals "beforeness" and the *inter-* of *interlude* "in-betweenness.")

Semantic Entailment

To see how the SATV tests students' grasp of semantic entailment, let's look at an item that comes at the very top (*dl5*) of its difficulty range. Semantic entailment, once again, involves seeing that the meanings of certain words are so to speak "built in" to the sense structure of others: to know that *Peter is a bachelor* must, to a competent speaker of English, be to know that *Peter is unmarried*. This is the sort of logical implication that comes into play in items like the following:

> Querulous: Complain

Here, as before, a great part of the "difficulty" is coming from the vocabulary: there are quite literally millions of students enrolled in American colleges and universities who could not tell you that a *querulous* person is one who *complains* a lot. But to a test-taker who does know that, the item will scarcely be more challenging than *preamble: statute*. A *querulous* person will be seen to *complain* a lot, one would want to say, as an *untruthful* person will be seen to *lie* a lot, or a *gluttonous* person will be seen to *eat* a lot. Here are the actual choices given for this item:

> (A) silent: talk
> (B) humorous: laugh
> (C) dangerous: risk
> (D) deceitful: cheat
> (E) gracious: accept

The answer, which in this instance is the sort of thing that gets you into an Ivy League college, is (D).

To get the basic idea of the SATV's reading comprehension sections, it's necessary only to look at a sample of the prose the test-taker is asked to read. The final section of the SAT we've been examining, for instance, is entirely reading comprehension: two passages followed by 12 questions and timed to take 15 minutes. Both passages are about the effects of TV news, with passage 1 arguing that it stimulates critical thinking because the viewer gets a direct view of events—the writer's example is the way images of civil rights sit-ins made Americans outside the South aware of segregation—and passage 2 arguing, to the contrary, that television trivializes events and the whole conception of public awareness or public duty, by presenting the news simply as entertainment. Passage 2 consists of four paragraphs. Here is the first paragraph and the beginning of the second:

> "Now . . . this" is a phrase commonly used on television newscasts to indicate that what one has just heard or seen has no relevance to what one is about to hear or see, or possibly to anything one is ever likely to hear or see. The phrase acknowledges that the world as mapped by television news has no order or meaning and is not to be taken seriously. No earthquake is so devastating, no political blunder so costly, that it cannot be erased from our minds by a newscaster saying, "Now . . . this." Interrupted by commercials, presented by newscasters with celebrity status, and advertised like any other product, television newscasts transmit news without context, without consequences, without values, and therefore without essential seriousness; in short, news as pure entertainment. The resulting trivialization of information leaves television viewers well entertained, but not well informed or well prepared to respond to events.
>
>   The species of information created by television is, in fact, "disinformation." Disinformation does not mean false information, but misleading information—misplaced, irrelevant, fragmented, or superficial information—that creates the illusion of knowing something, but that actually leads one away from any true understanding.

Whenever I discuss the SATV with students who got scores in the 700+ range, the reading comprehension items tend to elicit an incredulous grin. ("They tell you," one of my students said, "that the chicken crossed the road, then they ask 'What crossed the road?' and 'What did it cross?'") Yet when we recall that the SATV is designed to tell whether students who take the test are intellectually prepared for college, and that the ability to read at a certain level is more essential to college-level learning than any other factor, the reading comprehension sections make a good deal of sense. The way to grasp the point of items in this category, in short, is not to think about the small minority of students who find them embarrassingly easy, but about the hundreds of thousands who find them insuperably difficult.

Three questions from our sample SATV, all based on the passage quoted above, will show how the reading comprehension section works. The first asks whether the test-taker has understood a key word in the argument:

6. The word "mapped" in line 4 most nearly means _____

Since understanding *mapped* in line 4 simply involves seeing that it is a metaphor—i.e., that the writer is not talking about actual maps or geography here, but the way TV news defines social or cultural reality for its viewers—it's not easy to see where a wrong answer could come from. There are two possibilities, however, and they are precisely the ones that students with lower-level reading ability will tend to seize on. The first is that *mapped* is literal, having to do with maps and globes and measurement. In the list of answers below, (A), (B), and (C) play on this possibility. The second is that *mapped* does indeed mean something metaphorical, but the test-taker's vocabulary doesn't include one or more of the words given as choices, as might happen with (D) and (E) below. Here are the choices:

(A) plotted on a chart   (B) planned in detail   (C) measured   (D) defined
(E) verified

The answer is (D).

In the second item, the specialized meaning of a key term prompts the question. Even some students with good verbal ability will not be exactly clear on the difference between *disinformation* and *misinformation,* and, in fact, the writer is putting something of a spin even on the normal meaning of *disinformation* to drive home a point. So the question asks specifically how the writer is using the term:

8. According to Passage 2, the "disinformation" mentioned in line 13 affects television viewers by _____.

In this case, the wrong answers don't demand a lot of discussion. They are wrong either because they're nothing more than random or irrelevant associations with things mentioned in the passage, or because they directly contradict something in the passage, as when (A) gives the test-taker the option of filling in the blank with "leading them *to act on false information,*" while the writer of the passage has clearly said that "disinformation *does not mean false information*":

(A) leading them to act on false information
(B) causing them to become skeptical about television news
(C) giving them the mistaken impression that they are knowledgeable
(D) making them susceptible to the commercials that accompany the news
(E) turning them against certain political leaders

The answer is, of course, (C).

Finally, the SATV reading comprehension section includes a sort of summary item meant to see whether or not the test-taker has gotten the essential point of the passage as a whole or some major part of it. In principle, since any reasonably complex argument might be summarized in a variety of ways, these are the items that could most plausibly be attacked by critics hostile to the SAT. Yet in practice, the SATV minimizes ambiguity through the simple measure of listing four absurdly wrong possibilities along with one obviously right one. Here, for instance, is a question in this category:

6. According to Passage 2, television news is presented in a manner that serves to

_____.

Look again at the passage above, taking a moment to notice that the writer says that TV presents news "as pure *entertainment*," and that news-casts "leave television viewers well *entertained*, but not well informed." (Later on, in the part of the passage I haven't quoted, the writer says TV news "is packaged as *entertainment*, and that its viewers have been "*entertained* into indifference.") Here are the choices:

(A) hold leaders accountable for their policies
(B) entertain viewers
(C) define lies as truth
(D) make complex issues accessible
(E) exaggerate minor political blunders

The answer, as you may have guessed, is (B).

There, in a nutshell, is the SATV, the object of FairTest's wrath and the reservations of other, less strident critics. As I've tried to show, looking in detail at any actual SAT is likely to leave one wondering what the fuss is about. My own guess is that opposition to the SATV arises from two distinct sources. One is an instinctive dislike of "standardized" testing, with its implications of rigidity and impersonality, plus a suspicion that the SATV doesn't really measure anything important. Critics in this category could be satisfied, presumably, by being shown that the test does measure something real, and that its standardization, as with, say, the standard use of Olympic distances in athletic events held at different times and different locations, serves an obviously equitable purpose. The other category consists of critics who, despite the contrary assertions they so vociferously make for public consumption, are wholly aware that the SATV does measure verbal and cognitive ability, and oppose it on precisely that ground. I want to end by looking at critics in this category.

In the overcharged political atmosphere surrounding the SATV in recent years, with controversy focusing on such issues as the disparity between African American and white scores or the relation of SAT percentile to family income level, it has been easy to lose sight of an otherwise simple fact, which is that any student who has spent a great deal of time reading is virtually assured of a high SATV grade. In *A Is For Admission: The Insider's Guide to Getting into the Ivy League and Other Top Colleges*, in my opinion the best book on college admissions currently available, Michele A. Hernández, a former associate dean of admissions at Dartmouth College, returns to this point again and again. "It is not surprising," observes Hernández, "that the students who get 800 on the verbal SAT scores are always the ones who were read to a lot and then developed a real love of reading as they grew up. Even if they were not challenged in school, these children could read in their spare time and thus learn many of the skills necessary to succeed in college."

Coaching

The same observation, which is entirely borne out by my own twenty-five-year experience in the university classroom, bears on another controversial issue, the effect of SAT coaching on the scores of those, mainly students from the upper middle class, who can afford test preparation courses. Here the lines have been clearly drawn, with people like Princeton Review's Katzman claiming substantial score increases from coaching, ETS maintaining that the gains are, on average, inconsiderable. What almost never gets mentioned is Hernández's point that gains on the SATV, whatever their size, come mostly in the middle range: "It is not uncommon . . . to raise a verbal score from 450 to 600 or from 570 to 680. What is almost impossible is to jump into the 720 to 800 range, even if you are starting in the high 600s. With a few exceptions, the students who score over 740 or so are simply voracious readers, students who have been reading seriously since they were very young and have continued to do so all their lives."

One major reason that SAT coaching is able to yield such results in the middle range has to do with what experts call test familiarity: doing well not by paying attention to what is being tested, but how the test works. Princeton Review, for instance, has from the first concentrated on teaching its clients to "beat the test." An example described with evident relish by David Owen in *None of the Above*, for instance, consisted of a trick to be used on the SAT math test. Instead of doing mathematical calculations on geometry problems, Princeton Review students were taught to tear off a corner of their test booklet—a perfect 90° angle—and use it as a protractor, eliminating wrong choices on the answer list by eye measurement of the scaled diagram provided with the problem. On the SATV, students who don't know the answer to a question are taught various techniques to eliminate "obviously" wrong answers. Precisely as with card-counting in casino blackjack, this does effectively increase the probability of guessing right choices over an entire run of test items.

This sort of test-beating instruction has become less effective over the last few years, as ETS has worked to close the loopholes spotted by outfits like Princeton Review. But even when it was successful, such coaching might be viewed as amounting essentially to training in petty dishonesty, as though an Olympic coach, having found a loop on the course unsupervised by race officials, were to teach marathoners to turn in "faster" times by taking a short cut. (One suspects that this is why Katzman is so strident in his denunciations of the SAT: it's only by encouraging an utter cynicism about the test that Princeton Review's test-beating strategies can be made to look anything other than what some people might consider a bit shady.) Yet even Princeton Review gestures in the direction of substantive teaching, as with its famous "hit parade" of vocabulary items, based on a frequency analysis of past SATs and taught to its clients as preparation for the sentence completion and analogy sections.

Substantive Teaching

Our analysis of a sample SATV shows readily enough why this sort of thing will yield at least limited results. A sentence completion item we looked at earlier, for instance, required *interminable* as a correct answer. Even a student who knew the meaning of *interminable* purely through rote memorization would have a substantial advantage over a test-taker who had no idea what it meant. Among SAT coaches who carry this sort of substantive approach even farther, insisting that students spend an entire year learning the meaning of vocabulary words in context, the gains are even more dramatic. But then it is no longer clear that we are dealing with SAT coaching rather than simple, old fashioned, effective teaching. "People don't back their way into a good score," says Arun Alagappan, founder of Advantage Testing, a hugely successful tutoring operation that demands a great deal of its teenage clients. "Those who do well are conscientious students." Not surprisingly, Alagappan has a positive view of the SAT as a measure of cognitive ability.

Nonetheless, Michele Hernández's point that coaching gains come mainly in the middle range will leave even most of Advantage Testing's clients below the 750 SATV level, above which scores tend to measure a lifelong devotion to reading. "Every time I have seen a student with an 800 verbal score," reports Hernández, "there has been confirmation throughout the application that the student is a reader." "Teachers mention it," she adds, and "the student often talks about loving literature from a young age." Critics of the SAT sometimes manage to imply that large numbers of worthy students are being turned away from Harvard and Yale each year due to low scores, but this is not the case. As ETS likes to point out, over 90 percent of SAT-takers nationwide are admitted to the college of their first choice. In effect, this means elite colleges and universities draw their entering classes almost entirely from the small cadre of devoted readers Hernández describes. For everyone else, the test is largely a formality.

For colleges and universities themselves, however, a great deal hangs on SATV levels. A point almost never discussed by either side in the SAT controversy, for instance, no doubt because it is as much a political powder keg as the issue of natural cognitive ability, is that there is an average SATV level below which no institution can sustain a college-level curriculum, for the simple reason that such a curriculum will consist of materials beyond the comprehension of a student body with lower-level SATV scores. For any such curriculum will necessarily include not only writers like Aristotle, Thoreau, and Henry James, but history or economics or anthropology textbooks assuming college-level reading ability. My own analysis, based on difficulty levels of SATV items in relation to materials taught at Rutgers, suggests that a 580 SATV marks the lower limit of college-level reading comprehension, a combined 1130 SAT the minimum needed for college-level work.

Open Admissions

Yet many colleges and universities have mean or average SAT scores below this level, which is no doubt why one so often hears the complaint that many public institutions in America, operating essentially on a policy of open admissions, have become little more than glorified high schools. Statistics suggest that such pessimism is not unwarranted. Nationwide, points out Edwin S. Rubinstein in a recent survey, approximately 30 percent of incoming freshmen are today placed in at least one remedial course. At state universities remediation rates are even higher—35 percent, 48 percent, and 39 percent in New York, Kentucky, and Georgia, respectively. At a further extreme, nonselective admissions can actually produce a situation in which students read and write at a grade-school level, which no doubt explains the note of impatience in the voice of the mayor of New York as he called recently for an end to open admissions at CUNY: "Open enrollment is a mistake. . . . By eliminating any meaningful standards of admission and continually defining down standards for continuation, the entire meaning and value of a college education has been put in jeopardy for the many who are ready, willing, and able to meet and exceed higher standards."

In recent years, the competition to get into Ivy League and a few other selective colleges has been treated in the national press as little more than a frenzied pursuit of status by the middle class, a hysteria as irrational as the rush of lemmings to the sea. The competition is, indeed, ferocious, as witness Hernández's account of a recent Dartmouth class: "The average combined score for the admitted class of 2000 at Dartmouth was over 1410. In fact, for the class of 2000, the *average scores of all 11,400 applicants* who applied to Dartmouth (this includes all the weakest applicants in the pool) was 662V, 677M, almost 1340 combined." Yet to see this as perfectly rational behavior, it is necessary only to see that, for the roughly 10,000 students who got turned down, the application process was not only a struggle to get into Dartmouth, but also to *not* be compelled to attend a school where most students are incapable of meeting college level demands. This is another point that almost never gets mentioned in the national SAT controversy.

Demographics

Very bright students tend to think about getting into Harvard or Amherst or Dartmouth in the same way as a gifted violinist might hope someday to make the Chicago Symphony Orchestra or a gifted basketball player the NBA. Looking at such organizations from the outside, what one tends to hear about is their prestige. To those inside, however, prestige is almost always far less important than a chance to exercise natural ability or talent in a setting where others are equally talented. This serves to explain why demographic categories, so strongly depended on by critics of the SAT, are almost meaningless at this level. As it is impossible to predict in advance into what household a musical genius or NBA star will be born, it is virtually impossible to pinpoint where the sort of avid or insatiable reader described by Hernández will emerge.

At the highest level of performance, demographics can do no more than suggest the *conditions* under which talent or ability is likely to emerge, which in the cases we've been considering would include the degree to which a family or a culture emphasizes reading, music, or sports. This is the point, for instance, of the example of the National Basketball Association that is sometimes invoked in this connection. Though millions of young American males aspire to the celebrity and wealth that come with making the NBA—the average salary of an NBA player last year was $1.2 million—African Americans as a group are tremendously overrepresented while other groups (Jews, Hispanics) are underrepresented to the point of invisibility. Still, no one would waste a moment trying to argue that NBA selection is somehow biased in favor of African Americans and against Jews and Hispanics, if only because the need of professional teams to win guarantees that slots will be awarded to the best players. Yet a similar demographic disproportion at the higher levels of SATV performance is the entire basis of FairTest's argument that the test is culturally biased.

Nor is their argument without serious consequences for American society. For to take it seriously is to justify the sort of policies advocated by Derek Bok and William Bowen in *The Shape of the River*, or by Harvard president Neil Rudenstine in several widely reported speeches, which seek to correct demographic disproportion through brute force, rigging the admissions process at selective institutions to achieve desired results in racial and ethnic categories. It is against this background that it is salutary to recall the vision that originally motivated James Bryant Conant when he set out to open the university up to talented youngsters from across the United States, without regard to family income or educational background. The essence of Conant's notion of policy, especially as it involved the Harvard National Scholarships and the then newly-introduced SAT, was that it viewed America not in terms of demographic categories but of talented individuals.

Symbolic Value

Conant understood, in short, that factors like ethnicity and family income operate only as loose determinants of intellectual achievement. Nor is the point less valid today than during Conant's presidency of Harvard. Rich families and white families, we may suppose, will go on turning out their usual substantial quota of average and below-average offspring, children entirely happy to grow up in a world of MTV and skateboarding and total intellectual vacuity. Millions of other children, no matter what their socio-economic background, will choose to grow up in that same world. Even in a country that grants everyone twelve years of free education—a situation undreamt of in past centuries—few will want to read books. But scattered here and there in American society will be children who read their way through the public library. For them, as Conant foresaw, the SAT is less a test than a means of becoming visible to a world outside their own locality.

As Conant understood, the ultimate stakes have to do not with educational policy but with civic purpose. The symbolic value of the SAT lay, for him, in its power to remind an American society corrupted by the worship of wealth that its moral basis lay in rewarding talent or ability wherever found. This is why he instructed the Harvard National Scholarship project to cast so wide a net for what in Conant's generation were called promising youths. In a series of articles published in the *Atlantic Monthly* in the 1940s, Conant called this appeal to democratic or egalitarian principles a "new radicalism," by which he meant a return to the roots of American experience. Only against the background of such earlier idealism, perhaps, do we glimpse the sense in which FairTest and other groups who today demand abolition of the SAT would until very recently have been seen as, to borrow a famous phrase coined in Conant's own day, the enemies of promise.

Reflective Writing: *In defending the SAT, Dowling says, "The popularity of professional sports in American society, it is sometimes said, is due to their being the one domain in which we have somehow come to terms with the idea of natural ability. No American male is offended at being told that, no matter how hard he practiced, he could never be Michael Jordan or, indeed, a starting player in the NBA. Yet the thought that many students with good study habits and high aspirations do not have what it takes to do the work at Harvard or Berkeley remains a source of deep discomfort." What do you think Dowling is saying, in this quote and in his article as a whole, about the role of natural ability in educational success? What other factors do you think come into play and in what ways?*

More Testing, More Learning

Patrick O'Malley

Patrick O'Malley wrote this essay when he was a college freshman at a state university in California. In it, he proposes that college professors give students frequent brief examinations in addition to the usual midterm and final exams. Increasing the number of tests, he argues, will encourage students to study more and will, therefore, help them learn more. After discussing with his instructor his unusual rhetorical situation—a first-year college student advising professors—he decided to revise the essay into the form of an open letter that might appear in the campus newspaper.

To Consider: *O'Malley's essay may strike you as unusually authorative for a student writing. This air of authority is due in large part to what the author learned about the possibilities and problems of frequent exams from interviewing two professors and talking with several students. As you read, notice how he is able to anticipate professors' likely objections and their preferred solutions to the problem he identifies.*

It's late at night. The final's tomorrow. You got a C on the midterm, so this one will make or break you. Will it be like the midterm? Did you study enough? Did you study the right things? It's too late to drop the course. So what happens if you fail? No time to worry about that now—you've got a ton of notes to go over.

Although this last-minute anxiety about midterm and final exams is only too familiar to most college students, many professors may not realize how such major, infrequent, high-stakes exams work against the best interests of students both psychologically and intellectually. They cause unnecessary amounts of stress, placing too much importance on one or two days in the students' entire term, judging ability on a single or dual performance. They don't encourage frequent study, and they fail to inspire students' best performance. If professors gave additional brief exams at frequent intervals, students would be spurred to study more regularly, learn more, worry less, and perform better on midterms, finals, and other papers and projects.

Ideally, a professor would give an in-class test or quiz after each unit, chapter, or focus of study, depending on the type of class and course material.

311

A physics class might require a test on concepts after every chapter covered, while a history class could necessitate quizzes covering certain time periods or major events. These exams should be given weekly, or at least twice monthly. Whenever possible, they should consist of two or three essay questions rather than many multiple-choice or short-answer questions. To preserve class time for lecture and discussion, exams should take no more than 15 or 20 minutes.

The main reason why professors should give frequent exams is that when they do, and when they provide feedback to students on how well they are doing, students learn more in the course and perform better on major exams, projects, and papers. It makes sense that in a challenging course containing a great deal of material, students will learn more of it and put it to better use if they have to apply or "practice" it frequently on exams, which also help them find out how much they are learning and what they need to go over again. A recent Harvard study notes students' "strong preference for frequent evaluation in a course." Harvard students feel they learn least in courses that have "only a midterm and a final exam, with no other personal evaluation." They believe they learn most in courses with "many opportunities to see how they are doing" (Light, 1990, p. 32). In a review of a number of studies of student learning, Frederiksen (1984) reports that students who take weekly quizzes achieve higher scores on final exams than students who take only a midterm exam and that testing increases retention of material tested.

Another, closely related argument in favor of multiple exams is that they encourage students to improve their study habits. Greater frequency in test taking means greater frequency in studying for tests. Students prone to cramming will be required—or at least strongly motivated—to open their textbooks and notebooks more often, making them less likely to resort to long, kamikaze nights of studying for major exams. Since there is so much to be learned in the typical course, it makes sense that frequent, careful study and review are highly beneficial. But students need motivation to study regularly, and nothing works like an exam. If students had frequent exams in all their courses, they would have to schedule study time each week and gradually would develop a habit of frequent study. It might be argued that students are adults who have to learn how to manage their own lives, but learning history or physics is more complicated than learning to drive a car or balance a checkbook. Students need coaching and practice in learning. The right way to learn new material needs to become a habit, and I believe that frequent exams are key to developing good habits of study and learning. The Harvard study concludes that "tying regular evaluation to good course organization enables students to plan their work more than a few days in advance. If quizzes and homework are scheduled on specific days, students plan their work to capitalize on them" (Light, 1990, p. 33).

By encouraging regular study habits, frequent exams would also decrease anxiety by reducing the procrastination that produces anxiety. Students would benefit psychologically if they were not subjected to the emotional ups and downs caused by major exams, when after being virtually worry-free for weeks they are suddenly ready to check into the psychiatric ward. Researchers at the University of Vermont found a strong relationship between procrastination, anxiety, and achievement. Students who regularly put off studying for exams had continuing high anxiety and lower grades than students who procrastinated less. The researchers found that even "low" procrastinators did not study regularly and recommended that professors give frequent assignments and exams to reduce procrastination and increase achievement (Rothblum, Solomon, & Murakami, 1986, pp. 393, 394).

Research supports my proposed solution to the problems I have described. Common sense as well as my experience and that of many of my friends support it. Why, then, do so few professors give frequent brief exams? Some believe that such exams take up too much of the limited class time available to cover the material in the course. Most courses meet 150 minutes a week—three times a week for 50 minutes each time. A 20-minute weekly exam might take 30 minutes to administer, and that is one-fifth of each week's class time. From the student's perspective, however, this time is well spent. Better learning and greater confidence about the course seem a good tradeoff for another 30 minutes of lecture. Moreover, time lost to lecturing or discussion could easily be made up in students' learning on their own through careful regular study for the weekly exams. If weekly exams still seem too time-consuming to some professors, their frequency could be reduced to every other week or their length to 5 or 10 minutes. In courses where multiple-choice exams are appropriate, several questions take only a few minutes to answer.

Another objection professors have to frequent exams is that they take too much time to read and grade. In a 20-minute essay exam a well-prepared student can easily write two pages. A relatively small class of 30 students might then produce 60 pages, no small amount of material to read each week. A large class of 100 or more students would produce an insurmountable pile of material. There are a number of responses to this objection. Again, professors could give exams every other week or make them very short. Instead of reading them closely they could skim them quickly to see whether students understand an idea or can apply it to an unfamiliar problem; and instead of numerical or letter grades they could give a plus, check, or minus. Exams could be collected and responded to only every third or fourth week. Professors who have readers or teaching assistants could rely on them to grade or check exams. And the scantron machine is always available for instant grading of multiple-choice exams. Finally, frequent exams could be given *in place of* a midterm exam or out-of-class essay assignment.

Since frequent exams seem to some professors to create too many problems, however, it is reasonable to consider alternative ways to achieve the same goals. One alternative solution is to implement a program that would improve study skills. While such a program might teach students how to study for exams, it cannot prevent procrastination or reduce "large test anxiety" by a substantial amount. One research team studying anxiety and test performance found that study skills training was "not effective in reducing anxiety or improving performance" (Dendato & Diener, 1986, p. 134). This team, which also reviewed other research that reached the same conclusion, did find that a combination of "cognitive/relaxation therapy" and study skills training was effective. This possible solution seems complicated, however, not to mention time-consuming and expensive. It seems much easier and more effective to change the cause of the bad habit rather than treat the habit itself. That is, it would make more sense to solve the problem at its root: the method of learning and evaluation.

Still another solution might be to provide frequent study questions for students to answer. These would no doubt be helpful in focusing students' time studying, but students would probably not actually write out the answers unless they were required to. To get students to complete the questions in a timely way, professors would have to collect and check the answers. In that case, however, they might as well devote the time to grading an exam. Even if it asks the same questions, a scheduled exam is preferable to a set of study questions because it takes far less time to write in class, compared to the time students would devote to responding to questions at home. In-class exams also ensure that each student produces his or her own work.

Another possible solution would be to help students prepare for midterm and final exams by providing sets of questions from which the exam questions will be selected or announcing possible exam topics at the beginning of the course. This solution would have the advantage of reducing students' anxiety about learning every fact in the textbook, and it would clarify the course goals, but it would not motivate students to study carefully each new unit, concept, or text chapter in the course. I see this as a way of complementing frequent exams, not as substituting for them.

From the evidence and from my talks with professors and students, I see frequent, brief in-class exams as the only way to improve students' study habits and learning, reducing their anxiety and procrastination, and increase their satisfaction with college. These exams are not a panacea, but only more parking spaces and a winning football team would do as much to improve college life. Professors can't do much about parking or football, but they can give more frequent exams. Campus administrators should get behind this effort, and professors should get together to consider giving exams more frequently. It would make a difference.

References

Dendato, K. M., & Diener, D. (1986). Effectiveness of cognitive/relaxation therapy and study-skills training in reducing self-reported anxiety and improving the academic performance of test-anxious students. *Journal of Counseling Psychology, 33,* 131–135.

Frederiksen, N. (1984). The real test bias: Influences of testing on teaching and learning. *American Psychologist, 39,* 193–202.

Light, R. J. (1990). *Explorations with students and faculty about teaching, learning, and student life.* Cambridge, MA: Harvard University Graduate School of Education and Kennedy School of Government.

Rothblum, E. D., Solomon, L., & Murakami, J. (1986). Affective, cognitive, and behavioral differences between high and low procrastinators. *Journal of Counseling Psychology, 33,* 387–394.

Reflective Writing: *O'Malley advocates frequent brief exams as a solution to the problems of midterm and final anxiety, poor study habits, and disappointing exam performance. What do you think of his proposal in light of your own experience? Which of your high school or college courses have included frequent exams? Did you learn more because of them? What arguments against O'Malley's suggestions can you think of? For example, how mature, organized, and independent is the college student that he constructs?*

A Whole Lot of Cheatin' Going On

Mark Clayton

The problem of cheating on tests and assignments cuts across all levels of the U.S. educational system. Research reveals that cheating begins as early as kindergarten and continues through the highest levels of graduate and professional school. The problem is far more widespread than people may imagine. Cheating takes many different forms and is a major concern particularly when assessment results are used in making high-stakes selection, promotion, evaluation, or admission decisions. And with the rise of the Internet, where information can change hands with the mere touch of a keystroke, cheating has perhaps become even more of a temptation. This piece by higher-education reporter Mark Clayton, originally published in 1999 in the Christian Science Monitor *newspaper, examines the kinds of cheating some college students engage in, the reasons they cite for this behavior, and the responses of college faculty and administrators.*

To Consider: *How do the students interviewed by Clayton explain or justify their cheating? What reasons do college staff cite for their opposition to academic dishonesty?*

Sitting in the glow of his computer screen at 2 A.M. on Oct. 26, 1998, John Smolik, a University of Texas freshman, fires off an e-mail message to an online debate over academic cheating on the Austin campus.

Many of the 100-plus student messages argue that cheaters only hurt themselves. Not so says Mr. Smolik's missive, labeled "reality check!" "Cheating *is* an answer," he writes. "It might not be a good answer, but nonetheless it is an answer."

Actually, Smolik "disagrees with cheating" and was simply playing devil's advocate, he said in a recent interview. But he allows that his provocative message put forward a widely shared view. And researchers agree.

Across America, college students and college-bound high-schoolers appear to be cheating like there's no tomorrow, student surveys show.

The Center for Academic Integrity in Nashville studied 7,000 students on 26 small-to-medium-size college campuses in 1990, 1992, and 1995. Those studies found that nearly 80 percent admitted to cheating at least once.

316

"We've seen a dramatic increase in the more-explicit forms of test cheating" and illegitimate "collaboration," says Donald McCabe, associate provost at Rutgers University in Newark, who founded CAI and did its studies.

He and others blame poor role models and lack of parental guidance for the growing acceptance of cheating in colleges. Easy access to the Internet, with its vast and often hard-to-trace resources, is another factor.

Add to that a pervasive change in societal values, and students can easily be snared if they lack a strong moral compass—as well as a campus where peers and administrators take a firm stand against dishonesty.

"Nobody cheated [in the 1960s] because of the peer pressure and likelihood of being turned in," claims Johan Madson, associate provost for student affairs at Vanderbilt University in Nashville. "Students of this generation are reluctant to turn their classmates in. They feel everyone ought to have their own right to do their own thing."

The problem is hardly limited to college campuses. Critics also point to widespread cheating in high school as a reason for colleges' current woes.

Who's Who among American High School Students, which lists 700,000 high-achieving students, surveyed these top performers last year and found that 80 percent said they had cheated during their academic careers. Joe Krouse, associate publisher of the listing, says it is "the highest level we've ever seen."

Mr. Krouse taps adult behavior as a factor. "Because adults and role models in society do it, some students may have used those examples to rationalize cheating," he says. In a survey conducted in 1997–98, he also found that 66 percent of the parents of these top students said cheating was "not a big deal."

Colleges Are Watching More Closely

Whatever the reason for cheating, its sheer volume is capturing the attention of more than a few schools. Most, chary of their images, downplay dishonesty, unwilling to air dirty laundry in public. Yet a few are confronting cheating by making it highly public—on campus, at least.

The University of Texas is the nation's largest university with about 50,000 students. It has roughly 180 academic-integrity cases pop up annually, says Kevin Price, assistant dean of students. The school is trying to raise the profile of integrity issues during orientation with skits, a 10-page handout on plagiarism, and a newsletter called the *Integrity Herald* for faculty.

Another sign of academic stirring: the Center for Academic Integrity, founded in 1993, already has 175 member schools and is drafting a framework of principles that could be applied nationwide to lower student cheating.

Schools like Stanford University, Georgetown University, the University of Delaware, and a half-dozen others are also buffing up or introducing new honor codes.

But Mr. Madson at Vanderbilt University says what is most needed is for students themselves to take charge and reject the attitude that cheating can be justified.

Students say time and workload pressure are major factors spurring academic dishonesty, followed by parental pressure. "It's definitely what you get assigned—and how long you have to do it—that right there determines whether you're going to cheat," says Smolik, the University of Texas freshman.

Anne-Elyse Smith, another freshman at Texas, reasoned in an online debate that it may not be smart to cheat, but it could be educationally valuable.

"People should hold themselves accountable to a standard at which they are comfortable, and get out of the education what they can," she wrote. "If that involves looking at one answer on a quiz, I think the person is more likely to remember that one answer since they had to resort to cheating to obtain it."

A Little Imagination, a Lot of High Tech

Whether copying another student's homework, cheating on a test, or plagiarizing an essay, cheating is limited only by imagination—and technology. Some program their calculators with formulas, but rig them to show an empty memory if an instructor checks.

But what alarms some campus officials the most is the Internet's proven potential for explosive growth in negative areas such as pornography—and the possibility that plagiarism could be next. Web sites sporting names like "Cheater.com" and "School Sucks" offer tools for rampant plagiarism at the click of a mouse. "Download your workload" the latter site suggests, boasting more than 1 million term-paper downloads.

Such savvy borrowing may be lost on some educators, but others, like librarians, are catching up. "Students are finding it so easy to use these sources that they will dump them in the middle of the papers without any attribution," says John Ruszkiewicz, an English professor at Texas. "What they don't realize is how readily [professors] can tell the material isn't the student's and how easy it is for instructors to search this material on the Web."

Anthony Krier, a reference librarian at Franklin Pierce College Library in Rindge, N.H., is one such literary bloodhound. Last semester, he investigated nine cases of plagiarism, three of them involving the Internet. One student had downloaded and passed off as his own a morality essay, apparently unaware of the irony, Mr. Krier says.

Some colleges are fighting back with explicit warnings, more detailed orientations, and classes on how to cite sources—and lawsuits. Boston University sued five online "term-paper mills" in 1997. The case was rejected by a federal judge last month. School officials vow to refile.

Last fall, the dean of the school's College of Communication, Brent Baker, wrote a letter to students urging them to protect their "good name" by reviewing carefully the school's code of conduct. To drive home the point, he attached a listing of 13 unnamed cases and the penalties—probation, suspension, and expulsion—meted out.

Likewise, the 152 reports of academic dishonesty for 1997–98 at the University of Southern California in Los Angeles "is higher than previous comparable years beginning in 1991," wrote Sandra Rhoten, assistant dean in the office of student conduct, in a letter in the campus newspaper describing violations and sanctions assessed.

"We had a full-blown, two-year campaign [starting in 1995] to educate people about the problem," Ms. Rhoten says in an interview. "Sometimes faculty feel alone in this. We're reassuring them that we take this seriously too."

The Expectation of Honesty

Being blunt is the idea. Talking about the expectation of honesty is constant. And along with explicit warning shots, freshmen at USC are getting more intensive and detailed training in what constitutes plagiarism and other forms of cheating, Rhoten says.

The school passes out brochures on plagiarism, has regular coverage in the student paper on cheating cases, and has beefed up orientation courses with training to explain subtler issues like unauthorized collaboration—the largest area of student honor violation at USC and many other campuses, Mr. McCabe and others say.

For instance, Lucia Brawley, a senior majoring in English at Harvard University in Cambridge, Mass., does not believe cheating is a big problem at her school. But when asked about the collaboration issue, she is less sure.

"With people I know in the sciences, there's so much to do and so little time, they help each other," she says. "You go to a lecture today, I'll go next week. You do the reading this week, I'll do it next week. It's a gray area."

Ultimately, though, it is students who will have to uphold academic integrity themselves, many say.

The University of Virginia has a student-run honor code whose "single sanction" for violators is expulsion. It is one of the nation's strictest. Even after more than a century, it remains controversial on campus. Of 11 cheating cases last semester, five resulted in expulsion. But the code has also created an atmosphere of trust that means students can take unproctored exams. "Many of our alumni attribute their success in life to this school's honor code," says Cabell Vest, a graduate student who chairs UVA's honor council.

At Vanderbilt, which also has a strict code, 20 academic dishonesty cases are under review, Madson says—triple the number a few years ago. But he is confident the school is creating an atmosphere less tolerant of cheating. "You just can't have an academic enterprise that isn't based on integrity and honesty," he says. "Nobody wants somebody building bridges to take shortcuts."

Reflective Writing: *After reading this chapter carefully, write a response to it, relating your own interpretations, experiences, and observations to the information and portraits presented by author Mark Clayton. What picture of cheating emerges from the reading? Consider why the rate of cheating in colleges seems to be so high, and make some suggestions for ways to reduce the problem.*

College Students Speak
About ADD

Patricia O. Quinn, M.D.

ADD stands for Attention Deficit Disorder, a neurological condition that affects millions of students in the United States. Symptoms may include problems paying attention, impulsivity, hyperactivity, mood swings, and low frustration tolerance. Although students with this problem often experience great difficulty in school, with hard work and proper treatment many are able to become very successful. In this chapter from the book ADD and the College Student, *two students discuss their own experiences with the condition. The book is intended primarily for students who have the condition themselves but provides information that may be interesting and useful for others as well. The author is a developmental pediatrician and was formerly director of medicine at Georgetown University Child Development Center. She has a son who suffers from ADD.*

To Consider: *What problems did these students encounter, and what strategies and treatments helped them to overcome their difficulties? In addition, how were they treated by teachers, students, and administrators?*

The following pages contain personal commentaries from two young men with ADD. They tell about their experiences in high school and at college, and offer suggestions to assist you as you approach your college years. Since they wrote the following "letters," both of these young men have graduated from college, married, and are pursuing successful careers.

Erik

For most graduates, college is remembered as the best years of their lives. For others, college is a long, drawn-out affair that entails many changes, disappointments, and underachievement. I hope that most of you will remember college as a positive experience. During college, you stand to have the best time of your life, and you have the opportunity to learn and grow as you never have before.

It is a source of great pleasure to see myself change and mature, and notice how much of what I've been taught in class I've managed to retain

321

and use in my everyday life. Perhaps you've noticed my positive attitude toward college. This is a most important point. It is necessary that you view your education as *your* education. Intrinsic motivation is as vital to a student with ADD as it is to any other student. College is full of ups and downs, and take my word, there will be times when you need to motivate from within. But sticking it out and finishing are important.

For one thing, the majority of good paying jobs require a college education. This alone is a strong case for staying in school. Your chances of future employment and income level will rise dramatically. Besides, it's fun. Apart from the economics of the job market, other intrinsic factors make college an attractive choice.

When choosing a college, there are several things you owe it to yourself to consider. Your choice of the school you attend will be an important factor in your successful completion. One important issue to consider is the environment in which you will go to school. This obviously includes geography and weather preferences. More important, though, is the academic environment.

At Georgetown University, I was surrounded by what appeared to me to be an extremely competitive, conservative, motivated, intelligent, and often annoying and disconcerting student body. First of all, this environment contributed to a sense of intellectual insecurity. Many of the students liked to boast of their achievements. I soon learned that I was far from being the most intelligent person around. Not that I was the smartest guy in high school either, but I had been much closer to the top there. Also, the work was much harder than I had been prepared for in high school. Although this is often the case at college, it was particularly exaggerated at Georgetown. My grades not being as high as I had hoped contributed to my insecurities.

I was diagnosed as having ADD about the time I entered college, but did not begin taking medication at that time. My decline continued through the first semester of my sophomore year. At that time, I was reevaluated and decided to begin taking Ritalin upon the recommendation of a physician. The change was obvious. Almost immediately, my productivity increased tremendously. Also, my social life, which never had posed any problems, did not suffer. Social interactions can be an issue for many ADD individuals but fortunately were not a problem for me.

In looking back, there were a number of other factors contributing to my difficulties. Researchers often state that a stable, structured environment, in conjunction with Ritalin, is the most effective treatment of ADD and ADHD. I believe that nothing could be truer. Students must realize that when they leave home for college, they are also leaving behind the structure and balance that have made treatment most effective. Academic strains and the tendency of college students to maintain odd hours often disrupt regular hours. This often entails late nights and early classes. Diet and exercise are also compromised in the transition to college life.

While these conditions influence everybody, they especially affect ADD students. With even a little exercise every day, most students will notice a dramatic improvement in overall mental sharpness. I do 25 to 50 sit-ups daily, take vitamins, and make a conscious effort to eat a balanced diet. Occasionally, I'll swim or lift weights, but not very regularly. The difference is really quite surprising. Try it.

This is a logical point at which to address health issues related to the treatment of attention deficit disorder with stimulant medication. The increased treatment of ADD with stimulant medications has opened debate between the use of psycho-stimulants and the increased probability of drug use later in life. The long-term research clearly indicates no increase in drug abuse in later life if psychostimulants are taken during childhood or adolescence. Many people feel that ADD medication used appropriately can actually lower substance abuse because the person is not driven to seek relief from symptoms through self-medication with drugs and alcohol.

In addition, the warning label on your prescription should be heeded. Stimulants should not be used with alcohol or other drugs. In college, drugs are far more prevalent than in high school. Mixing stimulants and other illegal substances can pose a number of other problems. First, drugs will upset the balance you have achieved. Second, they will work to destroy your motivation and health. Third, the implications of addiction, outside the obvious physical ones, are very serious: expulsion from school, jail, or death. They pose a big risk to your chances for the future success that you as individuals with ADD or ADHD have worked harder than most to attain. Stay away.

In summary, a positive self-image, environmental factors, and mental and physical fitness are primary issues to be concerned with during college, particularly if you have ADD. In a certain sense, college is a Zen experience.

Chris

(The following letter was written while Chris was a 19-year-old college sophomore attending Davidson, a college near Charlotte, North Carolina.)

I was fortunate to be diagnosed as having attention deficit disorder early—in second grade—when my teachers began to realize that I was having problems zoning out in class. I met with a developmental pediatrician, and she started me on Ritalin. I was able to get control of my schoolwork very early on in high school.

As an ADD student, you can do a lot. It's certainly not something that needs to hold you back. I was class president during my sophomore, junior, and senior years in high school; I played football for four years; I ran track; and I became an Eagle Scout. I started a community service program at my high school to benefit the elderly, and I was on the honor roll for the last three years every quarter. I'm very proud that I was able to do all those things.

For the most part, my high school offered many favorable conditions for a student with ADD. The counselors were understanding, knowledgeable, and cooperative. Most teachers followed the recommendations of my counselors, my pediatrician, my parents, and myself. However, I cannot claim to have avoided the resistance of some teachers. A few were not very willing to assist me.

This resistance from teachers stemmed from, in my opinion, their ignorance of attention deficit disorder. They were misinformed on the subject, dismissive of the experts' claims, or completely unaware of the existence of ADD. I was passed off by many of them as being less than a hard worker, less driven than other students, and even lazy. It always frustrated me, because they didn't seem to understand how hard I actually had to work to accomplish the same things that the student next to me did, and that it took a lot more willpower and inner drive for me to do the work than they could ever understand. It was hard for me to communicate my frustration to them.

Many didn't believe that the diagnosis of ADD was valid, because the symptoms are common among many students. Everyone zones out in class once in a while. Everyone reads a page and says, "What did I just read?" And everyone can come to a problem on a test and have to skip it. But for a student with ADD, these problems are magnified. I would read an entire chapter and wonder, "What did I just read?" I would zone out constantly in class, and then I'd get called on and have to realize where I was. And when I got stuck on a problem, I could skip that problem, but then I'd get stuck with the next one; I'd skip that problem and get stuck with the next one. It's a lot worse for a student with ADD.

Other teachers doubted my need for special help because the symptoms weren't apparent in common conversation. Some teachers, when I'd tell them I had attention deficit disorder, would say, "Oh, okay, I can help you." Then they would speak loudly and slowly. I never said I was deaf, but there's such a vast misunderstanding.

Finally, some teachers assumed that I was going to abuse my special circumstances. I had to earn the trust of all my teachers, and that was very, very difficult. I did it, and you can do it as well simply by never cheating. I never cheated. Well, actually I cheated on one test in high school and felt so guilty that I turned myself in. I got a D, but I do think the teacher respected me. I never plagiarized a paper, and after a while, my teachers started to realize that I was honest. I earned their trust. When I needed extra time on a test, the teacher would say, "Okay, Chris, I trust you. Here, you just sit down here in this room by yourself and take it." My books could even be in the room with me, and there was never any problem.

Abuse of your circumstances is also something that is easily recognized by your peers, or at least by my peers. No matter what, some may be suspicious of you. I tried to keep it as secret as I could that I had ADD, but when everyone else has to turn in their test papers and I'm still working, and they come back an hour later and I'm still there, it looks suspicious to them. My friends would say, "Oh, if I had extra time, too, sure, I'd be able to do this."

It was hard for me to convince them that I would rather be in their shoes, that I'd much rather not have ADD and not need help than have ADD and need help. Because even if you have unlimited time on a test, after a while your brain just starts to go. If you have been sitting down and working on a test for three hours, believe me, the last thing you want to do is check your problems over and check everything a second time. You just want to get out of there. There were many times I would be taking a test and I knew I needed to spend more time to do well, but I felt I needed even more to get outside. I needed a breath of fresh air. There are different ways to deal with this, and I'll discuss them later.

The first problem in high school, then, is encountering resistance from your peers and teachers, but if you establish trust and respect, you can go far, very far.

As a student with ADD, I also encountered academic problems. These problems were in the areas of memorization of facts, problem solving, and reading comprehension. To aid in memorization of facts, I'd use different cue terms and poems and acronyms. I was careful to study definitions both ways (term to definition, and definition to term) because they could be presented either way on the test. I did not just use mental images, but knew the facts.

As for logic and problem solving, I think I could figure things out better than most people. The problem was that it took me a lot more time to do it. I needed to concentrate, and to keep down the mental fatigue as well.

Reading comprehension was much more of a problem. I would miss key terms or read over them in a paragraph. A paragraph could be in a completely different tense or totally different gender and I wouldn't even realize it. I would miss one word and need to keep going back and reading the passage over again and again. I'd read it, and it wouldn't make any sense. This was because I had missed the one word. You have to be really careful when you're reading, or at least I do, so that you don't miss anything.

Another problem I had with reading comprehension was my actual attention to the facts. If I wanted to retain all the facts in a given passage, I had to read them very slowly and almost examine every word, or else I would lose them. This can be a special problem with SATs and other standardized, timed tests. There is usually a reading comprehension section involving a passage to read, followed by questions about the passage. I usually had to read over these passages at least three times before I could answer the questions.

Besides reading comprehension, reading anything was really a chore because of the amount of time it took. It takes me about five minutes to read a page in a novel. It can take me up to 15 minutes to read one page in a textbook. This is an enormous amount of time—time that I often didn't have.

Here are the methods I came up with to help. If you're reading a novel, first read the *Cliff Notes* or some other summary, and then read the book itself. You read the summary first so that you have a basic idea of what is going on. Then if you miss a key word or key term, it doesn't throw you off. It is also important to discuss your reading with a friend after you've read the book. You may be looking at it from one perspective and he may be coming at it from another; if you share those perspectives, you'll gain a much better picture of the whole concept. It's rare that both of you will miss something entirely.

The same is true when reading textbooks. It's really helpful when there's a chapter summary before the chapter. It's also important always to read the bold print. If you read through all the bold print, all the highlighted information, and the outlines, then you'll understand what is going on. In addition, read any questions in the back of the book or chapter first, then read just to answer these questions. This will give you a good idea of the basic points. You can then skim through, and you will have all the facts that you're going to need.

And above all else, in everything you do, whenever you have a problem, talk to your teacher or professor. They enjoy teaching and like to talk to the students. This is especially true at the college level. Many college students feel intimidated about going to their professors' offices, or going to dinner or lunch with them. But your teachers really do want you to learn, and they can help you a lot. If you talk to your professors, you're going to do so much better. I wish more college students would realize that.

Other accommodations are also useful. The main accommodation I had to receive was extra time on tests. This, however, is not the only solution. Even though you have extra time, you still need to know all the material. Otherwise, you're going to be guessing. If you need to guess most of the time, you're going to find that your test takes hours and your brain is going to go to jelly. Basically, finish as quickly as possible so that you can avoid this mental fatigue. If you need to take a break, take a break. If you have to go to the bathroom, go to the bathroom. If you're hungry, get something to eat. If you're thirsty, go get a drink. You want to make it as comfortable for yourself as possible. If you have to go to the bathroom during a test but just sit there at your desk instead, you're not going to do as well. This may seem simple, but it is true, especially for someone with ADD. If you have something else on your mind, you're not going to do as well on the test. You want to remove any unnecessary distractions.

The SATs, I would say, were my biggest challenge. I took untimed SATs and I did very well. I got a 1480, but it took me eight hours! I mean, I was the only person there. This lady was so mad at me because I was making her stay there on Saturday. She checked her watch, I swear, every 30 seconds. Eight hours it took me, but I'm glad I stuck in there and took the extra time because it really helped me. When taking untimed SATs, the test proctors are generous about letting you eat, take breaks, and get drinks. You have to make sure that you have enough rest and a full stomach.

Well, that's how I got through high school. Now I would like to talk briefly about college. I decided to be a political science major, which requires a great deal of reading, but I'm doing what I want to do. I'm enjoying it, and I think that is really important. If you're going to do well, you have to enjoy what you're doing. If you don't enjoy it, you are going to lose your attention quickly. That's a problem I have always had.

I met regularly with my professors. I'd like to say something on behalf of small schools. I think there's more of a community atmosphere, and people and professors really want to help you. This may be true of large schools as well, but I am speaking from my own experience. Large schools may also have much larger facilities and resources to help you, but at a small school, there is a lot of personal attention for someone with ADD or a learning disability.

I also took medication. Very briefly, I want to relate my experience with Ritalin. It really helped me. I would probably describe it as a wonder drug. It's not a wonder drug for everyone who takes it, but it was for me. I started taking Ritalin in my sophomore year of high school and I maintained a steady 3.76 GPA, so something happened. I think it was the Ritalin; it helped me a lot. I do have side effects, though. I find that I have to take it on a full stomach, or else I have stomachaches. I also find that when I take it all year long and come off it for the summer, I have minimal withdrawal headaches and some stomachaches, which last about two or three days. I experience nothing that would keep me from participating fully in life's activities, and I think it did a lot of good for me. Whether it will for you, I don't know, but I hope so. I also hope that you can be successful and enjoy yourself as much as possible.

Reflective Writing: *After reading over these descriptions of learning disabled college students, how might you construct a portrait of a successful learning disabled student? What qualities would such a student require? What strategies would he or she need to employ? What types of institutional and peer support would be needed?*

Sorting Out
Which Students Have Learning Disabilities

Perry A. Zirkel

Over the past two decades, the number of college students officially designated as "learning disabled" has more than tripled. By virtue of federal law, these students are often entitled to certain accommodations, such as extra time, tutoring, and a quiet location when completing tests or other assignments. Professor Zirkel, an expert on education and the law, has been studying these trends in recent years, and he has worked with learning disabled students in his own classes. Professor Zirkel wishes to clarify the sometimes messy business of determining which students genuinely have a learning disability and what sorts of accommodations these students should receive.

To Consider: *What specific problems does Professor Zirkel see in the current policies regarding learning disabled students? What evidence does he provide? What remedies does he suggest?*

Although I've spent 30 years in higher education, it's been only in the past decade that I have received requests from students for extra time, and occasionally a quieter place, to take exams. My first such experience occurred when two students in my "Introduction to Law" class individually requested accommodations for the final exam, which consisted of 150 multiple-choice and true-false questions in a three-hour period. Both students had received clearance for certain accommodations from the assistant dean for academic support for students with disabilities.

One student, Jess, who had been identified as having a learning disability, was entitled to 50 percent more time. She explained to me in confidence that she did not want other students to know, and that if she needed her extra 90 minutes, she would wink once upon handing in her exam and then return immediately to finish after the other students had left.

The other student, Tom, had also been classified as learning-disabled since high school. As in most such cases, the school district had made the initial evaluation, and the college had deferred to it. On that basis, Tom was now entitled to twice as much time as most other students, along with a secluded exam site. He and I found a quiet and comfortable projection booth nearby.

329

On the day of the exam—after I had asked the students to put away their No. 2 pencils, and they had come up in a group to hand in their answer sheets—I couldn't detect whether Jess gave me her special wink. When she failed to return to the classroom after quite a while, I became worried and searched the campus for her. About an hour later, I finally found her in the snack bar. She explained to me that she thought she'd performed well on the exam and didn't need any extra time.

After I got back to my office to do some writing, I suddenly remembered Tom. I rushed back to the soundproof booth, only to find him in tears. His extra three hours had expired, and he was only halfway through the test. He lamented between sobs that he had stayed up all night studying, and that his father, a lawyer, would not allow him to stay at Lehigh University if he did not do well in the course.

What should I do? I wondered. What would be a fair, and legal, response?

Such a situation—and my quandary over it—is far from unusual. A recent national study conducted by the American Council on Education found that the proportion of full-time students with disabilities entering colleges and universities has more than tripled in the past two decades—from less than 3 percent in 1978 to 9 percent in 1998. Those figures are, in fact, encouraging. They reflect the positive effects of laws that require higher-education institutions to provide equal opportunities for students with disabilities. The laws are, specifically, the Individuals with Disabilities Education Act and Section 504 of the Rehabilitation Act, enacted in the mid-1970s, and the Americans with Disabilities Act, which went into effect in the early 1990s.

A closer examination of the data, however, reveals a lesser-known trend, one that conflicts with efforts to ensure that all students are treated fairly. The evidence points to a significant increase in "false positives," or students who do not truly qualify as having a disability.

According to the A.C.E. study, 41 percent of the freshmen who reported in 1998 that they had a disability came from the "learning disability" category, compared with 15 percent in 1988. Meanwhile, the percentage of students with more-traditional and visible disabilities had declined significantly. For instance, the proportion of visually impaired students went from 32 percent to 13 percent, and that of orthopedically impaired students from 14 percent to 9 percent.

What's most surprising is that compared with other freshmen with disabilities in 1998, those who were listed as learning-disabled had, on average, a significantly higher parental income and were, more often, white. At-risk factors for disabilities are usually connected with poverty, not wealth. The recent findings have led many observers to question whether a significant number of those students are truly learning-disabled or, rather, in the words of one college official, "upper-income game players."

In fact, an investigative article in the *Los Angeles Times* reported that high-school students who claim to be learning-disabled and ask for special accommodations—usually extra time—on the SAT are disproportionately clustered in well-to-do pockets along the Boston–New York–Washington and the San Francisco–Los Angeles–San Diego corridors. The percentage of students receiving such accommodations was not only exceptionally high in prominent public secondary schools, like Beverly Hills High School, but also more than four times the national average in prestigious prep schools, like the Rye (N.Y.) Country Day School and New York City's Dalton School. In sharp contrast, an analysis of 10 inner-city high schools in the Los Angeles area found that not a single student taking the SAT had received extra time or other accommodations.

My own experience has been similar. Although one must consider that the majority of students who attend Lehigh come from relatively affluent backgrounds—my sample is obviously skewed—no lower-income students in my classes have asked to receive testing accommodations like those afforded Jess and Tom.

Part of the reason for the growth in false positives among more-affluent students may be that the basic definition of a learning disability in the Individuals with Disabilities Education Act (IDEA), which has not changed in more than a decade, is not sufficiently specific. The specified criteria include a "severe discrepancy" between achievement and intellectual ability in at least one of seven designated areas (like basic reading skill or written expression) and the need for special education to help remedy the discrepancy. Both standards are fuzzy, and their interpretation varies, depending in significant part on parental pressure and sophistication.

For example, some parents shop around for psychologists or physicians until they find one who will diagnose their child as learning-disabled. It is not uncommon for parents to bring attorneys or disability advocates to a school or college and threaten legal action. Even when administrators believe that an accommodation is unwarranted, they have difficulty making tough decisions in the face of such pressure, given the costs of defending such suits and the possibility that as school leaders, they might infringe on the rights of a truly disabled child.

A recent state-by-state trend toward "high-stakes testing" has also encouraged school administrators to bow to parental demands. Scores on other standardized paper-and-pencil tests, in addition to the SAT, are being used as a basis for rewards or sanctions for schools as well as students. When schools, students, and parents view their own success as being dependent on test results, they may increasingly resort to questionable means to improve scores. Such costs are hidden, in contrast to litigation, but no less significant.

What's more, false positives may be on the rise as a result of regulatory changes and interpretations. The most recent report by the U.S. Department of Education to Congress revealed a whopping 315 percent increase from

1987 to 1997 in the most nonstigmatizing IDEA category: "other health impairment." In recent years, advocates for students have succeeded in arguing that attention-deficit disorder and attention-deficit hyperactivity disorder are implicitly covered under that category. The inclusion of A.D.D. and A.D.H.D. as allowable health conditions in the 1999 regulations for the act will certainly fuel even sharper growth in the number of false positives. Such conditions are particularly, although not exclusively, endemic to the wealthier regions of the country.

But many students who claim to have such learning disabilities are not disabled in the legal sense of the term. Under the IDEA law, having A.D.D. is not enough; the student must also need special education. As an alternative, parents, attorneys, and other advocates for psychologists' growing inventory of so-called invisible disabilities—not only A.D.D. and A.D.H.D., but also dyslexia (reading impairment), dyscalcula (math impairment), dysgraphia (writing impairment), dysthymia (mood disorder), obsessive-compulsive disorder, posttraumatic stress disorder, and multiple-chemical sensitivity, among others—have in recent years sought and secured identification of those disorders under the broader definition of disability contained in Section 504 and in the Americans with Disabilities Act. That definition requires a mental or physical impairment that limits a major life activity—and to a substantial extent. Prevailing school-district practice, often based on ignorance or parental intimidation, has been simply to acknowledge the impairment, like attention-deficit disorder, without considering whether it substantially limits a major life activity—especially if the parents threaten to sue.

In stark contrast, however, the courts have consistently interpreted "major life activity" as generic—for example, walking as general mobility rather than as specific variants, like crawling or running; and learning as a broad category rather than as a subset like spelling or test-taking. Most important, in recent years courts have narrowly interpreted the key criterion of "substantial" limitation with reference to the average student in the national population, and with—not without—mitigating measures, like medication.

Thus, as a legal reality, students with A.D.D. and A.D.H.D. at prestigious public and private schools—and, later, in college—often do not truly qualify as having a disability under Section 504 or the A.D.A. because they typically do not display a substantial limitation in learning (the relevant "major life activity" in SAT accommodations). Either with their medication (which is generally overprescribed), or even for those who do not use medication, the grade-point averages and standardized-test scores of such students do not suggest that they have a substantial learning impairment compared with the average student in the national population.

What can be done to preclude such students, who are not really learning-disabled, from receiving special accommodations—and, as a result, unfair advantages? The solution is multifaceted and does not include throwing out the precious baby of legally defensible disabilities with the bath water of inappropriate attempts to beat the system.

One part of the answer is that school districts and higher-education institutions, while giving parents notice of their legal rights, should learn to say respectfully, but firmly, No when it's appropriate. The courts and the Education Department's Office for Civil Rights have provided solid backing for such a response. For example, last year the United States Court of Appeals for the Ninth Circuit upheld the denial of learning-disabled eligibility under the Individuals with Disabilities Education Act to a fifth-grader in the Orinda Union School District, near Oakland, Calif., whom private evaluators had identified as having attention-deficit disorder. Why the denial? Because even if the inconclusive test results were interpreted as establishing a severe discrepancy between the student's ability and his achievement, his problems could be dealt with by making minor modifications in the regular education program. In other words, he did not need special education.

Similarly, the majority of recent rulings by the Office for Civil Rights under Section 504 and the A.D.A. have favored institutions of higher education, particularly with regard to academic adjustments for learning-disabled students, according to a recent dissertation by Margaret M. McMenamin, a faculty member at Lehigh Carbon Community College. The courts have also sided with defendants in a string of test-related Section 504 and A.D.A. suits brought by medical students and others—for example, *Wynne v. Tufts University School of Medicine* (1992), *Tips v. Regents of Texas Tech University* (1996), *Price v. National Board of Medical Examiners* (1997), *Tarum v. National Collegiate Athletic Association* (1998), *McGuiness v. University of New Mexico School of Medicine* (1998), *Gonzales v. National Board of Medical Examiners* (1999), and *Betts v. Rector and Visitors of the University of Virginia* (2000).

In *Price*, for example, three medical students whom the National Center of Higher Education for Learning Problems had diagnosed with attention-deficit hyperactivity disorder, as well as with other writing and reading disorders, sought extended time and a separate room for the first step of the national medical board's exam—which they had to pass to proceed to the third year of medical school. Deciding against them, a federal judge, Joseph Goodwin, concluded that "a 'learning disability' does not always qualify as a disability under the A.D.A," and that, inasmuch as those students were able to learn as well as the average person in the national population, they did not qualify for special test accommodations.

Colleges and universities can contribute to a solution by conducting research that helps systematically and objectively to identify students with disabilities. Institutions can also offer courses and conferences on learning-disability issues, like testing and measurement, and can establish learning-disability–evaluation centers in their towns. Thanks to the A.D.A. the IDEA, and Section 504, underidentification is largely a matter of the past. The focus should now be on defining and identifying false positives.

Such research-and-training efforts can help inform policymakers as well as practitioners. Congress or the Department of Education should clarify the legal definitions of disability, and officials of schools and colleges ought to interpret them more uniformly.

Of course, a certain amount of ambiguity and discretion is inevitable. The fundamental solution, therefore, is for school-district personnel, parents, the testing services, and college administrators and faculty members to avoid yielding to short-term pressure. To ensure long-term academic integrity and fairness for all students, higher-education institutions must have the courage to reserve special accommodations for those who truly have exceptional needs—even if it means investing in special evaluations or, as a last resort, litigation.

Colleges, along with primary and secondary schools and state governments, should also seriously examine the value and techniques of high-stakes testing. Colleges also should develop and apply defensible ways to determine the nature and extent of accommodations for those students who do have disabilities. For example, we might use multiple measures—performance portfolios, essays, and structured interviews, in addition to standardized, multiple-choice tests—for high-stakes accountability. We also could allow *all* students more time on tests, limiting the uniform time allocation only to the extent that it reflects an essential eligibility requirement. For example, in *Wynne v. Tufts University School of Medicine*, the court upheld timed, multiple-choice testing in medical school because doctors often must choose among multiple options within a limited time—say, when working in the emergency room.

The issues related to learning disabilities are evolving, and all of us in higher education should keep up with changing trends in disability regulations and practices. I know that I, as a professor, have already had to learn and adapt.

And what about Tom? What did I do about his emotion-laden request there in the projection booth? After quick consideration, I told him that another, unidentified student had been entitled to an extra 90 minutes, and that he could have her unused accommodation.

That was 10 years ago. I doubt that I'd make the same decision today. But if I saw Tom now and discovered that he was a lawyer, I'd recommend that he go into disability law. Litigation is booming, with a proliferation of lawsuits contesting whether the scores of any students who take extra time on their SATs should be flagged.

Meanwhile, I have halved the length of my exam, so that every student has ample time to finish—with or without winking.

Reflective Writing: *This essay by a noted professor of education looks at the complex issues involved in assessing learning disabled students. The essay discusses tests to determine the existence of a disability and the laws governing such assessments. But the author mainly focuses on the controversial issue of learning disabled students requesting special accommodations, such as extra time on tests in college* *courses. Zirkel argues that "To ensure long-term academic integrity and fairness for all students, higher-education institutions must have the courage to reserve special accommodations for those who truly have exceptional needs—even if it means investing in special evaluations or, as a last resort, litigation." What support does he provide for this position? What evidence does he offer that some students without exceptional needs now enjoy special accommodations? What arguments might be put forward by an advocate for more broadly defined accommodations for students identified as learning disabled?*

Grading Your Professors

Jacob Neusner

Throughout your college education, professors will be evaluating your work, making judgments about you that will affect your level of academic success and your prospects for admission to graduate programs and future employment. And yet, aside from end-of-course evaluations, students rarely have the opportunity to grade their professors in any systematic fashion. In this 1984 essay from the book How to Grade Your Professors and Other Unexpected Advice, *Jacob Neusner, professor of religious studies and author of more than 300 books, presents criteria by which he thinks college teachers ought to be judged. He distinguishes between average, good, and truly excellent instructors, based as much on faculty's attitude toward their subject matter as on the specific activities and syllabi they employ.*

To Consider: *As you read this piece detailing the qualities the author believes characterize A, B, and C professors, reflect on what Neusner claims most separates these different types of instructors. How does your own substantial experience as a student support and/or contradict Neusner's views? Also think about a parallel category system for students. What qualities, in your view, characterize A, B, and C students?*

Since professors stand at the center of the student's encounter with college learning, students ought to ask what marks a good professor, what indicates a bad one. The one who sets high standards and persists in demanding that students try to meet them provides the right experiences. The professor who gives praise cheaply or who pretends to a relationship that does not and cannot exist teaches the wrong lessons. True, the demanding and the critical teacher does not trade in the currency students possess, which is their power to praise or reject teachers. The demanding professor knows that students will stumble. But the ones who pick themselves up and try again—whether in politics or music or art or sports—have learned a lesson that will save them for a lifetime: A single failure is not the measure of any person, and success comes hard. A banal truth, but a truth all the same.

The only teacher who taught me something beyond information, who gave me something to guide my life, was the only teacher who read my work carefully and criticized it in detail. To that point everyone had given me A's. After that I learned to criticize myself and not to believe the A's. The teacher who read my writing and corrected not so much the phrasing as the mode of thought—line by line, paragraph by paragraph, beginning to end—and who composed paragraphs as models for what I should be saying is the sole true teacher I ever had. But I did not need more than one, and neither do you.

I do not mean to suggest that for each one of us there is one perfect teacher who changes our lives and is the only teacher we need. We must learn from many teachers as we grow up and grow old; and we must learn to recognize the good ones. The impressive teacher of one's youth may want to continue to dominate—as teachers do—and may not want to let go. The great teacher is the one who wants to become obsolete in the life of the student. The good teacher is the one who teaches lessons and moves on, celebrating the student's growth. The Talmud relates the story of a disciple in an academy who won an argument over the position held by God in the academy on high. The question is asked, "What happened in heaven that day?" The answer: "God clapped hands in joy, saying, 'My children have vanquished me, my children have vanquished me.'" That is a model for the teacher—to enjoy losing an argument to a student, to recognize his or her contribution, to let the student surpass the teacher.

In the encounter with the teacher who takes you seriously, you learn to take yourself seriously. In the eyes of the one who sees what you can accomplish, you gain a vision of yourself as more than you thought you were. The ideal professor is the one who inspires to dream of what you can be, to try for more than you ever have accomplished before. Everyone who succeeds in life can point to such a teacher, whether in the classroom or on the sports field. It may be a parent, a coach, employer, grade school or high school or art or music teacher. It is always the one who cared enough to criticize, and stayed around to praise.

But what about college professors? To define an ideal for their work, let me offer guidelines on how to treat professors the way we treat students: to give grades.

Professors grade students' work. The conscientious ones spend time reading and thinking about student papers, inscribing their comments and even discussing with students the strengths and weaknesses of their work. But no professor spends as much time on grading students' work as students spend on grading their professors as teachers and as people. For from the beginning of a course ("Shall I register?") through the middle ("It's boring . . . shall I stick it out?") to the very end ("This was a waste of time"), the students invest time and intellectual energy in deciding what they think, both about how the subject is studied and about the person who presents it. Since effective teaching requires capturing the students' imagination, and since sharp edges and colorful ways excite imagination, the professor who is a "character" is apt, whether liked or disliked, to make a profound impression and perhaps also to leave a mark on the students' minds. The drab professors, not gossiped about and not remembered except for what they taught, may find that even what they taught is forgotten. People in advertising and public relations, politics and merchandising, know that. A generation raised on television expects to be manipulated and entertained.

Yet the emphasis on striking characteristics is irrelevant. Many students have no more sophistication in evaluating professors than they do in evaluating deodorants. This should not be surprising, since they approach them both in the same manner. The one who is "new, different, improved," whether a professor or a bar of soap, wins attention. In this context people have no way of determining good from bad. I once asked an airline pilot, "What is the difference between a good landing and a bad one?" He replied, "A good landing is any landing you can pick yourself up and walk away from." To this pilot, the landing is judged solely by its ultimate goal—safely delivering the plane's passengers. Can we tell when a teacher has safely delivered the student for the next stage of the journey? Can we define the differences between a good teacher and a bad one?

Students have their own definitions of *good* and *bad*, and professors generally have a notion of the meaning of students' grades. Let us consider how students evaluate their teachers, examining in turn the A, B, and C professors. We will begin at the bottom of one scale and work our way up. Let us at the same time consider what kind of student seeks which grade.

Grade C Professors

The first type is the C professor. This is the professor who registers minimum expectations and adheres to the warm-body theory of grading. If a warm body fills a seat and exhibits vital signs, such as breathing at regular intervals, occasionally reading, and turning in some legible writing on paper, then cosmic justice demands, and the professor must supply, the grade of C or *Satisfactory*. The effort needed to achieve F or *No Credit* is considerably greater. One must do no reading, attend few class sessions, and appear to the world to be something very like a corpse.

The professor who, by the present criteria, earns a C respects the students' rights and gives them their money's worth. He or she sells them a used car, so to speak, that they at least can drive off the lot. At the very least the professor does the following:

1. Attends all class sessions, reaches class on time, and ends class at the scheduled hour.
2. Prepares a syllabus for the course and either follows it or revises it, so that students always know what topic is under (even totally confused) discussion.
3. Announces and observes scheduled office hours, so that students have access to the professor without groveling or special pleading, heroic efforts at birddogging, or mounting week-long treasure hunts.

4. Makes certain that books assigned for a course are on reserve in the library and sees to it that the bookstore has ample time in which to order enough copies of the textbooks and ancillary reading for a course.

5. Comes to class with a clear educational plan, a well-prepared presentation, a concrete and specific intellectual agenda.

6. Reads examinations with the care invested in them (certainly no more, but also no less) and supplies intelligible grades and at least minimal comments; or keeps office hours for the discussion of the substance of the examination (but not the grade); and supplies course performance reports—all these as duty, not acts of grace.

These things constitute student rights. No student has to thank a professor for doing what he or she is paid to do, and these six items, at a minimum, are the prerequisites of professional behavior. They are matters of form, to be sure, but the grade C is deemed by (some) students to be a matter of good form alone; the warm-body theory of this grade applies to professors and students alike.

"Tell me my duty and I shall do it" are the words of the minimally prepared. Just as students of mediocre quality want to know the requirements and assume that if they meet them, they have fulfilled their whole obligation to the subject, so mediocre professors do what they are supposed to do. The subject is in hand; there are no problems. The C professor need not be entirely bored with the subject, but he or she is not apt to be deeply engaged by it.

Grade C professors may be entertaining, warm, and loving. Indeed, many of them must succeed on the basis of personality, because all they have to offer is the studied technology of attractive personalities. They may achieve huge followings among the students, keep students at the edge of their seats with jokes and banter, badger students to retain their interest, but in the end what they have sold, conveyed, or imparted to the students' minds is themselves, not their mode of thinking or analyzing. Why? Because C professors do not think much; they rely on the analysis of others.

Above all, the grade C professor has made no effort to take over and reshape the subject. This person is satisfied with the mere repetition, accurate and competent repetition to be sure, of what others have discovered and declared to be true. If this sort of professor sparks any vitality and interest in students, then he or she will remind students of their better high school teachers, the people who, at the very least, knew what they were talking about and wanted the students to know. At the end of a course, students should ask themselves, Have I learned facts, or have I grasped how the subject works, its inner dynamic, its logic and structure? If at the end students know merely one fact after another, students should be grateful—at least they have learned that much—but award the professor a polite C. For the professor has done little more than what is necessary.

Grade B Professors

A course constitutes a large and detailed statement on the nature of a small part of a larger subject, a practical judgment upon a particular field of study and how it is to be organized and interpreted. The grade of B is accorded to the student who has mastered the basic and fundamental modes of thought about, and facts contained within, the subject of a course.

The grade B professor is one who can present coherently the larger theory and logic of the subject, who will do more than is required to convey his or her ideas to the students, and who will sincerely hope he or she is inspiring the minds of the students. B professors, as they continue to grow as scholars, are not very different from A professors; they might be described as teachers striving to become A professors. But they are definitely very different from C professors. Let us, then, move on to consider A professors, keeping in mind that B professors will probably become A professors.

Grade A Professors

Grade A professors are the scholar-teachers, a university's prized treasures among a faculty full of intangible riches. America has many faculties of excellence, groups of men and women who with exceptional intelligence take over a subject and make it their own, reshape it and hand it on, wholly changed but essentially unimpaired in tradition, to another generation.

The grade of A goes to student work that attends in some interesting way and with utmost seriousness to the center and whole of the subject of the course. Notice, I did not say that an A goes to the student who says something new and original. That is too much to hope, especially in studying a subject that for hundreds or thousands of years has appeared to the best minds as an intricate and difficult problem.

The grade A professors may have odd ideas about their subjects, but they are asking old-new questions, seeking fresh insight, trying to enter into the way in which the subject works, to uncover its logic and inner structure. What makes an effective high school teacher is confidence, even glibness. What makes an effective university teacher is doubt and dismay. The scholarly mind is marked by self-criticism and thirsty search; it is guided by an awareness of its own limitations and those of knowledge. The scholar-teacher, of whatever subject or discipline, teaches one thing: Knowledge is not sure but uncertain, scholarship is search, and to teach is to impart the lessons of doubt. What is taught is what we do not know.

On whom do you bestow a grade A? It is given to the professor who, stumbling and falling, yet again rising up and walking on, seeks both knowledge and the meaning of knowledge. It is to the one who always asks, *Why am I telling you these things? Why should you know them?* It is to the professor who demands ultimate seriousness for his or her subject because the subject must be known, who not only teaches but professes, stands for, represents, the thing taught. The grade A professor lives for the subject, needs to tell you about it, wants to share it. The Nobel Prize scientist who so loved biology that she gave her life to it even without encouragement and recognition for a half a century of work, the literary critic who thinks getting inside a poem is entering Paradise, the historian who assumes the human issues of the thirteenth century live today—these exemplify the ones who are ultimately serious about a subject.

One who has made this commitment to a field of scholarship can be readily identified. This is the one full of concern, the one who commits upon the facts the act of advocacy, who deems compelling what others find merely interesting. The scholar-teacher is such because he or she conveys the self-evident, the obvious fact that facts bear meaning, constituting a whole that transcends the sum of the parts. True, to the world this sense of ultimate engagement with what is merely interesting or useful information marks the professor as demented, as are all those who march to a different drummer. What I mean to say is simple. Anybody who cares so much about what to the rest of the world is so little must be a bit daft. Why should such things matter so much—why, above all, things of the mind or the soul or the heart, things of nature and mathematics, things of structure and weight and stress, things of technology and science, society and mind? Professors often remember lonely childhoods (for my part, I don't). As adults, too, professors have to spend long hours by themselves in their offices, reading books, or in their laboratories or at their computers, or just thinking all by themselves. That is not ordinary and commonplace behavior. This is what it means to march to a different drummer. A student earns an A when he or she has mastered the larger theory of the course, entered into its logic and meaning, discovered a different way of seeing. Like a professor, the student who through accurate facts and careful, critical thought seeks meaning, the core and center of the subject, earns the grade A.

Yet matters cannot be left here. I do not mean to promote advocacy for its own sake. Students have rights too, and one of these is the right to be left alone, to grow and mature in their own distinctive ways. They have the right to seek their way, just as we professors find ours. The imperial intellect, the one that cannot allow autonomy, is a missionary, not a teacher. Many compare the imperial teacher with the A professor, but if you look closely at their different ways of teaching, you will see that this is an error. The teacher leads, says, "Follow me," without looking backward. The missionary pushes, imposes self upon another autonomous self. This is the opposite of teaching, and bears no relevance to learning or to scholarship. The teacher persuades; the missionary preaches. The teacher argues; the missionary shouts others to silence. The teacher wants the student to discover; the missionary decides what the student must discover. The teacher enters class with fear and trembling, not knowing where the discussion will lead. The missionary knows at the start of a class exactly what the students must cover by the end of the class.

Grade A professors teach, never indoctrinate. They educate rather than train. There is a fine line to be drawn, an invisible boundary, between great teaching and self-aggrandizing indoctrination.

Knowledge and even understanding do not bring salvation and therefore do not have to be, and should not be, forced upon another. And this brings me back to the earlier emphasis upon scholarship as the recognition of ignorance, the awareness not of what we know but of how we know and of what we do not know. The true scholar, who also is the true teacher, is drawn by self-criticism, compelled by doubting, skeptical curiosity, knows the limits of knowing. He or she cannot be confused with the imperial, the arrogant, and the proselytizing. By definition, we stand for humility before the unknown.

A good professor wants to answer the question, Why am I telling you these things? A good student wants to answer the question, Why am I taking these courses? What do I hope to get out of them? Why are they important to me? I have not put before you any unattainable ideals in these questions. Some of us realize them every day, and nearly all of us realize them on some days. Just as students' transcripts rarely present only A's or *No Credits*, so professors rarely succeed all of the time. No one bears the indelible grade of A.

Reflective Writing: *How does Professor Neusner distinguish between high school and college instructors? How does his description fit your experience thus far in college? What qualities does Professor Neusner believe are most important in a college instructor? Based on these qualities, what theory of teaching do you think the author holds? If you were to develop your own theory of an ideal teacher, how might it be different from or similar to Neusner's? In what ways might such factors as the subject matter affect the quality or type of instruction?*

Possible Essay Topics

For this assignment, choose one of the following topics and write a three- to four-page essay. In your essay, be sure to draw significantly on readings from this unit or the anthology. Rather than merely summarizing or restating ideas from the essays, you will also want to add your own discussion and analysis of the readings and how they relate to your own ideas and experiences. Make sure your points are well developed and your prose carefully edited and proofread.

1. Read carefully Mark Clayton's article about cheating, and write responses from three different perspectives: that of a student, that of a teacher, and that of an ethics specialist. Consider your own experiences and observations on this subject. Conclude the essay with an overarching examination of how these three perspectives relate to one another and what you feel are the main implications of the author's findings. In all of your analysis here, be sure to talk about specific aspects and instances of cheating rather than to operate from a vague and general sense of the topic.

2. Two essays in this unit discuss grading. They include Patrick O'Malley's discussion of testing and learning and Jacob Neusner's suggestion for grading professors. Consider what these authors have to say and construct your own argument (drawing on personal experiences, observations, and ideas) about how grades function in high school or college—and how you believe they should function. Keep in mind that in different ways, grades are intended to serve various constituencies: students, educators, potential employers, and society as a whole.

3. College professor William Dowling argues that the SAT does indeed provide a helpful indication of students' potential to succeed in college. Peter Sacks and Brian Doherty argue instead that reliance on this test has had some very negative consequences to students and to society as a whole. Taking into account these differing views, provide your own perspective on this subject. What role has college entrance testing played in your own life? How accurate an indication of your own and others' academic ability do you think the test's results are and why? What do you see as the positive and negative implications of America's emphasis on standardized tests in determining admission to college?

4. Education professor Perry A. Zirkel argues that colleges need to do a better job of determining disability and devising more uniform policies for accommodating students with learning disabilities. Physician (and parent of a learning disabled student) Patricia O. Quinn takes a much more sympathetic view of learning disabilities. Write a response to the specific points author Zirkel makes, from the perspective of a learning disabled student.

5. Peter Sacks discusses the early history of standardized aptitude testing and its relation to the eugenics movement of the late nineteenth and early twentieth centuries. He argues that the eugenics movement culminated in the Nazis' mass murder of Jews and others whom they viewed as genetically inferior. Describe this early history of intelligence testing. What relationship, in your opinion, do the elitist and racist views of the early testers have to the current uses of college admissions testing? What vestiges, if any, of the early prejudices survive in today's testing applications? You may also want to draw upon other readings for the Unit, such as Doherty, Dowling, Quinn, or Zirkel.

Research Paper Assignment

The research paper is an investigation of a topic of interest and importance to you. Part of your challenge in writing the research paper is to make the material you write about interesting to your readers as well. An important part of the research project involves incorporating the ideas and inquiry of other people. You will read what others have written on the topic and will also talk with a specialist on the subject. However, your essay should definitely not be a mere collection of the ideas of others strung together into an essay. Rather, the paper should be a discussion of your overall research question (which will involve some subquestions), why and how you chose to investigate it, what you were able to find, and what further ideas and conclusions you came to as a result.

For this paper, you will investigate in some depth a major in which you are interested. You have some flexibility as to what aspects of the major you choose to investigate. However, there are several areas that you should be sure to examine. You will carry out this investigation using library research, World Wide Web–based inquiry, an interview with a specialist in the area, and possibly with other field research as well, such as observation and analysis of a work site.

Requirements

A. A major is not just a collection of disparate courses leading to a professional credential. It also comprises a way (or ways) of thinking, a set of strategies for problem solving, and a body of knowledge. As part of your paper, you should examine the conceptual underpinnings of your major.

B. A major field of study also exists in a social, political, and historical context. It makes certain contributions to the larger society. Your paper should include a discussion placing the field into this larger context.

C. In addition, a major is intended to prepare students for particular types of careers. You should investigate the relationship between the college course of study and the subsequent work people do in the field. Some questions to consider here include what aspects of the coursework seem to be most useful and in what ways, what sorts of careers people in this major typically go on to have, and what specifically their work involves.

D. Finally, you should draw some conclusions from your research that help you— and that may help others—better understand the field of study. Above all else, use this assignment as an opportunity to learn more about your planned direction in college and in life.

References

Bacon, Francis. "Of Studies." Reprinted in *The Mercury Reader*. Ed. Janice Neuleib, Kathleen Shine Cain, Stephen Ruffus, and Maurice Scharton. Needham Heights, MA: Pearson Custom Publishing, 1999.

Bowser, Benjamin and Herbert Perkins. "Against the Odds: Young Black Men Tell What It Takes." *Black Male Adolescents: Parenting and Education in Community Context*. Ed. Benjamin Bowser. Lanham, MD: University Press of America, 1991. 183–200.

Boyer, Ernest L. "Specialization: The Enriched Major." *College: The Undergraduate Experience in America*. The Carnegie Foundation for the Advancement of Teaching. New York: Harper and Row, 1987. 102–15.

Cahn, Steven. "The Democratic Framework" and "The Content of a Liberal Education." *Education and the Democratic Ideal*. Nelson-Hall: Chicago, 1979. 1–13.

Clayton, Mark. "A Whole Lot of Cheatin' Going On." *The Christian Science Monitor*, January 19, 1999. Reprinted in *The Presence of Others: Voices and Images That Call for Response*. Third Edition. Ed. Andrea Lunsford and John Ruszkiewicz. Boston: Bedford/St. Martins, 2000.

Doherty, Brian. "Those Who Can't, Test." *Mother Jones Magazine*, November/December 1998. Reprinted in *The Mercury Reader*. Ed. Janice Neuleib, Kathleen Shine Cain, Stephen Ruffus, and Maurice Scharton. Needham Heights, MA: Pearson Custom Publishing, 1999.

Dowling, William. "The SAT: A New Defense." *Current*, July 2000. 3–12.

Edmundson, Mark. "On the Uses of a Liberal Education: As Lite Entertainment for Bored College Students." *Harper's Magazine*, September 1997. 39–49.

Ehrlich, Thomas. "The University Serving the Community." *The Courage to Inquire: Ideals and Realities in Higher Education*. Bloomington: Indiana University Press, 1995. 71–92.

Freeland, Richard M. "The Practical Path, Too, Can Be High-Minded." *The Chronicle of Higher Education*, September 15, 2000. B11.

Jackson, Mark. "The Liberal Arts: A Practical View." *Free Falling and Other Student Essays*. Third Edition. Ed. Paul Sladky. New York: St. Martin's Press, 1997. 98–101.

Kaminer, Wendy. "Education: The Trouble with Single-Sex Schools." *The Atlantic Monthly*, April 1998. 22–36.

Karabell, Zachary. "The $10,000 Hoop: Has Higher Education Become an Exercise in Futility for Most Americans?" *Salon Ivory Tower*, 1998. http://www.salon.com/it/feature/1998/09/cov_14feature.html.

King, Jacqueline E. "Too Many Students Are Holding Jobs for Too Many Hours." *The Chronicle of Higher Education*, May 1, 1998. A72.

Loeb, Paul Rogat. "You Make Your Own Chances: Wealth as an Educational Goal," and "You Don't Have a Say: Individualism as Survival." *Generation at the Crossroads: Apathy and Action on the American Campus*. New Brunswick, NJ: Rutgers University Press, 1994. 11–26.

Meiland, Jack. "The Difference Between High School and College." *College Thinking: How to Get the Best Out of College*. New York: New American Library, 1981.

Neusner, Jacob. "Grading Your Professors." *How to Grade Your Professors and Other Unexpected Advice*. New York: Doubleday, 1984. 23–31.

Neusner, Jacob. "What People Learn in College: The Major." *How to Grade Your Professors and Other Unexpected Advice*. New York: Doubleday, 1984. 95–104.

O'Conor, Andi. "Who Gets Called Queer in School?" *The Gay Teen: Educational Practice and Theory for Lesbian, Gay, and Bisexual Adolescents*. Ed. Gerald Unks. New York: Routledge, 1995. 95–101.

O'Malley, Patrick. "More Testing, More Learning." *The St. Martin's Guide to Writing*. Third Edition. Ed. Rise Axelrod and Charles Cooper. Boston: St. Martin's, 1995.

Orenstein, Peggy. "Learning Silence: Scenes from the Class Struggle." *Schoolgirls: Young Women, Self-Esteem, and the Confidence Gap*. American Association of University Women. New York: Doubleday, 1995. 3–31.

Plato. "The Allegory of the Cave." *The Republic*. New York: Oxford University Press, 1945. 227–34. Reprinted in *The Mercury Reader*. Ed. Janice Neuleib, Kathleen Shine Cain, Stephen Ruffus, and Maurice Scharton. Needham Heights, MA: Pearson Custom Publishing, 1999.

Quinn, Patricia O. "College Students Speak Out About ADD." *ADD and the College Student: A Guide for High School and College Students with Attention Deficit Disorder*. New York: Magination Press, 1994. 39–50.

Randall, Michael. "A Guide to Good Teaching: Be Slow and Inefficient." *The Chronicle of Higher Education*, December 8, 2000. B24.

Reich, Robert B. "Hire Education: The Secretary of Labor Tells You Where the Jobs Are." *Rolling Stone*, October 20, 1994. 119–25.

Reich, Robert B. "How Selective Colleges Heighten Inequality." *The Chronicle of Higher Education*, September 15, 2000. B7–B10.

Rojstaczer, Stuart. "Lowering the Bar." *Gone for Good: Tales of University Life after the Golden Age*. New York: Oxford University Press, 1999. 13–26.

Sacks, Peter. "Inventing Intelligence: The Origins of Mental Measurement." *Standardized Minds: The High Price of America's Testing Culture and What We Can Do About It*. Cambridge, MA: Perseus Books, 1999. 17–34.

Shorris, Earl. "On the Uses of a Liberal Education: As a Weapon in the Hands of the Restless Poor." *Harper's Magazine*, September 1997. 50–59.

Solomon, Robert and Jon Solomon. "The Mission of the University." *Up the University: Re-creating Higher Education in America*. Reading, MA: Addison-Wesley, 1993. Reprinted in *The University Book: An Anthology of Writings from the University of Arizona*. Second Edition. Ed. Thomas P. Miller, Carol Nowotny-Young, Mark

Williams, Kat McLellan, Christine Hamel, Heather Brossard, and Ellen Price. Needham Heights, MA: Pearson Custom Publishers, 1999. 40–45.

Sommers, Christina Hoff. "The War Against Boys." *The Atlantic Monthly*, May 2000. 59–77.

Sperber, Murray. "Introduction." *Beer and Circus: How Big-Time College Sports Is Crippling Undergraduate Education*. New York: Henry Holt and Company, 2000. 3–11.

Suskind, Ron. "Something to Push Against." *A Hope in the Unseen: An American Odyssey from the Inner-City to the Ivy League*. New York: Broadway Books, 1998. 1–23.

de Toqueville, Alexis. "Why the Americans Are More Addicted to Practical Than to Theoretical Science." *Democracy in America*. New York: Washington Square Press, 1863/1964. 149–52.

Zirkel, Perry A. "Sorting Out Which Students Have Learning Disabilities." *The Chronicle of Higher Education*, December 8, 2000. B15–B16.